10-2-70

Blake's
Apocalypse

Blake's Apocalypse

A STUDY IN POETIC ARGUMENT

BY

HAROLD BLOOM

These leaves are the poem, the icon and the man.
These are a cure of the ground and of ourselves,

In the predicate that there is nothing else.

WALLACE STEVENS

CORNELL UNIVERSITY PRESS

ITHACA, NEW YORK

First printing, Cornell University Press, 1970

Standard Book Number 8014-0568-8
Library of Congress Catalog Card Number 63-8741
Printed in the United States of America

For
JEANNE

Contents

Preface

This book offers an introductory study of the argument of Blake's poetry. I have emphasized those elements that make Blake's poems more than documents in spiritual or intellectual history: continuity that is assured but often not discursive; polemic that is masterly but often not philosophical; style that is individual and exuberant. Blake's major poems often are discussed as if they were not poems at all, so that I have allowed myself the perhaps supererogatory function of indicating where they are beautiful, by evidencing how a masterful design is carried through into the minute articulations of each poem.

The poems are studied here in their probable order of composition, with only a few exceptions. More than half this book is given to the examination of *The Four Zoas, Milton,* and *Jerusalem,* Blake's epics. If this proportion is mistaken it is because even more emphasis should have been given to these major poems, for they are Blake's best.

I have slighted Blake's illustrations to his engraved poems, though to do so is to go against Blake's intentions and against what is now the accepted view among Blake scholars. Blake's poems, especially his epics, seem to me the best poetry in English since Milton, but about Blake's illustrations my judgment is uncertain. Some of them seem to me very powerful, some do not; but I am in any case not qualified to criticize them. As a critic I have tried to be true to my own experience in reading and enjoying Blake for fifteen years, and my experience is that the poems are usually quite independent of their illustrations. Contrary views to my own can be found very easily and I do not seek to convert anyone to my judgment on this matter; the detailed readings that follow, from *Songs of Innocence* through *Jerusalem,* are offered as justification for my procedure.

I have consulted originals or facsimiles of Blake's engraved poems and poems left in manuscript for almost all the texts I quote, as well as the standard edition of Sir Geoffrey Keynes. My quotations depart from the texts of Keynes particularly in punctuation, this being a vexed matter for any student of Blake, since the poet punctuated capriciously. Sometimes I have followed Blake's apparent punctuation, sometimes that of Keynes, sometimes an amalgam or a judgment of my own. In a few places, notably in *Jerusalem*, I am indebted to David Erdman's recovery of lines Blake altered or deleted. I am also grateful to Mr. Erdman for his kindness in allowing me to read his forthcoming study of the ordering of the sequence of plates in *Jerusalem* and for his reading of my proofs.

My specific critical debts are to the Blake studies of S. Foster Damon, J. Middleton Murry, David Erdman, and especially Northrop Frye. I have tried to indicate my borrowings from these and other writers, but it is unlikely that I have noticed all of them. To Mr. Frye's work I have a more pervasive obligation, for by reading him I learned to read Blake.

As a student I participated in seminars on Blake conducted by M. H. Abrams and W. K. Wimsatt, Jr., both of whom contributed to my understanding of the poet. More recently I have benefited by discussions of Blake with Martin Price, Geoffrey Hartman, Jerome Schneewind, Alvin Feinman, John Grant, Alice-Augusta Miskimin, and John Hollander.

I am grateful to Frederick A. Pottle for his kindness in reading and criticizing several of these chapters, and to Anne Freedgood for her patience and skill as an editor, and for a multitude of kindnesses besides.

I am also grateful to the Morse Fund of Yale University for a grant towards the preparation of the manuscript. Finally I wish to thank Barbara Chatfield for her continued good humor and patience in typing my manuscript.

Yale University
June 1962

PART I
The Minor Poems

CHAPTER ONE

Poetical Sketches: The Young Blake

Between 1769 and 1778, from his twelfth to twenty-first years, Blake wrote the poems he gathered together in *Poetical Sketches.* This volume was printed in 1783, probably under the patronage of the sculptor Flaxman, but not actually offered for sale. We have so little reliable biographical information about Blake that we can only surmise why he chose to reject the volume, engraving none of its contents in his maturer years. By 1788, judging from his annotations on other writers and his own early engraved tracts, Blake was very much himself. He knew by then what he wanted to say even if he did not always know the forms his expression might take. In 1783, at twenty-six, Blake was developed enough not to want a public for his apprentice work as a poet. Yet the best poems in *Poetical Sketches* are the work of a master, and even the worst can teach us much about the difficult poet who was to come.

Poetical Sketches begins with four landscape poems addressed to the seasons. Though arranged in stanzas, the poems are unrhymed, and are clearly indebted to James Thomson's blank verse descriptive poem, *The Seasons.* What is immediately evident is that Blake is already closer to eighteenth century poets later than Thomson (to Collins and Chatterton in particular) and that his practice as a landscape poet in the 1770's is premonitory of the work of Shelley and Keats fifty years later. Where Thomson's personifications are clear and simple, Blake's either approach a doubling or split between landscape and informing spirit as Collins's do, or else become actual mythmakings like Shelley's *West Wind* and Keats's *Autumn.*[1] Thomson's *Spring* opens:

> Come, gentle Spring, ethereal mildness, come;
> And from the bosom of your dropping cloud,
> While music wakes around, veiled in a shower
> Of shadowing roses, on our plains descend.

Here Spring as a personage, and as a season are clearly kept apart. The poet is thinking in seasonal images, and clothing his abstract goddess with them. Collins, in his *Ode to Evening*, a literary generation later, is thinking both abstractly and concretely at once, and describing the images of a lady and an evening in one another's terms:

> While Spring shall pour his show'rs, as oft
>   he wont,
> And bathe thy breathing tresses, meekest
>   Eve!
>   While Summer loves to sport,
>   Beneath thy ling'ring light:
> While sallow Autumn fills thy lap with
>   leaves . . .

The ling'ring light is the evening's, the lap the lady's, but the breathing tresses belong to both and cannot be assigned literally to either. This fusion substitutes a myth for the doubling of landscape and idea. We are being told a story about a creature other than human, in being a part of natural process, and more than natural, in being somewhat human. The next step towards mythmaking or the evanescence of the simile is taken in Blake's address *To Spring*:

> O thou with dewy locks, who lookest down
> Thro' the clear windows of the morning, turn
> Thine angel eyes upon our western isle,
> Which in full choir hails thy approach, O Spring!
>
> The hills tell each other, and the list'ning
> Valleys hear; all our longing eyes are turned
> Up to thy bright pavilions: issue forth,
> And let thy holy feet visit our clime.

> Come o'er the eastern hills, and let our winds
> Kiss thy perfumed garments; let us taste
> Thy morn and evening breath; scatter thy pearls
> Upon our love-sick land that mourns for thee.
>
> O deck her forth with thy fair fingers; pour
> Thy soft kisses on her bosom; and put
> Thy golden crown upon her languish'd head,
> Whose modest tresses were bound up for thee!

Spring here is like the "beloved" in the second chapter of the Song of Solomon. There, too, he comes upon the hills and looks forth at the windows, saying the winter is past and urging the love-sick land to rise up and come away with him. Blake's poem as thoroughly humanizes both the season and the earth, so much so that the abstract and the natural become subordinated to the image of sexual reunion.

In *To Summer*, the season is no longer a lover, but a youthful Apollo, a god of poetry incarnated again in a human form, whose "ruddy limbs and flourishing hair" suggest the first appearance in Blake of the visionary child later to be called Orc. The western isle of Britain, a love-sick land in *To Spring*, has now been sexually fulfilled into a poet's paradise:

> We lack not songs, nor instruments of joy,
> Nor echoes sweet, nor waters clear as heaven,
> Nor laurel wreaths against the sultry heat.

To Autumn is a dialogue between this poetic land and a mature harvest bard who sings a song of fruition:

> The narrow bud opens her beauties to
> The sun, and love runs in her thrilling veins;
> Blossoms hang round the brows of morning, and
> Flourish down the bright cheek of modest eve,
> Till clust'ring Summer breaks forth into singing,
> And feather'd clouds strew flowers round her head.

The assimilation of sexual joy to natural flowering here is so frequent in mythic thought as to be commonplace. What is more characteristic of Blake is the dual advent of song and achieved sexuality
in the stanza's final lines. *To Autumn* ends with a Miltonic reminder
(echoing the close of *Lycidas*) that our singer is season as well as
poet, or rather that our poet is as mortal as the season. But as Autumn leaves us his harvest, so the departing poet bequeaths us his
song:

> Thus sang the jolly Autumn as he sat;
> Then rose, girded himself, and o'er the bleak
> Hills fled from our sight; but left his golden
>   load.

This "golden load" of lyricism is totally abrogated by the harsh
clangor of *To Winter*:

> O Winter! bar thine adamantine doors:
> The north is thine; there hast thou built thy
>   dark
> Deep-founded habitation. Shake not thy roofs,
> Nor bend thy pillars with thine iron car.
> He hears me not, but o'er the yawning deep
> Rides heavy; his storms are unchain'd, sheathed
> In ribbed steel; I dare not lift mine eyes,
> For he hath rear'd his sceptre o'er the world.

Unlike the three earlier poems, the speaker here is a human individual, rather than the collective dwellers in a land or the land
itself. Here also, for the first time in this grouping of poems, a personal address to the season fails ("He hears me not") and conse-
quently the season becomes a hostile demon:

> Lo! now the direful monster, whose skin clings
> To his strong bones, strides o'er the groaning
>   rocks:
> He withers all in silence, and his hand
> Unclothes the earth, and freezes up frail life.

The songs are ended, and the withering results from the silence in which it takes place. Unlike Autumn, Winter *is* a personification, an abstraction clothed, even as he unclothes the earth. What can only be expressed, not addressed; spoken of, not to; is alien to us. Myth in relation to landscape requires an act of confrontation, but personification can exist only where there are unequal degrees of reality, in an inanimate universe or one where the animation is demonic, as in Blake's *To Winter*. At an astonishingly early age, Blake has grasped in sure potential all the fundamentals of his great program and theme. The natural must be transformed into the human, and mythmaking, the confrontation of life by life, a meeting between subjects, not subjects and objects—is the necessary mode of this transformation.

Therefore it is more than accident that Winter's appearance should anticipate that of Urizen, the fearful limiter of desire and oppressive sky-god of Blake's pantheon. Like Winter, Urizen's bones are more prominent than his flesh, his form more imposing than his substance. Like Winter, also, the cosmic demiurge is a spirit freezing up life, confining it in strict boundaries. Urizen's is the vision that emphasizes the *horizon* of thought (hence his name), the reductive tendency that wishes to bind us down to the gray particular of self-communing, the groaning rocks of a world in which we brood only on ourselves. Urizen's is the winter vision, Orc's the summer, and the songs of Blake's other seasons anticipate other aspects of cyclic struggle necessary before we are liberated into the immediacy of the human seasons.

Two small but subtle humanizing invocations follow, *To the Evening Star* and *To Morning*, both containing evidence of Spenser's influence on the young Blake.[2] *To the Evening Star* clearly echoes Spenser's *Epithalamion*, but where Spenser hails Venus as joying in the sight of married love, Blake makes the evening star a pastoral deity as well, covering the flocks with sacred dew and protecting them by its influence. The poem is an anticipation of the guarded pastoral world of Innocence, benignly adorned by natural process:

> scatter thy silver dew
> On every flower that shuts its sweet eyes
> In timely sleep. Let thy west wind sleep on

The lake; speak silence with thy glimmering eyes,
And wash the dusk with silver.

The soft sensuousness of these lines looks forward to the imagery
and tone of Blake's depictions of the state of being he will call "Beulah," the married land, or earthly paradise within nature and human
sexuality.[3] More characteristic even of Blake's later symbolism is the
other Spenserian fragment, *To Morning*:

O holy virgin! clad in purest white,
Unlock heav'n's golden gates, and issue forth;
Awake the dawn that sleeps in heaven; let light
Rise from the chambers of the east, and bring
The honied dew that cometh on waking day.
O radiant morning, salute the sun
Rouz'd like a huntsman to the chace, and, with
Thy buskin'd feet, appear upon our hills.

As before, Blake begins with an echo of Spenser's *Epithalamion*,
and recalls Psalm XIX, but both allusions are curiously ironic. Spenser's virgin bride comes out of her eastern chamber, like the sun, clad
in white, and ready for her marriage. The Psalm's sun emerges as a
bridegroom coming out of his chamber, and rejoicing as a strong man
to run a race. Blake's morning is a white-clad virgin goddess, but like
Diana she is a buskined huntswoman, not a runner, and she rouses
the sun like a huntsman to the chase. The association between the
hunt and virginity is for the mature Blake a sinister one, and the
unlocking of heaven's golden gates is another ambiguous image. There
is a suggestion that the classical Aurora, certainly no virgin, is becoming the first of Blake's elusive and demonic nature goddesses,
sadistic in her virginity, and mockingly cyclic in her effect upon mankind.

Just as Blake's morning compounds Diana and Aurora, so "the
prince of love" of the beautiful lyric "How sweet I roam'd from field
to field" is not just Cupid or Eros but Apollo the sun-god as well. The
singer of this song is enticed by the prince of love into his deceptive
"gardens fair," both a sexual paradise and a trap. Once secured, the
singer becomes an object for the sadistic satisfaction of the deceiving
god:

He loves to sit and hear me sing,
Then, laughing, sports and plays with me;
Then stretches out my golden wing,
And mocks my loss of liberty.

Partly this is an esoteric parable of the fall of nature, which Blake will expand on many years later. More simply, it is a first account of the movement from Innocence into Experience, with the deceptions of nature as the responsible agent of transition.

Most of the songs in the Elizabethan manner in *Poetical Sketches* are only technical exercises, charming but very slight. The exception is the remarkable *Mad Song*, in which Blake's genius for intellectual satire begins to manifest itself. *Mad Song* is the direct ancestor of poems like *The Tyger*, or the dramatic speeches of unintended self-revelation made by the mythic figures throughout Blake's major works. The singer of *Mad Song* is self-deceiving, like the chanter of *The Tyger*, but Blake intends us to discover this by ourselves:

The wild winds weep,
 And the night is a-cold;
Come hither, Sleep,
 And my griefs unfold:
But lo! the morning peeps
 Over the eastern steeps,
And the rustling birds of dawn
The earth do scorn.

The unfolding of griefs in dreams is being welcomed, in contrast to the aspiring birds' scorn of their nightly bed. The freedom they find above is an enclosed vault, a pavement over his head, for this dreamer:

Lo! to the vault
 Of paved heaven,
With sorrow fraught
 My notes are driven:
They strike the ear of night,
 Make weep the eyes of day;
They make mad the roaring winds,
 And with tempests play.

Though he tries to project a demonic universe, this madman recognizes a humanized nature whose roarings and tempests are created by himself. In a final thrust towards true madness he dehumanizes himself, choosing instead the hazy form of "a fiend in a cloud":

> Like a fiend in a cloud,
>   With howling woe,
> After night I do croud,
>   And with night will go;
> I turn my back to the east
> From whence comforts have increas'd;
> For light doth seize my brain
> With frantic pain.

Not content with having imprisoned himself in space, the singer now seeks a more limited sense of time as well. Blake's satirical tone emerges most surely in this stanza. The preference for night here is a wilful derangement; even the regular alternation of light and darkness is to be shunned. The comforts of the sun are rejected, and the "frantic pain" of daylight afflicts the singer's brain, not his eyes. His conceptualizations are grounded upon the night, so that he can forget the oppressiveness of time, even as his self-vaporization into a cloudy fiend rescues him from the intolerable vault of space. The grimness of Blake's irony is probably due to the little poem's satiric function as the young poet's warning to himself. The proper reaction to the cosmos of Newton for a visionary is not in the evading of consciousness, as it was for Cowper and Collins, but in a more energetic perception of the mental forms of space and time. The alternative is voluntary derangement, in which the imagination becomes only a shadow, a spectre of itself.

Much of the remaining work in *Poetical Sketches* is of historical interest only, useful for locating Blake in his own literary age, or for demonstrating the varied extent of his early ambitions. The fragmentary play, *King Edward the Third*, is evidently ironic in its intent, but its parody of Whig sentiments is dangerously close to the actual mixture of mercantilism and patriotism that makes a poem like Thomson's *Liberty* so unreadable.[4] Blake's *Gwin, King of Norway*, imitated from several ballads in Percy's *Reliques* and from Chatterton, is a vigorous though lengthy exercise in popular poetry. Gwin is a tyrant whose reign allows the nobles to feed "upon the hungry poor." A giant, Gordred, awakens from a long sleep in a cave and leads a bloody revolt of the oppressed to a presumably decisive conclusion. The ballad is perhaps most interesting for its crude handling of the social theme, as compared to the subtle emphasis Blake will learn to place upon the necessity for an inner and conceptual revolution.

Not much can be claimed for another of these early ballads, *Fair Elenor,* an exercise in Gothic horror again quarried from Percy's *Reliques. Blind Man's Buff* is a more genuine example of Blake's ability to make something lively out of an old form, here a winter pastoral that echoes Shakespeare and the genial manner of Goldsmith. The very experimental *Imitation of Spenser* introduces Blake's distaste for Augustan poetry:

> Midas the praise hath gain'd of lengthen'd ears,
> For which himself might deem him ne'er the worse
> To sit in council with his modern peers,
> And judge of tinkling rhimes, and elegances terse.

This disesteem is charmingly generalized in the gently mocking *To the Muses,* where the conventional diction of much eighteenth century poetry is turned on itself. Wherever the Greek Muses have gone, somewhere in a prettified and artificial nature, they have forsaken the British lyre:

> How have you left the antient love
> That bards of old enjoy'd in you!
> The languid strings do scarcely move!
> The sound is forc'd, the notes are few!

The poem, with its gracious irony, hints at the advent of Blake's own Muses, those Daughters of Inspiration who would replace the absent Daughters of Memory.

Three curious prose poems end *Poetical Sketches* and contain hints as to the prophetic mode Blake's Muses would revive in the country once adorned by Milton. *The Couch of Death* is poorly expressed, yet turns imaginatively upon a visionary intercession that mysteriously transforms the fear of mortality into joy. *Contemplation* opposes the conviction of mortality to the comforting cycle of nature. *Samson,* clearly influenced by Milton, is Blake's first exercise in contemplating the wiles and dark effects of what he was later to call the Female Will. None of these Ossianic pieces is as directly premonitory of Blake's later concerns as a *Song by an Old Shepherd,* copied into a presentation volume of *Poetical Sketches* a few years after the book was printed. The concept of Innocence makes its problematical appearance here as "a winter's gown" to help us abide the outward storm of life. The earliest *Songs of Innocence,* probably written in 1784, are involved in the same satirical complex of ideas that could find so striking an emblem for human potential as this equivocal gown, fashioned out of the poverty of ignorance against the natural storm of experience.

CHAPTER TWO

Early Tracts: Natural Religion
and Imagination

A satirical prose-fragment, *An Island in the Moon*, is the only sub-
stantial writing by Blake that we have between the *Poetical Sketches*
and the earliest engraved works, the tracts *There Is No Natural Religion* (two series) and *All Religions Are One*, etched about 1788.
An Island in the Moon sometimes suggests the influence of Sterne,
and hints at the kind of genial intellectual caricature that Peacock was
to achieve a generation later than Blake.

The *Island* is too much a fragment to be read for its own values,
but it is instructive in at least two respects towards a reader's apprehension of Blake. The fragment's victims are obsessed reasoners of
the reductive kind, all of them seeking to negate the full humanness
of existence. They are also compulsive singers, and their songs range
from a fine, vicious attack on the marriage-convention made by a
figure who probably represents Blake himself, to the first appearance
of three beautiful lyrics later to be engraved as part of the *Songs of
Innocence*. These first drafts of *Holy Thursday*, the *Nurse's Song* and
The Little Boy Lost are inserted in a purely satiric context, but they
instantly qualify that context by putting everyone into a still sadder
humor. They compel silence, and effectively disrupt the tone of the
larger work. We can surmise not only that the *Songs of Innocence*
have a hidden root in satire (as Frye and Erdman have done)[1] but
also that they helped turn Blake from developing his satirical gifts
too overtly in one of the eighteenth-century modes of satire. Blake
never ceased to be a satirist, and even *The Book of Urizen* is more
a satire on orthodox theogonies than a serious theogony in its own
right. But Blake is a very subtle and original blend of satirist and

visionary; he rarely presents satire unrelieved by the imaginative projection of worlds closer to his desire. One may guess that he abandoned the *Island* fragment because it did not allow him the scope for a contrary vision that his temperament demanded. As he contemplated the first drafts of his mature lyrics he perhaps came to understand the use he could make of their pastoral convention for a different kind of satire, in which whole states of existence could be portrayed as demonstrating one another's inadequacies.

Between this embryo of the *Songs of Innocence* and the realization of that complete work, Blake made two attempts to realize his emerging conceptual universe, one in prose in the tracts of 1788, and the other in the experimental poem *Tiriel* of 1789. Though the tracts are not really finished or consecutive works, Blake thought enough of them to keep engraving them in his mature canon. To read them now is to encounter the direct point at which Blake and a major eighteenth-century way of thinking first met in what was to be a lifelong and increasingly bitter conflict.

Blake's polemical title, *There Is No Natural Religion*, involves us in the problem of recapturing the special meaning that Natural Religion or Deism had for Blake. "Deism" is the dominant system of Error in Blake's poetry, and clearly Blake's Deism and historical Deism are not the same thing. Yet we need to know a minimum about the historical phenomenon if we are to understand Blake's mythic loathing for his "Deism."

As Descartes had resolved to doubt whatever could be doubted, so Blake in reaction resolved to find an image of truth in everything it was possible to believe. In Descartes it is God who sustains and regulates the relations between the antithesis of matter and soul, unthinking object and thinking subject. Yet the antithesis in Descartes is so sharp that the grounds of knowledge are withdrawn unless the sustaining and regulating agent, God, assumes a direct and concerned potency. Spinoza (in whom, Leslie Stephen observed, the essence of Deism was to be found)[2] solved the antithesis by bringing matter and soul together as counterparts, outer and inner, of one world. Spinoza's God, unlike the Jehovah of orthodoxy, is not separate from the universe. For later thinkers influenced by Spinoza it might seem that Stephen's witty summary was true: "The divine power seems to become a factor which enters on both sides of every equation, and may therefore be omitted."[3]

Deism so widened God as to follow Spinoza in making the God of the Churches unnecessary. The power of Spinoza's thought survives in Deism only as a strength of desperation, to be expected of a rationalism whose assumptions are outmoded. The ontology of Deism had been destroyed by Locke's attack on innate ideas, yet Locke retained a God proved by the idea of causation, a retention that could not honestly survive Hume. The Deists held earnestly to what they claimed was the objective fact of natural order and the subjective fact of man's reason even though Hume had demonstrated that order to be chance, and that reason to be custom. Blake could not rest in Humean skepticism or in Deistical deluded certainty. Blake's sketch of an escape from skepticism and from the tyranny of nature and reason was to assign to the imagination the power to create its own order in space, and its own consciousness in time.

The theological origins of English Deism, unlike the philosophical, are to be discovered in English traditions. Lord Herbert of Cherbury in his *De Veritate* (1624) had set down five fundamental propositions of natural religion (God exists; He ought to be worshipped; such worship depends on virtue as well as piety; repentance is proper for believers; some future state of rewards and punishments exists). The rational theology of Chillingworth and Tillotson, and the indirect ethical influences that led to Shaftesbury and Mandeville combined with the principles of Herbert of Cherbury to produce the Deist polemicists—Collins, Toland, Tindal.

By the time Blake was a young man, the Deist controversy was long over, but with some justice Blake decided that the Church of England had absorbed its defeated enemy and become Deist in spirit. From Blake's fierce viewpoint a book like Locke's *Reasonableness of Christianity* would have seemed no less Deist than Toland's *Christianity Not Mysterious*. Locke believed that God meant Christianity to give new authority to the dictates of reason, while Toland found finally that natural religion itself would vanish if *all* mystery were removed from Christianity. Blake must have taken a grimly ironical pleasure in such a conclusion, or in the claim of later Deists like Tindal and Voltaire that natural and revealed religion were necessarily the same.

Blake's reaction to Deism is neither that of the orthodox Bishop Butler, who refuted impudent rationalism by a demonstration of its mysterious limits, or the great mystical moralist William Law, whose *The Case of Reason* crushed Tindal and massively demonstrated the radical gap between natural religion and the divine arbitrariness of a revealed religion, whose God can never be approached by any human or natural analogy. Blake did not care about Critical Deism, that is, the attack on the historicity or unity or plausibility of the Bible. Defending the Deist Paine against the orthodox Bishop Watson, Blake pungently dismisses that side of the Deist Controversy:

> I cannot concieve the Divinity of the books in the Bible to consist either in who they were written by, or at what time, or in the historical evidence which may be all false in the eyes of one man & true in the eyes of another, but in the Sentiments & Examples, which, whether true or Parabolic, are Equally useful as Examples given to us of the perverseness of some & its consequent evil & the honesty of others & its consequent good.[4]

Blake's objection is to so-called Constructive Deism and its covert influence on the English Church. The God of Constructive Deism may not have been the mathematical diagram Blake felt him to be, but certainly he was a cold abstraction at best. Still worse, this God led finally to the Panglossian Deity who presided over a monstrous universe in which all the apparent evils were necessarily for the best. Blake may have read just enough of Butler's *Analogy of Religion* to discover that Deism was being refuted by the belief that nature reveals to us the same God as Christianity. The moral consequence might then be that all natural suffering was deserved punishment, a view against which Blake reacts violently in the *Songs of Experience*.

Blake's passion against the Deistic Anglicanism of his day was also based on his own sense of the parallel between Deism and neo-Classicism. Leslie Stephen, a very sympathetic critic of eighteenth century thought and literature, makes the point that "the most conspicuous literary phenomenon in the latter half of the eighteenth century in England is the strange decline of speculative energy."[5] Blake attributed this decline to Deism and its constricted vision of God as a divine watchmaker. In 1788 Blake attacks Deism with a fervor he was to maintain for forty years, in the conviction that Deism was the negation of Imagination.

The first tract denying Natural Religion is the simpler and less Blakean of the two. The desires and perceptions of man are not limited to objects of sense, and so man's desires and perceptions have an origin that transcends man as a natural organism or a reasoning power based upon nature:

> If it were not for the Poetic or Prophetic character the Philosophic & Experimental would soon be at the ratio of all things, & stand still, unable to do other than repeat the same dull round over again.

The "ratio" here is Blake's own word, rightly interpreted by Middleton Murry as "the mental abstract: that idea or abstract image of the thing, which serves, in the ordinary commerce of life and thought, for the thing itself."[6] The Philosophic and Experimental, left to themselves, would stand still or be trapped in cycle, with reason fed only by weakening memories of natural experience. The ratio of all things would be a mental abstract of all experience, and grossly inferior to the immediacy of the things themselves. But the creative energy of man, not natural in its dependency, is expressed in the Poetic or Prophetic character, and so a perpetual freshness of ideas is available for reason to build upon. There is then no Natural Religion because the religious ideas of man are Poetic in origin, and owe nothing to nature.

In the second series of aphorisms against Deism, Blake goes a step further into his own conceptual universe by identifying the ratio with the fallen or natural Selfhood of man, and both with reason. In style Blake suddenly becomes very difficult, and emphasizes gnomic expressiveness at some expense to clarity:

> IV. The bounded is loathed by its possessor. The same dull round, even of a universe, would soon become a mill with complicated wheels.

> V. If the many become the same as the few when possess'd, More! More! is the cry of a mistaken soul; less than All cannot satisfy Man.

VI. If any could desire what he is incapable of possessing, despair must be his eternal lot.

VII. The desire of Man being Infinite, the possession is Infinite & himself Infinite.

Application. He who sees the Infinite in all things, sees God.
He who sees the Ratio only, sees himself only.

Therefore God becomes as we are, that we may be as he is.

Proposition IV introduces the mill as Blake's symbol of the static
natural cycle. In V, we hear one of Blake's characteristic exaltations
of the infiniteness of human desire. Desiring more is a mistake, for
once we possess the many they will become as the few, for when
possessed they are bounded, and the bounded is loathed by its possessor. Only the cry for All! is truly a cry deserving the honorific title
of human. The lineaments of gratified desire will come to man only
when he possesses the infinite power of God, for Whom desire and
fulfillment are one. To see the Infinite in all things is to see God, and
to see the Infinite within one is to see God in one. But to see the
negation of the Infinite, the bounded mental abstract or ratio, is to
see only one's own divided self. God is man, but man is not altogether
or always God. In a humanistic displacement of the doctrine of the
Incarnation, Blake daringly concludes by having God becoming altogether as we are, infinite desire, that we may be as he is, infinite
fulfillment.

Since the desire and fulfillment alike come from the Poetic character (Blake may be thinking of Collins's *Ode* on that subject when
he uses this phrase), the next step must be to identify the Poetic
character with the true or real Man who is also the source of the true
God. This is the burden of Blake's third tract, *All Religions Are One,*
in which he hints at the mythological counterpoint between religious
traditions that was to become part of his symbolism. In this third
tract, Blake prefigures the rejection of dualism he was to proclaim in
The Marriage of Heaven and Hell. What the orthodox have called
the soul is the Poetic Genius, and "the body or outward form of Man
is derived from the Poetic Genius," that is, the body is that part of
the soul that natural sense can perceive.

The most acute analysis this tract has received is by Middleton Murry, who sees that in it Blake is identifying the individual creativity or Poetic Genius in every man with the principle of individuation itself.[7] But the self or ratio is in every man also, and its brutishness is made manifest in the laws of society the Deists have extracted from the laws of nature. The Jewish and Christian testaments are derived from the Poetic Genius, but so are the testaments of all other religions. Blake's implication is that no law should be founded on the "probable impossibilities" of these poems. In the first poem by Blake that followed his awakening against natural religion, *Tiriel* (1789), we see the horrible results of the rule of law founded on a faith in the divine tyranny and uniformity of nature.

CHAPTER THREE

Tiriel: The Voice in the Wilderness

Tiriel (1789) is the harshest of Blake's poems before *Jerusalem*. Tiriel's name may contain a reference to the Prince of Tyre in Ezekiel 28:13–16. That Prince, once a guardian of the Ark of God, becomes the Covering Cherub who constitutes a barrier between man and the re-entry into Paradise. More simply, Tiriel's name may compound the Greek root of 'tyrant' and the Hebrew *El* for "the Almighty," one of the names of God.

In the mythic background of the poem *Tiriel* are the stories of Shakespeare's King Lear and Lear's friend Gloucester, and perhaps of Sophocles' Oedipus. All these are fathers who curse their children, become crazed or blind, and are doomed to wander under the guidance of a daughter or a son-like fool, or a son concealed by simulated madness. Tiriel curses his children, is mad and blind, and is forced to use a daughter as his guide. In the historical allegory, the story of Tiriel probably does have some reference to the madness of George III. But Lear and Oedipus serve Blake's purpose better than any contemporary monarch could. Lear and Oedipus move finally into the emancipation of a tragic resolution. They reconcile themselves, purged, to a higher nature within themselves before they die. Tiriel's story ends in negation. Having awakened to his own intellectual error, Tiriel can only die in despair. The errors of Lear and Gloucester are errors of passion, and their largeness of feeling first entraps and finally liberates them. But Tiriel's error is one of reason, and Tiriel, who is an early version of Urizen, is slain by the reason's horror of the consequences of its own supremacy over will and feeling.

Tiriel is an aged monarch lapsing into senility. The blindness of

Oedipus is voluntary, being both self-punishment and a judgment upon the deceptions of nature. Tiriel's blindness is the involuntary and ironic consequence of a vision totally unconcerned with the reality of other selves. Tiriel was King of the West, the realm of man's body in Blake, and therefore the gate back to Eden, since it is by an increase in sensual fulfillment that man is to recover himself. But Tiriel was a restrictive and moralizing ruler of the body, as his name of the Almighty Tyrant symbolizes. In his old age, he stands "before the Gates of his beautiful palace," already excluded from the center of his domain. His wife, the fire or spirit of his existence, fades in death, leaving Tiriel as a strictly isolated selfhood. The sons of Tiriel are presumably, like the sons or cities of Urizen, his imaginative achievements. As such they are "sons of the Curse," and a Curse incarnate is the role of Tiriel all through the poem.

Having been Law incarnate, the degeneration of Tiriel's activity into the passive one of cursing suggests that Blake's allegorical intention is the quite daring one of showing us the tragedy of Jehovah, the God of the Law, portrayed as if he were Lear roaring out on the heath. Blake's theme in this poem might well be simplified as: "God is dying. Will he learn a different conception of himself before he dies?" *Tiriel* is a very dramatic poem, and may be a Blakean attempt at a new form of passion play, in which a conception of divinity purges itself, and dies of its own understanding.

Tiriel has cursed too often in the past for his further threats to affright his sons, for whom the eldest speaks:

> Were we not slaves till we rebell'd? Who cares
> for Tiriel's curse?
> His blessing was a cruel curse; his curse may
> be a blessing.

Yet Tiriel continues almighty in that his curses are realized. Since his irascibility is very near madness, his curses are in excess of their provocation. Blake does not give us a cause for Tiriel's wrath; most probably, as with Lear, there is a cause only in nature and not in circumstances. The eldest son's reference to having rebelled is probably to be understood in a purely domestic context, in terms of the poem's narrative. But domestic disobedience for this fading God-King is an intolerable sin, especially when offered to him by beings he has created. Previously he had cast out his brother Zazel, and cursed all that brother's descendants. Zazel is possibly the Hebrew Azazel ("scapegoat") and Blake's interest in the uncanonical and apocalyptic *Book of Enoch* would have reminded him that the first "demon" cast off there by Jehovah is called Azazel.[1] Like a castoff scapegoat, and like Lear, Gloucester, and Oedipus, Tiriel now is "to wander like a Son of Zazel in the rocks." Ironically, the tyrant chooses the fate he has first invented for others.

The second section of the poem explains Tiriel's desire to cast himself out into the wilderness. Faced by approaching extinction, he has a crucial choice. He can alter his understanding of his own self, and thus be twice-born into an imaginative existence, or he can seek a mere cyclic renewal of the natural existence he has so horribly experienced. He chooses the self-defeat of the latter quest, and goes back to the unborn state Blake in this poem calls "the vales of Har," and was later to name the lower level or limit of Beulah. Thel, in her book, lives in the vales of Har, as Har and Heva in *Tiriel* do. The condition of Har and Heva, imbecilic infancy or aged ignorance, is the state Thel chooses for herself when she flees back unhindered into the vales of Har at the close of her poem. Har and Heva are the proof that Beulah, dwelled in too long, becomes what Blake will call Ulro—that the state of Innocence cannot be sustained but becomes finally a self-absorbed bower of solipsistic bliss, unless it is outgrown.

"Har" is the Hebrew for mountain. In Blake, the creature called Har is the ironic negation of the prophetic cry that every valley shall be exalted. Instead of the exaltation of the valley, Blake gives us the fall of the mountain into a vale. Har's wife is Heva, which suggests that Har is Adam, but Adam in Blake is the limit of Contraction, the point beyond which mankind cannot fall. So Adam comprehends more than Har; he has life and eternity in him as well as death and time. But Har is in the endless time of a second and lunatic infancy; he has never been born into life. He cannot of course die, but this is merely because he has never lived. Frye's identification of Har as the Selfhood is therefore altogether likely, for the Selfhood is an individual man's idea of his own separateness from others or, at last, his own death.[2] Tiriel goes to Har seeking eternal life, and can find in

him only the living death of the undeveloped natural foetus that has
been frozen at one stage of its growth into the human. Having fled
death-in-life, the tyrant finds life-in-death. The ironic hint is that Tiriel's quest represents religion's attempt to posit a literal immortality
which repeats but does not renew life. The Body wants to be resurrected, but the Body's ruler, Tiriel, can find for it only a zombie's
destiny.

Har and Heva are tended by a nurse who is Blake's prophecy of
the nurse, Nature, in Wordsworth's *Intimations* Ode. Blake's figure,
Mnetha, whose name suggests both Athena or wisdom and Mnemos-
yne or memory, is established as imperceptive when she refuses to
recognize, in the poor blind man before her, the tyrant she remembers
in his joy. Tiriel, as he contemplates the nature of the vale of Har
and its inhabitants, comes to understand that he cannot abide in
this place either, for in its vision his desperate quest is reduced to
the alternative goals of death or deathless imbecility. When Har
fears the newly arrived Tiriel, he describes the quester in preternatural
terms:

> For he is the king of rotten wood & of the
> bones of death;
> He wanders without eyes & passes thro'
> thick walls and doors.

When Har has ceased to fear Tiriel, the descriptive terms become
natural, and the affectionate gruesomeness goes beyond the supernatural projection in unconscious horror:

> God bless thy poor bald pate! God bless thy
> hollow winking eyes!
> God bless thy shrivel'd beard! God bless
> thy many-wrinkled forehead!
> Thou hast no teeth, old man! & thus I kiss
> thy sleek bald head.

With this imbecilic blessing on his head, Tiriel turns from the
"pleasant" vale to seek the rocks and weary hills again. As he wanders
in the wastelands of what is to be the Ulro, he encounters Ijim, who

is a satyr or wild man, brutalized not so much by nature as by the presences he has confronted in a world animized by himself.[3]

Where Har and Heva have seen Tiriel as being his own aged father, Ijim sees him as a phantom usurper of Tiriel's form. To the eyes of those who have not passed through Experience, negative holiness cannot fade. To one who has known only the nightmares of Experience, negative holiness or moral restriction may appear to have lost its force, but the appearance of such spiritual bankruptcy cannot be accepted as reality.

The blinding irony of Blake's poem is concentrated in its subsequent images of dramatic misunderstanding. The savage Ijim, carrying the exhausted tyrant on his back, enters the gate of Tiriel's palace and demands of the terrified sons of Tiriel that they fetch their father to behold his phantom double. As they stand confounded, Tiriel begins to curse them again; he has learned something about life and death, but nothing as yet about himself. His curses are effectual, and his sons are either slain by natural disturbances or else cower, waiting for inevitable death.

In destroying his sons, Tiriel has destroyed the form of his own creations, and is left alone with the external nature his own curses have done so much to brutalize. His five senses are his only remaining connectors to a humanized reality outside of himself. But he curses four of his daughters, symbolic of his senses, and having chosen thus to increase his blindness, is left only with Hela, his sense of touch or sexuality. Her name (the Eddic for "hell") indicates his initial attitude towards her, and his crisis is hardly designed to make him more forgiving. He curses her for her desperate defiance, and she becomes a hideous Medusa, a final projection of horror onto the human identity. With even his sense of touch disordered, and sexuality reduced to a necessary but minimal form of life, Tiriel gropes his way back to the imbecile paradise of Har. Now, at the last, a hysteria of sudden and dreadful understanding comes upon Tiriel. He repudiates the vision of holiness as negative virtue that he has inherited from Har, and denounces also the repressive wisdom he has founded upon that heritage. Har is Tiriel's father, as Adam, the natural man or selfhood, was Jehovah's. The state of unorganized Innocence or ignorance has made a monster from its vision of the fatherhood of God and the childhood of man. The dying God, Tiriel, casts out all belief in uniformity, in natural limitation, but can find nothing to replace such "idiot's wisdom," and so dies cursing the natural Man, Har, who has made God in his own foolish image.

Blake did not engrave *Tiriel*, though he had made sketches to illustrate it. The last of these shows Tiriel lying dead in a vineyard, with Hela staring down at his corpse. As Tiriel speaks, in the poem's final lines, of existing on "a drear sandy plain," it is evident that Blake intended the final illustration to be ironic.

The poem is a masterpiece, if irony alone is sufficient to make one, but Blake had little regard for intellectual satire as such, powerful as his gifts were for it. Though he is second only to Swift as an English satirist, Blake was too much an apocalyptic thinker to abide even momentarily in any merely satiric vision. *Tiriel* is a very uncomfortable poem to read, and one can guess that it made even Blake uncomfortable. The poem is uncompromisingly exuberant in its negations, and this impression of imaginative energy saves the poem from the ugliness that its sustained quest of moral idiocy necessarily seeks. The death of even the falsest conception of God made a part of Blake's imagination uneasy, for a poet knows the aphorism of Wallace Stevens to be true: the death of one god is the death of all.[4] Blake spared himself, and us, the mocking laughter of Nietzsche's Zarathustra. He abandoned *Tiriel* and its too-overtly satirical vision of Innocence for the more ambiguous and aesthetically gratifying vision of Beulah. He began to gather together and engrave a group of his lyrics as the *Songs of Innocence*.

CHAPTER FOUR

The Pastoral Image

Songs of Innocence

Of the traditional "kinds" of poetry, Blake had attempted pastoral and satire at the very start, in the *Poetical Sketches*, though the satire there is subtle and tentative. In *Tiriel*, satire and tragedy are first brought together in a single work by Blake. *Songs of Innocence* is Blake's closest approach to pure pastoral, but an even subtler form of satire seems to be inherent in these famous visions of a childhood world, as their genesis out of *An Island in the Moon* might suggest.

Pastoral as a literary form is generally associated with the antithetical relationship of Nature and Art, which on a social level becomes an opposition between country and town.[1] Art and the urban world come together as an image of experiential Fall from Nature's Golden Age, a sad manhood following a glorious childhood. This pastoral association, which held from Theocritus and Virgil until the seventeenth century, has no relevance to *Songs of Innocence*.

Blake's shepherds are not types of the natural life as such, but rather ironically accepted figures, whose joys testify to the benevolent maternalism of the world as it supposedly is when viewed by the Deistical temperament. The Nature of *Songs of Innocence* is viewed softly, and seems to offer back the soft comfort implicit in the earliest Christian pastoral, as well as its eighteenth century adaptations. The Christ of St. John is the good shepherd who knows his sheep and is known of them, and who offers his pastoral call to the scattered flocks. Behind this shepherd is the pastoralism of the Song of Solomon, where an allegory of divine love is presented as a song of human marriage set "beside the shepherds' tents." Blake also sets a desired good in the simple context of pastoral convention, but then demonstrates that no value can be sustained by that context. The purity and wisdom of the child or natural man is for Blake not the reflection of environment, but a self-consuming light that momentarily transforms natural reality into an illusion of innocence. The human child of *Songs of Innocence* is a changeling, reared by a foster nurse who cannot recognize his divinity, and whose ministrations entrap him in a universe of death.

Blake's reading of literary pastoral centered in Spenser and Milton, but included (in translation) Virgil, who inaugurated the tradition by which the young poet aspiring towards epic begins with allegorical pastoral. Late in life, Blake executed a beautiful series of woodcuts for Thornton's version of Virgil's pastorals. In these woodcuts, which strongly affected the younger painters Samuel Palmer and Edward Calvert, Blake presents a remarkably Hebraized Virgil, who has more in common with Bunyan, Spenser, and Milton than with his own Roman world.

In so thoroughly absorbing Virgil into an English Puritan vision of innocence, Blake made a startling but successful continuance of the long tradition by which European pastoral had turned Virgil to its own purposes.[2] The idealization of an Arcadian existence in nature became assimilated to Adam's loss of Eden, and to his descendants' nostalgia for that blissful seat. The theme of heroic virtue in the Puritan Saint could not readily be associated with longings for a naturalistic repose in an earthly paradise. The Protestant poet's solution was to dream of two paradises, an upper and a lower, a heavenly city and a breathing garden. So Bunyan's Pilgrims saw "the Countrey of *Beulah* . . . within sight of the City they were going to," Beulah being a land where "the shining Ones commonly walked, because it was upon the Borders of Heaven."[3] So Spenser, whose Red-Crosse Knight is allowed only a distant glimpse of the City he is going to, nevertheless allows himself and his readers a detailed view of the Gardens of Adonis, a place where Spring and harvest are continual, both meeting at one time.[4] Michael Drayton in his *Muses' Elizium*, the Spenserian culmination of visionary pastoral in English before Milton, secularizes these Gardens into a Poet's Paradise, an allegory of poetry's solace rendered by poetry itself. Milton is Blake's direct ancestor in pastoral

as he was in epic, and Milton's early poetry is the likely source for
Blake's version of the *locus amoenus*, the lovely place upon which a
visionary landscape centers.

Milton's earlier poetry, from *On the Morning of Christ's Nativity*
to *Lycidas* and *Comus*, failed to resolve its creator's inner conflicts
between the other-worldly religion of a Puritan believer and the desire of the greatest of Renaissance Humanists to free man's thought
and imagination. Unlike Calvin, Milton insists always that the will
of a regenerate man is made free by his rebirth in the spirit. Again
unlike Calvin, Milton is not a dualist; the outward form of man as
well as the human soul is made in God's image. Arthur Barker summarizes Milton's position by emphasizing that dualism "was unpal-
atable to one whose highest delight was the integration of form and
substance in poetry. Man must therefore be regarded as an indivisible
unit."[5] Yet, as Barker emphasizes again, Milton turned to prose in
his middle period because his early pastorals did not fulfill this desire
to integrate nature and spirit within himself.

Blake recognized this aspect of Milton's experience, and profited
by it to the extent of approaching pastoral in a spirit of subtle irony.
The *Songs of Innocence* are the songs *of* the innocent state; they are
not songs *about* Innocence. For Blake's "Innocence" is from the start
an equivocal term. The root meaning of innocence is "harmlessness";
hence its derived meanings of "freedom from sin" and "guiltlessness."
Blake's first use of Innocence is in the *Song by an Old Shepherd*
he added to *Poetical Sketches*, where the quality of Innocence serves
as a winter's gown that enables us to abide "life's pelting storm."
In annotating the moralist Lavater, probably in 1788, Blake speaks of
one who is "offended with the innocence of a child & for the same
reason, because it reproaches him with the errors of acquired folly."
Neither of these uses of Innocence make it an opposite of sin or
harmfulness or guilt, but rather of experiential life, its storms and its
acquired follies. So, by 1789 when he engraved the *Songs of Innocence*, Blake already seems to have anticipated joining them together
with songs that would show the "Contrary State of the Human Soul,"
as he did five years later. Innocence is a state of the soul that warms
our hearts against experience, and reproaches the errors of a supposedly mature existence. So far this is easily assimilated to the Arcadian state of the soul presented by the Virgilian pastoral and its

descendants. But Blake could not stop with a study of the nostalgias, or with a simple reproach to adult readers. The next step in understanding his concept of Innocence is to begin examining some of its songs.

The *Introduction*, "Piping down the valleys wild," is a poem of immediate knowledge, and evidently celebrates a kind of unsought natural harmony. The pure reactions of the child to the piper are those of the spirit as yet undivided against itself, free of self-consciousness. The child has not sundered itself to self-realization, and his natural world shares the same unity, as the little poem, *A Dream*, indicates.

The same theme, of a primal oneness between the human and the natural, is exemplified in the traditional Christian pastoral of *The Lamb* and *The Shepherd*, but a disturbing element begins to enter as well. The Lamb dressed in its own wool is described as wearing "clothing of delight," in an overly anthropomorphized image, and the Shepherd inspires a confidence in his flock which is entirely dependent upon his actual presence. *The Little Girl Lost* and *The Little Girl Found*, transferred by Blake to *Songs of Experience* in 1794, relate the theme of Innocence as primal unity with the animal creation, to the romance convention of the lost child cared for by beasts of prey. The transfer to Experience was probably based on *The Little Girl Lost's* opening stanzas:

> In futurity
> I prophetic see
> That the earth from sleep
> (Grave the sentence deep)
>
> Shall arise and seek
> For her maker meek;
> And the desert wild
> Become a garden mild.

As a prophecy of a return to Innocence, this was clearly out of place *in* the realm of Innocence. So was the implied sardonicism that climaxes *The Little Girl Found*, when the seeking parents lose their fear and make their home in the land of lions and tygers where their daughter is found:

Then they followed
Where the vision led,
And saw their sleeping child
Among tygers wild.

To this day they dwell
In a lonely dell;
Nor fear the wolvish howl
Nor the lions' growl.

This is an escape from Experience, as Blake recognized when he transposed the poem into that state of existence. The genuine ambiguities of Innocence begin to reveal themselves in *The Blossom:*

Merry, Merry Sparrow!
Under leaves so green
A happy Blossom
Sees you swift as arrow,
Seek your cradle narrow
Near my Bosom.

Pretty, Pretty Robin!
Under leaves so green
A happy Blossom
Hears you sobbing, sobbing,
Pretty, Pretty Robin,
Near my Bosom.

The repeated phrase, "A happy Blossom," in the third line of each stanza is a clear mark of the inadvertence of the natural world to suffering even when the grief ought to be its own. The Blossom is equally happy to grow on the same tree that cradles the sparrow's merriness, or that merely shades the robin's sobbing. It is enough that the joy or the sorrow takes place near its bosom. In *The Ecchoing Green* a day's cycle moves from spontaneous sounds of happiness in the first stanza to the nostalgic laughter of the old folk in the second, to the total absence of any sound in the conclusion:

Till the little ones, weary,
No more can be merry;
The sun does descend,
And our sports have an end.
Round the laps of their mothers
Many sisters and brothers,
Like birds in their nest,
Are ready for rest,
And sport no more seen
On the darkening Green.

The refrains of the first two stanzas were of sport seen, in present and then in past time, on an *Ecchoing* Green. Now, with no sport to be seen upon it, the Green has lost its echoes also, and the darkening upon it is the shadow of mortality, recognition of which will end Innocence as a state. *The Divine Image* sets forth the virtues of that state at its most confident:

For Mercy has a human heart,
Pity a human face,
And Love, the human form divine,
And Peace, the human dress.

Then every man of every clime,
That prays in his distress,
Prays to the human form divine,
Love, Mercy, Pity, Peace.

The human form divine is the God of Innocence, but this God is not presented as a visual form or the image of the title, but rather as a monster of abstractions, formed out of the supposedly human element in each of Innocence's four prime virtues. What is the face of Mercy, or the heart of Pity, we are expected to wonder. In what dress does the human form of Love present itself, and what is the form of Peace? Until its matching contrary comes to it in *Songs of Experience*, the poem's prime characteristic is its deliberate incompleteness.

The same incompleteness, but expressed as an inability to make a necessary moral judgment, dominates *The Chimney Sweeper* of Innocence, where for the first time the inadequacy of the unsundered state is stressed. The voice of the Piper is replaced by the voice of the Chimney Sweeper, a charity child sold into bondage by his father and the Church:

> When my mother died I was very young,
> And my father sold me while yet my tongue
> Could scarcely cry " 'weep! 'weep! 'weep! 'weep!"
> So your chimneys I sweep, & in soot I sleep.

The coming together of "sweep" and "weep" here introduces the cry of Experience, which is "weep!". Blake is returning to the rhetorical art of his *Mad Song*; as readers we need both to understand the limitations of the poem's dramatic speaker, and yet to feel also the poignance attained by the intensity of that speaker's Innocence:

> There's little Tom Dacre, who cried when his head
> That curl'd like a lamb's back, was shav'd:
>   so I said
> "Hush, Tom! never mind it, for when your head's
>   bare
> You know that the soot cannot spoil your white
>   hair."

This is the Lamb, called by Christ's name, who became a little child, only to have his clothing of delight shorn by the exploiter of Experience. But more is in this stanza; the child's illogic mounts to a prophetic and menacing sublimity. The bare head remains adorned by an unspoiled white hair, comparable to the "naked & white" appearance of the children in their own liberating dream:

> And so he was quiet, & that very night,
> As Tom was a-sleeping, he had such a sight!
> That thousands of sweepers, Dick, Joe, Ned,
>   & Jack,
> Were all of them lock'd up in coffins of black.

> And by came an Angel who had a bright key,
> And he open'd the coffins & set them all free;
> Then down a green plain leaping, laughing, they
>   run,
> And wash in a river and shine in the Sun.
>
> Then naked & white, all their bags left behind,
> They rise upon clouds and sport in the wind;
> And the Angel told Tom, if he'd be a good boy,
> He'd have God for his father & never want joy.

The black coffins are at once confining chimneys and the black ragged forms of the sweeps, in the death of the body which has become their life. The Angel's promise is the loving fatherhood of God which, with the loving motherhood of Nature, is one of the prime postulates of Innocence. But the Angel's promise is also the direct projection, as dream-fulfillment, of the Church's disciplinary promise to its exploited charges. The final stanza, more powerful for its lack of consciously directed irony on the child's part, beats, with a new fierceness for Blake, against the confining and now self-deceiving trust of Innocence:

> And so Tom awoke and we rose in the dark,
> And got with our bags & our brushes to work.
> Tho' the morning was cold, Tom was happy &
>   warm;
> So if all do their duty they need not fear harm.

The sourness of that last line as a moral tag becomes sourer still in the last line of the *Holy Thursday* of Innocence:

> 'Twas on a Holy Thursday, their innocent faces
>   clean,
> The children walking two & two in red &
>   blue & green,
> Grey-headed beadles walk'd before, with wands
>   as white as snow,
> Till into the high dome of Paul's they like
>   Thames' waters flow.

O what a multitude they seem'd, these flowers of
    London town!
Seated in companies they sit with radiance all
    their own.
The hum of multitudes was there, but multitudes
    of lambs,
Thousands of little boys & girls raising their
    innocent hands.

Now like a mighty wind they raise to heaven the
    voice of song,
Or like harmonious thunderings the seats of
    Heaven among.
Beneath them sit the aged men, wise guardians
    of the poor;
Then cherish pity, lest you drive an angel
    from your door.

On Ascension Day the charity children are led into St. Paul's to celebrate the charity of God, that loving pity of which human charity is intended as a direct reflection. The voice of this song is not a child's, but rather of a self-deceived onlooker, impressed by a palpable vision of Innocence, moved by these flowers of London town. The flowing metre is gently idyllic, and the singer gives us two stanzas of Innocent sight, followed by the triumphant sound of Innocence raising its voice to Heaven.

The ambiguity of tone of Blake's songs is never more evident than here, and yet never more difficult to evidence. One can point of course to several disturbing details. The children's faces have been scrubbed clean, and are innocent, in a debased sense—because they ought to appear brutalized, which they are, and yet do not. The children are regimented; they walk two and two, and the beadles' wands are both badges of office and undoubtedly instruments of discipline in a savage British scholastic tradition. The children are dressed in the colors of life; the beadles are grey-headed and carry white as a death emblem. It is the fortieth day after Easter Sunday, forty days after Christ's ascension into Heaven, yet the children, his Lambs, still linger unwillingly in the wilderness of an exploiting society.

Though they flow like Thames' waters, this is not a mark of their freedom but of the binding of the Thames, which is already the 'chartered' river of the poem *London* in *Songs of Experience*. The prophet Joel, crying that man's wickedness was great, called for "multitude, multitudes in the valley of decision." The hum of multitudes is in St. Paul's, but these are multitudes of lambs, and their radiance is "all their own"; it has nothing to do with the Church. Their voice rises like a wind of judgment, and thunders harmoniously among the seats of Heaven. *Beneath* the children, spiritually as well as actually, are the seats of Heaven upon which sit the beadles. If these guardians of the poor are wise, it is not with the wisdom of Innocence, and their wisdom is epitomized in the last line, at once one of the bitterest in Blake by its context, and one of the most seemingly Innocent in its content.

This contrast between context and content is prevalent. The childish patter of *Infant Joy* is meaningful only when we realize how much the poem's voice imposes its sentimentality upon the helplessly mute infant. A *Cradle Song* has a surface of even more exquisite sentimentality, as it identifies the lovely infant with the Christ Child for whom "all creation slept and smil'd." The poem's enigmatic beauty hovers in the juxtaposition of its final stanzas with the milkiness that has gone before:

> Sweet babe, in thy face
> Holy image I can trace.
> Sweet babe, once like thee,
> Thy maker lay and wept for me,
>
> Wept for me, for thee, for all,
> When he was an infant small.
> Thou his image ever see,
> Heavenly face that smiles on thee,
>
> Smiles on thee, on me, on all;
> Who became an infant small.
> Infant smiles are his own smiles;
> Heaven & earth to peace beguiles.

The tears of the Christ Child were not an image of infant help-lessness, but a lament for all mortality, for the transience of Inno-cence. Yet the mother singing A *Cradle Song* will not see this, but converts the infant god of Innocence very rapidly into a father god of the same state, with a supposedly inevitable movement from "Wept for me, for thee, for all" to "Smiles on thee, on me, on all." The tense shifts from past to present, for Christ's incarnation, to the Mother of Innocence, is a past moment, and his heavenly smiles a perpetual present.

The more elaborate patterning of *Night* is a clearer testimony to the ambiguities of Innocence. The best definition of Innocence may be that it is that state of the human soul in which we ascertain truth as immediate knowledge, for the knower and the known share an unsought natural harmony. In *Night* that harmony is apprehended with a loving wonder, edged by the consciousness of how precarious such harmony must be. The guardian angels of the childhood world may not avert all natural calamity, but what they cannot prevent, they translate into new worlds:

> When wolves and tygers howl for prey,
> They pitying stand and weep;
> Seeking to drive their thirst away,
> And keep them from the sheep.
> But if they rush dreadful,
> The angels, most heedful,
> Recieve each mild spirit,
> New worlds to inherit.

This is a gentle irony, but an irony nevertheless. The confiding simplicity of tone reminds us of the paradox of how the spiritual must be sundered from the natural, for the spiritual "new worlds" cannot exist unless the condition of nature surrenders itself, to be absorbed in the higher angelic condition. However gently, Blake be-gins to hint that Innocence is not enough, that realization depends upon a severing between the natural and the human.

Nor can concord be won in nature or Innocence again, as *The Little Boy Lost* and *The Little Boy Found* exist to show us. The lost child weeps to see his father vaporize into the dark night, but his

tears vanish at the appearance of the God of Innocence, a white likeness of the father who has abandoned him. Led by this ghostly father
back to his pale and weeping mother, the little boy is back where he
started, in a helpless dependence on a state of being where any darkness can vaporize the forms of his protection. We have here the
prelude to the entrapments of Experience, as the songs there of *The
Little Boy Lost* and *The Little Girl Lost* will show. The *Nurse's Song*
of Innocence is another of these delicate premonitions of the sundered state. Here the poem's meaning is in the implied time-to-be,
when the voices of children are no longer heard on the green, and
the heart ceases to rest in their laughter. Yet to *become* as little children is not always to remain children, and to find *knowledge* of delight we need to discover sorrow. *On Another's Sorrow* gets this
exactly (and deliberately) backwards. Here the poem's progression
depends on a rather grim little cycle in which Christ's incarnation is
ascribed to his pity for the helplessness of infancy's natural grief. The
communion of sorrow is the only vision available to Innocence of the
mature consciousness of sin in Experience:

> He doth give his joy to all;
> He becomes an infant small;
> He becomes a man of woe;
> He doth feel the sorrow too.
>
> Think not thou canst sigh a sigh,
> And thy maker is not by;
> Think not thou canst weep a tear
> And thy maker is not near.
>
> O! he gives to us his joy
> That our grief he may destroy;
> Till our grief is fled & gone
> He doth sit by us and moan.

The poem in *Songs of Innocence* that most clearly forebodes that
state's lament against its destruction is *The School Boy* (later transferred to *Songs of Experience*), where the child's voice undergoes a
transition from the sweet company of the sounds he hears in a sum-

mer morn to the anxious sighing and dismay of his schooling. The
bafflement of instinct presents questions which Experience will not
answer:

> How shall the summer arise in joy,
> Or the summer fruits appear?
> Or how shall we gather what griefs destroy,
> Or bless the mellowing year,
> When the blasts of winter appear?

The epitome of *Songs of Innocence*, and the best poem in the
series, is *The Little Black Boy*, one of the most deliberately misleading and ironic of all Blake's lyrics. A detailed reading of this poem
will serve here as a temporary farewell to Blake's vision of Innocence,
until we can return to it by juxtaposition with *Songs of Experience*.

The Little Black Boy speaks his own poem, and his voice rises to
an intensity of innocent love in the final stanza, where he seeks to
apply his mother's teachings to the dilemma of his own condition.
His mother's wisdom fuses together the hopeful beliefs of Innocence: the loving fatherhood of God, the saving identity of maternal
guidance and the natural world, and the brotherhood of all children
born from Nature under God. The child accepts all this as truth, and
his clear and sweet urge to work out the consequences of such truth
reveals the inadequacy of Innocence, of the natural context, to sustain any idealizations whatsoever.

The first stanza presents a categorical dualism which is at once
philosophical and social, and vicious, to Blake, in either sphere:

> My mother bore me in the southern wild,
> And I am black, but O! my soul is white;
> White as an angel is the English child,
> But I am black as if bereav'd of light.

The English child is white, angelic, and all soul. The Little Black
Boy is a ghost in a machine, a white soul in a black body, as if
bereav'd of light. "Bereaved" here has the force of "dispossessed" or
"divested"; the myth of the Fall has entered the poem.

My mother taught me underneath a tree,
And sitting down before the heat of day,
She took me on her lap and kissed me,
And pointing to the east, began to say:

"Look on the rising sun: there God does live,
And gives his light, and gives his heat away;
And flowers and trees and beasts and men receive
Comfort in morning, joy in the noonday."

To be taught underneath a tree is to learn the lessons of life beneath the shrouding of Nature, the Tree of Mystery, as it will come
to be called later in Blake. The mother instructs her child before the
heat of day, in the comfort of morning, not in the naturalistic joy
of noonday. God gives both his light and his heat away, but the
mother is not altogether of one mind about the heat of divine love:

"And we are put on earth a little space,
That we may learn to bear the beams of love;
And these black bodies and this sunburnt face
Is but a cloud, and like a shady grove.

"For when our souls have learn'd the heat to bear,
The cloud will vanish; we shall hear his voice,
Saying: 'Come out from the grove, my love &
     care,
And round my golden tent like lambs rejoice.'"

Our time here on earth is not the immediate *now* of Eternity for
the mother, but only a little space in which we learn to *bear* the
force of God's love. The spatial concept is allied to the mother's ob-
session with the blackness of the body, the fallen form or debased
extension of the soul. An imagination so flawed is ironically incapable of even an accurate empirical association of cause and effect.
The black bodies and sunburnt face are somehow not to be desired, and yet are the consequences of having borne the beams of
love. They are a cloud which will vanish, and yet are created by a
cloudless sun, emblematic of God. Yet even the mother does not
deceive her stronger instinct; the blackness has the providential as-

pect of a shady grove, and is therefore both trial and comfort. The God of Innocence, when his love has been fully endured, will call mother and child out of their bodies, out from the grove, and into the golden tent of his heaven.

On the basis of this unintentionally equivocal teaching, the Little Black Boy makes explicit the full irony of his mother's confused vision:

> Thus did my mother say, and kissed me;
> And thus I say to little English boy:
> When I from black and he from white cloud free,
> And round the tent of God like lambs we joy:
>
> I'll shade him from the heat till he can bear
> To lean in joy upon our father's knee;
> And then I'll stand and stroke his silver hair,
> And be like him and he will then love me.

Nothing in Blake that we have so far encountered has the rhetorical force of that tremendous line in which all the ambiguities of Innocence are implied: "When I from black and he from white cloud free." The Little Black Boy does not know all that he is saying, and it is too much of an irony that so many of Blake's readers have chosen not to know either. To be free of the body's separation from the soul will not liberate us, if the soul continues to be separate from the body. The Little Black Boy knows what his mother evidently cannot know, that:

> Labour is blossoming or dancing where
> The body is not bruised to pleasure soul.

To have a white body is not to have borne enough love, and so in God's revelation the little English boy will need his black friend's body to shade him from the heat of that full noonday. Yet Blake is already too bitter, too much aware of the confining menace of a merely natural context, to allow himself to end the poem with so radiant an insight. Having been instructed by confusion, the Little Black Boy ends in that state. By his own logic, he ought to say that the English boy will be like himself at the last, but instead he gives us the opposite notion, the pathos of unfulfillable wish:

And be like him and he will then love me.

Brooding on the unresolved antinomies of Innocence, Blake must have undergone that most subtle of artistic dissatisfactions, the realization of imaginative incompleteness, a knowledge that the state he had shown was potentiality and not reality. The garden of natural childhood was both vision and illusion, poem and deception. No more than *Poetical Sketches* and *Tiriel* could these isolated *Songs of Innocence* please the prophetic humanist in Blake. Like Milton, he desired to identify all of man's capabilities with imaginative redemption. Not for another five years did Blake arrive at the necessary complement to Innocence, the myth of the contrary state of Experience. But he worked steadily at the problem of the destiny of his pastoral vision, and the progress of those labors can be seen in the poems written between 1789 and 1793. In 1789, even as he engraved the *Songs of Innocence*, Blake attempted a fuller projection of an unrealized world, in the delicately beautiful engraved poem *The Book of Thel*. Here the paradise of Innocence attains the full dimensions of myth, and pastoral poetry in English finds one of its most assured later triumphs.

The Book of Thel

In *The Book of Thel*, Blake uses the fourteener again, the long line that he made as much his own as Spenser did his stanza, or Milton blank verse. Though scholars have believed Blake derived the line from Elizabethan poetry (George Chapman's version of Homer's *Iliad*, William Warner's *Albion's England*), or else from Macpherson's *Ossian* (printed as prose, but clearly verse), it may be that the King James Bible is the true source, as it had been for Christopher Smart's *Jubilate Agno* and was later to be for Whitman and D. H. Lawrence.

Blake's great poetic desire was to write a prophetic epic, as Spenser and Milton had done before him. But Blake's temperament is that of an orator who moves rapidly between rhetorical climaxes, and he clearly felt encumbered in his Spenserian stanza and blank verse experiments in *Poetical Sketches*. Both forms must have seemed to him to be too ceremonial and ornate for his purposes. The fourteener or septenarius had associations with popular poetry, in ballads from the Middle Ages on. Blake is more like Bunyan and the ballad-writers in his social origins and in the emotional temper of his religion than he is like Spenser and Milton, though he sees himself as the direct inheritor of those Puritan epic poets. The rhythms of Bunyan's prose and of Blake's verse alike resemble the rhythms of the King James Isaiah and Song of Solomon. It is not far from this passage, chosen at random, to the movement of *The Four Zoas*:

> Who is this that cometh from Edom, with dyed
>   garments from Bozrah?
> This that is glorious in his apparel, traveling
>   in the greatness of his strength?
> I that speak in righteousness, mighty to save.

In its first appearance in Blake, the fourteener achieved the limited success of *Tiriel*, where the poet seems a little unsure as to the possibilities of his wavering line. In *Thel*, the fourteener has been naturalized, and Blake has full confidence in his flexible control of what he must have felt to be his triumphant answer to the number, weight, and measure of the Augustan couplet, or the haunted Miltonizings of Thomson's and Cowper's blank verse.

Thel's name is from the Greek for "wish" or "will" and Thel herself has been well characterized by P. F. Fisher as "the wilful rather than the willing spirit,"[6] a creature who will venture nothing unless she is assured in advance that experience cannot alter her. *The Book of Thel* begins with her enigmatic motto:

> Does the Eagle know what is in the pit?
> Or wilt thou go ask the Mole?
> Can Wisdom be put in a silver rod?
> Or Love in a golden bowl?

The Mole is in the pit of Experience, and knowledge of Experience must be sought there with him. Wisdom and Love must be put into a rod and bowl of flesh, organs of human generation. The questions are Thel's, but she refuses the answers.

Tiriel returned to the paradise of Innocence, the eastern "vales of Har," after a life in the West, the experiential body of man. Finding only aged idiocy there, and not an instructive Innocence, he went forth again into the wilderness. Returning to Har at the moment of his death, he tried in his desperate last speech to instruct Innocence in the lesson he had learned, finally, from Experience. Part of that speech is Thel's motto also: "Can Wisdom be put in a silver rod? Or love in a golden bowl?" But when Tiriel uttered this, the meaning was very different, and the question was purely a rhetorical one. The answer was 'No,' but coming from Tiriel in his death agony, this was a negative irony, for Tiriel represented the failure of Experience, even as Thel represents the failure of Innocence. Both Tiriel and Thel serve to remind us of the motto's probable source in Ecclesiastes 12:

> . . . and desire shall fail: because man goeth to
> his long home, and the mourners go about the
> streets:
> Or ever the silver cord be loosed, or the
> golden bowl be broken, or the pitcher be broken
> at the fountain, or the wheel broken at the
> cistern.
> Then shall the dust return to the earth
> as it was. . . .

The golden bowl, in Blake, may be womb or brain; probably the former for Thel, the latter for Tiriel. Tiriel had descended into the pit, but his wisdom was certainly put in the wrong organ, and love did not exist for him. He returns to the earth as it was, but Thel refuses to go to her long home, and thus desire in her fails even more radically. We see her first as the youngest daughter of the Seraphim, in a pastoral world of the unborn, where her sisters tend the flocks of the sun. Though in a state of pre-existence, since she lives in the vales of Har, her state is a mortal one, for time is in her garden, just as it was in Spenser's Gardens of Adonis (which may account for Thel lamenting "down by the river of Adona"). Her justified fear is that hers is doomed to be a "morning beauty." The images of her lament are Shelleyan; they center on the evanescences of nature. As she projects her own transience Blake gives us a startling echo of Genesis:

> Ah! gentle may I lay me down, and gentle rest
>   my head.
> And gentle sleep the sleep of death, and gentle
>   hear the voice
> Of him that walketh in the garden in the
>   evening time.

In Genesis 3:8 Adam and Eve, fallen and ashamed, heard the voice of God walking in the garden in the cool of the day, and they hid themselves. The echo here in Blake's poem serves initially to suggest an identity between Thel's world and the Garden of Eden; they are places to fall from, if the experiential world is to begin. Yet the echo is more plangent and complex. Unlike Adam and Eve, fearful and disgraced, and hiding from the judgment of death, Thel is sadly resigned. Gentle she will hear the voice that marks the evening of her beauty. Innocence can be maintained, and this unbodied child can die a child, to be absorbed into the natural cycle of her paradise.

Yet she could choose a better way, at the price of a birth into suffering and fallen reality. What *The Book of Thel*, by its very form, makes clear is the human limitations of the state of Innocence. Here is born what the engraved tracts had foretold: Blake's dialectics of Nature, or his argument about the relative values of Innocence and Experience. Innocence is a higher state than Experience, but you cannot progress in it, for where there are no oppositions of spirit, the spirit stagnates. There are no truths in Innocence because there are no falsehoods, and no vision but stasis, because the only contrary to desire is mere cycle. The destiny of man in Eden is repetition, the circle of natural organicism. Thel's Innocence is natural ignorance; she abides in a Mystery, and her very form is a reflection in a glass, a shadow in the water, an infant's dream.

If we examine the form of *The Book of Thel*, we come very quickly to the realization of Blake's immense care in putting together this fragile and almost symmetrical poem. It opens with the lamentation of Thel we have already encountered. Then come three dialogues, between Thel and a "Lilly," a Cloud, and a Clod of Clay in that sequence. Thel then enters Experience, but flees from it after hearing another lament, uttered from "her own grave plot." The dialogues form the bulk of the poem; the framing laments, by their ironic relationship to one another, shape the poem's final significance, which is the inadequacy of an Innocence that refuses the birth into generative sorrow, the rigors of human incarnation.

The dialogues themselves are very formalized. Blake had already characterized the mythmakings of a childlike universe, in which life everywhere confronts life, so that there are no objects to experience, but only answering subjects, in the *Songs of Innocence*. But Thel's world is still more Innocent, being unborn. Blake's technical problem was enormous, in attempting so extended a lyrical poem set in an unborn state, but his solution to the problem is triumphant. A flower, a cloud, the clay itself, speak also in the state of Innocence, but in the vales of Har they are so naturalized as to have distinctive accents. The Lilly of the valley's voice is gentle and modest, and even her most intense aspirations are fulfilled by the smile of the sun. Her decay is in natural cycle, and her joyous essence is in acceptance of that cycle:

> Yet I am visited from heaven and he that smiles
>   on all
> Walks in the valley and each morn over me
>   spreads his hand,
> Saying, "Rejoice, thou humble grass, thou
>   new-born lilly-flower,
> Thou gentle maid of silent valleys and of
>   modest brooks;
> For thou shalt be clothed in light and fed
>   with morning manna;
> Till summer's heat melts thee beside the
>   fountains and the springs,
> To flourish in eternal vales."

In a brilliant descriptive touch, this "wat'ry weed" reacts to her vision of her own dissolution by smiling in tears. The firmness of Blake's tone here is admirable, for any paraphrase will make this passage into the namby-pamby sentimentalism it surely does not contain. Thel is impressed, as she should be, by the flower's faith, but she cannot accept this as comfort. The flower gives to those that cannot crave, to the pastoral animals of this paradise, but Thel is only a presiding shepherdess, ornamental yet useless, "a faint cloud kindled at the rising sun." The flower, baffled as comforter, calls on such a cloud to descend for Thel's reassurance. The flower's transience is closer to Thel's condition than the cloud's, but the intensification of mutability in the cloud makes it a more eloquent apologist for the process of natural decay:

> "O virgin, know'st thou not our steeds drink
>   of the golden springs
> Where Luvah doth renew his horses? Look'st
>   thou on my youth,
> And fearest thou because I vanish and am seen
>   no more,
> Nothing remains? O maid, I tell thee, when I
>   pass away,
> It is to tenfold life, to love, to peace and
>   raptures holy:
> Unseen descending, weigh my light wings upon
>   balmy flowers,
> And court the fair-eyed dew to take me to her
>   shining tent:
> The weeping virgin, trembling kneels before the
>   risen sun,
> Till we arise link'd in a golden band and never
>   part,
> But walk united, bearing food to all our tender
>   flowers."

This is the first appearance in Blake's work of one of his Giant Forms, the living being or Zoa called Luvah, who has or should have the sexual life of man and nature in his control. Here Luvah is primarily the renewer of the sexual cycle of Innocence, but as this is an undeveloped sexuality, it lacks all possibility of consciousness, and by intending no objects, lacks all purpose. All that the cloud has expressed is a touching faith in a mystery, and "the weeping virgin" is fittingly the vaporizing half of the water-cycle in nature, for her tears are the essence of the cloud's existence. The irony is gently stated and yet sardonic. The "fair-eyed dew" trembles with sexual repression, and the hint is that the cloud-cycle is based upon this sexual timidity.

Though the cloud participates in the most infantile of sexualities, at least he and the dew-virgin "arise link'd in a golden band and never part." But Thel bears no food of union whatsoever, and her lament begins to verge upon both bitterness and fear:

> But Thel delights in these no more because I
>   fade away;
> And all shall say, "Without a use this shining
>   woman liv'd,
> Or did she only live to be at death the food of
>   worms?"

To soothe Thel, the cloud calls up the feared worm. The worm is at once the phallic emblem of the generative world that Thel dreads entering, and the final devourer of that world. What Thel views then is both the body and the death of the body, and yet the phenomenon seen appeals powerfully to her repressed maternalism:

> "Art thou a Worm? Image of weakness, art thou
>   but a Worm?
> I see thee like an infant wrapped in the Lilly's
>   leaf.
> Ah! weep not, little voice, thou canst not
>   speak, but thou canst weep.
> Is this a Worm? I see thee lay helpless &
>   naked, weeping
> And none to answer, none to cherish thee with
>   mother's smiles."

The creative mind of Blake verges on the sinister in the subtle transition that now turns the course of the poem. The state of Innocence is a world of deceptive reflections, a shadowy looking glass where two appearances of the one reality will seem equally true. Thel's worm is the infant image of weakness it seems, but the mother's embrace it invites will be an embrace of Experience and death. It is not the worm that replies to Thel, but a clod of Clay, the worm's environment and fruit alike, the clay from whose red outline Adamic man is to be formed. The worm does not reply because it cannot speak and only weeps in its infant sorrow, but its tears are ambiguous and menacing, as Thel cannot quite know. The link between the human, of which Thel is the embryonic form, and the clay is the worm: through it, earth becomes man, and man again becomes earth. This is a grimmer mystery than the cycle of dew and cloud, and one that the Clod of Clay cannot understand:

> "O beauty of the vales of Har, we live not
>   for ourselves.
> Thou seest me the meanest thing, and so I am
>   indeed.
> My bosom of itself is cold, and of itself is dark;
> But he that loves the lowly, pours his oil
>   upon my head
> And kisses me, and binds his nuptial bands
>   around my breast,
> And says: "Thou mother of my children, I have
>   loved thee
> And I have given thee a crown that none can take
>   away."
> But how this is, sweet maid, I know not, and I
>   cannot know;
> I ponder, and I cannot ponder; yet I live and love."

Almost without notice, we are again involved in what can be called visionary satire. The crown that none can take away is no part of the earth's understanding, for all that is given to it is perpetually taken away again. Earth is conscious of its lack, not alone of knowledge, but of the means of knowledge, and its puzzled pondering leads only to a realization of how poorly it can ponder. Trapped in these limitations, earth surrenders to its own ignorance, and trusts in the mystery of Innocence: "yet I live and love."

With characteristic irony, Blake allows Thel to be comforted by this obscure resolution of her problem. The God of Innocence cherishes even a worm through the ministrations of "the matron Clay." Cannot Thel trust this earth to be a loving foster mother?

> And I complain'd in the mild air, because I fade
>   away,
> And lay me down in thy cold bed, and leave my
>   shining lot.

In answer, earth proposes that Thel attempt the experience of that cold bed. The proposal emphasizes that the entrance into a generative existence will be merely tentative:

> Wilt thou, O Queen, enter my house? 'Tis
>   given thee to enter,
> And to return: fear nothing, enter with thy
>   virgin feet.

That final phrase hovers upon irony again, for only Thel's feet will experience the sorrows of generative life. From the start, Thel sees Experience with a shock scaled to the unknown intensities she now encounters:

> The eternal gates' terrific porter lifted the
>   northern bar:
> Thel enter'd in and saw the secrets of the land
>   unknown.
> She saw the couches of the dead, & where the
>   fibrous roots
> Of every heart on earth infixes deep its restless
>   twists:
> A land of sorrows & of tears where never smile
>   was seen.

The symbolism of the éternal gates here is one of the few genuine and indisputable borrowings on Blake's part from Neoplatonic tradition.[7] Homer, in *The Odyssey* (Book XIII), describes the Cave of the Naiades, through which Odysseus re-enters his native Ithaca:

> To which two entries were—the one for man
> (On which the North breath'd), th'other for
>   the gods
> (On which the South), and that bore no abodes
> For earthy men, but onely deathlesse feete
> Had there free way.
>
> (Chapman's version, XIII, 164–68)

Porphyry, in his commentary on this Cave, read it as an allegory of the descent of the soul. The same allegory of double gates associated with an earthly paradise Blake would have found in Spenser's Garden of Adonis, the closest prototype of Thel's garden. Spenser's porter is "Old *Genius*, the which a double nature has"; Blake's "terrific porter" is not identified, but he is later established as Los, the primal being of imaginative perception, in a similar passage in the prophetic epic *Milton* [26:16–18]. Passing out of her unborn paradise by the northern gate is for Thel to identify herself as incarnate Man, descending into the fallen world of Experience. The north later in Blake (in *The Book of Urizen*) will become the area where Urizen perpetuates his errors of the selfish intellect, and where the fall of man and our creation in our present form will take place. Thel finds herself surrounded by evidences of this simultaneous fall and desperate creation, in a world where every human heart is a mysterious natural growth, with restlessly twisted roots. Wandering in this world, listening to its sepulchral voices, she comes at last "to her own grave plot," where she sits down. This grave plot represents both the natural body she can still refuse to assume, and also her final destiny on earth, the literal resting place for her body after it has known Experience. From the hollow pit there breathes the lamentation that climaxes the poem:

"Why cannot the Ear be closed to its own destruction?
Or the glist'ning Eye to the poison of a smile!
Why are Eyelids stor'd with arrows ready drawn,
Where a thousand fighting men in ambush lie!
Or an Eye of gifts and graces show'ring fruits
    and coined gold!
Why a Tongue impress'd with honey from every
    wind?
Why an Ear, a whirlpool fierce to draw creations
    in?
Why a Nostril wide inhaling terror, trembling,
    & affright?
Why a tender curb upon the youthful burning boy?
Why a little curtain of flesh on the bed of our
    desire?"

This is the voice of Thel herself, as she would be at the latter end
of Experience, should she maintain herself in the fallen world. The
vocabulary of this lament is drawn from Elizabethan conventions of
erotic poetry. These are the ambuscades of the awakened senses, with
Eye, Tongue, Ear, and Nostril working to deceive. Against the excessive and tempting strengths of these senses Thel protests, for they
have whirled her to destruction. But, in a startling reversal, she laments not the active strength, but the passive weakness of the fifth
and more properly sexual sense of touch. The other senses were too
strenuous in enticement, but the actualizing sense was too timid, and
by a grim irony the Thel of Experience has gone to her death still a
virgin. The little curtain of flesh has curbed the ardor of her lover;
the final trap of Experience is the waste of its repressive morality.
Confronted by the realization that she will have suffered life only
to have attained again to a state of unrealized potential, Thel chooses
not to have lived:

> The Virgin started from her seat, & with a
>   shriek
> Fled back unhinder'd till she came into the
>   vales of Har.

The word "unhinder'd" is used ironically, for Thel's return is only a mode of self-hindrance, of the barren restraint of an unborn nature. Thel's fate, because of her choice, is one we have seen already in *Tiriel*. Dwelled in too long, the fragile Vales of Har become more a self-enclosed prison than a paradise. Thel will become like Har and Heva, an aged imbecile immured in a nightmare of unorganized Innocence, a perfection of ignorance. Yet that is not the tone, though it is the implied meaning, of *The Book of Thel*. We remember, not the pathos of Thel's mistaken choice, but the exquisite form of the poem, its success in representing a very beautiful but less than real world. With the fearful retreat of Thel, Blake left his pastoral image behind him, and turned to the French Revolution of actual experience.

CHAPTER FIVE

Revolution and Prophecy

The French Revolution

This poem, unlike any other mature creation by Blake, came down to later generations as neither manuscript nor engraved work, but as a printed page proof. Set up in type by the Radical printer Joseph Johnson in 1791, it was never published, presumably because of Johnson's (or Blake's) prudence. This poem's uniqueness among Blake's similar visions of revolution (*A Song of Liberty, America, Europe, The Song of Los*) is that it has no overt references to any symbolism not fully presented by its own text.

Though the title page speaks of the poem as having seven finished books (and promises the six remaining in their proper order) it seems certain that Blake wrote only the single book we have, which is in any case quite a finished work, though probably not so in Blake's judgment, since he never chose to engrave it.

The French Revolution opens with the brooding presence of a pestilence-bearing mist, like the one Tiriel calls down upon his sons. The tyrannies of law, the "slumbers of five thousand years" of fallen history, find their end signalized in this apocalyptic fog. Though the poem, in its historical aspect, deals with social unrest, its images are of a natural world collapsing, and human forms being crowded from that world by an army of preternatural portents. It is not the pattern of events that compels Blake's imagination, but the hint that some revelation is at hand, a rough beast whose appearance may cleanse natural appearance and force history to its crisis.

In a poem all of whose presages are of a final judgment being

imminent, it is not surprising that little rhetorical distinction is
made between historical oppressors and aspiring rebels, or between
the mental states of warders and victims. The nightmare of history
is expressed in the mind-forged manacles that can be heard alike in
every voice and every ban. The Governor of the Bastille stalks like
a mad lion from one to another of his seven towers—Horror, Darkness, Bloody, Religion, Order, Destiny, and God. These seven pillars of the creation of Law hold up among them the social and the
natural worlds, the body of man as imprisoned in society and the
body of man as immured in nature. The human victim chained
within each tower manifests, in his condition, the tyranny of being a
natural man, rather than just the marks of his punishment:

> And the den nam'd
> Horror held a man
> Chain'd hand and foot; round his neck an iron
> band, bound to the impregnable wall;
> In his soul was the serpent coil'd round in his
> heart, hid from the light, as in a cleft
> rock:
> And the man was confin'd for a writing prophetic.

The serpent of the heart, imprisoning one by a band within, is
the prophecy that has been hidden, however involuntarily, from the
light. This inner binding of the outcasts is matched by the similarly
figurative outer binding of their oppressors, the Nobles:

> Each stern visage lock'd up as with strong bands
> of iron, each strong limb bound down as
> with marble.

The *inner* bonds of the Nobles, and *outer* chains of their victims,
are equally real, but Blake takes these to be evident. In a world over-
ripe for apocalypse, the inner and the outer have become confused.
The body and the spirit rapidly assume one another's attributes, and
the strict forms of reality tend to dissolve. That is why the dominant
image of *The French Revolution* is the cloud, which represents at

once the failure of vision to achieve a clear form, and the failure of less imaginative perception to form a clear image. As the events of the Revolution ensue, the protagonists behold neither what might be nor what is, but only what was and what will be no more.

The King, lamenting his own loss of nerve, is comforted by a sight of his armies: "then his bosom expanded like starry heaven." The starry floor is given to man until the break of day: if the King's armies can hold back the human dawn that the Revolution presages, then the starry heaven which is the floor above us will expand. So the royal henchman, Burgundy, whose associations are with a harvest of blood, directly compares threatened authority to a cosmic order put in jeopardy by resurrected Titans:

> Shall this marble-built heaven become a clay
>   cottage, this earth an oak stool, and
>   these mowers
> From the Atlantic mountains mow down all this
>   great starry harvest of six thousand
>   years?

Here, in two lines, Blake epitomizes both the imagery and the theme of his poem. The marble-built heaven is both the *Ancien Régime* and the cosmic vision of the being later called Urizen; the clay cottage is at once a peasant's dwelling and the real form of the starry heavens, a human immediacy. The earth of tyranny is to be transvalued by revolution into a human artifact, and the transvaluers or levelling mowers of revolution are at once the forces successful in America, and the unfallen Titans of Atlantis, restored from undersea to their mountain-status of liberty. The great starry harvest of six thousand years is the aristocratic accumulation of privilege based upon man's exploitation of man since the Creation-Fall. Though this burden of meaning is ironic, since it is expressed defiantly as a rhetorical question by Burgundy, its dramatic strength is very real, and the Duke has a sinister dignity. The Archbishop of Paris shares in this dignity, and his peroration expresses still more powerfully the static vision of an orthodoxy that will not yield to a prophetic event:

Hearken, Monarch of France, to the terrors of
    heaven, and let thy soul drink of my
    counsel!
Sleeping at midnight in my golden tower, the
    repose of the labours of men
Wav'd its solemn cloud over my head. I awoke;
    a cold hand passed over my limbs, and
    behold!
An aged form, white as snow, hov'ring in mist,
    weeping in the uncertain light.
Dim the form almost faded, tears fell down the
    shady cheeks; at his feet, many cloth'd
In white robes; strewn in air censers and harps;
    silent they lay prostrated;
Beneath, in the awful void, myriads descending
    and weeping thro' dismal winds;
Endless the shady train shiv'ring descended
    from the gloom where the aged form wept.
At length, trembling, the vision sighing, in a
    low voice like the voice of the grass-
    hopper, whisper'd:
"My groaning is heard in the abbeys, and God, so
    long worshipp'd, departs as a lamp
Without oil; for a curse is heard hoarse thro'
    the land, from a godless race
Descending to beasts; they look downward and
    labour and forget my holy law;
The sound of prayer fails from lips of flesh,
    and the holy hymn from thicken'd tongues;
For the bars of Chaos are burst; her millions
    prepare their fiery way
Thro' the orbed abode of the holy dead, to root
    up and pull down and remove,
And Nobles and Clergy shall fail from before me,
    and my cloud and vision be no more."

The weeping form is the Jehovah of orthodoxy, the sky-god Urizen,
a pillar of cloud by night. The mist and the uncertain light are nec-

essarily satiric details, for they refer to a minimal Reason, self-assured of its own validity. The voice of revolt is heard as coming from a place at the bottom of the graves, and is associated with a fire breaking from chaos into order. This is the orthodox vision of the fire of Hell, which is an exuberant energy seeking its own liberation. The contrary vision is presented by a noble champion of the Revolution, "Orleans, generous as mountains":

> O Princes of fire,
>> whose flames are for growth, not
>> consuming,
> Fear not dreams, fear not visions, nor be you
>> dismay'd with sorrows which flee at the
>> morning!
> Can the fires of Nobility ever be quench'd, or
>> the stars by a stormy night?
> Is the body diseas'd when the members are
>> healthful? can the man be bound in
>> sorrow
> Whose ev'ry function is fill'd with its fiery
>> desire? can the soul, whose brain and
>> heart
> Cast their rivers in equal tides thro' the great
>> Paradise, languish because the feet,
> Hands, head, bosom, and parts of love follow
>> their high breathing joy?

The opening distinction here, between flames for growth and for consuming, is that of *The Marriage of Heaven and Hell,* between the Prolific and the Devourer, as we will see. The rest of this beautiful passage turns on the metaphor of society as a human form, in which the delight of integration must be at one with the delight of each function's gratification. The balance is in the finest statement of Orleans, still to come: "for fire delights in its form." This is not just energy's eternal delight in itself, but also Blake's definition of true, as opposed to conventional, form. As fire rages into first one shape and then another, so the content of vision, expressed in society or art, impels first one form and then another, with the impulse always generating itself afresh from within.

The clash of contraries between Burgundy and Orleans prepares us for the authentic voice of revolution, represented in Blake's poem by the Abbé de Sieyès:

> When the heavens were seal'd with a stone, and
>   the terrible sun clos'd in an orb, and
>   the moon
> Rent from the nations, and each star appointed
>   for watchers of night,
> The millions of spirits immortal were bound in
>   the ruins of sulphur heaven
> To wander enslav'd; black, deprest in dark
>   ignorance, kept in awe with the whip
> To worship terrors, bred from the blood of
>   revenge and breath of desire
> In bestial forms, or more terrible men; till the
>   dawn of our peaceful morning,
> Till dawn, till morning, till the breaking of
>   clouds, and swelling of winds, and the
>   universal voice;
> Till man raise his darken'd limbs out of the
>   caves of night. His eyes and his heart
> Expand: Where is Space? where, O Sun, is thy
>   dwelling? where thy tent, O faint
>   slumb'rous Moon?

Here the emphasis is at last where Blake desires it to be: on revelation, the uncovering of a human form heretofore enshrouded by the illusion of Space. This is what makes *The French Revolution* so uniquely a Blakean poem, though it lacks the cosmic myth which elsewhere is the mark of Blake's individuality. The French Revolution, as an event in human consciousness, cannot come to fullness unless it expands our consciousness of the human, and this expansion must be at the expense of the natural limitations of creation. Man under the tyranny of the Law is most tyrannized by the darkening and enclosure of his limbs, eyes, and heart. Breaking of clouds means more than break of day, just as the fall of the terrible towers of the Bastille means an overthrow of more false orders than those canonized by social law.

Blake's poem ends without taking this vision farther than the departure of the King's army from Paris, which leaves the Assembly free to deliberate on the means of revolution. The poem ends on a token of fulfillment, with the revolutionaries, who "in peace sat beneath morning's beam." Blake had nothing to add, and the course of events had little to add to Blake's desired consummation.

The French Revolution is composed in long anapaestic lines, which makes it again unique among Blake's poems. The cumulative rhythm of the anapaest, with its sense of mounting intensity, is handled well by Blake, but evidently he was unhappy with this technical experiment. His next works ranged through a variety of forms—the mixed free verse and prose of *The Marriage of Heaven and Hell*, the prose-poetry of *A Song of Liberty*, and the regular stanzaic forms of the poems in the Rossetti Manuscript. The years 1790 to 1793 were a ferment for Blake;—in outer events, and in his practice as a poet. In 1793 he found himself technically again, returning to the sure fourteeners of *Visions of the Daughters of Albion* and *America, A Prophecy*. By 1793 he had also formulated his myth: *America* introduces the symbolic beings and states of existence that will dominate Blake's major poems. The great transitional work, written in 1790, is the famous polemic *The Marriage of Heaven and Hell*. The intellectual daring of the early engraved tracts fuses here with Blake's sense of his own spiritual maturity, to produce a masterpiece of satiric vision.

The Marriage of Heaven and Hell

About 1788, Blake read and annotated Swedenborg's *Wisdom of Angels Concerning Divine Love and Divine Wisdom*. Blake was not brought up a Swedenborgian, that being one of the many biographical myths about him that David Erdman has demonstrated to be inaccurate or irrelevant.[1] Much in Swedenborg must have seemed unimaginative to Blake from the start, but clearly Blake progressed from feeling some affinity with Swedenborg to a strong sense of outrage, as he realized how limited the affinity actually was. Blake read as he lived, painted, and wrote: to correct other men's visions, not into Blake's own, but into forms that emphasized the autonomy of each human imagination, both as against "nature" or what our eyes see when they are tired and deathly, and as against any received notions that might seek to set limits to perception. So, to Swedenborg's "In all the Heavens there is no other Idea of God than that of a Man," Blake added:

> Man can have no idea of any thing greater than Man, as a cup cannot contain more than its capaciousness. But God is a man, not because he is so perciev'd by man, but because he is the creator of man.[2]

Swedenborg touches upon a religious humanism, but halts his imagination before realizing its potential. Blake, as an artist, knows that his own best being is in his creations. So God, whose best creation is man, must find *his* own best being in man. Man is the form that God creates and loves, and so God must be a man. That the converse is not always true, that man is only partly God, is the burden that Blake's poems exist to lighten, and hope at last to annihilate.

Swedenborg, though he ended as a visionary and the founder of yet another Christian sect, had begun as a reasoner from nature, and his reports of what he took to be the spiritual world read now like parodies of the eighteenth century search for a science of sciences. The result is that the direct satirical basis of much in *The Marriage of Heaven and Hell* has lost its point. Even if Swedenborg had any relevance to our condition now, we would not need Blake to satirize him. But Blake has much in common with Swift as a satirist. The satire in each has survived its victims, because the structure of that satire comprehends eternal types of intellectual error and spiritual self-deception. A reader of *The Marriage of Heaven and Hell* needs to know of Swedenborg only what Blake took him to be:

> O Swedenborg! strongest of men, the Samson
> shorn by the Churches,
> Shewing the Transgressors in Hell, the proud

> Warriors in Heaven,
> Heaven as a Punisher, & Hell as one under
> Punishment . . .
>
> *Milton*, 22:50–52

> He [Swedenborg] shews the folly of churches,
> & exposes hypocrites, till he imagines that all
> are religious, & himself the single one on earth
> that ever broke a net.
>
> *The Marriage*, 21

Swedenborg is the eternal type of the prophet who becomes a new kind of priest, and by becoming a church loses his imaginative strength, until he concludes by renewing the religious categories of judgment he came to expose as impostures. The psychological root of this ironic cycle of transformation is in the prophet's growing and pernicious conviction of his absolute uniqueness. The contempt of Blake for this kind of self-deception is based on a conviction that the entire process is another triumph of nature over the integrity of vision. Whatever faults of passion Blake possessed, and he recognized each of them in turn as they became relevant to his poetry, he never allowed himself to believe he was "the single one on earth that ever broke a net" of religious orthodoxy.

The literary form of Blake's *Marriage* is best named by Northrop Frye's term, an *anatomy*, or more traditionally a Menippean satire, characterized by its concern with intellectual error, its extraordinary diversity of subject-matter, a mixed verse-and-prose form, and a certain reliance on a symposium setting.[3] Relentless experimenter as he was, Blake created in the *Marriage* what may even have surprised himself, so original is the work in its structure. It opens with a free-verse "Argument," and then passes to a statement of creative oppositions that Blake calls "Contraries." Two sets of contraries are then stated in a passage headed "The voice of the Devil," which concludes by a remarkable brief reading of Milton's *Paradise Lost*. Following is the first of five "Memorable Fancies," clearly originating as parodies of Swedenborg's "Memorable Relations," in which the Swedish visionary had described the wonders of the spiritual world. The first

Memorable Fancy leads to the famous "Proverbs of Hell," seventy
aphorisms unmatched in literature for their intellectual shock-value.
The remainder of the *Marriage* alternates Memorable Fancies with
groupings of apocalyptic reflections. The first of these gives a brief
history of religion; the next relates Blake's art to the "improvement of
sensual enjoyment" that will precede the Apocalypse; and the final
two deal with the strife of contraries again, and with the errors of
Swedenborg. After the final Memorable Fancy, the whole work ends
with a proverb previously gasped out in Tiriel's death agony: "One
Law for the Lion & Ox is Oppression."

The unity of this structure is a dialectical one, and depends upon
a progression in understanding, as one proceeds from engraved plate
to engraved plate of the work. The title plate shows a sexual embrace
amid flames, in its lower half; the upper part depicts wanderers between twisted trees, and a loss of Innocence beneath two trees of
Mystery, with a raven overhead. The center of the plate features
lovers rising upward from the flames, but aspiring towards the roots
of the sinister trees above. The visual process is purely ironic; to rise
away from the sexual fire can only lead to loss. This picture epitomizes the rhetorical emphasis of the *Marriage*, with its "diabolical"
preference for desire over restraint, energy over reason. But the
sequence of plates transcends this antinomian rhetoric, and demonstrates the necessity for both sets of creative oppositions. The Argument states the problem of the work's genesis: the breakthrough of
the contraries into history. The Memorable Fancies are all on the
rhetorical side of the "Devil," though they continually qualify the
supposed demonism of that party. The sections between the Fancies
carry forward the dialectic of the work; they exist to clarify the role
of the contraries. Blake asks of his reader a subtle alternation of
moods; to move constantly from a defiant celebration of heretofore
repressed energies to a realization that the freed energies must accept
a bounding outline, a lessened but still existent world of confining
mental forms.

Our actual reading of *The Marriage of Heaven and Hell* can begin
with a consideration of the title itself. Annotating Swedenborg's *Wisdom of Angels Concerning Divine Love and Divine Wisdom* in
1788, Blake came to a particular statement urgently needing ironic
correction by a restatement ostensibly in agreement with it:

SWEDENBORG: Man is only a Recipient of Life. From this Cause it is, that Man, from his own hereditary Evil, reacts against God; but so far as he believes that all his Life is from God, and every Good of Life from the Action of God, and every Evil of Life from the reaction of Man, Reaction thus becomes correspondent with Action, and Man acts with God as from himself.

BLAKE: Good & Evil are here both Good & the two contraries Married.[4]

It is probable that this interchange is the seed of *The Marriage of Heaven and Hell*. Blake perceives in Swedenborg an instance of the two moral contraries of good and evil being so held in relation to each other that they exist in harmony without losing their individual characteristics. The key term in the Swedenborg passage is "correspondent"; in the Blake comment it is "contraries." In Swedenborg, "correspondent" means that the Reaction and Action of the passage do subsume one another; they become for pragmatic purposes a unity of mutual absorption. But Blake's "contraries" never absorb one another; and his point is that the "Good & Evil" of Swedenborg were never really moral good and moral evil, but merely forms of the good in the first place. For Blake's Man creates life, and does not only receive it from God. All contraries are born within the human existence: Blake's last note on Swedenborg's *Divine Love* is: "Heaven & Hell are born together." Yet Swedenborg either forgot or had never learned this. Reading Swedenborg's *Divine Providence* two years later, in 1790, Blake is outraged at the flowering of Swedenborg's error into the dead fruit of the doctrine of Predestination. From this outrage the title of Blake's *Marriage* takes its origin.

Blake's title also has ironic reference to Swedenborg's *Heaven and Hell and their Wonders*, though his annotated copy of that book is lost. So is his copy of Swedenborg on the *Last Judgment*, where it was declared that:

. . . the evil are cast into the hells, and the good elevated into heaven, and thus that all things are reduced into order, the spiritual equilibrium between good and evil, or between heaven and hell, being thence restored. . . . This Last Judgment was commenced in the beginning of the year 1757 . . .

That was the year of Blake's birth, and so Swedenborg's heaven and Blake's hell were born together. In 1790, Blake was thirty-three years old, and thirty-three years had elapsed since the Last Judgment in the spiritual world. The outward apocalypse had been slow in coming, but by 1790 it must have seemed to Blake that the prophesied time-of-troubles that must precede apocalypse was surely at hand. We have seen Blake tracing those portents in his poem *The French Revolution*. Though the satiric motive for the *Marriage* is Blake's desire to expose Swedenborg, the work has a half-serious religious and political impulse within it as well. The French Revolution and the British reaction to it suggest to Blake a contemporary manifestation of the ancient turning over of a prophetic cycle. The *Marriage's* Argument begins:

> Rintrah roars & shakes his fires in the
>   burden'd air;
> Hungry clouds swag on the deep.

As with the appearance of Luvah in *The Book of Thel*, and Urizen in *Visions of the Daughters of Albion*, here we encounter another introduction of a symbolic personage before Blake is quite ready to make full use of him. What this suggests is that Blake may have formulated a large part of his mythology some years before he incorporated it into his poetry. Rintrah is Blake's Angry Man, a John the Baptist or Elijah figure, the wrathful spirit of prophecy driven out into the wilderness. The outcry and fires of Rintrah are in the burdened clouds, hungry with portents, that heavily sink down on the deep that separates France from England. The cycle of human existence turns over, and the just man is driven out by the villain:

> Once meek, and in a perilous path,
> The just man kept his course along
> The vale of death.
> Roses are planted where thorns grow,
> And on the barren heath
> Sing the honey bees.

Then the perilous path was planted,
And a river and a spring
On every cliff and tomb,
And on the bleached bones
Red clay brought forth;

Till the villain left the paths of ease,
To walk in perilous paths, and drive
The just man into barren climes.

Now the sneaking serpent walks
In mild humility,
And the just man rages in the wilds
Where lions roam.

The meek just man begins by regulating his course in that perilous path of life that always is shadowed by death. Yet that path is already involved in existential contraries; roses and thorns come up together, and the honey bees sing on a heath with no provision for them. The joy and grief of this existence are woven too fine; the course kept by the just man is *planted*, and becomes a natural custom, or falls into vegetative existence. Yet this naturalizing of the just man is a creation as well as a fall. The barrenness of cliff and tomb yields to a water that people may drink, and on the bleached bones of an earlier world the red clay that is Adam is brought forth.

But a turning natural cycle is an invitation for the villain, who leaves the paths of ease(which must be in a realm of non-existence, since for Blake existence is a struggle) and usurps the just man's place. Very likely on the social level this is a parable of exploitation. The villain becomes the sneaking serpent or "Angel" of mild humility, who stalks through the now ironically titled "perilous paths," and the just man becomes the "Devil" or outcast prophet, menaced by everything in nature that fears prophecy. The contraries of natural cycle are not true contraries, else the cycle could not go on unchanged. So Blake breaks off his "Argument" and begins to state the laws of progression:

> As a new heaven is begun, and it is now thirty-three years
> since its advent: the Eternal Hell revives. And lo! Swedenborg
> is the Angel sitting at the tomb: his writings are the linen
> clothes folded up. Now is the dominion of Edom, & the re-
> turn of Adam into Paradise. See Isaiah xxxiv & xxxv Chap.

Blake is thirty-three, and remembers that Christ rose in the body
at that age. Swedenborg sits at the tomb, Angel to Blake's Devil,
to testify that Blake has awakened from the error of death into the
more abundant life of the risen body. Poor Swedenborg's writings
are but the linen clothes folded up, neatly put aside by Blake, who
does not need the coverings of death to shield his passionate body
from apocalyptic light. For the prophesied times are come; the dominion of Edom is at hand. The blessing of Esau, the red man of
Edom, was that he should some day have dominion over Jacob. The
prophet Isaiah saw this red man coming from Edom, with the day
of vengeance in his heart, and knew this to be the troubled time
before the Judgment, when Adam would at last return into Paradise.
In 1790 Edom is France, and the red man will soon be identified as
Blake's Orc, Spirit of Revolt, who seems a creature from Hell to those
dwelling at ease in the Jacob or Israel that is Pitt's England.

The red man comes into Isaiah's vision late, at the start of Chapter
63, where the judging climax begins to gather together. Blake's own
reference is earlier; to two contrary chapters, 34 and 35, for some
historical progression will be necessary before England attains to its
climax. In Chapter 34 the indignation of the Lord is upon all nations,
and the wild beasts of the desert come to possess the world. But in
Chapter 35 the troubles yield to revelation: the eyes of the blind are
opened, waters break out in the wilderness, and the perilous path
becomes the highway of holiness upon which the redeemed shall walk.
Both states, the outcast and the redeemed, are crucial; to us and to
one another. For:

> Without Contraries is no progression. Attraction and Repul-
> sion, Reason and Energy, Love and Hate, are necessary to Hu-
> man existence.

From these contraries spring what the religious call Good & Evil. Good is the passive that obeys Reason. Evil is the active springing from Energy.

Good is Heaven. Evil is Hell.

The philosopher Heraclitus condemned Homer for praying that strife might perish from among gods and men, and said that the poet did not see that he was praying for the destruction of the universe.[5] The vision of Heraclitus is of an attunement of opposite tensions, of mortals and immortals living the others' death and dying the others' life. Blake read little with any care besides the Bible and Milton; he is not likely to have derived anything really central to him from ancient philosophy, or from the theosophy of the Cabala or Boehme. His doctrine or image of contraries is his own, and the analogues in Heraclitus or in Blake's own contemporary, Hegel, are chiefly interesting as contrasts. For Heraclitus, Good and Evil were one; for Blake they were not the inseparable halves of the same thing, but merely born together, as Milton had believed. For Hegel, opposites were raised to a higher power when they were transcended by synthesis; for Blake, opposites remained creative only so long as each remained immanent. Good and Evil could not refute one another, for each was only what the religious called Good and Evil, passive and active, restrained and unrestrained.

The usual misinterpretation of Blake's contraries (stemming from Swinburne) is that they represent a simple inversion of orthodox moral categories.[6] Blake is then pictured like Milton's Satan on Mount Niphates, passionately declaiming: "Evil be thou my Good." Blake of course is doing nothing of the kind; he is denying the orthodox categories altogether, and opposing himself both to moral "good" and moral "evil." Frye usefully remarks that the Swinburnean error in interpretation "ignores the fact that Blake attaches two meanings to the word 'hell,' one real and the other ironic."[7] The real hell is in the fearful obsessions of the Selfhood; the ironic one is that just quoted from the *Marriage*: an upsurge of desire whose energetic appearance frightens the Selfhood into the conviction that such intensity must stem from an external hell.

From this point on, the vocabulary of the *Marriage* is altogether ironic, and requires close attention. If Hell is the active springing from Energy, and the Eternal Hell revives with Blake's assumption of the Christological role, then "The voice of the Devil" that follows is Blake's own, but diabolical only because it will seem so to Sweden-borg or any other priestly Angel. The Devil's voice attacks the dual-ism of Christian tradition, the negation of setting the body's energy as evil against the soul's reason as good. Against these "Errors" the Devil Blake sets his contraries:

1. Man has no Body distinct from his Soul; for that call'd Body is a portion of Soul discern'd by the five Senses, the chief inlets of Soul in this age.

2. Energy is the only life, and is from the Body; and Reason is the bound or outward circumference of Energy.

3. Energy is Eternal Delight.

Blake is not saying that the soul is part of the body, but that the body is the outward circumference or boundary of the soul. In former ages, Blake implies, the more numerous and enlarged senses of man were able to discern a larger portion of the soul than the five senses can now. But what *can* be discerned of the soul now is chiefly the body; if the body is inadequate, it is nevertheless by necessity the way back to the soul. Asceticism is then exactly the wrong way to handle the body. It is by an increase and not a diminishment of sensual en-joyment that we can begin to expand our souls to their former dimensions. Donne in *The Extasie* affirms that the soul must repair first to the body before it can flow into another soul, but Donne's language is paradoxical and his remarkable poem abides in a philosophical dualism. But Blake really does believe that Energy is the only life, and is from the body, so that the greater wealth of a more abundant life, a more capable soul, must be the body's gift. The body's exuberance is the eternal delight that Coleridge and Wordsworth were to identify as the joy that alone made possible any artistic creation. For Blake, the running-down of that delight defines the place of reason in the creative life; the outward circum-ference where a vision recedes into merely natural light. In an ironic play upon an ancient Christian adage, the mind of the archetypal creator is for Blake an everlasting circle whose exuberant center is everywhere, and whose reasonable circumference is nowhere.

The archetypal creation, for Blake, was not the outward nature of the Coleridgean Primary Imagination, but the complete vision exuberantly manifested in the King James Bible. If a single poet since the Prophets and Jesus had incarnated that archetypal creative mind for Blake, surely that poet could only be John Milton. The *Marriage* passes therefore to the failure (as Blake saw it) of final exuberance in the maker of *Paradise Lost*. Plates 5 and 6 are a reading of the great English epic deliberately, which is to say ironically, from a Devil's point of view. Why did Milton restrain his poet's desire, and how did the restrainer, or reason, usurp desire's place and come to govern the unwilling poet?

Those who restrain desire, do so because theirs is weak enough to be restrained; and the restrainer or reason usurps its place & governs the unwilling.

And being restrain'd, it by degrees becomes passive, till it is only the shadow of desire.

The history of this is written in Paradise Lost, & the Governor or Reason is call'd Messiah.

And the original Archangel, or possessor of the command of the heavenly host, is call'd the Devil or Satan, and his children are call'd Sin and Death.

But in the Book of Job, Milton's Messiah is call'd Satan.

For this history has been adopted by both parties.

It indeed appear'd to Reason as if Desire was cast out; but the Devil's account is, that the Messiah fell, & formed a heaven of what he stole from the Abyss.

This is shewn in the Gospel, where he prays to the Father to send the comforter, or Desire that Reason may have Ideas to build on; the Jehovah of the Bible being no other than he who dwells in flaming fire.

Know that after Christ's death, he became Jehovah.

> But in Milton, the Father is Destiny, the Son a Ratio of the
> five senses, & the Holy-ghost, Vacuum!
>
> Note. The reason Milton wrote in fetters when he wrote of
> Angels & God, and at liberty when of Devils & Hell, is because
> he was a true Poet and of the Devil's party without knowing it.

Few passages of literary analysis, and this is surpassingly excellent
analysis, have been as misread as Blake's excursus on *Paradise Lost*.
The traditional misinterpretation, with its distinguished lineage from
Swinburne to C. S. Lewis, holds that Blake's reading is an antinomian
one.[8] But Blake is as uninterested in moral evil as he is in moral good;
neither category seems imaginative to him. *Paradise Lost* and the
Book of Job are theodicies; they seek to justify the existence of moral
evil by asserting the ultimate reality and providence of moral good.
Against such theodicies, with their final appeal to the necessity of
fallen nature, Blake makes a double attack, on the one hand rhetorical and ironic, on the other argumentative and prophetically serious. The rhetorical attack *seems* antinomian, but is actually aesthetic,
and concerns the relative failure (in Blake's view) of both *Paradise
Lost* and Job. The prophetic attack is as serious as Blake can make it,
and seeks to correct Milton's error in vision.

Paradise Lost, Blake judges, is written out of Milton's despair of
his earlier apocalyptic hopes, and is a Song of Experience, a poem
that accepts the fallen world's restraint of human desire. Milton is
willing to restrain the desires of Satan and Eve, or see them punished
for not accepting such restraints, because his own desires for knowledge and for the complete fulfillment of his imaginative potential
have become weak enough to be restrained. Reasoning from nature
usurps the place of imaginative desire and governs Milton's visionary
powers, though they are unwilling to be so governed. By degrees,
Milton's exuberance of invention becomes passive, until it is only the
shadow of the power that creates the opening books of *Paradise Lost*
and the past prophetic glory of *Areopagitica*.

The inner history of this psychic process of repression is written
in *Paradise Lost*, where it is externalized as the progressive inhibition
of Satan, who is degraded by his fall, from active rebellion into

passive plotting against the restraints of Right Reason. The restrainer, called Messiah by Milton, is called Satan in the Book of Job. Here Blake is at his most subtle. Milton's Messiah drives Satan out of Heaven with fire, and "Eternal wrath/Burnt after them to the bottomless pit." Hell is thus created by an act of Messiah. In the Book of Job a hell of external torment is created for Job by Satan, who serves as God's Accuser of sins, going to and fro in the earth to impute sin to the righteous.

This crucial resemblance between Milton's Christ and Job's Satan —that each creates a world of punishment, a categorical judgment that militates against mutual forgiveness of every vice—inspires Blake's blandest irony: "For this history has been adopted by both parties." The two parties are Devils—or true poets who write to correct orthodoxy, and Angels—or ruined poets and theologians who write to uphold moral and religious conventions. According to Blake, Milton was like Swedenborg in that he aged from a Devil into an Angel. It indeed appeared to Milton the theologian, that Satan or Desire was cast out into Hell, but the true poet or Devil, working away *within* Milton and the authors of the Bible, gave another account—though to read that account now we need to read Milton and the Bible in their "diabolical" sense.

This infernal sense of meaning is to Blake *the* poetic sense of Milton or Job or the Gospels. If it appeared to the curbers of desire that all illicit energies had been cast out into an abyss of heat without light, it appears to the supposed outcasts that the heaven of restraint, abandoned behind them, is only a stolen and frozen form, out of the many living forms constantly being created in the "abyss" of realized desires. The heaven of orthodoxy, or idea of restraint, was formed by the Messiah or Reason, but to get the stuff of creativity he had to "fall" into the energetic world of imaginings, or else Reason could have no ideas to build on. So the Gospel promise to send the comforter is a desire for Desire, and the answering Jehovah of imagination, the Jehovah of the Bible, is a creator who dwells in flaming fire, not in the cold light of Milton's static heaven. If the Son was truly human desire, and the Father, Desire removed from all encumbrances, then their identity in the resurrection of the human body is an identity of fire, of an impeded desire flaming into that which delights in its own form. But in Milton, the Father is not the self-determining form of fire, but the determined form of Destiny. The Son is not the human desire to attain a more imaginative body, but a Ratio of the five senses, a reductive argument from the limitations of natural perception. And the comforter or Holy Ghost is not a mediating desire binding man to his envisioned fulfillment, but rather a vacuum, for he is not there at all, in a poem that places all positive action in the past, and assigns to its historical present a choice only of obedient passivity or demonic defiance. Yet, as Blake's altogether ironic *Note* to this section adds, Milton the poet could not be content with this desperate quietism. Energy and desire enter into the poem when Milton writes at liberty, for Milton's greatness was, at last, in spite of himself. Because he was a true poet, his creative exuberance burst the fetters of Right Reason, and the Satan who dominates the first third of the poem came into his powerful existence.

As a reading of *Paradise Lost*, there is much to be said against this, and more to be said for it than most contemporary critics of Milton would now acknowledge. But whether Blake's reading of Milton is correct is not altogether relevant to a reader's understanding of the *Marriage*. What matters is that momentarily he learn to read the poem as Blake read it.

When Milton's Satan goes off on his perilous journey through chaos to the earth in Book II of *Paradise Lost*, his fallen host remains behind him in Hell, where they busy themselves with their equivalents of Olympian games, with composing and singing poems on their fate, with metaphysical and ethical discussions, and with explorations of their sad new world. One need not endorse Milton's theology to feel the force of his point: detached from God, such activities are demonic, and these enjoyments of fallen genius are sterile because they seek to serve as their own ends. But Blake's next section, the first of his Memorable Fancies, is an apt reply to Milton. Blake goes "walking among the fires of hell, delighted with the enjoyments of genius, which to Angels look like torment and insanity." To walk among those fires is to compose a poem or engrave a picture, and to collect the Proverbs of Hell, as Blake proceeds to do, is to express the laws of artistic creation in a series of aphorisms. When Blake came home from his proverb-collecting:

. . . on the abyss of the five senses, where a flat sided steep frowns over the present world, I saw a mighty Devil folded in black clouds, hovering on the sides of the rock: with corroding fires he wrote the following sentence now percieved by the minds of men, and read by them on earth:

How do you know but ev'ry Bird that cuts
    the airy way,
Is an immense world of delight, clos'd by
    your senses five?

The Devil is the artist William Blake, at work engraving the *Marriage*, and the corroding fires refer metaphorically both to his engraving technique and the satiric function of the *Marriage*. The flat sided steep, frowning over the present world, is fallen human consciousness, and Blake is an old Rocky Face like the Yeats of *The Gyres* whom he influenced. The stony cavern of the mind has been broken open by Blake's art; the imagination rises from the mind's abyss and seeks more expanded senses than the five making up that abyss. The gnomic couplet etched by the Devil Blake is adapted from one of Thomas Chatterton's best poems, and is meant to serve as an introductory motto to the following Proverbs of Hell.[9] In thus using Chatterton, Blake precedes Keats in honoring that Rimbaud of the English eighteenth century as a prophet of later poets' sensibilities.

Chatterton, for Blake, knew in his life, if not altogether in his work, that every object of natural perception contained an immense world of delight, closed off from us by the inadequacy of our five senses as we tended to use them in our minimal perceptions. The idea of raising our intensity of perception and so triumphing over nature *through nature* is the central idea of the Proverbs of Hell. Sexual exuberance, breaking the bounds of restraint and entering a fullness that Angelic Reason considers excess, will lead to a perception of a redeemed nature, though this perception itself must seem unlawful to fallen reason. The Proverbs emphasize an antinomian rhetoric, but expect the reader to recognize the implicit argument that underlies and finally absorbs this fierce vocabulary. Blake is not saying that active evil is morally better than passive good, though he wants the shock value that such a statement would have. Blake's good is the active springing from energy; there is therefore no such thing as a passive good, except to the Angels who identify act and evil. Blake's definition of an act is only implied in the *Marriage*, but had been set down clearly by him in 1788 when he annotated the aphorisms of his contemporary, the Swiss poet and theologian Johann Kaspar Lavater:

> There is a strong objection to Lavater's principles (as I understand them) & that is He makes every thing originate in its accident; he makes the vicious propensity not only a leading feature of the man, but the stamina on which all his virtues grow. But as I understand Vice it is a Negative. It does not signify what the laws of Kings & Priests have call'd Vice; we who are philosophers ought not to call the Staminal Virtues of Humanity by the same name that we call the omissions of intellect springing from poverty.
>
> Every man's leading propensity ought to be call'd his leading Virtue & his good Angel. But the Philosophy of Causes & Consequences misled Lavater as it has all his Cotemporaries. Each thing is its own cause & its own effect. Accident is the omission of act in self & the hindering of act in another; This is Vice, but all Act [from Individual propensity] is Virtue. To hinder another is not an act; it is the contrary; it is a restraint on action both in ourselves & in the person hinder'd, for he who hinders another omits his own duty at the same time.
>
> Murder is Hindering Another.
>
> Theft is Hindering Another.
>
> Backbiting, Undermining, Circumventing, & whatever is Negative is Vice. But the origin of this mistake in Lavater & his cotemporaries is, They suppose that Woman's Love is Sin; in consequence all the Loves & Graces with them are Sin.[10]

Of all Blake's annotations upon other writers, this seems to me the most profound, and the most central for a reader's understanding of Blake himself. Here indeed is the imaginative seed of not only the Proverbs of Hell but the whole of the *Marriage*, and of Blake's ideas of good and evil to the end of his life. What is hindrance and not action is evil, whether one hinders the self or another. Restraint for Blake is a mode of indecision, and proceeds from a mind in chaos. Decision, true act, proceeds from the whole man, the imaginative mind, and must be good, for whatever is negative is a restraint upon another, and not an act. Act stems from the only wealth, from life, but restraint is an omission of intellect, and springs from the poverty of lifelessness, the absence of the exuberance of mind delighting in its own forming powers. The paradoxes of Blake's Proverbs of Hell nearly always arise from an ironic awareness of the gap between "what the laws of Kings & Priests have call'd Vice" and what an artist sees as Vice: "the omission of act in self & the hindering of act in another."

In form, Blake's Proverbs parody what he might have called the "Proverbs of Heaven," the Book of Proverbs in the Hebrew Bible, which claim "to give subtility to the simple, to the young man knowledge and discretion." In contrast, Blake's Proverbs exist to break down orthodox categories of thought and morality. To accomplish this end Blake employs an apparent dissociation of customary meanings, both within many of the Proverbs and in their curious disarrangement. Since the Proverbs seek to destroy a pattern of preconceived responses, they rely on a final association of meanings after the initial dissociation has done its work.

The reader can arrive at this association by considering the Proverbs as falling into four overlapping groups, largely defined by their imagery. The first is clearly and intensely sexual, so intense that in it the act of sexual union assumes the mythic dimension familiar to us from the work of D. H. Lawrence. In the Proverbs, this sexual imagery is presented in a variety of ironic disguises, including the sacraments of baptism and communion, with their water and wine symbolism, and a complex association of plowing and harvest imagery with the idea of the fulfillment of prayer. Thus, "In seed time learn, in harvest teach, in winter enjoy" looks like a traditional description of man's life, but refers also to the sexual rites of initiation. To "Drive your cart and plow over the bones of the dead" is to renew human life by a refreshment of sexuality, even at the cost of defying the codes of the past. In the third Proverb, "The road of excess leads to the palace of wisdom," a second grouping of ideas and images are introduced. To increase sexual fulfillment is to take what the Angels consider the road of excess that will lead one to the palace of the diabolical principle. But this excess Blake considers as the contrary to the deliberate self-frustration of the Angels, expressed in the next Proverb, which is a brilliant allegorical story in one sentence: "Prudence is a rich, ugly old maid courted by Incapacity." Repressed energy culminates in neurosis: "He who desires but acts not, breeds pestilence." But what is genuinely acted upon may be injured yet is augmented: "The cut worm forgives the plow," an unequivocal image of phallic plenitude.

The themes of sexuality and excess meet in "Dip him in the river who loves water," for this cleansing baptism is the total immersion of the soul in the body's sexual wealth. Sexual excess as initiator meets its apocalyptic result in the following Proverbs, as the two further imagistic groupings, turning upon antinomianism and increased perceptiveness, make initial appearances. "A fool sees not the same tree that a wise man sees," for the wise man, as a creative Devil, sees the tree in a context more exuberant than any an unvitalized nature could sustain. The fool is self-condemned to a status of minimum vitality in nature, for "He whose face gives no light, shall never become a star." We see the light we emanate, and our creativeness is responsible not only for a different tree than the fool sees, but a different time in which vision takes place, for "Eternity is in love with the productions of time," not with time's passivities. In creation the oppressiveness of clock time vanishes, for "The busy bee has no time for sorrow" and "The hours of folly are measur'd by the clock; but of wisdom, no clock can measure."

In creative or human time, the restraints of fallen experience, the nets and traps of natural morality, tend to lose their immediacy, and desire and gratification are near-allied, an intimation of psychic health because "All wholesome food is caught without a net or a trap." The psychic abundance of the creative life scorns the conventionalizing forms of tradition, whether in the social elaborations of manners or the closed couplet of Augustan poetic decorum, for restricted forms ration the meager, not the prolific: "Bring out number, weight & measure in a year of dearth." The net of convention is broken by the imagination capable in itself, and in the consciousness of its own powers: "No bird soars too high, if he soars with his own wings." As

for the offended conventions, they can do no harm, for "A dead
body revenges not injuries."

So far the Proverbs of Hell have mostly been assaults upon conventional evasions of human energies. But Blake is not content to
attack timidity; he desires also to replace the tired mind's naturali-
zations of its own best moments, by showing that mind the meaning
of its own rejected strengths. In the human confrontation of another human, in the moment where the self acknowledges the full
reality of another self, the relationship of equal immediacies is a recognition of the imaginative act itself: "The most sublime act is to
set another before you."

We have considered, so far, the first seventeen of the seventy Proverbs of Hell. To go through each of the Proverbs in this way would
be to usurp the reader's individuality of response, for the Proverbs
should mean a variety of things, quite correctly, to different readers.
There is perhaps more potential value in exploring the general pattern of the remaining Proverbs. The sexual and harvest images lead
to the vision of excess, by which apparent foolishness culminates in
the wisdom of a further horizon of human aspiration. This aspiration
is emphasized obliquely in the group of antinomian Proverbs that
concern animal powers and violently revenge stifled energies upon
the restraints of Law and Religion. Hence: "The wrath of the lion is
the wisdom of God," and "The tygers of wrath are wiser than the
horses of instruction."

When this antinomian intensity is carried over into a human admonition, the result is deliberately shocking: "Sooner murder an infant in its cradle than nurse unacted desires." A moment's reflection
grimly clarifies Blake's meaning: to *nurse* an unacted desire is to
feed a monster, after already having murdered the cradled infant desire, and the unacted desire, nursed to full size, will be a demon of
destruction. The only way out of this cycle of repression and torment
is through a perception that transforms time into the eternity of a
creative *now*, and that renders space as form until nature itself becomes art. These abstractions are mine, not Blake's, who prefers the
more palpable particulars of his Proverbs. "Exuberance is Beauty,"
and "Where man is not, nature is barren," for exuberance is the stuff
of human desire, and the dull round of nature can bear nothing unless man will marry it with the animation of his overflowing energy.

The coda to the Proverbs of Hell is a brief account of the hardening of poetic myth into priestcraft. The ancient Poets, who were one with the titanic ancient men, animated all sensible objects because they perceived them with "enlarged & numerous senses." The weak in courage, being strong in cunning, chose forms of worship from these poetic tales: "Thus men forgot that All deities reside in the human breast," and thus the contraries of priestly Angels and prophetic Devils sprang into existence.

A Memorable Fancy follows, in which Blake entertains two prophetic predecessors, Isaiah and Ezekiel, at dinner and questions them as to their certainty of being divinely inspired. Isaiah expresses his "firm perswasion" that an honestly indignant human voice is the voice of God, while Ezekiel more directly stresses the necessity for extreme action if the prophet is to raise other men into a perception of the infinite, the human reality that masks as natural appearance. This prophetic encouragement inspires one of Blake's most passionate perceptions: the natural world is on the point of being purged by fire. The fire here is the fire of intellect and art, which must begin "by an improvement of sensual enjoyment." The active intellect of the artist, raised to its full powers by sexual completion, will consume the whole creation and bring man back to the tree of life, driving away the lesser fire of the guardian cherub's flaming sword. But this sexual completion cannot begin without expunging the pernicious Angelic notion of dualism, and for such work the visionary satirist like Blake is essential. His engraved poems, like the *Marriage*, will be salutary and medicinal corrosives. Even as he creates his plates by melting apparent surfaces away, so the function of his art will be to display the hidden infinite, hid in the phenomenal world. To imitate the artist is to see as he sees:

If the doors of perception were cleansed every thing would appear to man as it is, infinite.

For man has closed himself up, till he sees all things thro' narrow chinks of his cavern.

This cavern is the skull of fallen man, or in a larger dimension the whole of his fallen body. To see more, we must cleanse the doors of perception we still have, the five senses, but to cleanse them, for Blake, means to begin by raising them to the heights of their sensual power. You do not expand your sense of touch by avoiding sexuality, but only by rising *through* it, and to see more, you must begin by seeing everything you can.

This insistence on the role of increased sensual enjoyment in creation is followed by a sardonic Memorable Fancy confirming that role. Blake is "in a Printing house in Hell," a six-chambered establishment that serves as an allegory of the creative process. In the first chamber is a phallic Dragon-Man "clearing away the rubbish from a cave's mouth," and so cleansing the human sense of touch. Within, other dragons are at work "hollowing the cave," widening the body's potential for imaginative knowledge. Art ensues in this aggressive sexuality, but the next chamber introduces the censorious restrainer, "a Viper folding round the rock & the cave," seeking to confine man within his fallen limits. But a Proverb of Hell comes to our aid: "When thou seest an Eagle, thou seest a portion of Genius; lift up thy head!" So in the next chamber an Eagle combats the Viper by causing "the inside of the cave to be infinite," and the artists who share in a portion of Genius are seen as "numbers of Eagle-like men who built palaces in the immense cliffs." We remember the mighty Devil Blake of an earlier plate, where he hovered on the sides of the rock and wrote sentences in corroding fire. The Eagle-like men prepare us for the fourth chamber of the creative mind, where the archetypes are seen as "Lions of flaming fire, raging around & melting the metals into living fluids." These metals were introduced by the restricting Vipers of reason; now they are melted down into the basic fluids of imaginative life. In the fifth chamber the metals are cast into the expanse of human existence by "Unnam'd forms," who are like the smiths of Yeats's Byzantium. Hell's Printing house ends in a sixth chamber where men take on the forms of books, and the finished creation is at last evident.

These men appear again, in an interlude directly after the Printing house fantasy, as "the Giants who formed this world in its sensual existence, and now seem to live in it in chains." They are our buried energies, our waking appetites, our more than natural resources. Blake now terms them a class of men called the Prolific, and their cunning contrary the class called the Devouring:

Thus one portion of being is the Prolific, the other the Devouring: To the Devourer it seems as if the producer was in
his chains; but it is not so, he only takes portions of existence
and fancies that the whole.

But the Prolific would cease to be Prolific unless the Devourer,
as a sea, received the excess of his delights.

In this beautiful passage Blake's concept of contraries undergoes
a change into a more balanced theory of human existence than was
first set forth by "The Voice of the Devil." If ever Blake speaks
straight, forgoing all irony, in the *Marriage*, it is here. Reason is
still only the outward bound or circumference of Energy, and still
fancies that its reductive idea of existence is the whole, rather than
a part, of the Human. But the productive Prolific would cease to be
itself, would stifle by its own exuberance of invention, if the Devourer ceased to be a primal sea of forms into which the excess of
Prolific delights could be received. We are hearing not the Devil's
story, and certainly not an Angel's, but the law of human process
itself. The Devourer is an outer limit of the Prolific, even as Freud's
ego is of his id, but unlike the ego, the Devourer can never manifest
itself independently, for Blake will never recognize the validity of a
physical world different from the self. Yet the *appearance* of an independent Devourer mocks Blake's Prolific by assuming the shadowy
form Blake will later call the Spectre. The process of assumption is
remarkably like the constitution of Freud's super-ego, as set forth by
Philip Rieff:

The ego is but an outer portion of the id—crystallizing independently as soon as the infant becomes aware of a physical
world different from the self. Then, onto this acceptance of
reality lodged in the perceptual system, are superimposed the ex-
hortations of society: first embodied in the figures of the parents
and later constituted as a part of the personality, the superego.[11]

As repression is the function of the Devourer, so is it of the
Freudian ego. But the Prolific, unlike the id, is not chaotic; it can

become chaotic if it lacks all bounds, but this chaos will be an over-flux, a superabundance of creativity. By re-stating the contraries as classes of men, Blake has transformed his psychic terms into social ones, and his equivalent of Freud's "civil war" that takes place within the mind now becomes a conflict within culture:

> These two classes of men are always upon earth, & they should be enemies: whoever tries to reconcile them seeks to destroy existence.

> Religion is an endeavour to reconcile the two.

Orthodox religion seeks to transcend the strife of existential con-traries by absorbing the Prolific into the Devourer, the energies of men into the organizing categories of the Church. The religious be-lieve that God alone is the Prolific; but Blake is a pragmatic human-ist on this issue: "God only Acts and Is, in existing beings or Men." And Blake's Christ, ironically like "Satan or Tempter," is identified in the *Marriage* as another of "the Antediluvians who are our En-ergies," the Titans repressed by the Sky-gods of reductive reason.

Blake's demonic impiety in making this identification provokes an Angel into commencing the next and longest of the Memorable Fancies, a Swiftian exercise in direct satire. The Angel warns Blake of the dungeon in hell awaiting him. Blake asks to see it:

> So he took me thro' a stable & thro' a church, & down into the church vault, at the end of which was a mill: thro' the mill we went, and came to a cave: down the winding cavern we groped our tedious way, till a void boundless as a nether sky ap-pear'd beneath us, & we held by the roots of trees and hung over this immensity; but I said: "if you please, we will commit our-selves to this void, and see whether providence is here also: if you will not, I will:" but he answer'd: "do not presume, O young man, but as we here remain, behold thy lot which will soon appear when the darkness passes away."

> So I remain'd with him, sitting in the twisted root of an oak; he was suspended in a fungus, which hung with the head down-ward into the deep.

The stable may be either the home of the tamed "horses of instruction" of the Proverb (Foster Damon's suggestion)[12] or simply the stable of Christ's birth, ironically leading into the grander structure of the Church. The vault is emblematic of Christ's burial. In the resurrection of the body Christ passes out of the vault, but the Angel and Blake go to the vault's other end which aptly leads into a mill, mechanical symbol of reductive reason. Once through the mill, and we are in the winding cavern of the fallen mind, in which any groping yields a way that is both downward and tedious, until we hang with Blake and the Angel over the abyss of nature, the unimaginative chaos of reductive intellect. The roots of trees hold us on to the minimal vegetative forms that precariously abide in this mental void. Blake at least has an oak's twisted root for support; his vision paradoxically has a stubborn attachment to natural fact, but the ascetic Angel is properly suspended in a fungus, since those who deny nature for the soul live as parasites *on* the body, not as natural forms within the body. What Blake and the Angel see is the Angelic vision of hell as a torture chamber, complete with a sun giving heat without light, tormenting spiders, and the great Leviathan of Job coming out of the burning East of unrestrained passion, "tinging the black deep with beams of blood, advancing toward us with all the fury of a Spiritual Existence." But the Angel, though a Spiritual Existence himself, climbs back from his fungus into the mill; retreating from this king over all the children of pride into the windings of theology. Left alone, Blake finds that the horrible vision is no more:

. . . but I found myself sitting on a pleasant bank beside a river by moonlight, hearing a harper, who sung to the harp; & his theme was: "The man who never alters his opinion is like standing water, & breeds reptiles of the mind."

The metaphysics of Angels creates Leviathans, but Blake's vision, to which the Angel must now submit, makes monkeys out of theologians:

"Here," said I, "is your lot, in this space—if space it may be call'd." Soon we saw the stable and the church, & I took him to the altar and open'd the Bible, and lo! it was a deep pit, into which I descended, driving the Angel before me; soon we saw seven houses of brick; one we enter'd; in it were a number of monkeys, baboons, & all of that species, chain'd by the middle, grinning and snatching at one another, but withheld by the shortness of their chains: however, I saw that they sometimes grew numerous, and then the weak were caught by the strong, and with a grinning aspect, first coupled with, & then devour'd, by plucking off first one limb and then another, till the body was left a helpless trunk; this, after grinning & kissing it with seeming fondness, they devour'd too; and here & there I saw one savourily picking the flesh off of his own tail; as the stench terribly annoy'd us both, we went into the mill, and I in my hand brought the skeleton of a body, which in the mill was Aristotle's Analytics.

The "seven houses of brick," as Swinburne surmised, are the seven churches in Asia to whom St. John the Divine addressed his revelation.[13] To reach these temples, Blake takes in his hands Swedenborg's weighty volumes, that Devil and Angel may sink together into the holy void. The gruesome lewdness of Blake's vision of a theological monkey-house has not lost its shock-value; it still offends orthodoxy. Swift himself could not have done better here, in the repulsive projection of an incestuous warfare of rival doctrines, ground together in the reductive mill of scholastic priestcraft.

The smack at Swedenborg is sharpened in Blake's next interlude, where we are given an invaluable guide to Blake's notions of cultural precedence:

. . . Any man of mechanical talents may, from the writings of Paracelsus or Jacob Behmen, produce ten thousand volumes of equal value with Swedenborg's, and from those of Dante or Shakespear an infinite number.

But when he has done this, let him not say that he knows better than his master, for he only holds a candle in sunshine.

This little passage not only dismisses Swedenborg and all systematic reasoners in spiritual matters with him, but quietly implies a truth about Blake that many of his more esoteric scholars might have pondered; Dante and Shakespeare are valued infinitely above the theosophists Paracelsus and Boehme (Behmen), for the great poets are a sunshine in which any mystical writer is only a candle.

The last full section of the *Marriage* is the wisest of its Memorable Fancies, illustrating the Proverb Angels generally will not learn: "Opposition is true Friendship." Blake sees a Devil in a flame of fire rising before an Angel sitting on a cloud. The fire-cloud opposition is premonitory of the symbolic figures into which the Devil and Angel will develop, the fiery Orc of desire and the cloudy Urizen of restraint. Blake's Devil defines the emergent religion of the *Marriage*:

> The worship of God is: Honouring his gifts in other men, each according to his genius, and loving the greatest men best: those who envy or calumniate great men hate God; for there is no other God.

Greatness here means artistic greatness. As God is a Man, for Blake, and finds his being in human acts of creation, so any man who achieves greatness in art is God to the extent of being himself constituted by his own creative acts. The outraged Angel invokes the Ten Commandments and the visibility of God in Jesus Christ, only to hear the Devil proclaim that Jesus was one of the antinomian party:

> I tell you, no virtue can exist without breaking these ten commandments. Jesus was all virtue, and acted from impulse, not from rules.

Blake is resorting again to the rhetoric of shock, as he did at the start of the *Marriage*. As argument, this last Memorable Fancy is weak, but we are not intended to take it as more than a fiery polemic, uttered for its fire and not its light. The Angel at least is drawn to it, embraces the fire, is consumed, and rises again as the archetypal prophet or Devil, Elijah. With an ironic "Note," Blake closes this last section of his gnomic work. The Angel-turned-Devil is the poet's

particular friend; together they read the Bible in its infernal or diabolical—that is, in its originally poetic—sense. If the world behaves
well, Blake blandly insinuates, they shall have this reading, but in
any case they shall receive from Blake "The Bible of Hell," or canon
of his engraved poems.

As he works upon writing and engraving the *Marriage*, Blake evidently arrives at the central organizing principle of his life's work.
The experiments in pastoral of *Poetical Sketches* and *Songs of Innocence* suggest an emulation of the classical kind of canonical
principle, as Blake follows Virgil, Spenser, and Milton in preparing
for epic by explorations in man's golden age. But now, in the *Marriage*, Blake declares himself a Biblical poet, in the tradition of the
later Milton who repudiated the classical Muses and sought Zion's
springs instead. The English Bible, as Blake read it, began with a
Creation that was also a Fall, proceeded to the cycle of history,
with alternate movements of vision and collapse, and achieved the
pastoral art of the Song of Solomon, the tragedy of Job, and the
triumphant prophecy of greater poets like Isaiah and Ezekiel. The
entrance of this poetry into history in the Gospels was culminated
in the Apocalypse, and set a pattern for the Christian poem, a pattern that Milton, in Blake's view, had almost succeeded in emulating.

But the proper poetic use of this pattern, for Blake, depended
upon an achieved freedom from the interpretative tradition of priestcraft. The Protestant passion for the Bible as an individual possession, to be read finally by the inner light of each believer's spirit, is
Blake's most direct heritage from the radical element in English religious tradition. Blake's Bible of Hell, the sequence of his engraved
poems, is the first of the great Romantic displacements of the Biblical revelation into the poetic world of an individual creator, the first
of the heterocosms.

Blake chooses not to end the *Marriage* with this promise of his
own oncoming world, but with an emblem of the negation of vision.
The nightmare of Nebuchadnezzar, fallen from great Babylon
down to a dwelling with the beasts of the field, is the nightmare of
history unrelieved by the prophet's transforming vision. The *Marriage's* last plate is dominated by a picture of the metamorphized
king with the prophecy fulfilled upon him:

The same hour was the thing fulfilled upon Nebuchadnezzar: and he was driven from men, and did eat grass as oxen, and his body was wet with the dew of heaven, till his hairs were grown like eagle's feathers, and his nails like birds' claws.

DANIEL 4:33

Blake's picture suggests this, and also the great beast of Yeats's *The Second Coming*, with lion body and the head of a man, portending the coming of "mere anarchy" upon the world. Beneath the horror of Nebuchadnezzar, Blake inscribed, as covering Proverb, the dying tyrant Tiriel's gasp of wisdom: "One Law for the Lion & Ox is Oppression." With this outcry against the imposition of any code of uniformity upon contrary individualities, Blake brings *The Marriage of Heaven and Hell* to its proper conclusion. We are left with the memory of the Voice of the Devil, crying aloud in the desert places of a repressive society, and reminding society that it tempts the fate of Nebuchadnezzar, a fall into dazed bestiality, if it will not heed the warnings of vision.

A Song of Liberty

Engraved in 1792, this vigorous prose poem was associated by Blake with *The Marriage of Heaven and Hell*, to the extent that he sometimes bound it as a coda or pendant to the greater work. In language and conception, *A Song of Liberty* suggests a mature (and politically minded) Rimbaud, exchanging his season in Hell for a summer of unbounded exuberance and imaginative passion. Indeed Blake's *Song* is written in an effective kind of imaginative shorthand, as though the rising enjoyment of poetic fulfillment does not allow time for expansion into even a short romance or prophecy. What Blake gives us is a kind of scenario for an ode of revolutionary triumph. I suspect that *A Song of Liberty* was intended originally as a separate emblem book, in twenty or more plates, and that the twenty numbered sentences of the work were each meant to serve as caption for an individual plate. Certainly each sentence concentrates on a separate image, or an adumbration of an image, until the total image is gathered together in the *Song's* Chorus:

Let the Priests of the Raven of dawn no longer, in deadly
black, with hoarse note curse the sons of joy! Nor his accepted
brethren—whom, tyrant, he calls free—lay the bound or build
the roof! Nor pale religious letchery call that Virginity that
wishes but acts not!

For everything that lives is Holy!

The Raven of dawn is the sky-god Urizen, associated with the
Raven because that is the emblematic bird of Odin, the sky-god of
Northern mythology. Urizen's accepted brethren are the vested
powers of Europe, who lay the boundary for man's liberty and build
the roof of the orthodox heaven above man's head. The whiteness of
religious chastity is the paleness of sexual repression, murderously
nursing unacted desires. But all true desire is sacred, for everything
that *lives* is holy. A *Song of Liberty* reaches this conclusion by a
rhapsodic mythic narrative that outlines the main characters and
events of more finished prophetic poems by Blake. In attaching it to
The Marriage of Heaven and Hell, Blake provides us with an introduction to poems like *Visions of the Daughters of Albion, America, Europe,* and *The Book of Urizen.*
A *Song of Liberty* begins with the groaning in childbirth of an
Eternal Female, later to be named Enitharmon, the Queen of
Heaven. She is giving birth to a "new born fire," Orc, a muttering
shiver among the tyrannies of Europe, for the temporal manifestation of this fire is the French Revolution. But the "new born terror"
is not powerful enough to overcome Urizen, "the starry king":

8. On those infinite mountains of light, now barr'd out by the
Atlantic sea, the new-born fire stood before the starry king!

Blake is introducing his version of the myth of lost Atlantis, later
to be developed in *America.* The confrontation between Orc and
Urizen takes place in the unfallen world, from which we are separated by the Atlantic, chaotic sea and sinister emblem of our minimal notions of space and time. Orc seems to lose the battle, and like
Lucifer is hurled down flaming into the abyss. But the falling fire

makes an ironic appearance on earth as the Revolution, the active springing from energy that seems diabolical to orthodox society.

Urizen and his host fall also, so that Blake's version of Milton's Fall of the Angels brings down both Jehovah-Urizen and Lucifer-Orc. With fine irony, Blake parallels Urizen's gathering together of his forces with Satan's rallying of his host in *Paradise Lost*. In a more daring analogue, worthy of the Bible of Hell, the figure of Moses is invoked as the next stage in Urizen's career:

18. With thunder and fire, leading his starry hosts thro' the waste wilderness, he promulgates his ten commands, glancing his beamy eyelids over the deep in dark dismay,

19. Where the son of fire in his eastern cloud, while the morning plumes her golden breast,

20. Spurning the clouds written with curses, stamps the stony law to dust, loosing the eternal horses from the dens of night, crying:

EMPIRE IS NO MORE! AND NOW THE LION & WOLF SHALL CEASE.

The Ten Commandments are set here in the most negative of contexts, and their close association with Empire marks the passage as one of the most antinomian in Blake. Yet even at his most turbulent and rebellious, Blake does not altogether forget the necessity of contraries. The dens of night, from which Orc looses the horses, releasing them from Instruction to Wrath, are referred to earlier in A *Song of Liberty* as "Urthona's dens," where Urizen and his starry host lie all night beneath the ruins. Urthona is the unfallen or eternal name of the being who will evolve into the hero of Blake's myth, Los, the imaginative shaper who must be the agent of a human apocalypse. To be in Urthona's dens is to have fallen into the lowest regions of creativity, and yet to be still within a possibility of further creation. A *Song of Liberty* therefore does not simply describe a conflict between tyrannizing restraint and revolutionary desire, with all our sympathies given to desire, but hints at the conflict as being a clash of creative forces, blindly striving against a background that Blake has yet to clarify.

CHAPTER SIX

Torments of Love and Jealousy

The Notebook Poems

In February 1793, war began between England and France. At about
the same time Blake went through an inner turbulence, almost certainly involving sexual conflict with his wife. We have little clear information about this, and Blake's biographers do not help matters by
their inventiveness. What we do have is Blake's notebook, traditionally called the Rossetti Manuscript. Originally the possession of
Blake's beloved brother Robert, the notebook was very dear to
Blake, and served him first as a sketchbook and then as a kind of
poetic workshop. Most of the *Songs of Experience* (all but four)
exist in earlier drafts in the notebook, as do some forty other lyrical
poems and fragments. The notebook's relation to the *Songs of Experience* implies that Blake's concept of Experience grew from a
concern with the threat of jealousy, which to Blake meant the selfish
possessiveness of the natural heart.

The notebook poems begin with an intense bitterness, based upon
the supposed perversity of female nature. Their first message is the
Yeatsian "never give all the heart," for woman yields to some measure of indifference. Blake does not rest long in this convention, and
fortunately it tires him before it does us. He is driven to work back
from the female will (in what to him seems its derangement) to the
causes in society, restrained reason and fallen nature, of that will. The
triumph of society, reason, and nature is the religion that justifies the
union of these concepts in one psychic apparatus of repression:

> I saw a chapel all of gold
> That none did dare to enter in
> And many weeping stood without
> Weeping mourning worshipping.

The God to whom this chapel is built is Nobodaddy, not the loving father of Innocence, but the nobody's father of Experience:

> Why are thou silent & invisible
> Father of Jealousy?
> Why dost thou hide thyself in clouds
> From every searching Eye?
>
> Why darkness & obscurity
> In all thy words & laws
> That none dare eat the fruit but from
> The wily serpents jaws?
> Or is it because Secresy gains females' loud
>   applause?

To understand this grim little poem is to be able to connect what are for some of us incompatibles, but for Blake were a unified system of mind-forged monstrosities, stiflers of man's one life, his desire. What men and women require in one another are "the lineaments of Gratified Desire." What, for Blake, are the outlines or external features of fulfillment? For Blake the only valid mark of an individuality is the clarity of its bounding outline, but the true outline is formed from within, and is reached only when the energy within finds itself delighted by the form it has attained. The lineaments of *gratified* desire manifest themselves in a delighted countenance and the measure of gratification is taken when the human face can be seen as what Milton called it in a moving passage that greatly influenced Blake, as a "human face divine."[1] The negation of this face is the invisible, cloud-hidden Nobodaddy of the notebook poem.

The deliberate obscurity of this hidden, faceless divine is manifested also in all its dark words and laws, which give the lie to passionate being, to the human truth of sexual freedom. The masterpiece of Nobodaddy is his association of sexuality and sin, fruit

eaten from the serpent's jaws. Blake's poem to Nobodaddy is a series
of questions as to this god's wilful mysteriousness, followed by the
poet's guess at an answer. Nobodaddy is the god of the female will,
and secrecy gains for the silent divinity the loud applause of female
kind.

There is enough direct sexual bitterness in Blake's notebook to
keep us from assuming that this "female" is as yet what she will later
become in Blake's work, the natural as opposed to the imaginative,
rather than woman as opposed to man. By at least the Autumn of
1793, Blake had transvalued the word in that way; the female in
Songs of Experience is the natural world and the generative process,
and the male represents the human, both man and woman. We can
see Blake learning this lesson, and repenting of any anti-womanly
feelings, in another engraved poem of 1793, the magnificent *Visions
of the Daughters of Albion*. In the *Visions* a woman, Oothoon, is
the embodiment of desire and advocate of free love, and her two
stupidly brutalized men are tormented by jealousy and a Nobodaddy-
inspired doctrine of repression. The notebook lyrics, with all their
bitter irony, were to modulate into the complex ironies of the frequently satiric *Songs of Experience*. But the fire within Blake early
in 1793, his longing for a full freedom in sexual expression, receives
its final and perfect statement in *Visions*, a tragic but exultant hymn
to the exuberant beauty of sexual release.

Visions of the Daughters of Albion

The motto to this poem is "The Eye sees more than the heart
knows," emphasizing the primacy of perception over the limited wisdom of the natural heart. More significantly, the motto relates this
poem to its predecessors *Tiriel* and *Thel*. Tiriel learned too late that
his hypocrisy of intellect was "the idiot's wisdom & the wise man's
folly," and his eye at last saw more than his mind had ever known.
Yet even at the end, little had moved his heart. Thel's eye always
saw more than her heart knew, but her attempt to gain experience
of the heart ended in hysterical failure. The experience of Tiriel and
the innocence of Thel could make no fruitful meeting with one another, and so neither of their lives could progress. The natural heart,

for Blake, is redeemed by organizing its innocence into that subtle
state so well described by the contemporary British philosopher John
Wisdom: "We need to be at once like someone who has seen much
and forgotten nothing; and also like one who sees things for the first
time."[2] The heroine of *Visions*, Oothoon, attains this state of innocence carried over into experience at the very beginning of her
poem, and she attains it as the *Marriage* had prophesied it must be
attained, "by an improvement of sensual enjoyment." The heart that
knows less than the eye sees is not her own but that of her self-
tormented lover, Theotormon, and perhaps of her momentary or cas-
ual lover and exploiter, Bromion.

In the *Visions*, we are not yet involved in Blake's own mythology
to any vital degree, as we will be in *America*, the next poem to be
considered, and the first of Blake's poems altogether in the mythmaking mode that is to lead on to the epic *Jerusalem*. The *Visions*
takes place in a cosmos precariously balanced between our own and
Blake's more individual world. Oothoon's "Argument" places her initial world for us, and introduces all the characters of her poem:

> I loved Theotormon
> And I was not ashamed;
> I trembled in my virgin fears,
> And I hid in Leutha's vale!
>
> I plucked Leutha's flower,
> And I rose up from the vale;
> But the terrible thunders tore
> My virgin mantle in twain.

Though she loved Theotormon (the man tormented by his own
idea of God, as his name indicates), and had pride in her love, nevertheless Oothoon confesses that her lack of sexual experience resulted
in ambiguous fears, so that she hid herself in the vales of a female
sub-deity called Leutha. Leutha appears in *Europe*, engraved a year
later than *Visions*, as a "lureing bird of Eden" sent among mankind by her mother Enitharmon, a kind of courtly-love Queen of
Heaven, so as to take away from man his "lineaments of gratified
desire." Leutha is at once a "soft soul of flowers" and a "sweet smil-

ing pestilence," a "silken queen" whose "blushing light" will darken the clear outlines of man's fulfillment. In the same poem, directly after invoking this faintly sinister temptress, Enitharmon reproaches her other daughter, Oothoon, in a clear reference to *Visions of the Daughters of Albion:*

> I hear the soft Oothoon in Enitharmon's tents;
> Why wilt thou give up woman's secrecy, my
>   melancholy child?
> Between two moments bliss is ripe.
> O Theotormon! robb'd of joy, I see thy salt
>   tears flow
> Down the steps of my crystal house.

The cruelty of her mother Enitharmon, rejoicing at the frustrations and jealousies that provoke male tears, is the negation of Oothoon's attitude, for Oothoon's whole quest is to find bliss ripe in the moment, not in the female evasiveness that takes place "between two moments." Enitharmon teaches the bondage of time; her generous daughter seeks to offer eternity, by not letting the ripe moment of sexual fulfillment go. Oothoon desires to kiss the joy as it flies; Enitharmon wishes to bind to herself a joy, and thus destroy the winged life of an immortal moment.

If we return to *Visions* from this excursion into *Europe* and the notebook, we ought to be able to grasp decisively the poem's argument and its action. Oothoon (her name is modeled on the heroine of Ossian's *Oithona*, but only as a protest or parody) hides in the valley of sexual evasiveness and denial, until she suddenly wills the courage that Thel could never achieve. She plucks one of Leutha's flowers and rises up from the vale into the openness of sexual generosity. But, as the Argument goes on to imply, this free offering of herself is betrayed before she can present herself to her lover. She is raped by a thunder Titan Bromion (the name refers to the Greek for a "roaring one" and not to an alternative name of Bacchus), and this rape is her involuntary introduction into the sexual experience she had voluntarily sought with another.

The poem proper acts out this Argument in its first seventeen lines,

but with a remarkable and illuminating difference in tone. This tone
is set by the opening lines:

> Enslav'd, the Daughters of Albion weep; a
>   trembling lamentation
> Upon their mountains; in their valleys,
>   sighs toward America.

> For the soft soul of America, Oothoon,
>   wander'd in woe
> Along the vales of Leutha, seeking flowers
>   to comfort her.

The poem, as its title indicates, consists of what these Daughters
of Albion *see*. But who are they? Their father Albion, the archetypal
or unfallen Man, Blake's equivalent of Milton's Adam, does not play
any central part in Blake's mythmaking for another two years, until
the epic concerning him, *The Four Zoas*, begins to be composed in
1795. To find a comment by Blake on his Albion which will be relevant to the *Visions*, we need to go all the way ahead to Blake's "Descriptive Catalogue" for his Exhibition of paintings held in 1809, by
which time nearly the entire canon of Blake's engraved poems was
complete. Commenting on his painting, now unfortunately lost, of
"The Ancient Britons," Blake related his Albion to the Titan
Atlas: "The giant Albion, was Patriarch of the Atlantic; he is the
Atlas of the Greeks, one of those the Greeks called Titans."
    If Albion is Atlas, then his Daughters, with their sighs towards the
liberty of America, are the Daughters of Atlas, the Hesperides. They
are associated with Hesperus, the Western Star, sacred to Aphrodite
and still called Venus in our heavens. Their father, Atlas, after the
fall of the Titans, was condemned to hold up the heavens in the
Far West. His daughters live in the Western Island, a last remainder
of the Lost Atlantis, where they have in their keeping a golden apple
tree, the wedding gift of Mother Earth to Hera, the bride of Zeus.
In his Eleventh Labor, Hercules is required to secure fruit from this
tree, which is also guarded by a serpent. Hercules slays the serpent,
and departs with the golden fruit. This fruit becomes the Apple of

Discord over which Athena, Aphrodite, and Hera quarrel, and so it is the ultimate cause of the Trojan War.

In his adoption of Hesperidean symbolism, Blake is likelier to have been influenced by Spenser and Milton than by any classical or esoteric source. The last temptation of Guyon, the knight of Temperance and hero of Book II of *The Faerie Queene*, is to be offered Hera's apple tree by the tempter Mammon:

> For those, which *Hercules* with conquest bold
> Got from great *Atlas* daughters, hence began,
> And planted there, did bring forth fruit of gold.

Both Spenser and Milton interpreted Hercules's conquest of the serpent as being a classical version of the Christian story that Christ should break the serpent's head, and conquer the power of Hell. So the Christ of Milton's *Paradise Regained*, after he completes his victory over Satan's temptations, is compared to Hercules. The tree of Hera, like the tree of Knowledge, brought strife into the world, and is associated by Spenser at least with the Garden of Proserpina, Queen of Hell. The Oothoon of Blake's *Visions* may be thought of as a kind of Proserpina, but only in being opposed to Enitharmon, who is Blake's Hera, not as the heroine of a Neoplatonic fantasy that some Blake scholars have read into her poem.

This long mythological excursus is justified if it can explain the scene-setting and basic event of Blake's *Visions*. The Daughters of Albion represent human spirits of the fallen world, inhabitants of a sexual Eden that has become the sexual barrier or prison-paradise of Leutha. Their sister, Oothoon, "the soft soul of America," breaks through this barrier, even as the political revolutions of Blake's age first manifest themselves in America. Oothoon plucks a flower, the bright Marygold, from Leutha's vale, which is the equivalent of escaping the Western Island with a Golden Apple. The Marygold, like the Apples of Hesperidean legend, is sacred to the sun. Oothoon puts the flower between her breasts, symbolizing her receptivity to Experience, and flies eastward over the Atlantic, which is spoken of as being "Theotormon's reign." The fallen Atlantis has become the chaotic Atlantic, sea of time and space, and a good emblem of the chaos of Theotormon's mind.

On the political level of meaning, Oothoon's flight eastward would take her to Britain, Albion's land, where her enslaved sisters, the soft souls of Blake's countrymen, are still awaiting their liberation in 1793, a year of warfare. But the political allegory of the *Visions* seems to me of secondary importance in reading the poem, and has in any case been worked out with finality by David Erdman.[3] If Oothoon can reach Theotormon and give herself to him, and if that confused lover could accept the gift, then the fallen nature of the Atlantic would be raised to a golden status, and as in the Apocalypse of the New Testament, there would be no more sea. The ethics of sexual release, as in the *Marriage* or Shelley's *Prometheus Unbound*, would renovate mankind and end all mind-forged tyrannies, not just the political ones. But none of this is yet to be, and the poem's delighted aspirations collapse into the realm of the roaring thunderer Bromion, who hovers over the Atlantic as a surrogate for his god, Nobodaddy, the Father of Jealousy, first introduced in this poem under his Blakean name of Urizen, but whom we have met before in Blake as Winter, Tiriel, Restraint, the Devourer and the Nobodaddy who successfully masquerades as God the Father in *Songs of Innocence*.

Bromion's morality is familiar to us because it is our own; the morality of a slave-driving society that first rapes and then condemns the exploited victim as being far gone in harlotry. But Blake makes it quite clear that Bromion's monstrous morality is engendered by his bad conscience:

> Bromion rent her with his thunders; on his
>   stormy bed
> Lay the faint maid, and soon her woes appall'd
>   his thunders hoarse.

Though appalled by Oothoon's woes, both in the usual intransitive sense of "appalled" and in the sense of those woes darkening his thunders (the same pattern is in the *London* of *Songs of Experience*, where the chimney sweepers' cries of woe appall the blackening Church, inwardly and outwardly), Bromion blusters his conscience away in an accusation of harlotry and a taunting invitation to Theotormon, Oothoon's betrothed lover:

. . . "Behold this harlot here on Bromion's bed,
And let the jealous dolphins sport around the
    lovely maid!
Thy soft American plains are mine, and mine
    thy north & south:
Stampt with my signet are the swarthy children
    of the sun;
They are obedient, they resist not, they obey
    the scourge;
Their daughters worship terrors and obey the
    violent.
Now thou maist marry Bromion's harlot, and
    protect the child
Of Bromion's rage, that Oothoon shall put forth
    in nine moons' time."

The uneasy violence of Bromion has its sexual origins in the sadism
of a slave-owning morality and the inverted sensuality of debased
Puritanism that Lawrence was to call "sex in the head." Bromion has
detected in the tortured writhings of his unwilling victim an awakened sensibility, a more abundant life coming into being, in spite of
his brutalities. In the political allegory, the bondage of the "soft
American plains" is an indication that the Revolution in the West,
Tiriel's realm of the body, has not progressed far enough. More directly and poetically the "soft American plains" is a sexual reference,
and Bromion hints at a masochistic yielding in Oothoon that also
leads him, madly enough, to call her a harlot. Bromion's address to
Theotormon concludes with a genuine slave-owner's irony. Oothoon
will be an improved property for a marriage between slaves, as she
may bear the child of Bromion's rage.

The response of Theotormon is a troubled torment of jealousy and
love, the chaotic anguish of one who, as H. M. Margoliouth observed, can now neither bear to accept Oothoon nor bear to let her
go.[4] Geographically, Theotormon is the abyss of the Atlantic, desiring the liberated form of America but held back from his desire
because he accepts the morality of the thunder-demons of the sky.
What Theotormon *sees* is not reality, but the watery vision of corrup-
tion. To his eyes, Bromion and Oothoon are an "adulterate pair/

Bound back to back in Bromion's caves." These caves of self-enclosure and mental limitation are in fact the inner dwelling place of Theotormon's consciousness. Trapped in his own "black jealous waters," the ocean-titan weeps the secret tears that in *Europe* will flow as salt tears down the steps of Enitharmon's crystal house, the demonic structure of the unassailable Female Will. The waves of the disturbed ocean reverberate their jealous turbulence in an oppressed world:

> At entrance Theotormon sits, wearing the
> threshold hard
> With secret tears; beneath him sound like
> waves on a desert shore
> The voice of slaves beneath the sun, and
> children bought with money,
> That shiver in religious caves beneath the
> burning fires
> Of lust, that belch incessant from the summits
> of the earth.

These difficult and brilliant lines presage Blake's later and more characteristic condensed style in *Jerusalem*. The jealousy-tormented sea catches up in its sound the voice of others tormented by the same false morality of restriction; of literal slaves, of the Church's chimney sweeps (children bought with money), of all those who hide from the liberating fires of desire in the frozen caves of religious repression, so as to "save" themselves from what the religious call "burning fires of lust." Yet these fires, which Blake will identify in *America* with the rebel of desire, Orc, cannot be long restrained, but burst forth, volcano-like, and incessantly.

What follows in the *Visions* is Blake's most remarkable and dramatic poetry up to this time. Oothoon's first reaction to the outrageous situation created by her monstrous and pathetic lovers is to accept the sado-masochistic morality of defilement and repentance which is all they offer her:

Oothoon weeps not; she cannot weep! her tears
    are locked up;
But she can howl incessant writhing her soft
    snowy limbs
And calling Theotormon's Eagles to prey upon
    her flesh.

"I call with holy voice! Kings of the sounding
    air,
Rend away this defiled bosom that I may reflect
The image of Theotormon on my pure transparent
    breast."

The Eagles at her call descend & rend their
    bleeding prey:
Theotormon severely smiles; her soul reflects
    the smile,
As the clear spring, mudded with feet of
    beasts, grows pure & smiles.

Blake is very subtle here, and the lines require close attention, for they are certainly ironic. Oothoon's tears are not locked up because of shock, but because in fact she does not really believe her first sexual experience, though involuntary, was a defilement of any kind. But she does not yet consciously know this, and does her best to simulate the anguish of despair, though an "incessant writhing" of "her soft snowy limbs" really indicates ungratified but fully aroused sexual desire. Blake is quite subtly but definitely implying that the situation could have been saved instantly, if Theotormon had reached out now to possess her himself. But he does not, and both he and Oothoon experience instead the deviant sexual pleasure of seeing her supposedly defiled bosom rent unto blood by Promethean eagles of remorse. Blake's irony becomes very overt in Oothoon's belief that only her supposedly lost purity can reflect the image of the still virgin Theotormon, in Theotormon's sadistic severe smiles, and most of all in the simile by which Oothoon's reflection of that smile is compared to a clear spring reassuming its form after having been mudded by bestial feet. The brazen conventionality of that simile is Blake at his most deceptive, mocking orthodox morality with its own moral idiocies.

This is Oothoon's most exploited and deceived moment, but her liberated passion does not permit her, or us, to abide in it. After a repetition of the choral line: "The Daughters of Albion hear her woes, & eccho back her sighs," Oothoon suddenly awakens and ceases all sighing. For the rest of the poem her voice gradually intensifies in prophetic urgency, even as her vision of love realizes itself with expanding clarity. She has passed out of Innocence by the sexual gate, but triumphantly she has carried that Innocence with her into a context that sets it off with apocalyptic violence in a radiant contrast.

> Arise, my Theotormon, I am pure
> Because the night is gone that clos'd me in
>   its deadly black.
> They told me that the night & day were all
>   that I could see;
> They told me that I had five senses to inclose
>   me up,
> And they inclos'd my infinite brain into a
>   narrow circle,
> And sunk my heart into the Abyss, a red, round
>   globe, hot burning,
> Till all from life I was obliterated and erased.

The night that is gone belonged to both Leutha and Bromion, virgin temptress and brutal rapist, mirror images in a demonic world masquerading as Innocence. By her increase in sensual enjoyment Oothoon has done what Thel failed to do—broken through the philosophy of the five senses, not by ascetic avoidance, but by expanding the crucial sense towards an infinite of desire. If she has surpassed Thel's quest, Oothoon has also triumphed where Tiriel failed, for she has awakened also, in the fullness of her life, to the lesson of the unique individuality of every being that Tiriel only learned in his death agony. If every being is unique, then no single code of restraint, no binding laws of sexual morality, are relevant to man. Unlike Thel, who merely lamented down by the river of Adona, Oothoon has reached the delta, as Frye observes,[5] and she is new baptized "by the red earth of our immortal river."

In response to Oothoon's passionate insistence on her liberation, both Theotormon and Bromion utter final speeches of desperate self-justification. Theotormon is of little faith and cannot believe in the revelation that is offered him. To the fierce rhetorical questions of Oothoon, he replies with the broken rhetorical questions of baffled timidity:

> "Tell me where dwell the thoughts forgotten
>   till thou call them forth?
> Tell me where dwell the joys of old? & where
>   the ancient loves,
> And when will they renew again, & the night
>   of oblivion past,
> That I might traverse times & spaces far
>   remote, and bring
> Comforts into a present sorrow and a night of
>   pain?
> Where goest thou, O thought? to what remote
>   land is thy flight?
> If thou returnest to the present moment of
>   affliction,
> Wilt thou bring comforts on thy wings, and
>   dews and honey and balm,
> Or poison from the desert wilds, from the eyes
>   of the envier?"

Oothoon claims by her experience to have rediscovered the human joys of old, the union of Innocence and Experience that results from a Marriage between the Hell of Desire and the Heaven of Restraint. But Theotormon cannot believe this, for his own senses have not made the sexual journey of discovery. He cannot believe that Oothoon's discovery is in the here and now available to him, for he exists only in "the present moment of affliction," bounded by his sexual envy, and therefore will not trust the gifts his beloved would bring to him.

Theotormon is merely stupid in his pathos—though moving

enough, for all men have suffered his jealousy. But Bromion's reaction is more complex and even impressively sinister, for Bromion is neither an ordinary hypocrite nor an unthinking sadist but an insane rationalist, who justifies his obscene morality by an appeal to man's supposed necessity for uniform laws to govern the chaos of experience:

"Thou knowest that the ancient trees seen by
     thine eyes have fruit,
But knowest thou that trees and fruits flourish
     upon the earth
To gratify senses unknown? trees, beasts and
     birds unknown;
Unknown, not unperciev'd, spread in the infinite
     microscope,
In places yet unvisited by the voyager, and in
     worlds
Over another kind of seas, and in atmospheres
     unknown:
Ah! are there other wars beside the wars of
     sword and fire?
And are there other sorrows beside the sorrows
     of poverty?
And are there other joys beside the joys of
     riches and ease?
And is there not one law for both the lion and
     the ox?
And is there not eternal fire and eternal
     chains
To bind the phantoms of existence from eternal
     life?"

The dramatic power of Blake, with which we so little credit him, is responsible for the extraordinary appeal of this speech, despite its being a perfect summary of attitudes Blake seeks to burn away. Bromion does not deny the reality of Oothoon's experience, as Theotormon did, but he admits to fearing the implications of that reality. Oothoon *has* seen the ancient trees that once were visible to unfallen men, and she does know that these trees still have fruit to gratify her awakened senses. But Bromion claims that Oothoon has opened a Pandora's box of chaotic experience that will upset the perilous balance by which the eighteenth century has learned to live. Other trees and fruits exist in the infinite abyss of the unbounded and prolific world of experience, to provoke and gratify senses best left unknown.

Bromion is a kind of Deist version of Milton's affable archangel, Raphael, warning against forbidden knowledge. In the infinite microscope of the human potential for perception there are all too many unexplored worlds, and Bromion insists that they must all be excluded from consciousness. Yet he is moved despite himself as he meditates the possibility of intellectual wars, and of sorrows and joy existing beyond the universe of economic determinism. To repress his momentary emotion, he calls on the supreme wisdom of his restrictive vision: "And is there not one law for both the lion and the ox?" Tiriel learned better, and the *Marriage* ends with Blake's answer to such wisdom: "One Law for the Lion & Ox is Oppression." Bromion refuses to learn and is willing to oppress; he is an Angel of Urizen and is cheered by the prospect of an orthodox vision of Hell, an eternal fire in which the harlot Oothoon shall burn for having dared to recognize not only her own sexual pleasure, but the worlds awaiting her after she has taken the Western path through the gates of wrath, into the body's wisdom.

With Bromion's expedient exclusion of man's freedom the poem ends its second movement. For a day and a night Oothoon waits in silence. Then, having gathered within herself that voice of honest indignation that is prophecy, she begins a one-hundred-line chant that makes up the remainder of the poem and is one of Blake's greatest achievements, a rhapsody of such force and distinction as to surpass any of Blake's previous poetry, and all but match the best that was to come.

The chant begins with the kind of insight we demand from a prophetess. In one imaginative leap, Oothoon passes beyond Bromion and Theotormon to the being they worship:

> O Urizen! Creator of men! mistaken Demon of
>   heaven!
> Thy joys are tears, thy labour vain to form
>   men to thine image.

How can one joy absorb another? Are not
    different joys
Holy, eternal, infinite? and each joy is a
    Love.

    Urizen is the creator of men, not as they were or should be, but as
they are now. Yet though he rules most men, Urizen is simply mistaken; his quest to form men to his own image cannot be realized, for
individualities cannot be reduced, only obscured. The minute particulars of joy crowd Oothoon's chant: the laughing mouth, the
vigorous joys of morning light, the moment of desire. Oothoon is
now open to the experience of life wherever the beauty of a unique
identity appears:

    If in the morning sun I find it, there my eyes
        are fix'd
    In happy copulation; if in evening mild,
        wearied with work,
    Sit on a bank and draw the pleasures of this
        free born joy.

    The moment of desire! the moment of desire!
        The virgin
    That pines for man shall awaken her womb to
        enormous joys
    In the secret shadows of her chamber: the
        youth shut up from
    The lustful joy shall forget to generate &
        create an amorous image
    In the shadows of his curtains and in the folds
        of his silent pillow.
    Are not these the places of religion, the
        rewards of continence,
    The self enjoyings of self denial? Why dost
        thou seek religion?
    Is it because acts are not lovely that thou seekest
        solitude
    Where the horrible darkness is impressed with
        reflections of desire?

This is not a demonstration, and certainly in no sense an argument. What Bromion calls morality is simply not relevant to Oothoon. Bromion fears what nature could be, and so accepts the moral law of Urizen, founded on a minimal vision of natural existence. Oothoon's nature begins as the sexual nature of all creation, but as she liberates that nature from morality she still more remarkably accomplishes a transmemberment of nature itself. Blake's dialectics of nature have about them a beautiful, laughing irony; only gratified desire can liberate us from the torments of desire. We exult, in the passage quoted above, at the contrary human statement to the negative wisdom of St. Augustine, or the transcending denials of the Buddha's Fire Sermon. Oothoon's eye is on fire, but in the burning perception that fixes that eye "in happy copulation" (one of Blake's most daring and successful verbal figures), it is nature and not the human that burns away. If the burning be denied, as the ascetics would have it, then indeed the religion of orthodoxy will be established, in a triumph of natural limitation and a defeat of the human in us. The secret places of religion are truly the rewards of continence, and the mystical experience inevitably results from the repression of the only desire by which nature can find renovation and self-transformation.

Against the cycle of religion and nature, one founded on the secret thwarting of the other, Oothoon cries out for a progression through contraries, the meeting of creative oppositions that is the freedom of love:

> I cry: Love! Love! Love! happy happy Love!
>   free as the mountain wind!
> Can that be Love that drinks another as a
>   sponge drinks water,
> That clouds with jealousy his nights, with
>   weepings all the day,
> To spin a web of age around him, grey and
>   hoary, dark,
> Till his eyes sicken at the fruit that hangs
>   before his sight?
> Such is self-love that envies all, a creeping
>   skeleton
> With lamplike eyes watching around the frozen
>   marriage bed.

With absolute clarity she sees now what Blake in the torments of his notebook poems was prompted to see. The final weapon of reason, nature, and morality against the realization of the human identity is that disguise of love "that drinks another as a sponge drinks water." To seek to possess, to appropriate another, is to diminish a human subject into a natural object. For all love is the meeting of mutual confrontation, and only a shared reality can be reality. And no love can be diminished by another:

> But silken nets and traps of adamant will
> > Oothoon spread,
> And catch for thee girls of mild silver, or
> > of furious gold.
> I'll lie beside thee on a bank & view
> > their wanton play
> In lovely copulation, bliss on bliss, with
> > Theotormon:
> Red as the rosy morning, lustful as the
> > first born beam,
> Oothoon shall view his dear delight, nor
> > e'er with jealous cloud
> Come in the heaven of generous love, nor
> > selfish blightings bring.

This is the culmination of Oothoon's achieved humanity. If we are convinced, Theotormon is not, but continues to sit "upon the margin'd ocean conversing with shadows dire." He loves his own grief, and his sexual pleasure is complete in contemplating his jealousy. The abyss of nature, the black incessant waters of the Atlantic, will not surrender itself to freedom. The tyranny of nature is self-perpetuating, and the sexual illness of mankind will not seek the only cure that is not death. Blake needs to explain why, and he turns to a myth of his own making for that explanation. *Visions of the Daughters of Albion* hesitates on the threshhold of mythopoeic poetry. With his next poem, *America*, Blake enters into his mythic world, not to escape but to seek again the secrets of the psyche, the processes that tempt the human to the self-enjoyings of self denial.

CHAPTER SEVEN

The Prophecy of Orc

America: A Prophecy

The "Preludium" of *America* has about it the special excitement that attends a great poet coming into the proper practice of his art. Here, for the first time, Blake finds the *kind* of poem he is most himself in writing. In *The Marriage of Heaven and Hell*, Blake attained his full intellectual maturity and proclaimed his spiritual freedom, at the age of thirty-three. Now, three years later, in 1793, Blake has his true *annus mirabilis*. He finishes engraving the *Marriage*, and perhaps the great design known both as *The Dance of Albion* and *Glad Day*, where the poet himself is now identified both with the self-sacrificing archetypal man, Albion, and the rising Apollo figure of the revolutionary Orc. In the same year, he writes and engraves *The Gates of Paradise* in its earlier form, and *Visions of the Daughters of Albion*, *America: A Prophecy*, and many of the *Songs of Experience*. The manuscript poems of this year are uniformly powerful; the engravings have a new strength of line and boldness of color. We have none of Blake's letters written between October 1791 and December 1795 —which is as much as to say that we have little reliable information as to his inner life in 1793, beyond the essential life we can study in the artistic work of that year.

The unprejudiced reader of poetry, who begins on a reading of *America* for the first time, usually experiences a shock of surprise at the strangeness of the poem. The shock is genuine and warranted, and is itself a prelude to imaginative discernment and enjoyment, if it is properly recognized for what it is. At the opening of *America*, in the "Preludium," Blake has found his way back to some of the roots of poetry and myth. A poem, whose announced subject is the American Revolution, begins with a tremendous image of sexual torment, followed by a fierce image of sexual release. The personages who make up this image are called the shadowy Daughter of Urthona and red Orc. The names need not bother the reader; their relevance will be clear later. Only the situation matters, here at the start. The daughter of a tyrant and the tyrant's imprisoned victim confront one another in a context that blends the primitive and the sacred, the fundamental postulates of early human myth:

> The shadowy Daughter of Urthona stood before
>   red Orc,
> When fourteen suns had faintly journey'd o'er
>   his dark abode:
> His food she brought in iron baskets, his
>   drink in cups of iron.
> Crown'd with a helmet & dark hair the
>   nameless female stood;
> A quiver with its burning stores, a bow like
>   that of night,
> When pestilence is shot from heaven: no other
>   arms she need!
> Invulnerable tho' naked, save where clouds
>   roll round her loins
> Their awful folds in the dark air: silent
>   she stood as night;
> For never from her iron tongue could voice
>   or sound arise,
> But dumb till that dread day when Orc assay'd
>   his fierce embrace.

The mythic world suggested is the Northern one of Odin and Thor, the Eddic literature known to Blake through Mallet's *Northern Antiquities* (translated by Bishop Percy) and the poems and translations of Thomas Gray. The nameless female carries what Blake considered to be iron age utensils and wears a helmet. She is the daughter of a smith, who is Blake's equivalent of Thor and who serves a tyrannical sky-god, even as Thor served Odin. The world dwelt in (and created by) this smith is one just barely come into life. Darkness, shadows, clouds are the images of this world, which adds to its minimal light a preternatural silence and the failure of self-realization indicated by namelessness. The smith who has hammered out the iron communion vessels for human food and drink has endowed his daughter with an iron tongue. The imprisoned youth, fed from iron baskets and iron cups, has reached a stage in his natural cycle where his expanded desires compel him to attack his environment at its crucial center, the female who ministers to him.

The name Orc is formed from the Latin "Orcus" which is a name for Hell, and Blake is not the first English poet to so name what seems to be a monstrous spirit.[1] That the name of Blake's Orc is ironic is clear from the very first line of his existence, which is the first line of *America*. The female is shadowy, but Orc is definite; he has what the later Romantic poet Beddoes was to call "the red outline of beginning Adam." A reading of *America* from its very first line can begin by utilizing anyone's best hint for reading William Blake: every female personage finally relates to, or is, a form of nature; every male at last represents humankind, both male and female. If we try this out upon the first line of *America* then we have a good start into the poem: a shadowy nature stands before a red human; a mothering and generating impulse confronts a growing organism about to attempt to tear itself free of the Adamic red clay from which it has been formed.

The remaining nine lines of this first passage are as primordial in mythic meaning as they are powerful in expression. The "fourteen suns" indicate Orc's sexual maturity, but as they also take him halfway through a lunar cycle, there is a hint that his impending liberation is condemned to be cyclical, not final. If Orc is reviving organic life, he will at last wane, for organic life is part of a wheel of births and deaths. But now, in an act of intensifying life, his desire is opposed to the Urizenic clouds that enfold the loins of his captor's daughter. These clouds of dogma provoke Orc to break his chains, that he may see and possess his shadowy beloved. Spiritually he is already unbounded; the orthodoxies of the eighteenth century identify him with the lively forces, natural and political, that threaten their perilous balance. He is eagle, lion, whale, and serpent—all patriotic emblems of revolt.[2] He seeks to give his voice, and his passion, to silent nature:

> Silent as despairing love, and strong as
>   jealousy,
> The hairy shoulders rend the links; free are
>   the wrists of fire;
> Round the terrific loins he siez'd the
>   panting, struggling womb;
> It joy'd: she put aside her clouds &
>   smiled her first-born smile,
> As when a black cloud shews its lightnings
>   to the silent deep.

Though she can now both smile and speak, she is not redeemed from the intellectual basis of her father's errors. She vows not to let Orc go and recognizes in him the image of God, but her sexual pleasure does not overcome the inhibiting effect of the instruction she had long received. The embraces she welcomes are nevertheless felt by her as torment:

> O what limb rending pains I feel! thy fire
>   & my frost
> Mingle in howling pains, in furrows by thy
>   lightnings rent.
> This is eternal death, and this the torment
>   long foretold!

With this anguished outcry, the "Preludium" to *America* ends in most copies of the poem. In some, the stern Bard who has sung this grim song of the Iron Age is so ashamed of the shadowy female's reaction that he smashes his harp, turns silently away, and wanders off, lamenting. Blake may have cancelled these lines because the poem proper offers enough of an inconclusive hope to make the Bard's disgust premature.

The action of *America* begins with two opposing visions, one of the King of England as a dragon form, the other of the unbound Orc as a Promethean portent rising over the Atlantic and giving off "heat but not light," the token of the Miltonic or orthodox fires of hell. The King is called Albion's Angel, as against the Devil Orc, the vocabulary being derived from the *Marriage*. The Angel stands "beside the Stone of Night," the essential building block of the opaque world of matter that Blake will later call Ulro, a really Satanic region of solipsistic monologues and death-wishes. The Stone of Night is both the pillow of the sleeping Jacob, who dreamed of a ladder up to heaven, and the tablets of the Mosaic Law.[8] The Angel is called a Spectre, that is, a shadow of desire, and his dragon length stains his temple of natural religion with "beams of blood," in a parody of the bright light of the Miltonic God. The voice of the Promethean Orc comes forth and shakes the temple with a prophetic poem:

"The morning comes, the night decays, the
        watchmen leave their stations;
The grave is burst, the spices shed, the
        linen wrapped up;
The bones of death, the cov'ring clay, the
        sinews shrunk and dry'd
Reviving shake, inspiring move, breathing,
        awakening,
Spring like redeemed captives when their bonds
        and bars are burst.
Let the slave grinding at the mill run out into
        the field,
Let him look up into the heavens & laugh in
        the bright air;
Let the inchained soul, shut up in darkness and
        in sighing,
Whose face has never seen a smile in thirty
        weary years,
Rise and look out; his chains are loose, his
        dungeon doors are open;
And let his wife and children return from the
        oppressor's scourge.
They look behind at every step & believe
        it is a dream,

Singing: 'The Sun has left his blackness,
    and has found a fresher morning,
And the fair Moon rejoices in the clear &
    cloudless night;
For Empire is no more, and now the Lion &
    Wolf shall cease.' "

This great speech is one of the central passages in Blake's poetry. It recapitulates the opening of *The Marriage of Heaven and Hell*, the end of *A Song of Liberty*, and the chants of Oothoon, and it looks forward to Blake's vehement presentation of the Last Judgement in Night the Ninth of *The Four Zoas*.

Orc begins by identifying his release and the subsequent start of the American Revolution with the resurrection of Jesus. Like Jesus, Orc is a revived God who is also Man, and Orc's renewal is as radical as that of the Jesus of orthodoxy. Orc has burst not only the grave and all its properties, but the limitations of the fallen body as well. This act of self-liberation momentarily restores nature as well, but Albion's Angel does not admit even a temporary defeat. To his eyes, the Revolution is "serpent-form'd," one of Blake's fine ironies, as the Angel is actually the devouring dragon or serpent of death, whom the rebel Orc desires to slay. To any Angel, the infinite spirit of Revolution is a threat to the dominion of the Queen of Heaven, Enitharmon, the orthodox projection of a fallen and limited spatial universe.

Orc's reply to the Angel's denunciation again echoes *A Song of Liberty* and Oothoon's passion and introduces a crucial reference to Nebuchadnezzar's dream in the apocalyptic Book of Daniel:

The Terror answer'd: "I am Orc, wreath'd
    round the accursed tree:
The times are ended; shadows pass, the
    morning 'gins to break;
The fiery joy, that Urizen perverted to ten
    commands,
What night he led the starry hosts thro' the
    wide wilderness,

That stony Law I stamp to dust; and scatter
   religion abroad
To the four winds as a torn book, & none
   shall gather the leaves;
But they shall rot on desert sands, & consume in bottomless deeps,
To make the desarts blossom, and the deeps
   shrink to their fountains,
And to renew the fiery joy, and burst the
   stony roof;
That pale religious letchery, seeking Virginity,
May find it in a harlot, and in coarse-clad
   honesty
The undefil'd, tho' ravish'd in her cradle
   night and morn;
For everything that lives is holy, life
   delights in life;
Because the soul of sweet delight can never
   be defil'd.
Fires enwrap the earthly globe, yet man is
   not consum'd;
Amidst the lustful fires he walks; his feet
   become like brass,
His knees and thighs like silver, & his
   breast and head like gold.

Orc ascribes his serpent-appearance in Angelic eyes as being due to his attempt to pull down nature, the accursed tree of Mystery we will see developed in *Songs of Experience* and *The Book of Urizen*. As in *A Song of Liberty*, Urizen is identified with the Jehovah of Exodus, perverting the fiery Prolific of human energy into ten Devouring commandments. Orc stamps those tablets into dust, and scatters the Bible of Heaven as so many withered leaves of the tree of Mystery. Like the dead leaves of Shelley's revolutionary *Ode to the West Wind*, they will serve to quicken a new birth. But Blake's image is more radical: the world reacts to the end of restriction as it does in *Prometheus Unbound*, rather than in the deliberately ambiguous *Ode*. "The deeps shrink to their fountains"; the seas of chaos are restored to their life-giving functions. Religious lechery, still nursing its unacted desires, finds its idealized Virginity in a harlot perpetually ravished but always undefiled, like Oothoon. The fires of desire consume nature but not man, for man is like the walkers in the furnace of Daniel, Chapter 3. Yet more vital, man was once the image dreamed and then forgotten by Nebuchadnezzar, who suffered for his forgetfulness. This image, of terrible brightness, is described in the second chapter of Daniel:

This image's head was of fine gold, his breast and his arms of silver, his belly and his thighs of brass,

His legs of iron, his feet part of iron and part of clay.

Thou sawest till that a stone was cut out without hands, which smote the image upon his feet that were of iron and clay, and brake them to pieces.

Then was the iron, the clay, the brass, the silver, and the gold, broken to pieces together, and became like the chaff of the summer threshingfloors; and the wind carried them away, that no place was found for them: and the stone that smote the image became a great mountain, and filled the whole earth.

Daniel interprets this as a story of the dividing and destruction of Nebuchadnezzar's kingdom. In Blake's symbolic reading, the image is of his archetypal man Albion, and the breaking of the image is the fall of Albion, as we will see when we come to consider this myth in *The Four Zoas*. In *America*, Blake uses the image because the destructive stone is a good analogue to the Angel of Albion's Stone of Night, and also because it enables Orc to prophesy a renovated man greater than the image. Orc's man is one stage higher than Nebuchadnezzar's image: the feet of iron and clay have become brass; the thighs of brass have become silver; the silver breast has joined the head in being golden. The allegorical suggestion is that the risen body is improved in its values, and indeed the heart and the brain have been made equal.

The Angel's response is a speech of mounting hysteria, a cry of reaction that attempts to rouse the thirteen Angels who represent the

American colonies against the threat of Orc. Washington, Franklin, Paine, and the other leaders of revolution, mentioned earlier in the poem as rising up in the night of oppression, now stand "with their foreheads rear'd toward the east," threatening the Urizenic world of England and Europe. The same speech of Albion's Angel gives a vivid picture of Orc as a serpent-devourer of his mother, the shadowy female of the "Preludium." If Orc's beloved indeed bore him, then as the mother of his mortal part, she is probably to be named as Tirzah, the maternal principle to whom the last of the *Songs of Experience* is addressed. But Blake is not willing to assign the American Revolution, symbolically more essential to him than the French, merely to the organic world of cyclic energy's reaction to repression. So, for the first time in his poetry, he tries to visualize the Golden world, in the Atlantean symbolism first indicated in *Visions of the Daughters of Albion*:

> On those vast shady hills between America &
>   Albion's shore,
> Now barr'd out by the Atlantic sea, call'd
>   Atlantean hills,
> Because from their bright summits you may pass
>   to the Golden world,
> An ancient palace, archetype of mighty Emperies,
> Rears its immortal pinnacles, built in the
>   forest of God
> By Ariston, the king of beauty, for his stolen
>   bride.

Blake's sources for this beautiful passage may include Plato, Herodotus, Spenser, and Bacon, but the amalgam is his own.[4] Most of Atlantis sank beneath the waves, leaving Britain on one side of the resulting chaos, and the American wilderness on the other. The spiritual center joining the two continents is lost, but Orc's prophecy includes the rejoining of the shattered halves of the world, even as Isaiah's did. In Blake's fantasy, somewhere amid the Atlantic wastes still rise up the bright summits of the Atlantean hills, on which are built the Golden world's archetypes of Eternity. Ariston, the "best" of Greeks (by his name) built the particular palace in which the

American Angels now meet. The "forest of God" is an ambiguous phrase, suggesting a mistake on Ariston's part, as Blake's forests, like Spenser's and Dante's, are mazes of error. Ariston is "the king of beauty," but his bride, who presumably incarnates that beauty, is a stolen one. I suspect that Blake, who was a resentful Platonist when he was a Platonist at all, is suggesting that the Platonic realm of ideal forms or lost Atlantis was derived or stolen from a British and Hebrew original. Something of this ought to be clearer when we encounter Blake's Druidic symbolism in his epic poems.

In *America* this meeting of Angels in the palace of archetypal beauty suffices to transform them into "Devils" like Orc. Led by Boston's Angel, the thirteen rend off the robes and throw down the scepters of English tyranny and natural religion. They combine with the rebellious colonists and prepare to withstand the assault of Albion's Angel. With typical irony, Blake has the Angel send against America the plagues that Jehovah sent against Egypt. There is a crisis:

> Then had America been lost, o'erwhelm'd by
>   the Atlantic,
> And Earth had lost another portion of the
>   infinite;
> But all rush together in the night in wrath
>   and raging fire.
> The red fires rag'd! the plagues recoil'd!
>   then roll'd they back with fury
> On Albion's Angels: then the Pestilence began
>   in streaks of red
> Across the limbs of Albion's Guardian; the
>   spotted plague smote Bristol's
> And the Leprosy London's Spirit, sickening
>   all their bands:
> The millions sent up a howl of anguish and
>   threw off their hammer'd mail,
> And cast their swords & spears to earth,
>   and stood, a naked multitude:

Erdman summarizes the theoretical basis of Blake's *America* as being the transvaluation of revolutionary war into "a harvest sacrifice made by people with opened eyes and an enlightened social program for cultivating the earth as a garden paradise."[5] That is certainly an important aspect of the poem's meaning, and explains the vision just quoted, of the English people exposing themselves as "a naked multitude" to the plagues returned upon them. The plagues are chaotic in their nature; they threaten to drown America beneath the Atlantic sea of Space and Time. But the red fire of creative desire, the shaping imagination, turns the chaos back, and changes its nature, so that it is spotted with red streaks of forming energy when it re-encounters the English. The enormous plagues that now come upon England are plagues only to the orthodox, for these fires of hell expose the Angels as the serpents they genuinely are. The Bard of Albion or Poet Laureate of the orthodox is forced to shield himself against the imaginative fires by taking on his dragon form, and the Priests are driven into their dens:

> The doors of marriage are open, and the Priests,
> in rustling scales,
> Rush into reptile coverts, hiding from the
> fires of Orc,
> That play around the golden roofs in wreaths of
> fierce desire,
> Leaving the females naked and glowing with the
> lusts of youth.

As in a similar moment in *The French Revolution* the weeping Jehovah of state religion now appears, this time exposed as Nobodaddy or Urizen:

> Over the hills, the vales, the cities, rage the
> red flames fierce:
> The Heavens melted from north to south; and
> Urizen, who sat
> Above all heavens, in thunders wrap'd, emerg'd
> his leprous head
> From out his holy shrine, his tears in deluge
> piteous
> Falling into the deep sublime.

The hypocritical tears descend as the icy deluge to be expected from this outraged deity, and they succeed for a time in obscuring the triumph of the American Revolution:

> Weeping in dismal howlings before the stern
> Americans,
> Hiding the Demon red with clouds & cold mists
> from the earth,
> Till Angels & weak men twelve years should
> govern o'er the strong;
> And then their end should come, when France
> reciev'd the Demon's light.

The twelve years of continued Angelic restraint in Europe are followed by France's reception of Orc's light. Blake's poem ends in the midst of cataclysms, with the united Angels of Europe vainly striving to stem Orc's fires:

> They slow advance to shut the five gates of
> their law-built heaven,
> Filled with blasting fancies and with mildews
> of despair,
> With fierce disease and lust, unable to stem
> the fires of Orc.
> But the five gates were consum'd, & their
> bolts and hinges melted;
> And the fierce flames burnt round the heavens,
> & round the abodes of men.

These gates are the gates of perception, the five senses that Blake's art seeks to cleanse of their fancies and mildews. Blake brilliantly closes his poem not on its political level, but on its apocalyptic program for action. Whether or not Orc is to win (and history and Blake's poetry alike will prove that he cannot) his effect upon human faculties is a permanent one. Desire shall fail, but the gates are consumed, and man is opened to infinity if he will but see his own freedom. Blake's last line is precise and foreboding: the flames burnt *round* the heavens and men's abodes. For the flames to burn *through* the heavens would liberate mankind from spatial limitations, but also from the security of its fixed conceptual position. *America* is at once Blake's fiercest tribute to our Promethean potential and yet also a warning that to be unbound will be an experience that must be paid for by a loss of the comforting certainties of most fallen experience. The terrors of such comfort are explored definitively in the *Songs of Experience*, engraved by Blake probably just after *America*, and before continuing the story of Orc in *Europe* and *The Book of Urizen*.

Songs of Experience

Blake wrote the *Songs of Experience* between 1789 and 1794, engraving them in the latter year but probably not often as a separate work. Though I have discussed the *Songs of Innocence* in their chronological position, Blake clearly wanted the two groups of songs to be read (and viewed) together. The title of the 1794 engraved work is *Songs of Innocence and of Experience, Shewing the Two Contrary States of the Human Soul,* and the *Songs of Experience* do not in fact exist for us in a single copy without the preceding work. To some extent the discussion here of Blake's most famous work will recapitulate that of the earlier songs, but from another aspect.

Magnificent as the best of the *Songs of Experience* are, it is unfortunate that they continue to usurp something of the study that should be given to Blake's more ambitious and greater works. Their relative conventionality of form has made them popular for some of the wrong reasons, and they frequently tend to be misread. It is as though Milton were to be esteemed for *Lycidas* alone, and *Lycidas* to be read as a tormented mystic's outcry against the harshness of an existence that devastates the dreams of childhood. Even learned readers, who can laugh at such a possibility, are willing to see the *Songs of Experience* as Blake's greatest achievement, and to see it also as a lamentation for lost Innocence.

Songs of Experience begins with a powerful *Introduction* addressed to Earth by a Bard, and follows with *Earth's Answer*. This

Bard of Experience has considerable capacity for vision, and has much in common with Blake, but he is *not* Blake, and his songs are limited by his perspective. They are songs *of* the state of Experience, but Experience is hardly Blake's highest and most desired state of existence.

We can see the distance between the Bard of Experience and Blake in the second stanza of the *Introduction*. The first stanza tells us that the Bard sees the "Present, Past & Future," but this is not the statement that will be made later in *Jerusalem:* "I see the Past, Present & Future existing all at once Before me." The later statement is true vision, for it makes the prophetic point that compels clock time to become imaginative or human time: If not now, when? The Bard of Experience sees what is, what was, and what is to come, but he does not necessarily see them all as a single mental form, which is the clue to his tragic mental error throughout the *Introduction*. His ears *have heard* the Holy Word that *walk'd* among the ancient trees, but he does not hear that Word now. This is made altogether clear when he refers to the Soul as having lapsed:

> Calling the lapsed Soul,
> And weeping in the evening dew;
> That might controll
> The starry pole,
> And fallen, fallen light renew!

The Holy Word is God-as-Man, Jesus, who once walked in the Garden of Eden "in the cool of the day." The Word calls and weeps, and if the Word were heeded, the Fall could be undone, for "the lapsed Soul" still has the potential that might control nature. But the Bard, though he sees all this, thinks of man as a "lapsed Soul," and Blake of course does not, as the *Marriage* has shown us. Blake knows that when man is raised, he must be raised as a spiritual body, not as a consciousness excluded from energy and desire.

The Bard's error takes on an added poignancy as he emulates Milton, in deliberately echoing the desperation of the prophet Jeremiah.[6] He tries to tell the very soil itself what her inhabitants are deaf to, urging the Earth to hear the word of the Lord and to return:

O Earth, O Earth, return!
Arise from out the dewy grass;
Night is worn,
And the morn
Rises from the slumberous mass.

In this precisely worded stanza, Earth is being urged to arise literally out of herself; to abandon her present form for the original she has forsaken. If the morn can rise in its cycle, cannot Earth break the cycle and be herself at last?

Turn away no more;
Why wilt thou turn away?
The starry floor,
The wat'ry shore,
Is giv'n thee till the break of day.

What the Bard urges is what ought to be, but Earth can no more arise "from out" the grass than man's "lapsed soul" can rise from the "slumberous mass" of his body. The Bard's dualism, traditional in orthodox Christian accounts of apocalypse, divides still further an already dangerous division. If Earth returns it must be in every blade of grass, even as man must rise in every minute particular of his body. The starry roof of the spatially bound heavens ought to be only the floor of Earth's aspirations, just as the wat'ry shore marking Earth's narrow border upon chaos ought to be a starting point of the natural, and not its end. But it is again a not fully imaginative hope, to believe that a world of matter is given to Earth only until the apocalyptic break of day. Blake's heaven, unlike the Bard's, is a radical renewal of *this* world, an Earth more alive to the awakened senses than the one that so fearfully turns away.

The Bard is neither the prophetic Devil nor the timeserving Angel of the *Marriage*, but the ancestor of and spokesman for a third class of men in Blake, the almost-imaginative, who will later be termed the Redeemed. The parallel names for Devil and Angel will be the Reprobate and the Elect respectively, and clearly all three names are as ironic as Devil and Angel. The Reprobate are the prophets who appear reprobate to society; the Elect are dogmatists of societal values, as self-deluded as the Calvinist chosen; the Redeemed are those capable of imaginative redemption who still stand in need of it. The central irony of the *Songs of Experience* has proved too subtle for most of Blake's readers; the songs sung directly by the Bard are only in the Redeemed, and not the Reprobate category. That is, just as most of the *Songs of Innocence* are trapped in the limitations of that vision, so are many of the *Songs of Experience* caught in the dilemmas implicit in that state. The Bard's songs are, besides the *Introduction*, notably *The Tyger*, *A Poison Tree*, and *A Little Girl Lost*. Blake's own songs, in which he allows himself a full Reprobate awareness, are *Holy Thursday*, *Ah! Sun-Flower*, *London*, *The Human Abstract*, and the defiant *To Tirzah*. The remaining poems in *Songs of Experience* belong to various other Redeemed speakers.

One of this group is *Earth's Answer* to the Bard. A Reprobate prophet would take a tone less optimistic than that of the Bard, and Earth is too experienced to react to optimism with less than an immense bitterness. Earth is exactly like the Earth of Act I of Shelley's *Prometheus Unbound*, dominated by a "stony dread" of what Jupiter or "Starry Jealousy" may yet do to her, though that Nobodaddy has already done his worst. Grimly, Blake's Earth refers to her jealous jailer as "the Father of the ancient men," a title Blake would never grant him. Earth is in despair, and will not believe that the oppressive sky-god is merely a usurper of power. Even in despair she allies herself to Oothoon's questionings:

> Selfish father of men!
> Cruel, jealous, selfish fear!
> Can delight,
> Chain'd in night,
> The virgins of youth and morning bear?
>
> Does spring hide its joy
> When buds and blossoms grow?
> Does the sower
> Sow by night?
> Or the plowman in darkness plow?

Blake's most distinguished commentator remarks that "Earth is not saying, as some critics accuse her of saying, that all would be well if lovers would only learn to copulate in the daytime.""⁷ But one ought not to leave Blake's image too quickly, since it dominates both these stanzas. The contrast to a dark secret love must be a bright open one, and the dark secret love that destroys is destructive because the dark secrecy is psychic rather than just physical; the concealment is being practiced upon elements within the self. To expose love to the light is a combative image, that takes its force from the social association usually made between night or darkness and the sexual act, an association with a tradition of orthodox Christian imagery behind it.

The issue between the Bard and Earth intensifies in Earth's last stanza:

> Break this heavy chain
> That does freeze my bones around.
> Selfish! vain!
> Eternal bane!
> That free Love with bondage bound.

The Bard sought to put the burden upon nature, urging Earth to turn away no more. Earth gives the burden back to whom it belongs: the Bard, and all men, must act to break the freezing weight of Jealousy's chain. If they can free Love, then nature will respond, but the sexual initiative must be taken by and between humans, for they need not be subject to natural limitations.

The themes announced in these two introductory poems are the principal themes of the entire song cycle. *The Clod & the Pebble* opposes two loves, the Clod's of total sacrifice, and the Pebble's of total self-appropriation. The irony is that the opposition is a negation, for neither love can lead to the progression of contraries that is a marriage. The Clod joys in its own loss of ease; the Pebble in another's loss, but there is loss in either case. Heaven is being built in Hell's despair, Hell in Heaven's despite. Both Clod and Pebble are caught in the sinister moral dialectic of exploitation that is a mark of Experience, for neither believes that any individuality can gain except at the expense of another.

This dialectic of exploitation expands to social dimensions in *Holy Thursday*, which matches the earlier *Holy Thursday* of Innocence. But the ambiguity of tone of the earlier song has vanished:

Is this a holy thing to see
In a rich and fruitful land,
Babes reduc'd to misery,
Fed with cold and usurous hand?

Is that trembling cry a song?
Can it be a song of joy?
And so many children poor?
It is a land of poverty!

Two contrary readings of the first *Holy Thursday* were equally true, but from the stance of Experience only one reading is possible. This second poem goes so far as to insist that the charity children live in an "eternal winter" without the fostering power of nature's sun and rain, since the dazed mind cannot accept poverty as natural. *The Chimney Sweeper* of Experience has the same childlike logic, with the peculiar rhetorical force that "because" takes in this context:

Because I was happy upon the heath,
And smil'd among the winter's snow,
They clothed me in the clothes of death,
And taught me to sing the notes of woe.

The second *Nurse's Song* affords a remarkably instructive contrast to the first. The Nurse of Experience reacts to the sound of children's voices on the green by recalling her earlier vision, and her face "turns green and pale," as well it might, in comparing the two states, for the movement is from:

Come, come, leave off play, and let us away
Till the morning appears in the skies.

to:

Your spring & your day are wasted in play
And your winter and night in disguise.

This is neither realism nor cynicism replacing Innocence, but an existence both lower and higher, less and more real than the undivided state of consciousness. The morning does not appear again, and so the generous expectations are self-deceptions. But the wisdom of Experience is at its best too much the wisdom of the natural heart, and we cannot altogether accept that the play was wasted. Nor are we meant to forget that the final waste will be in the disguise of death, which is the culmination of the cruder deceptions of Experience.

The subtler deceptions of Experience are presented in *The Sick Rose*, one of Blake's gnomic triumphs, a profound irony given to us in the ruthless economy of thirty-four words:

> O rose, thou art sick!
> The invisible worm
> That flies in the night,
> In the howling storm,
>
> Has found out thy bed
> Of crimson joy,
> And his dark secret love
> Does thy life destroy.

The first line expresses a shock of terrible pity, but what follows puts a probable tonal stress on the "art," for the rose is not blameless, and has an inner sickness that helps bring on the outer destructiveness of the worm's "dark secret love." The worm is borne to the hidden rose bed (it must be "found out") by the agency of nature ("the howling storm"), and his phallic passion devours the rose's life. Dark secret love is the jealous lust for possession of the Devourer, the reasonable Selfhood that quests only to appropriate. Yet the worm is scarcely at fault; by his nature he is the negation, not the contrary of the rose. The rose is less Innocent; she enjoys the self-enjoyings of self-denial, an enclosed bower of self-gratification, for her bed is already "of crimson joy" before it is found out. The rose is a Leutha-figure subservient to the Enitharmon of nature, and the frustrations of male sexuality strike back in the worm's Orc-like destructiveness.

The Fly is a less ferocious emblem-poem, but it also turns upon unexpected ironies. The insect here is probably a common housefly, and the speaker a man awakening to mortality, to the precariousness of human existence in the state of Experience:

> Little Fly,
> Thy summer's play
> My thoughtless hand
> Has brush'd away.
>
> Am not I
> A fly like thee?
> Or art not thou
> A man like me?
>
> For I dance,
> And drink, & sing,
> Till some blind hand
> Shall brush my wing.
>
> If thought is life
> And strength & breath,
> And the want
> Of thought is death;
>
> Then am I
> A happy fly,
> If I live
> Or if I die.

It may be that Blake is recalling *King Lear*, and the frightening reflection that the gods kill us for their sport, even as wanton boys kill flies. If so, Blake uses the recollection to help us realize that we need to free ourselves of those gods. The want of thought is death; the thoughtless hand is therefore murderous. The blind hand of a god will thus be a thoughtless hand when it brushes us away. If Nobodaddy is the deity, then we are at best happy flies (because deluded ones), whether we live or die. To seek a heavenly father beyond the skies is to find a moral chaos, and to abrogate the pragmatic distinction between life and death, and so to dehumanize oneself. What makes *The Fly* so effective a poem is that this grim and humanistic sermon is conveyed in a deliberate sing-song, as light and wayward as a fly's movements.

The Angel, My Pretty Rose Tree, and *The Lilly* are a group of slight but exquisite exercises upon the frustrating theme of natural modesty or female concealment. *The Lilly* celebrates that flower's openness to love, in contrast to the thorny Rose Tree, for the sake of which an offering greater than natural, "as May never bore," was unwisely rejected. *The Angel* gains in meaning if the reader will remember the kind of orthodox evasion of passion that Blake associates with Angelic mildness.

With the greatest of these poems, *The Tyger,* the Bard of Experience returns, in all the baffled wonder of his strong but self-fettered imagination:

> Tyger! Tyger! burning bright,
> In the forests of the night:
> What immortal hand or eye
> Could frame thy fearful symmetry?

Nobody staring at Blake's illustration to this would see its Tyger as anything but a mild and silly, perhaps worried, certainly shabby, little beast. Blake uses the same irony of contrast between text and design that he has in at least one place in *America,* where Orc is being described by Albion's Angel as a fierce monster while two sleeping children are shown nestling against a peaceful ram.[8] The Tyger of the design is not in the forests of the night, but in the open world of clear vision. The forests are "of" the night in belonging to it; the Bard of Experience is in mental darkness. He sees a burning beast against a bordering blackness, and his own mortal eye is framing the Tyger in a double sense: creating it, and surrounding it with an opaque world. But from the start he desires to delude himself; the first of his rhetorical questions insists on a god or demon for its answer.

Blake evidently derived the notion of confronting a mythic beast and having it serve as the text for a series of increasingly rhetorical questions that will help to demonstrate an orthodox theodicy from the Book of Job. The Tyger is a precise parallel to the Behemoth and the Leviathan, emblems of the sanctified tyranny of nature over man. The Bard's Tyger is also "the chief of the ways of God: he that made him can make his sword to approach unto him."

Fearful and awed, the Bard learns the logic of Leviathan: "None is so fierce that dare stir him up: who then is able to stand before me?" Jehovah proudly boasted of Leviathan that he was a king over men, those deluded children of pride. Though he worships in fear, the Bard also is proud to reveal the Tyger's power. Melville's Moby Dick is another Tyger, but Ahab strikes through the mask, and asserts the Promethean defiance of an Orc. The Bard of Experience is confused, because this world in many of its visible aspects seems to have been formed both in love (the Lamb) and fright (the Tyger). The Bard is one of the Redeemed, capable of imaginative salvation, but before the poem ends he has worked his frenzy into the self-enclosure of the Elect Angels, prostrate before a mystery entirely of his own creation.

To trace this process of wilful failure one need only notice the progressive limitation of the poem's questionings. The second stanza asks whether the Tyger was created in some "distant deeps" (Hell) "or skies" (Heaven). If a mortal were the creator in either case he must have been an Icarus ("On what wings dare he aspire?") or a Prometheus ("What the hand dare sieze the fire?"), both punished by the sky-gods for their temerity. Behind the Tyger's presumably lawful creation must be the blacksmith god who serves as a trusty subordinate to the chief sky-god. His furnace, and not the human brain, wrought the Tyger's deadly terrors, including that symmetry so surprisingly fearful. What Blake called "Deism" is entering the poem, but inverted so that an argument from design induces a question that the Bard cannot wish to have answered:

> When the stars threw down their spears
> And water'd heaven with their tears:
> Did he smile his work to see?
> Did he who made the Lamb make thee?

We will come upon this image later in Blake, but its Miltonic background is enough for our understanding. When the fallen Angels were defeated, when their tears and weapons alike came down as so many shooting stars, did the same god, who is now taken to be an answer to the poem's earlier questionings, smile at his victory? And is that god, clearly the creator of the tyrants of Experience, Tyger and Leviathan, also the god of unsundered Innocence, of which the Lamb is emblematic? The Bard abandons the issue and plunges back into the affrighted awe of his first stanza, but with the self-abnegating change of "Could frame thy fearful symmetry" to "Dare frame." I do not think that Blake meant it to remain an open question, but also he clearly did not want a premature answer. All deities, for him, resided within the human breast, and so, necessarily, did all Lambs and Tygers.[9]

The ironies of apprehension mount in the remaining *Songs of Experience*. The reader learns in time that what these poems demand is a heightened awareness of tonal complexities. Here is the limpid *Ah! Sun-Flower*, so evidently a study of the nostalgias, and yet as cruel a poem as Blake ever wrote:

> Ah, Sun-flower! weary of time,
> Who countest the steps of the Sun,
> Seeking after that sweet golden clime
> Where the traveller's journey is done:
>
> Where the Youth pined away with desire,
> And the pale Virgin shrouded in snow,
> Arise from their graves, and aspire
> Where my Sun-flower wishes to go.

Blake himself speaks here, and is a little weary of his own pity for those who will not learn to free themselves from the ascetic delusion—the dualistic hope that a denial of the body's desires will bring about "that sweet golden clime," a heaven for the soul. The whole meaning of this poem is in another of Blake's descriptions of heaven, as "an allegorical abode where existence hath never come."[10] The Sun-flower is weary of time because of its heliotropic bondage; nature has condemned it to the perpetual cycle of counting the steps of the sun. Each twilight it watches the sunset, and desires to be in that sweet golden clime on the western horizon, where all journeys would seem to be done. It is the next stanza that establishes the little poem's pungency, for the three "where"s are the same. The Sun-flower desires to go where the sun sets; that heaven is where the Youth and Virgin are resurrected to the rewards of their holy chastity. They arise, and they still aspire to go to their heaven, but that is where they already are. They have not escaped nature, by seeking to deny it; they have become monuments to its limitations. To repress energy is to join the sunset, and yet still to aspire after it. The flower is rooted in nature; the Youth and the Virgin were not, but have become so. To aspire only as the vegetative world aspires is to suffer a metamorphosis into the vegetative existence.

The Garden of Love offers a simpler and poetically less effective bitterness, so much less so that it seems to me the poorest of the *Songs of Experience*, and might perhaps have been better left in the notebook. *The Little Vagabond*, much less famous, is not only a better poem, but spills more of the blood of the oppressive Church. Blake's tone is his most popular, and most bitterly jovial, in the sudden vision of a humanized God replacing Nobodaddy in the last stanza.

> And God, like a father, rejoicing to see
> His children as pleasant and happy as he,
> Would have no more quarrel with the Devil
>   or the barrel,
> But kiss him, & give him both drink and
>   apparel.

Nothing jovial exists in the remaining *Songs*. *London* is a prophetic cry in which Blake turns upon Pitt's city of oppression as Amos turned upon Uzziah's. The epigraph might well be from Amos: "The Lord hath sworn by the excellency of Jacob, surely I will never forget any of their works." But we mistake the poem if we read it as an attack upon oppression alone. Blake is a poet in whom the larger apocalyptic impulse always contains the political as a single element in a more complex vision. Of the four stanzas of *London* only the third is really about the oppression of man by society. The other three emphasize man's all-too-natural repression of his own freedom. The street is charter'd by society (both bound and, ironically, supposedly granted liberties) but the Thames is bound between its banks as well. There are marks of woe in every face, but marks of weakness are mentioned first. Every voice and every ban (Pitt's bans against the people—but every vow authorized by society including those relating to marriage) has in it the sound of mind-forged manacles, but that mind is every mind, and not just the mind of Pitt. It is because all men make and accept mental chains, that the Chimney-sweeper's cry ("'weep! 'weep!' in notes of woe") makes the perpetually blackening Church yet blacker:

> How the Chimney-sweeper's cry
> Every black'ning church appalls;
> And the hapless Soldier's sigh
> Runs in blood down Palace walls.

"Appalls" means "drapes in a pall" here; in its intransitive sense it hints, not that the exploiting Church is at all unhappy about the sweeper's servitude, but that it trembles involuntarily at the accusing prophecy of the cry. The hapless Soldier, enforcing a ban he has not the courage to defy, releases a breath that is a kind of prophetic handwriting on the wall of the Palace, foretelling the King's punishment and the suffering of all society before the storm of revolution and subsequent apocalypse. But most of all, Blake hears the consequences of the societal code that represses sexuality:

> But most thro' midnight streets I hear
> How the youthful Harlot's curse
> Blasts the new-born Infant's tear,
> And blights with plagues the Marriage hearse.

Two readings, at least, are possible here, and may reinforce one another. One is that the blasting of the tear refers to prenatal blindness due to venereal disease, the "plagues" of the poem's last line. A closer reading gives what is at first more surprising and yet finally more characteristic of Blake's individual thinking. Most of *London* is *sounds*; after the first stanza, Blake talks about what he hears as he walks the streets of his city. In the midnight streets of the city, he hears a harlot's curse against the morality of the Bromions, who speak of her with the authority of reason and society and, as they would suppose, of nature. But it is her cry, from street to street that weaves their fate, the winding sheet of their England. They have mistaken her, for she is nature, and her plagues are subtler than those of venereal disease. A shouted curse can *blast* a *tear* in a quite literal way; the released breath can scatter the small body of moisture out of existence. Blake knows his natural facts; he distrusted nature too much not to know them. The tear ducts of a new born infant are closed; its eyes need to be moistened before it can begin to weep. Blake ascribes a natural fact to the Harlot's curse, and so the Harlot is not just an exploited Londoner but nature herself, the Tirzah of the last Song of Experience. In this reading, *London's* concluding line takes a very different and greater emphasis. The curse of nature that blights the marriage coach and turns it into a hearse is venereal infection in the first reading. But Blake is talking about *every* marriage, and he means literally that each rides in a hearse. The plagues are the enormous plagues that come from identifying reason, society, and nature, and the greatest of these plagues is the Jealousy of Experience, the dark secret love of the natural heart.

The heart of Experience is the theme of *The Human Abstract*, a matching poem to *The Divine Image* of Innocence. Blake's title is probably not to be understood in terms of the Latin *abstractus* ("separated," "drawn apart"), for the contrast between the two poems is not between the integral and the split human nature, but rather between the equal delusions of Innocence and Experience as to the relationship of the human to the natural. *The Divine Image*, as we have seen, is no image at all but a deliberately confused tangle of abstractions, as befits the limitations of the Innocent vision. *The Human Abstract* is an image, the organic and terrible image of the Tree of Mystery, growing out of the human brain and darkening vision with thickest shades:

> Pity would be no more
> If we did not make somebody Poor;
> And Mercy no more could be
> If all were as happy as we.

And mutual fear brings peace,
Till the selfish loves increase:
Then Cruelty knits a snare,
And spreads his baits with care.

The virtues of *The Divine Image* are exposed as being founded upon the exploiting selfishness of natural man. Not content with this inversion, the death-impulse of Cruelty traps the self-approving heart through the most dangerous of its smugnesses, Humility:

He sits down with holy fears,
And waters the ground with tears;
Then Humility takes its root
Underneath his foot.

From this root there soon spreads "the dismal shade of Mystery," the projection of Experiential man's fears upon the body of nature, and the subsequent identification of those fears with the Mystery of the Incarnation. The poem climaxes in the Deceit of natural religion, with images drawn from Norse mythology:

And it bears the fruit of Deceit,
Ruddy and sweet to eat;
And the Raven his nest has made
In its thickest shade.

The Gods of the earth and sea
Sought thro' Nature to find this Tree;
But their search was all in vain:
There grows one in the Human Brain.

Odin, the Norse Nobodaddy, hanged himself upon Yggdrasil, a Tree of Mystery, self-slain as a sacrifice to himself, that he might gain knowledge of the runes, a key to mystery. The fruit of Deceit includes the runes and the apple of Eve's fall, the natural entrance to the negations or moral good and moral evil, the ethical mazes of Urizen. The Raven is Odin's emblem, a Devourer who nests within the tree waiting to consume the Prolific of man's sacrificed desires.

The last stanza evidently refers to an adumbration of the Norse myth of Balder's death. The other gods seek vainly for the mistletoe, a branch of which had slain Balder; but the Tree of Death is now not in nature but within the human mind.

Much the same tree appears in the slighter *A Poison Tree*, first entitled *Christian Forbearance*, a grisly meditation on the natural consequences of repressed anger. *Infant Sorrow* and *A Little Boy Lost* are less successful, for Blake does little in them to guard himself against his own indignation, against nature in *Infant Sorrow*, against priestcraft in *A Little Boy Lost*. *A Little Girl Lost* is saved by its simplicity, by the very starkness of its contrast between two kinds of love, that which can "naked in the sunny beams delight" and the jealous paternal "loving look" that strikes terror even as the restrictive Bible of Heaven can.

Perhaps as late as 1805, Blake added a final poem to the *Songs of Experience*, together with an illustration depicting the raising from death of the Spiritual Body. This poem, *To Tirzah*, is a condensed summary of the entire cycle of *Songs of Innocence and of Experience*. Tirzah we will meet again later in Blake, but all we need to know of her for this poem is in her name. Tirzah was the capital of the kingdom of Israel, the ten lost tribes, and therefore opposed to Jerusalem, capital of Judah, the two redeemed tribes. By 1801, Jerusalem, for Blake, symbolizes Milton's Christian Liberty, the spiritual freedom of man. Tirzah therefore stands for man's bondage to nature:

> Whate'er is Born of Mortal Birth
> Must be consumed with the Earth,
> To rise from Generation free:
> Then what have I to do with thee?

As Jesus denied his mother and so declared his freedom from mortal birth, so Blake now denies the motherhood of Tirzah. Whatever is mortal will be consumed, when the Earth is enabled to heed the opening plea of the Bard of Experience. Consumed by the revelation of the human, with natural disguise fallen away, the generative cycle can cease:

The Sexes sprung from Shame & Pride,
Blow'd in the morn; in evening died;
But Mercy chang'd Death into Sleep;
The Sexes rose to work and weep.

Blake is not saying that the sexual act sprang from the Fall, but he is insisting that sexual division in its present form must be the result of a "Shame & Pride" that were not originally human. In *The Book of Urizen*, Blake identifies the Fall with the Creation of man and nature in their present forms. They came together in the morn of history and would have died already, but for the Mercy of time's potential, which allows the imagination to convert the deathly nightmare of history into the sweet and bitter sleep of human survival, the generative struggle of sexual labor and lamentation. But that struggle, if it is to turn into a progression, must be freed of its mortal patroness:

Thou Mother of my Mortal part,
With cruelty didst mould my Heart,
And with false self-decieving tears
Didst bind my Nostrils, Eyes, & Ears;

Didst close my Tongue in senseless clay,
And me to Mortal Life betray:
The Death of Jesus set me free:
Then what have I to do with thee?

Nature restricts the heart and four senses; she cannot bind or close the fifth sense, the specifically sexual sense of touch. The Atonement set Blake free, not from the orthodox notion of original sin, but from the deceits of natural religion. Blake understands the Atonement as the triumph of the imaginative body over the natural body, a triumph *through* touch, an improvement in sensual enjoyment. *To Tirzah* repudiates Innocence and Experience alike, for Tirzah is the goddess of both states, the loving mother of one and the mocking nature of the other. But *To Tirzah* is a later poem, and in 1794, Blake could not so triumphantly dismiss the nightmare of history.

The symbolic lyrics of the *Songs of Experience* have shown us the world into which the energy of Orc had to enter, to be tried by the challenge of entrenched error. In *Europe*, another engraved poem of 1794, Blake resumed the story of Orc's effect upon human history.

Europe: A Prophecy

The text of *Europe* opens with a statement of the wilful human confinement of the sensual life:

> "Five windows light the cavern'd Man: thro'
>   one he breathes the air;
> Thro' one hears music of the spheres; thro'
>   one the eternal vine
> Flourishes, that he may recieve the grapes;
>   thro' one can look
> And see small portions of the eternal world that
>   ever groweth;
> Thro' one himself pass out what time he please,
>   but he will not;
> For stolen joys are sweet & bread eaten in
>   secret pleasant."

We are in a cavern closed up by ourselves, and we see all things through chinks in it. We can pass out of that cavern when we please, but only by the fifth sense of touch, which to Blake is ultimately exemplified by a freely fulfilled sexuality. Yet, as the final line of this passage observes, we choose not to do so. In one of Blake's flashes of insight, our motive is identified as the perverse pleasure we take in the forbidden—in stealth and secrecy. A debased hedonism, and not the overt values supposedly involved in moral restriction, is the cause of sexual inhibition.

The "Preludium," setting the tone of *Europe*, follows. As in the "Preludium" to *America* we are confronted by a "nameless shadowy female," but she is one stage further onwards in the sorrow of the natural cycle. Having mated with Orc in the *America* "Preludium," here she rises from out his breast. His love has liberated her voice,

and she raises it in a passionate lament to Enitharmon, the Queen
of Heaven, patroness of fallen human history. The shadowy female
is the mother of all that is mortal in man, lamenting the fact of that
mortality. Frye gives the fine analogue from the prophet Ezekiel
(8:14) of the "women weeping for Tammuz," who "represent the
nature who has once more been cheated, once more left unawakened
by her lover and abandoned."[11] This is also the Thammuz of Milton (*Paradise Lost*, I, 446–57):

> Whose annual wound in Lebanon allur'd
> The Syrian Damsels to lament his fate
> In amorous ditties all a Summer's day

Orc, like Tammuz, is a dying god, and Enitharmon is willing to
see him brought forth in cycle after cycle. Against this recurrent misery, the shadowy natural world protests in anguish:

> My roots are brandish'd in the heavens, my
>   fruits in earth beneath
> Surge, foam, and labour into life, first
>   born and first consum'd!
> Consumed and consuming!
> Then why shouldst thou, accursed mother,
>   bring me into life?

The tree of life has been uprooted and reversed; its fruits surge
into the cycle of the Prolific, which chokes on the excess of its delights, consumed and consuming, as the French Revolution and parallel social cycles foamed into self-destruction, "howling terrors, all
devouring fiery kings, devouring and devoured." It becomes clear
that *Europe* repeats the action of *America*, but sees that action in
another and more ironic perspective. The rebirth of Orc in Blake's
own time is part of a second coming of Jesus, but is the eighth birth
of Orc in history. *Europe's* scope in time is that of the eighteen
Christian centuries between the birth of Jesus and the American
and French revolutions, or the seventh major Orc cycle in Blake's
vision of history. So, when the "Preludium" and its outraged cry of

defrauded nature is done, *Europe* proper opens with a parody of Milton's Christmas Hymn, *On the Morning of Christ's Nativity:*

> The deep of winter came,
> What time the secret child
> Descended through the orient gates of the
> eternal day:
> War ceas'd, & all the troops like shadows
> fled to their abodes.

This advent of peace upon earth is necessarily deceptive, as the secret child descending through the eastern gate of sexual birth is a new incarnation of energy and desire, whom nature will attempt to compass with swaddling bands. Enitharmon binds the infinite precisely because her fallen existence is predicated upon the notion of spatial limitation. Her male counterpart, Los, who in his best aspect can transform time into redemption, is at a low point of imaginative fervor when the secret child is born. He is at rest, content as the supposed possessor of the moon, and he joys in the peaceful night as a time "that strong Urthona takes his rest." But he is deceived, and the Urthona, or full imagination in him, verges on the stony sleep of death. The ironic mark of Los's confusion is his reaction to the omens that accompany the new birth of his son Orc:

> And Urizen, unloos'd from chains,
> Glows like a meteor in the distant north.
> Stretch forth your hands and strike the
> elemental strings!
> Awake the thunders of the deep!

Urizen is Lucifer, the morning star. Blake is parodying Milton's Nativity Hymn again:

> The Stars with deep amaze
> Stand fixt in steadfast gaze,
>   Bending one way their precious influence,
> And will not take their flight,

For all the morning light,
   Or *Lucifer* that often warn'd them thence;
But in their glimmering Orbs did glow,
Until their Lord himself bespake, and bid them go.

The child's birth has interrupted the normal functioning of natural cycle. Milton recognizes this as another indication that the birth is greater than natural, but Los regards the morning star as an intruder upon the naturally ordained night of repose. Urizen's response to Orc's birth is at least one of opposition, but Los's song misinterprets not only the reaction but the birth itself:

The shrill winds wake,
Till all the sons of Urizen look out and envy Los.
Seize all the spirits of life, and bind
Their warbling joys to our loud strings!
Bind all the nourishing sweets of earth
To give us bliss, that we may drink the
     sparkling wine of Los!
And let us laugh at war,
Despising toil and care,
Because the days and nights of joy in lucky
     hours renew.
Arise, O Orc, from thy deep den!
First-born of Enitharmon, rise!
And we will crown thy head with garlands
     of the ruddy vine;
For now thou art bound,
And I may see thee in the hour of bliss, my
     eldest-born.

Urizen's motive is not envy but a justified fear; he and his sons represent the intellectual limits of the fallen world, and they understand "the sparkling wine of Los," red Orc, as an inundation of blood and chaotic life to mock the hard-won limits of existence. To Los his son, properly bound in Enitharmon's swaddling bands, represents the fulfillment of paradise and the promise of its continuance.

The magnificent rhetorical irony of crowning the child "with garlands of the ruddy vine" is altogether unconscious on the part of
Los. Orc rises as Urizen would picture him: a demon or fiend at-
tended by red stars of fire, whose garlands are made of the grapes
of wrath and whose blood will be the apocalyptic vintage of revolutionary wars.

The greater irony belongs to Enitharmon, the remote and mocking Virgin, to be worshipped throughout European history as a
beauty who must be approached through a courtly love ritual. From
her ambiguous "crystal house," the elusive human dream of heaven,
Enitharmon now descends into the red light of the bound Orc, singing her triumph over man's aspirations:

> Now comes the night of Enitharmon's joy!
> Who shall I call? Who shall I send,
> That Woman, lovely Woman, may have dominion?
> Arise, O Rintrah! thee I call, & Palamabron,
>   thee!
> Go! tell the Human race that Woman's love is
>   Sin;
> That an Eternal life awaits the worms of sixty
>   winters,
> In an allegorical abode where existence hath
>   never come.
> Forbid all Joy; & from her childhood shall
>   the little female
> Spread nets in every secret path.
> My weary eyelids draw towards the evening;
>   my bliss is yet but new.

Rintrah has already been introduced by Blake as a John the Baptist figure in the verse Argument to *The Marriage of Heaven and
Hell*. Throughout Blake's work, Rintrah represents the wrath of
prophecy, associated with Hebraic tradition. Palamabron (here introduced) is the civilizing pity of art, other than prophetic art, sometimes of traditions other than Hebraic. Enitharmon sends her sons,
who are the primal artists, to corrupt both Jewish and Greek culture

with the doctrines that sexual love is sinful, that worship of virginity will take one to the allegorical abode of heaven, and that this heaven constitutes eternal life. Acceptance of these doctrines contributes to a repressive morality, and such codes will result in the dominion over man of "Woman, lovely Woman." So, from the start, the Queen of Heaven seeks to separate male and female in each civilization. Rintrah's bride is "the lovely jealous Ocalythron," who becomes a goddess of sexual jealousy. On the level of historical allegory, Ocalythron represents the religious jealousy of Jewish prophecy, insofar as it had any tendency toward nationalist restrictiveness. Palamabron, who appears as the horned priest of pagan religion, is accompanied by Elynittria, a "silver bowed queen" and therefore a Diana figure, emblematic of religious chastity. With her power thus distributed, Enitharmon happily falls into a sleep of eighteen hundred years, the supposedly Christian centuries created by a fusion of Jewish and Greek traditions. Man is reduced to Enitharmon's dream, and lives only in "the night of Nature." This nightmare of history is fittingly presented as a phantasmagoria:

> Shadows of men in fleeting bands upon the winds
> Divide the heavens of Europe
> Till Albion's Angel, smitten with his own
>   plagues, fled with his bands.
> The cloud bears hard on Albion's shore,
> Fill'd with immortal demons of futurity:
> In council gather the smitten Angels of Albion;
> The cloud bears hard upon the council house,
>   down rushing
> On the heads of Albion's Angels.

We are back at the close of *America*, but we now view those events with an archetypal detachment, for they are no longer presented as being concerned only with the American Revolution. The king and his stricken host are identical with the starry king and his followers in *A Song of Liberty*, momentarily buried beneath the ruins of their mental world:

> One hour they lay buried beneath the ruins of
>   that hall;
> But as the stars rise from the salt lake,
>   they arise in pain,
> In troubled mists, o'erclouded by the terrors
>   of strugling times.

Both this and the passage previously quoted are satiric, but the satire is deliberately muted as suits the conscious speed and glancing movement of *Europe. Europe* is perhaps Blake's most experimental poem of middle length, and it attempts so many new techniques that it has seemed the most confusing of Blake's "minor prophecies." Yet it is organized with extraordinary care and is exquisitely subtle in many of its effects. Even its metres are more startling than in Blake's other poems; the seven-stress line which is Blake's staple is alternated with what looks like free verse, but tends to be four-stress lines with the unstressed syllables freely omitted. Such passages, like the one beginning "Shadows of men in fleeting bands upon the winds" quoted above, are generally used to mark sudden transitions in the time-scheme of the poem, or in its spatial dimensions.

The satiric aspect of history as Enitharmon's dream centers on the cyclic irony of eternal recurrence, a mere repetition of events that blurs all differences between Angels and Demons, orthodox or unorthodox, fallen individuals and groups. The discomfited band of Albion's Angels can be King George, Pitt, and their subordinate ministers, or they can be Satan, Beelzebub, and their host in *Paradise Lost*. Either way, the plague-bearing cloud and the troubled mists represent severe mental confusion, brought on by the attempted defeat of an opposing energy that has rebounded upon its repressors. Satan and his host sought to redress their anguished condition by building the palace of Pandemonium. Albion's Angels repair to a giant temple for their comfort:

> In thoughts perturb'd they rose from the bright
>   ruins, silent following
> The fiery King, who sought his ancient temple,
>   serpent-form'd,

That stretches out its shady length along the
    Island white.
Round him roll'd his clouds of war; silent the
    Angel went
Along the infinite shores of Thames to golden
    Verulam.
There stand the venerable porches that
    high-towering rear
Their oak-surrounded pillars, form'd of massy
    stones, uncut
With tool, stones precious; such eternal in
    the heavens,
Of colours twelve, few known on earth, give
    light in the opake,
Plac'd in the order of the stars when the
    five senses whelm'd
In deluge o'er the earth-born man; then turn'd
    the fluxile eyes
Into two stationary orbs, concentrating all
    things:
The ever-varying spiral ascents to the heavens
    of heavens
Were bended downward, and the nostrils' golden
    gates shut,
Turn'd outward, barr'd, and petrify'd against
    the infinite.

For the first time, we encounter the Druid element in Blake's
mythmaking. Even when we come to consider *The Four Zoas*, we
need know very little about either the historical Druids (the priests
of the old Celtic religion in Britain) or what the eighteenth century
speculative mythologists thought about them. The "ancient temple,
serpent-form'd" of this passage may be based on a Druid temple at
Avebury, that probably was built in the shape of a serpent. For
Blake, Druidic religion is natural religion in its least disguised form;
a religion of human sacrifice to placate the ferocity of nature.[12] Since
Albion's Angels are preparing to sacrifice the human in a war against
Orc and his demons, they repair naturally to a Druid temple. But

the poetry here transcends either its possible antiquarian sources or its possible references to England's crusade against revolutionary France (upon which Erdman has an elaborate commentary).[13] I tend to sympathize here with Middleton Murry's bias against political interpretation, even though he overstates the case for a mythic reading when he asserts that "Albion has nothing to do with the England of George III and Pitt."[14] Clearly Albion has much to do with them; in the historical allegory he is to be identified with them, or very nearly. But in Blake as in Spenser the political allegory and the moral allegory or mythic meaning tend to exist on intersecting but quite distinct levels. Most readers, interested in Blake as an imaginative maker, can afford to ignore the historical allegory in its detail, provided that they acquire a general sense of the poetry in its historical relationship.

Europe will end with an impending "strife of blood" that clearly involves war between England and France, and for the general pattern of the poem's symbolism, this fact is worth knowing, as Erdman insists.[15] But if Albion represented only the English powers of reaction in 1793, then Blake would have been well advised to risk political pamphlets rather than poetry in that year, for only historians would want to read him now. Murry rightly insists that the serpentine temple is "coextensive with the land of Albion itself; and Albion has become the symbol of the Eternal Man in his fallen state."[16] It is this identification that makes lines 71–85 of *Europe* reverberate so greatly, for their main emphasis is on the self-deluded and monstrously unnecessary Fall of the human potential into the uncountable miseries of the buried life.

Read closely, this marvelous passage is a microcosm of the process by which our power to see as much as we can see is restricted to empirical observation of the supposedly real world. Verulam is the entrance to the snaky temple because it was the home of Sir Francis Bacon, whose intellectual influence Blake despised with wonderful passion. Bacon was an experimenter who insisted on the necessity for the rational dissection of what we see, an attitude that Blake would have had no quarrel with, except that Bacon (and his followers) lost sight of the human in their obsessed pursuit of the true shape of the natural. Blake would have it that the Baconians carved up vision as the Druids religiously dismembered their victims, with

the stony knives of Moral Virtue.[17] Bacon's Urizenic moral wisdom
in the *Essays* did not much delight Blake either, nor did Bacon's
political career please the poet who snorted: "King James was Bacon's Primum Mobile."

Bacon's empiricism is for Blake a primal basis for natural religion,
and is associated in lines 71–85 of *Europe* with the Zodiac, the fixed
order of the stars, that attempts tyrannically to regulate the life of
man. The Zodiac forms the pillars of the serpent-temple, and the
serpent shape itself is associated with the Leviathan world of matter,
the chaotic sea of time and space that deranged the five senses of
man when his vision lost control of infinity. The stricken senses
poured the chaotic welter of their undisciplined impressions over
Adamic man, and in self-defence the golden gates of eyes and nostrils
shrank into forms "petrify'd against the Infinite." That Infinite was
once the *here*, even as the Eternal was the *now*, both identified with
the majestic immediacy of man's phenomenal body. But man lost
this psychic health, and developed a world of neuroses instead. Not
Freud but the phenomenologists are the modern parallel to Blake's
insights here:

> Thought chang'd the infinite to a serpent,
>   that which pitieth
> To a devouring flame; and man fled from its
>   face and hid
> In forests of night: then all the eternal
>   forests were divided
> Into earths rolling in circles of space, that
>   like an ocean rush'd
> And overwhelmed all except this finite wall
>   of flesh.
> Then was the serpent temple form'd, image of
>   infinite,
> Shut up in finite revolutions, and man became
>   an Angel,
> Heaven a mighty circle turning, God a tyrant
>   crown'd.

If man falls, then his four principal relationships fall with him. These relationships are to his world, to his body, to other men, and to his own past and future. The thought of fallen man alters his space and time even as it has confined his apprehensions and marred his sense of brotherhood with other men. Unfallen, according to Blake, we *are* our bodies; fallen we only *have* them, and finally we are possessed and imprisoned by them. The world is human until the fall, but then becomes the hostile "forests of night" in which the Bard of Experience encountered his Tyger. The pre-reflective time of Eternity, like the pre-reflective space of Infinity, becomes the Druid Serpent of fallen nature. Reflection changes the Prolific, "that which pitieth" in unfallen human brotherhood, into the devouring flame of Angelic charity, the pity dependent upon our first making somebody poorer and less happy than ourselves. The final result is the phenomenal perspective that leads to Deism; man is a "finite wall of flesh" rolling on a little earth "in circles of Space," and doomed to be "shut up in finite revolutions," this last word being used ironically, for Blake already understands the cyclic nature of political revolutions. The final consequence is the culmination of error; we are left with Angels (in the *Marriage of Heaven and Hell* sense), with Heaven as a recurrent circle of destiny, and with God as Urizen.

With this mythic foundation established, *Europe* returns to its sardonic action. Albion's Angel, now called "the ancient Guardian" of the Druid shrine, arrives at the temple's southern porch. In accordance with a directional symbolism that Blake always seems to have had in mind but did not employ fully until *The Four Zoas*, the south is the intellectual quarter of man, while the north is the imaginative, the west the instinctual, and east the emotional. The ancient Guardian approaches the temple (which is archetypal man's fallen body) by an entrance of debased intellectuality (Bacon's Verulam). The entrance is planted thick with a forest of error, in a dark vale that encloses the Stone of Night, the Jacob's Pillow and Decalogue of *America*. The Stone stands oblique, probably for the same reason that Urizen swerves oblique as he comes down in his Creation-Fall in *The Book of Urizen*.

It is now relevant to notice that the frontispiece to *Europe* is Blake's famous painting "The Ancient of Days," in which we see

Urizen bent over the fallen world, marking out its limits with compasses. His Stone of Night is overhung with poisonous flowers and
berries, an image of the tropical heat of unfallen intellect ("that
sweet South, once open to the heavens") now gone bad. In a daring
alternative image, the Stone is the human skull, once the golden head
of Urizen in the south, but now turned upside down in a whirlpool
of destruction:

> Once open to the heavens, and elevated on the
>   human neck,
> Now overgrown with hair, and cover'd with a
>   stony roof.
> Downward 'tis sunk beneath th' attractive
>   north, that round the feet,
> A raging whirlpool, draws the dizzy enquirer
>   to his grave.

The roofed-over mind is a parody of the myth of Plato's Cave; the
whirlpool is the imagination out of position and therefore an eddy
that dazes the misplaced enquirer, just as the visionary is shut in
where he does not belong, in the mind's cavern.

Reaching the Stone, the Angel mounts it to survey the world's situation:

> Albion's Angel rose upon the Stone of Night.
> He saw Urizen on the Atlantic;
> And his brazen Book,
> That Kings & Priests had copied on Earth,
> Expanded from North to South.

The brazen book is the Bible of Heaven, and the copies of it are
the codes of kingdoms and churches, expanding from imaginative
origins to systems of intellectual error. Suddenly, with line 107,
Blake shifts back to Enitharmon's dream of history, with cycle after
cycle of revolt and reaction. In one of Blake's most brilliant passages,
we hear the triumphant laughter of the Female Will:

> Enitharmon laugh'd in her sleep to see (O
>   woman's triumph!)
> Every house a den, every man bound: the
>   shadows are fill'd
> With spectres, and the windows wove over
>   with curses of iron:
> Over the doors "Thou shalt not", and over
>   the chimneys "Fear" is written:
> With bands of iron round their necks fasten'd
>   into the walls
> The citizens, in leaden gyves the inhabitants
>   of suburbs
> Walk heavy; soft and bent are the bones of
>   villagers.

Against this petrified background Urizen and Orc, repression and rebellion, enact their cyclical struggle, pillar of cloud against pillar of fire, night against day. Aroused by this senseless suffering, a "red-limb'd Angel," stimulated by Orc's fires, tries to bring on the apocalypse, but is incapable of blowing "the trump of the Last Doom," though he tries three times. Blake's usual figure for such a role is Rintrah, the Hebrew genius for prophecy, invoked earlier in the poem by Enitharmon, but for debased purposes. Now the prophetic tradition, weary of the cycles of Orc's incarnations and crucifixions, makes three attempts to convert history into linear progression.

The numerical symbolism here is probably based upon the Book of Daniel again. Three figures go walking in the furnace and are not consumed, but Nebuchadnezzar, or natural man, cannot be redeemed until he peers within and sees a fourth figure walking in the flames, a shape like the Son of God. In the same way, "seven times" must pass over Nebuchadnezzar before he can be changed back from a beast to a man. So in *Europe* there must be seven comings of Orc and seven struggles in history before the eighth and final coming, and there must be three attempts to sound the apocalypse in fire before the enormous blast can be blown at the fourth attempt:

> A mighty Spirit leap'd from the land of Albion,
> Nam'd Newton: he seiz'd the trump & blow'd
>   the enormous blast!

Yellow as leaves of autumn, the myriads of
    Angelic hosts
Fell thro' the wintry skies, seeking their
    graves,
Rattling their hollow bones in howling and
    lamentation.

This passage is one of the most surprising, and most satiric, in all Blake's poetry. Sir Isaac Newton, who with Bacon and Locke is one of Blake's unholy trinity, ushers in the Last Judgement. In part, as Frye observes, Blake is being unkind about Newton's attempts to write a commentary on Revelation.[18] Primarily, Newton prepares for apocalypse by bringing about the triumph and self-revelation of error, in the sense that his genius reveals the cosmos of Deism in its full horror, from Blake's point of view, or full sublimity, from a Deist's. When Newton blows the trump, that is, explains the universe, the Angelic hosts are revealed as dying leaves, as creatures with hollow bones overready for their graves. In a sense, Blake's lines are a deliberately bad joke; the Angels learn their gravity through Newton's trumpet blast, and the earth pulls them down into its abyss. More profoundly, Newton's discoveries at once testify to the grandeur of Urizen as Nature's God, and are a final kind of naturalistic reductiveness, since they demonstrate to Blake how remote nature really is from Blake's ideal human. Frye finely invokes the opening image of *The Marriage of Heaven and Hell* here: Newton has revealed nature to be a stone that sleeping humanity can roll away from its tomb, if only it would rise in the body and so awaken.[19]

With exquisite irony, Newton has forced history to its crisis, for Enitharmon wakes. The Christlike birth of Orc shown in *Europe's* opening had led to Enitharmon's chant in which she began to call up her children. Now everything between lines 55 and 150 is revealed as a recapitulation of her dreams; the torments of the Muse of history. She summons her children, one after another, to torment mankind, but Orc deceives her this time, and menaces her sway; and for the first time she weeps. The poem ends, with obviously deliberate indecision, in the Europe of early 1793, on the eve of the wars with Edom (or France) that should herald the coming of the Last Day:

But terrible Orc, when he beheld the morning
    in the east,
Shot from the heights of Enitharmon,
And in the vineyards of red France appear'd
    the light of his fury.

The Sun glow'd fiery red!
The furious terrors flew around
On golden chariots raging with red wheels
    dropping with blood!
The Lions lash their wrathful tails!
The Tigers couch upon the prey & suck the
    ruddy tide;
And Enitharmon groans & cries in anguish
    and dismay.

Then Los arose: his head he rear'd, in snaky
    thunders clad;
And with a cry that shook all nature to the
    utmost pole,
Call'd all his sons to the strife of blood.

Morning in the East means that the fires of the West (the body's energy and the American Revolution) have now appeared in man's emotional life and in the French Revolution. The vineyards of France are where the grapes of wrath are stored, and the vintage of blood is the apocalyptic wine that means both war and an ambiguous brotherhood of death. Blake was somewhat equivocal about Orc in *America*, but now he clearly distrusts not only the English preparation to fight France but what has happened to France herself. Nature is full of portents, and its goddess Enitharmon weeps perhaps hypocritical tears as the badly misled Titan of the Imagination, Los, is finally roused from the dogmatic slumbers he enjoyed so profoundly at the start of the poem. Los is not yet Blake, the inspired poet, but a long-sleeping creative principle rousing himself to what for a time will be befuddled action. Imagination too suddenly awakened may appear at first as if it might better have been left asleep. Los is still part of the Druid Serpent of time and space, and still reverberates with Urizen's thunder. But his *cry* transcends his confused will, and shakes all nature to the utmost pole. The sons of Los are called to the ambiguous strife of blood; they may drown in the mire, or they may beget fresh images from the images of destruction. In this unresolved intensity the most audacious poem Blake had yet written arrives at the most inconclusive of his conclusions. The nightmare of history has been vividly exposed, but no cure for bad dreams has been suggested.

The Song of Los

Blake engraved this poem about 1795, a year in which he completed two sequences of his myth and began on the epic intended as the myth's justification, *Vala*, later recast as *The Four Zoas*. *The Song of Los* completes the mythic sequence of Orc, in that its two parts, *Africa* and *Asia*, give the background for the action of *America* and *Europe*. In the same way, *The Song of Los* gives the background for what Frye has termed "the Orc cycle," the contest between Orc and Urizen set forth in *The Book of Urizen* (1794) and continued in its overlapping sequels of 1795, *The Book of Ahania* and *The Book of Los*. The *America-Europe-Africa-Asia* sequence, dealt with in this chapter, concerns the prophecy of Orc, and is set in the historical world of human experience, just as *The Songs of Experience* are. The *Urizen-Ahania-Book of Los* sequence is purely mythic, and neglects history for theogony. Reading *The Song of Los*, one can see that it is the connecting link between the two series of poems. Indeed, its first section, *Africa*, seems to have been written for the single purpose of filling out the explanatory detail of Blake's early myth, as it attempts to provide information towards the structure of narrative in all of Blake's poems from *Tiriel* on. *Africa* is more of a catalogue than it is a poem, and has little aesthetic value. But *Asia*, which follows it in *The Song of Los*, and adds little to Blake's myth, is one of Blake's most powerful Biblical chants, a prophetic denunciation worthy of Amos or Jeremiah.

Africa precedes *America* in its historical action. Blake makes this clear by having *Africa* end with the first line of *America*: "The Guardian Prince of Albion burns in his nightly tent." Unfortunately, the burden of religious and intellectual history from Adam and Noah to

Rousseau and Voltaire is rather too much for a poem of fifty-two
lines, and a reader is likely to be irritated by Blake's haste in *Africa*.
Probably Blake was so hurried because *Africa* is such a ghastly succession of disasters, demonstrating the progressive dominion of the
laws of Urizen over all cultures. The outline of history shows a mounting tendency towards abstraction in metaphysics and belief, according
to Blake, until "a Philosophy of Five Senses was complete." This
natural philosophy is Urizen's masterpiece, and excites him to hypocritical tears as he gives it into the hands of his prophets, Newton
and Locke.

One turns with relief to the poetic vigor of *Asia*, which chronolog-
ically follows the action of *Europe* in the sequence. The spider-kings
of Asia run out of their webs, dreading "the thick-flaming, thought-
creating fires of Orc." In bitterness of soul they cry out a remarkable
defence of their threatened tyranny, doubly effective in that it is a
mirror-distortion of the prophetic indignation of an Amos or a Blake:

> Shall not the Councellor throw his curb
> Of Poverty on the laborious,
> To fix the price of labour,
> To invent allegoric riches?
>
> And the privy admonishers of men
> Call for fires in the City,
> For heaps of smoking ruins,
> In the night of prosperity & wantonness?
>
> To turn man from his path,
> To restrain the child from the womb,
> To cut off the bread from the city;
> That the remnant may learn to obey.

This very effective three-stress metre is probably adopted from the
King James Amos or Isaiah, and it is a pity that Blake did not do
more with it, as it finely accommodates this sort of prophetic irony,
the emphatic statement of tyranny revealing itself as such. Blake's
satire becomes almost too overt, in Urizen's shuddering response to
this complaint of his regents. The Ancient of Days flies from Europe
to Judaea to protect the fastnesses of his power, but the combined

effect of his own despair and the heat of Orc's fires is too much for him:

> And his Books of brass, iron & gold
> Melted over the land as he flew,
> Heavy-waving, howling, weeping.

By the time Urizen asserts his ancient place over Jerusalem, in stretching out a pillar of cloud, his natural world has begun to shrink away from Orc's pillar of fire. The poem ends in the turbulence of things falling apart, as the Grave shrieks with delight, and the blood-dimmed tide of an apocalyptic vintage is loosed upon the world. To understand Urizen better, and to begin to see why Blake grows so dubious about Orc as a liberator, we need to turn back a year, and read a finer poem, the satire on orthodox accounts of creation and fall that Blake created in the longest and most ambitious of his earlier poems, *The Book of Urizen*.

CHAPTER EIGHT

Eternal Recurrence: The Orc Cycle

The Book of Urizen

The sequence of poems examined in the last chapter dealt with the relation between history and myth; individual history in the *Songs of Experience*, political and cultural history in *America*, *Europe*, and *The Song of Los*. In the sequence of poems to be considered now, Blake completed the structure of his earlier canon by three creations in pure myth, the books of *Urizen*, *Ahania*, and *Los*. These poems set forth the beginnings of myth; they are the Genesis and Exodus of Blake's "Bible of Hell." In form, they are allied by still another of Blake's metrical experiments; they are all written in four-beat verse, and give an effect of nervous passion, even of affrighted alarm. The lyricism of *Europe* is absent here; Blake wants a harsh clangor, a call-to-arms of emerging universes.

The Book of Urizen is not as subtle a poem as *Europe*, but its greater energy gives it a more masculine beauty than Blake has achieved before. Blake's genius for intellectual satire, subordinated since *The Marriage of Heaven and Hell*, finds full expression again in *Urizen*, and largely accounts for the poem's startling tone. Like *The Tyger*, the tone is one of shuddering awe, for Urizen is both fearfully mistaken and genuinely fearful. Urizen is Tiriel developed on a cosmic scale, a Nobodaddy of winter and repression at last exposed in a properly gigantic portrait.

Urizen is horrible, but he has a horrible dignity, as befits a god who will rule the heavens of all religious and philosophical orthodoxies. On one level Urizen is a parody, both of the Jehovah of Genesis and of Plato's Demiurge in the *Timaeus*. Yet Blake's quarrel is with himself, not merely with other men's ideas of order. The Urizen of Blake's myth is as much (and as little) Blake himself as are the other characters of the myth, and Blake's satire in *The Book of Urizen* is not directed at Urizen alone.

The illustrations to *The Book of Urizen* are among Blake's finest, and have been more admired than the poem itself, which nevertheless is superior to them. Even the frighteningly self-absorbed stony old man of the famous frontispiece is not really adequate to Blake's magnificent conception. By a very grim paradox, Urizen, the limiter of energy, is himself an indomitable energy, for the reasoning mind is the most terrible force in nature, and the mind of Urizen is truly the great poem of winter.

The "Preludium" of *Urizen* is one of Blake's simplest:

> Of the primeval Priest's assum'd power,
> When Eternals spurn'd back his religion,
> And gave him a place in the north,
> Obscure, shadowy, void, solitary.
>
> Eternals! I hear your call gladly.
> Dictate swift wingèd words & fear not
> To unfold your dark visions of torment.

Blake's subject is the primordial history of priestcraft, and clearly the adjective "assum'd" is equivocal. The reference to the north is an ironic allusion to Satan's revolt in *Paradise Lost*, V, where the great rebel gathers his host "into the limits of the North" to plot against the hierarchy of heaven. Blake's Muses are the unfallen Eternals, themselves actors in the story of Urizen's fall.

The poem begins greatly, with the sudden rise of a shadow in Eternity. In a world of open consciousness there appears a spirit who divides, differentiates, appropriates for himself. Urizen begins his revolt against his brethren by withdrawing into himself, becoming "unknown, unprolific, self-clos'd, all-repelling." To the other Eternals he seems a void or vacuum, but to his priests who will write Genesis he will seem a being overflowing with creative generosity. This self-di-

vided Demiurge is the brooding power that moved over the face of
the abyss, but his creativity is viewed here from quite another perspective:

> For he strove in battles dire,
> In unseen conflictions with shapes
> Bred from his forsaken wilderness
> Of beast, bird, fish, serpent, and element,
> Combustion, blast, vapour, and cloud.

Blake again parodies Milton's God who created by retraction—"I
uncircumscribed myself retire"—but Urizen's retraction is an aban-
donment that allows nightmare shapes to spring from a "forsaken
wilderness." Urizen is fighting himself, and the darkness he moves
within is an invisible ninefold, a number associated with nightmare
images throughout every European mythical tradition. Urizen's creativity is negative because it is solipsistic, and Blake hints strongly
that the solitary male principle of God in Genesis is equally entrapped in a prison of self:

> Dark, revolving in silent activity:
> Unseen in tormenting passions:
> An activity unknown and horrible,
> A self-contemplating shadow,
> In enormous labours occupied.

Blake continues to build tension, by delaying Urizen's direct manifestation in the work. We see, with the Eternals, the formation of a
"petrific abominable chaos," a rock upon which orthodoxy will be
built. Within that stony maelstrom the Nobodaddy of superstition
is preparing, evolving the future of our illusion:

> His cold horrors, silent, dark Urizen
> Prepar'd; his ten thousands of thunders,
> Rang'd in gloom'd array, stretch out across
> The dread world; & the rolling of wheels,
> As of swelling seas, sound in his clouds,

In his hills of stor'd snows, in his mountains
Of hail & ice; voices of terror
Are heard, like thunders of autumn,
When the cloud blazes over the harvests.

This is the god of natural religion, rather like the Power of Coleridge's *Hymn before Sunrise*, a mountain Leviathan, white with the colorless all-color of the indefinite.[1] Having presaged the human meaning of this dread being, Blake gives a brief glimpse of the world Urizen first disrupts:

Earth was not: nor globes of attraction;
The will of the Immortal expanded
Or contracted his all-flexible senses;
Death was not, but eternal life sprung.

Earth and the other planets are cyclic images of a fallen world. The single Man who was Immortal had full control of his potential for perception, and so the final contraction we call death could not be. But a trumpet sounds in the heavens, and thundering words burst forth. Urizen speaks, and we know at last the tragedy of his motives:

From the depths of dark solitude, from
The eternal abode in my holiness,
Hidden, set apart, in my stern counsels,
Reserv'd for the days of futurity,
I have sought for a joy without pain,
For a solid without fluctuation.
Why will you die, O Eternals?
Why live in unquenchable burnings?

He has invented the idea of the holy, an idea Blake hated with an altogether humanistic passion, for everything that lives is holy, and no individuality can be more holy than another. And with the sickness of holiness Urizen has invented also the affliction of futurity, not the future as it is now rushing forward to meet one, but the future as the indefinite, menacing and remote. Urizen knows himself, all too well, for he has wearied of the strife of contraries. He desires not an exuberant becoming, but a repose of unchanging solidity, a joy unperplexed from its human neighbor, pain. The passions of the life of Eternity are to Urizen so many separate deaths, intolerable dissolvings of his solidity. Enshrined in his petrification he longs for the glorious withering of monologue, not the "unquenchable burnings" that define the human state of imagination. The element of fire, burning upward as Promethean emblem, must be forced downward and inward into the abyss of the consuming self:

> First I fought with the fire, consum'd
> Inwards into a deep world within,
> A void immense, wild, dark & deep,
> Where nothing was—Nature's wide womb;
> And self-balanc'd, stretch'd o'er the void,
> I alone, even I! the winds merciless
> Bound; but condensing in torrents
> They fall & fall; strong I repell'd
> The vast waves, & arose on the waters
> A wide world of solid obstruction.

There is an allusion here to the Chaos through which Milton's Satan so courageously travels, a "wild Abyss, the Womb of nature and perhaps her grave." Unlike the external Chaos of *Paradise Lost*, the abyss of Urizen is all within, but the journey of Satan and the inner strife of Urizen are genuinely parallel, for each will bring destruction to man. The firmament of Jehovah in Genesis, divided off from the waters, is one with Urizen's "wide world of solid obstruction," spun out as a barrier against energy.

Blake is taking us back to the ironic identifications of the *Marriage*: Jehovah, Satan, and Urizen are one, three demiurges desperately shaping worlds out of tortured expediencies. But Urizen is the most cunning and comprehensive of this trinity. In his introspection he has discovered the "Seven deadly Sins of the Soul" and to counter these he must unfold his darkness. On the rocky world he has formed (we have met it before, in *Europe*, as the Stone of Night) he proceeds to found a Decalogue, the "Book of eternal brass." The brazen laws are those we have had expounded to us by Bromion in *Visions* and earlier by the aged Tiriel:

> One command, one joy, one desire,
> One curse, one weight, one measure,
> One King, one God, one Law.

In reaction to Urizen's self-righteousness, the other Eternals yield to the temptation of moral outrage, and by this fierce irony they rather than Urizen are responsible for the next stage of the Fall. The pretensions of a self-congratulatory moral intellect are answered by the unforgiving wrath of the affronted human faculties of emotion, instinct, imagination. Again the parody is directed towards *Paradise Lost*, where the Divine Wrath burning down the abyss upon the falling Satanic host created the heat without light of Hell. Against this black fire Urizen is forced to emulate the desperate labors of Plato's Demiurge. He digs up mountains and hills (an ironic allusion to Angelic activity in Milton's heavenly war) and piles up a stony womb in the shape of a globe, thus obstructing the vision of Eternity. By closing himself off, Urizen has effected a total separation from the being he is closest to, the imaginative shaper, Los, whom we have encountered previously in *Europe*. The analytical mind cannot go mad without distorting the imagination, and the anguish of Los is a bitter refrain throughout the rest of the poem.

Urizen, sundered from reality, has become indefinite, "unorganiz'd," and is sunk in a "stony sleep" like the beast in Yeats's *The Second Coming*. Confronted by this formlessness, Los rouses his fires, hoping to reshape Urizen into some semblance of his former existence. But Urizen, like Nebuchadnezzar, must have seven ages of change pass over him, seven lengthy days of Creation-Fall, until at last the Eternal mind will appear as the mind of Deism, the human intellect struggling in the context of an imprisoning nature.

If the mind collapses into perpetual winter, it takes the inventing vision with it. Los, struggling to make the falling mind more definite in its outline, is in the unhappy position of the Deist poet who feels he must stoop to truth and moralize his song. As Urizen "his prolific delight obscur'd more and more," Los reacted by "numb'ring with links hours, days and years." Clock-time is invented in the hope of somehow organizing a chaos, and to meet an imaginative dearth, Los is bringing out number, weight, and measure. In the ghastly comedy of a falling creation, the well-meaning Los and the solipsistic Urizen are equally blunderers.

The changes of Urizen, presented in a rhetoric of horror, are only the forming of our own natural body, the shrinking-up of flexible senses into the confinements of our cavern. When the process is complete, the fallen Urizen faces west, towards the ironic completion of death. Horrified by his failure to arrest Urizen's fall, Los momentarily gives up, drops his hammer, and silently merges with Urizen.

Blake's aesthetic complexity is fully revealed in this reunion of Urizen and Los. In part Blake's point is again satiric; the poetry of an age yields to that age's minimal ideas of order, when the poet is making his most extended effort to transform that order back into its original and larger form. The naturalization of a system of thought, its actual embodiment, causes the shaping spirit of imagination to despair, and then to merge itself with the body of nature that is the idea of order incarnate. Here in 1795 Blake profoundly anticipates the crisis in Wordsworth's and Coleridge's creative lives that took place a decade later.

This crisis of Los joining Urizen is satirical only insofar as it is allegorical; read in its own terms it is a direct statement of Blake's creative psychology. Pity, as we have seen in *The Human Abstract*, is not for Blake an unequivocal virtue, and pity enters the mythic word of *The Book of Urizen* out of Los's dismay at the disaster suffered by solipsistic intellect. Los becomes the image of the death he pities, and so divides his being in two. The crisis of the imagination produces "the first Female form now separate," the Enitharmon of *Europe*. Blake's meaning is becoming involved enough to retard the poem's action before bringing it to its unresolved crisis.

The Book of Urizen is essentially an ironic explanation of how both man and nature fell into their presently botched condition. Milton's explanation is being constantly parodied by Blake, for Milton is the greatest of English Christian visionaries before Blake in Blake's view. In *Paradise Lost* all created nature was perfect until Satan fell. From that fall and Satan's subsequent activities, all natural creation at length becomes debased. But in *The Book of Urizen*, the natural creation does not begin until after the genuinely Satanic Urizen has fallen. And that creation achieves no absolutely human lineaments, recognizable as such by us in clearly descriptive terms, until the Divine capacity for vision and imaginative making falls also.

Los and Enitharmon are Blake's fallen Adam and Eve, but from the start, they are made to plague and not to comfort one another. The sight of a separate female form is a horror for the unfallen Eternals. Confronted by this division into nature, they react by repudiating Los as they have already denied Urizen. The powers of Los are the powers of perception, just as the unfallen Urizen controlled the Eternal basis of conceptualization. The evolving Urizen is dwindling down to the minimal mental process of abstraction, and the sundered Los shrinks to a fixed perception of time even as the Enitharmon split from his side hardens into a materialized perception of space. The stupidity of the surviving Eternals (presumably Tharmas and Luvah, instinctual impulse towards unity and emotional consciousness respectively) is that they complete the fall of man, by passionately rejecting both the self-ruined intellect and the self-divided power of perception. By first weaving the woof they call Science, and then fastening it down over Urizen, Los, and Enitharmon as a tent, they give unnecessary substance to fallen ideas of space and time. They objectify an order of fallen nature when all they seek is to be rid of it.

Within this newly confined world Los and Enitharmon enact the torments of love and jealousy. She perversely flees, he follows, and:

> Eternity shudder'd when they saw
> Man begetting his likeness
> On his own divided image.

Yet the divided image must regenerate the human in time, for the Eternals cannot. Orc is born from Enitharmon in the shape of time's serpent, a new birth of organic energy evolving out of a lower into a higher nature. The fierce child is too much for the Eternals to bear, though he is not the Shadow they take him for, but a fresh desire they cannot comprehend. To protect themselves, they close down the tent of space, and rob Los of his right to behold the eternal world.

With the birth of Orc and its consequences, *The Book of Urizen* has reached its crisis. The remaining three sections of the poem (VII–IX) are superior in vigor and relevance to the earlier parts, for Blake now has the advantage of dealing with an experiential world, though in its primitive stages.

The terror of familial strife begins with Los's jealousy of his first-born. Perhaps because the child has cost him Eternity, perhaps out of possessive love for Enitharmon, Los begins to be afflicted by a tightening chain around his bosom. He breaks it each night, but it forms again each day, in imitation of the chain called "Devouring" that bound the titanic Loki in the Eddic literature. As the castoff chains fall down on Urizen's rocky world they lock together into a linked Chain of Jealousy, and Los uses what nature has made for him:

> They took Orc to the top of a mountain.
> O how Enitharmon wept!
> They chain'd his young limbs to the rock
> With the Chain of Jealousy,
> Beneath Urizen's deathful Shadow.

There is a sense of an archetype being renewed here; of Oedipus being exposed to die by Laius's command, of Abraham preparing to sacrifice Isaac. The poetic principle fathers fresh life upon nature, and yet cannot accept that life, resents it, and prepares to offer it up to the death-shadow of a deformed moral intellect. Yet life has its voice, and the freshness of an infant cry can sting nature out of its sleep of death, and rouse even Urizen from dogmatic repose:

> The dead heard the voice of the child,
> And began to awake from sleep;
> All things heard the voice of the child,
> And began to awake to life.

> And Urizen, craving with hunger,
> Stung with the odours of Nature,
> Explor'd his dens around.

The remainder of the poem is concerned with Urizen's exploration of his dens, one of the major events in Blake's reading of the history of man's primordial consciousness. Urizen begins by emulating the

God of the Book of Proverbs and *Paradise Lost*; he forms golden compasses and other instruments to assist him in measuring and dividing up the Abyss he is responsible for having formed.[2] It is as though the onset of new generative life has warned him that there are forces still to be confined, energies that threaten his "solid without fluctuation." His prime motive in drawing apart from other beings was to avoid the life of Eternity, with its "unquenchable burnings"; now he fears the burnings of Orc's flames of desire. Other flames are set against him (and against Orc as well):

> But Los encircled Enitharmon
> With fires of Prophecy
> From the sight of Urizen and Orc.
>
> And she bore an enormous race.

The myth of the beautiful woman surrounded by a ring of fire is most familiar today in its Wagnerian form. Blake's source here may be from Northern mythology but the meaning of these lines has little to do with tradition, for they are satiric. The fires or creative movements of Los ought to be prophetic in function, but here they are only possessive. Los encircles part of the human, but the encircling necessarily naturalizes, and ensures that the enormous race of descendants will be ensnared within natural limitations.

Urizen exploring his dens displays the negative moral courage of Milton's Satan questing through chaos, but Urizen is capable of self-education where Satan is not. This makes it the more heinous that Urizen should always learn the imaginatively mistaken lessons. What Urizen sees quite properly sickens him, yet he fails to assume responsibility for such horrors. He sees the grief of his children, elemental forms of fallen existence, and his reaction to such grief is the blind cursing of a Tiriel:

> He in darkness clos'd view'd all his race,
> And his soul sicken'd! He curs'd
> Both sons & daughters; for he saw
> That no flesh nor spirit could keep
> His iron laws one moment.

As he contemplates his creation, he weeps the hypocritical tears of abstract pity, parodying the mercy of the destructive Jehovah. As in *The Human Abstract* pity breeds a monstrous growth:

> Cold he wander'd on high, over their cities,
> In weeping & pain & woe;
> And wherever he wander'd, in sorrows
> Upon the aged heavens,
> A cold shadow follow'd behind him
> Like a spider's web, moist, cold & dim,
> Drawing out from his sorrowing soul,
> The dungeon-like heaven dividing,
> Wherever the footsteps of Urizen
> Walk'd over the cities in sorrow.

This is the Net of Religion, the flytrap of moral virtue, the rightly reasonable knowledge of good and of evil. Blake's barely controlled indignation menaces the tone of this passage, for he feels the tactile repulsion of the "moist, cold, and dim" rather too strongly. This web is, as he powerfully remarks, "a Female in embryo," the origin of the Female Will that dreams the poem *Europe*, and that will dream the nine Nights of the epic *Four Zoas*. "No wings of fire," not the most inspired of poets, can break the web:

> So twisted the cords, & so knotted
> The meshes, twisted like to the human brain.

After this the poem settles into the lamentable defeat of man's culmination in Fall, properly assigned to its ninth and most sinister chapter. The descendants of Urizen shrink "beneath the dark Net of infection," and this shrinking primarily affects their senses. The climax is reached in the rhetorical shudder of a ghastly parody of the Sabbath:

> Six days they shrunk up from existence,
> And on the seventh day they rested,
> And they bless'd the seventh day, in sick hope,
> And forgot their eternal life.

Urizen's explorations have resulted in man's invention of death, which is only an exhaustion based on deliberately narrowed perceptions:

> No more could they rise at will
> In the infinite void, but bound down
> To earth by their narrowing perceptions
> They lived a period of years;
> Then left a noisom body
> To the jaws of devouring darkness.

We die because we want to die, because we refuse the effort of vision that would take us out of a perversely comforting universe of death. That universe of death is allegorically named Egypt in the Bible. Blake identifies it with the englobed chaos of the salt Ocean, product of Urizen's hypocrisy and terrible weeping. *The Book of Urizen* ends with the departure of a saving remnant from this Egypt, led by Fuzon, Urizen's fiery son. Fuzon's revolt from Urizen begins the next poem in this series, *The Book of Ahania*, where Fuzon takes the place of Orc as the titanic emblem of organic energy. Blake originally entitled *Urizen* the *First Book of Urizen* and thus clearly intended the poem to be incomplete in itself, a Genesis requiring an Exodus and a subsequent canon. What the alert reader takes away from *Urizen* as a poem in its own right is a strong sense of the internal menace embodied in that fallen angel of thought. Urizen is within us as he was within Blake, and there is even a self-mocking aspect of his poem, demonstrating how uncomfortable Blake was in trying to keep the compass-wielding categorizer in his place. Even a parody of an orthodox cosmology begins to be overly involved in the Urizenic spirit, and Blake may have begun to worry that as a true poet he might be of Jehovah's party without knowing it. Satan did not seduce Milton and Urizen did not entrap Blake, but both poets undoubtedly felt the appealing force of their negative creations.

The Book of Ahania

The Orc of *The Book of Urizen* was last seen as a Promethean child bound to the barren rock, but raising his voice and so moving nature to some life and Urizen to the analytical exploration of his confined universe. The cyclic contest of Orc and Urizen is fully developed in Blake's first epic, *The Four Zoas*, where the mythic pattern demonstrates a grim aging of the young rebel into the old tyrant, a perpetual failure of the creative impulse to rid itself of organic decay. In *The Book of Ahania*, one of the most beautiful of Blake's poems, Orc is replaced by Fuzon, whose name seems to mean "the fire of nature," and who is Urizen's own son.[3] Perhaps Blake displaced Orc by Fuzon because he intended a more hopeful prophecy than *Europe* or *The Book of Urizen*, and saw Fuzon as having a better prospect of victory. But, faithful to the imaginative structure of his myth, he abandoned this hope, and Fuzon suffers the fate of Orc, an immolation that echoes the martyrdoms of Prometheus, Balder, and Christ, and perhaps also of David's son Absalom, caught in the thickets of the natural world and slain as a sacrifice to God's righteousness.[4]

The Book of Ahania is in two parts, four sections being devoted to the revolt and fall of Fuzon, and a final one to the haunting lament of Urizen's abandoned female counterpart, Ahania, a wisdom goddess as her name, apparently founded on Athena, would indicate.

Fuzon is the "Son of Urizen's silent burnings," and rises with the murderous wrath of unacted desires. His first defiance of his father finely states a potentially humanist dismissal of Mystery:

> "Shall we worship this Demon of smoke,"
> Said Fuzon, "this abstract non-entity,
> This cloudy God seated on waters,
> Now seen, now obscur'd, King of sorrow?"

The allusion here to the creation in Genesis heightens Fuzon's rejection of natural limitation, as does his contempt for a god devoted to concealment. But the son is all too like the father; his fire is only a natural one, and his weapons therefore are his father's. Even as Urizen marked out globes, dimensions of circularity, so Fuzon forms a globe of wrath as his weapon. As it flies burning towards Urizen it lengthens into a hungry beam, phallic in its implications. Urizen puts up a disk to protect himself against his son's fury but:

> laughing, it tore through
> That beaten mass, keeping its direction,
> The cold loins of Urizen dividing.

As Urizen is Jehovah, and Fuzon a strangely Titanic Moses, we are suddenly startled by the audacity of Blake's myth, more radical than Freud's suggestions in *Moses and Monotheism*. The conflict of Urizen and Fuzon is sexual, in that the son has sought to wound and thus awaken the cold loins of his father. But the effect is radically opposite, for the afflicted Urizen rejects his sexuality, and dismisses his female counterpart as Sin:

> Dire shriek'd his invisible Lust!
> Deep groan'd Urizen; stretching his awful hand,
> Ahania (so name his parted soul)
> He seiz'd on his mountains of jealousy.
> He groan'd, anguish'd, & called her Sin,
> Kissing her and weeping over her;
> Then hid her in darkness, in silence,
> Jealous, tho' she was invisible.

This is a complex rejection, founded on the jealous possessiveness of a father shielding a mother from her child, but also isolating the intellect's delight in itself from the passions of creation. The mind's pleasures, rejected, breed Pestilence, the moon-worship of a separate female principle:

> She fell down a faint shadow wand'ring
> In chaos and circling dark Urizen,
> As the moon anguish'd circles the earth,

> Hopeless! abhorr'd! a death-shadow,
> Unseen, unbodied, unknown,
> The mother of Pestilence

The fiery beam of Fuzon, its chaotic work accomplished, becomes "a pillar of fire to Egypt," guiding earth-wanderers, until the creativity of Los shall hammer it into unity with the sun, and so present human passion and nature combined as an ambiguous emblem of divinity.

Separated from his capacity for joy, Urizen prepares his revenge upon his son. In his dire self-communings he has bred a serpent of mortality from his own forsaken wilderness. He slays this serpent and makes its corpse into a black bow. The serpent's blood is used to poison a rock, and the rock is then sent as an arrow against Fuzon. Unaware that his father's rejected sexuality is murderously approaching him, Fuzon is already in the ironic process of becoming his father:

> While Fuzon, his tygers unloosing,
> Thought Urizen slain by his wrath.
> "I am God!" said he, "eldest of things."
>
> Sudden sings the rock; swift & invisible
> On Fuzon flew, enter'd his bosom;
> His beautiful visage, his tresses,
> That gave light to the mornings of heaven,
> Were smitten with darkness, deform'd,
> And outstretch'd on the edge of the forest.
>
> But the rock fell upon the Earth,
> Mount Sinai in Arabia.

The murder of this rebel Moses is an archetypal act, celebrated in a triumph of Blake's intellectual symbolism. The poetic excellence of this passage is a function of its astonishing concentration, and of the sudden flashing out of mythic analogues. Fuzon unlooses his tygers of wrath, but those powers of insight are restrained by his self-instruction, his attempt to identify himself as God. The rock enters his bosom as the mistletoe slew Balder or the lance entered the side of Christ, to overcome divinity by nature. Like Absalom caught by his hair "between the heaven and the earth" to be slain upon the oak, so Fuzon is entrapped, destroyed by his father. Blake's symbolism goes further, for Fuzon's light-giving tresses become identical, in their deformation, with the foliage of the forest. Balder dead meant the dawn gone out of the heavens, and Fuzon struck down means the darkening of nature into the forest of the night, where the Tyger of mysterious wrath will affright the eye of the Bard of Experience. In this great passage's climax the rock which has served as a negation of an arrow of desire falls upon the earth to become Mount Sinai, the rock of the Law. The Mosaic dispensation is converted into the commandments of Urizen, and the Moral Law itself has slain the Moses who tried to lead Urizen's surviving children out of Egypt.

Urizen annoints his wounded loins, and the mixed blood and balm flows down into the void, to become the snake's poison of Experience, the moral negations of absolute good and absolute evil. The body of Fuzon is nailed by Urizen to the topmost stem of the Tree of Mystery we have already encountered in *The Human Abstract*. As an image of crucifixion this recalls both Christ and the Odin on the Tree, self-slain to attain the runes, the knowledge of Mystery. But since Fuzon has been slain by a serpent-bow, and there is a later hint that he himself becomes a serpent upon the tree, there is also an allusion to the brazen serpent raised by Moses in the spiritual wilderness. No more than time's serpent does Fuzon altogether die; he becomes a "pale living corse on the tree," a raised serpent of Jehovah-Urizen's will to chaos. For the forty years of Israelite wandering Blake substitutes forty years of reptilization, while Fuzon groans upon the dead tree. At the end of those forty years, "Asia arose in the pendulous deep," and the next cycle of history began, a repetition of conflict already discussed in *The Song of Los*.

With this fresh defeat of the spirit of organic energy, Blake had carried the events of his myth as far as he could, without utilizing the full structure of epic. The remainder of *The Book of Ahania* is the seventy-line chant in which Ahania laments her separation from Urizen. This chant is the equivalent of Oothoon's great lament, and deliberately echoes *Earth's Answer* in the *Songs of Experience*. Ahania's grief begins as a longing for lost sexual fulfillment:

> To awake bright Urizen, my king,
> To arise to the mountain sport,
> To the bliss of eternal valleys;

> To awake my king in the morn,
> To embrace Ahania's joy
> On the bredth of his open bosom,
> From my soft cloud of dew to fall
> In showers of life on his harvests.

The imagery of Ahania is drawn from Solomon's Song, and from the fragment "Thou hast a lap full of seed" in Blake's Notebook. The mind in its unfallen relation to reality was itself a sexual principle, and the activity of intellect was rewarded by the delight of sexual completion:

> Swell'd with ripeness & fat with fatness,
> Bursting on winds, my odors,
> My ripe figs and rich pomegranates,
> In infant joy at thy feet,
> O Urizen, sported and sang.
>
> Then thou with thy lap full of seed,
> With thy hand full of generous fire,
> Walked forth from the clouds of morning;
> On the virgins of springing joy,
> On the human soul to cast
> The seed of eternal science.
>
> The sweat poured down thy temples,
> To Ahania return'd in evening;
> The moisture awoke to birth
> My mothers-joys, sleeping in bliss.

The loss of pleasure on Urizen's part is clearly the cause of a psychic impotence that devours the mind's prolific joy. The state of dejection that ensues is the reigning atmosphere of Experience's universe of death. The poem ends with Ahania's echoing of the language of *Earth's Answer*:

> But now alone over rocks, mountains,
> Cast out from thy lovely bosom,
> Cruel jealousy, selfish fear,

> Self-destroying! how can delight
> Renew in these chains of darkness,
> Where bones of beasts are strown
> On the bleak and snowy mountains,
> Where bones from the birth are buried
> Before they see the light?

Few images, even in Blake, are grimmer than that final vision of mental infanticide. The Wisdom of the eighth chapter of Proverbs, who was daily Jehovah's delight, "rejoicing always before him," has become now so pale a wanderer as almost not to exist. "Doth not wisdom cry? and understanding put forth her voice?" But Blake's Wisdom weeps upon the void, "distant in solitary night."

The Book of Los

So far Blake has dealt mostly with Orc and with Urizen. His eternal Prophet, Los, the figure of poetic genius, is also involved in the fall of Urizen, but we have not yet seen that fall from his perspective. *The Book of Los* (1795), the last of Blake's minor poems to be discussed here, centers its story of the fall on the role of Los, beginning in the midst of the action of Chapter IV of *The Book of Urizen*. Unfortunately, *The Book of Los* is fascinating in conception but not always eloquently expressed and, with the *Africa* part of *The Song of Los*, seems to me poetically the poorest of Blake's important works, inferior to both *Urizen* and *Ahania*. There is an exhaustion evident in the language of *The Book of Los*, as if the strenuous quality of Blake's inspiration cannot accommodate itself any longer to a three- or four-beat line, and to the limiting context of a shorter poem. The visualizations of *The Book of Los* are of epic intensity and require the larger form of *The Four Zoas*. Precisely because of the strain between its form and its content, *The Book of Los* can teach us much about Blake and the conceptual scope of his poetry. He was ready to cease experimenting and to create the full dimensions of his mythic world, to speak with the full authority of his own Word. The tone of *The Book of Los* is impatience, and remorselessly the poem hurls itself to its climax, the collapse of prophetic power into the body's singular mixture of imagination and irrelevance. Blake as a poet and prophet is aware that the descent of Los into the sublime absurdity of our mortal body is the story of his own incarnation in eighteenth-century England.

The poem begins with the song of an "aged Mother," Eno, who guides "the chariot of Leutha." Eno is evidently a mother of fallen existence, and her song expresses deep yearning for those "Times remote" when the four qualities of Covet, Envy, Wrath, and Wantonness did not rage in the world. Leutha we have met already, as a sexual temptress of the kind of Spenser's Acrasia, guardian of a world from which Oothoon had to escape. To be reduced to guiding Leutha's chariot is to be involved, however unwillingly, in the deceptiveness of a sexual masquerade, which explains Eno's chagrin. The poem she chants is one of Blake's most ironic, for it is a parable of how the imagination goes wrong for all its contrary intentions.

The action of *The Book of Los* begins with that moment in *Urizen* when the fiery rage of the other Eternals set Los the hateful work of watching Urizen's decay. The psychic allegory is instructive, if read with tact. When the mind insists on detaching itself from the human integral, and so achieves a self-congratulatory chaos, the fury against the mind felt by the emotional and instinctual life will damage the imagination. Los is asked to be a passive guardian of the "Solid without fluctuation" that Urizen has desired and now all too literally achieved. But this unbearable passivity almost ruins him, as it is alien to his active perceptiveness. Confronting a world of walled-in conceptualization, Los is made desperate by the cold and dark fires of abstract brooding. His "expanding clear senses" finally can bear the hard bondage no longer, and he rends Urizen's mock-cosmos into fragments, to fall with them into the abyss:

> Falling, falling, Los fell & fell,
> Sunk precipitant, heavy, down, down,
> Times on times, night on night, day on day—
> Truth has bounds, Error none—falling, falling,
> Years on years, and ages on ages:
> Still he fell thro' the void, still a void
> Found for falling, day & night without end;

For tho' day or night was not, their spaces
Were measur'd by his incessant whirls
In the horrid vacuity bottomless.

His falling motion has begun the regulating process of marking out the spaces of time, and so his great labor of somehow forming man's world has begun, though with ironic inadvertence. He begins to contemplate his fall, and it "chang'd oblique"; even a swerve acquires the significance of creation in a downward-borne reality. Los has begun the incessant labors that will occupy him on through Blake's definitive poem, *Jerusalem*, labors finding their direct analogue in Blake's own acts of artistic creation, organizing the inchoate strife of the poet's mind into the intellectual warfare of prophecy.

What is first created on the heaving sea of emergent space and time is an undifferentiated mass of organic life, sardonically termed "the white Polypus." Los battles the waters, and, in a parody of the basic forms of cosmogony, separates "the heavy and thin," as God in Genesis divided the darkness from the light. This act of distinction revives the light of darkened desire, and by such reillumination Los beheld:

Forthwith, writhing upon the dark void,
The Backbone of Urizen appear
Hurtling upon the wind
Like a serpent, like an iron chain,
Whirling about in the Deep.

Aside from its parody of the Mosaic glimpse of the back parts of Jehovah, this startling passage's main import is in its terrifying effect upon Los. Grotesque as Urizen has become, his astonishing manifestation suggests to Los that even so serpentine a creature can be molded into a definite form. Los builds the panoply of a divine smith, including furnaces (like those in the Book of Daniel) and an Anvil and Hammer (as in *The Tyger*) and begins to shape Urizen into something more definite.

Los is now more like the Demiourgos of Plato's *Timaeus* than Urizen ever was, but Los is not being praised, as Plato's harried shaper evidently was meant to be. For Los is mistaken, fearfully mistaken; the shaping spirit has been forced into error. He forms "an immense

Orb of fire," our sun, condensing it from the flowing-down fires of eternal desire. This sun is an image of circularity, of sinister cycles formed in the "infinite wombs" of Los's furnaces throughout nine ages of misled prophetic framing. When the sun is ready, Los smiles, and binds the vast spine of Urizen "down to the glowing illusion." It is an illusion of eternity, an artifice that will enchain the fallen mind to the circular pulsation of natural recurrence. From this truly dead sun's encounter with the mind's remnants, the most terrible of imaginative errors is completed. The "Human Illusion" or Adamic Man is formed as an inadequate substitute for the Man who beheld Eternity:

> But no light! for the Deep fled away
> On all sides, and left an unform'd
> Dark vacuity: here Urizen lay
> In fierce torments on his glowing bed;
>
> Till his Brain in a rock & his Heart
> In a fleshy slough formed four rivers,•
> Obscuring the immense Orb of fire,
> Flowing down into night; till a Form
> Was completed, a Human Illusion,
> In darkness and deep clouds involv'd.

The four rivers of Eden are the fallen senses of mankind, flowing down into the night of unnecessary sensory bondage. Urizen becomes Adam, and so fallen God too literally becomes fallen Man. Yet Urizenic Man at least has fierce torments, and his earth is a glowing bed. But only for a while; then the limit of contraction is reached, as the brain becomes lodged in the skull's cavern, and the heart forms the minimal perceptiveness that obscures even the natural sun. At the end, all Los's labors have resulted in Urizen's triumph; the Deist existence enshrouded in the deep clouds of abstract contemplation.

Blake could not leave the story there, but could also do no more with the figures of Orc, Urizen, and Los alone. The conflicts of energy, reason, and imagination could not account for the complexities of human existence; a larger picture of the psyche was required. By 1795, Blake had been experimenting endlessly with his poetry. He had been a poet for twenty-five years, and was approaching middle age. Like Milton, he had been long choosing, and now he was ready to begin. For nearly a decade, until some time in 1804, he worked at the epic poem he called first *Vala* and later *The Four Zoas*. Though he finally left the poem in manuscript, he found himself in it, and prepared himself by it for the double-epic he completed and engraved, the poems *Milton* and *Jerusalem*. To cross over from the minor prophetic poems to *The Four Zoas* is to leave Blake's tentative work for his masterpieces, and to encounter the most fully articulated myth ever invented by a single imagination.

PART II
The Major Poems

CHAPTER NINE

The First Epic: *Vala,* or *The Four Zoas*

The Completed Myth

The latent hero of *The Four Zoas* is archetypal Man, called Albion, the patriarch of Britain, who does not appear in any of the engraved poems of 1789–95. Sometime between 1795 and 1797, Blake tentatively completed the mythic structure he had labored so long to create. The manuscript of *The Four Zoas* presents many problems for the Blake scholar, and was in a sense rejected by Blake himself, and yet I believe the poem, with all its variants and shifts in sequence, remains an imaginatively coherent and very beautiful work. What this chapter presents is an attempt at a full reading of *The Four Zoas* in its final shape as Blake left it. Embedded within the manuscript is the earlier poem *Vala,* conjecturally restored in the edition of H. M. Margoliouth.[1] I will refer to *Vala* as my discussion proceeds, but my working text here is essentially the full version of *The Four Zoas* manuscript in the British Museum, available in the editions of Sloss and Wallis, and of Geoffrey Keynes.

The full title of *The Four Zoas* includes the finely descriptive *The Torments of Love & Jealousy in the Death and Judgement of Albion the Ancient Man.* "Zoas" is Blake's own coinage, from the Greek for "beasts" in Revelation 4:6, where "four beasts full of eyes before and behind" surround the throne of God. These beasts are derived from the "four living creatures" that "had the likeness of a man" in Ezekiel's vision of the Chariot of God. The Zoas are the four Eternals whose unity constitutes Albion, the archetypal man, in his original integrated form. Blake's epic describes how Albion fell into the sleep of death, and how his four elements or sons fell into involvement in temporal strife. The Zoas are in every man as they were in the first man, and they are the rulers of the darkness of this world. Blake's epigraph to *The Four Zoas* is Ephesians 6:12, which states that our strife is not against flesh and blood, but against spiritual wickedness in high places, the powers and principalities of blind cosmic rule, responsible for the darkness of our world. The Zoas—Urizen, Tharmas, Luvah, and Urthona—are these powers and principalities in Blake's myth. Urizen we already know a great deal about, and Urthona is the unfallen name of Los, even as Luvah is the name Orc was called in Eternity. Tharmas, like Albion, is a new figure in Blake, and a brief discussion of the completed myth necessarily must center on Albion and on Tharmas.

Spenser and Milton both mention Albion as the father of the British people. This Albion is a giant son of Neptune, who calls the island after his own name. Blake's Albion is not Neptune's son, but rather the primordial being, faintly resembling the *Adam Kadmon* or Divine Man of Jewish Cabbalist tradition. One can pursue analogues and possible sources for Blake's Albion and his other "Giant Forms" at considerable length, but I have never found a knowledge of Blake's supposed esoteric sources to be of much use in reading *The Four Zoas* or other poems by Blake. Usually the hunt for those sources is all too successful in its results, and the reading of the sources takes the place of reading Blake's poems as poems. One can imagine Blake's unhappiness at having a "tradition" of hidden wisdom or a "perennial philosophy" substituted for the meanings of his very original poems, but he would have understood, wryly, the tendency that attempts "to realize or abstract the mental deities from their objects." Many scholarly readers of Blake have worked hard at "choosing forms of worship from poetic tales," but they are doing Blake's work after him in an ironic sense only.

Albion is not a speculative product of the Platonizing imagination. He is a character in an epic poem, albeit a visionary epic, concerned with what man was and might be again, as well as what he is now. Albion in his original form is a greater Adam, a man who contains all of reality within himself, and who is therefore human *and* divine, male *and* female, and a fourfold balance of the faculties of intellect, imagination, emotion and the instinct that holds the first three faculties together in the unsundered harmony of organized Innocence. That instinct for wholeness Blake names Tharmas, certainly the most difficult of the Zoas to visualize. Urizen is a snowy old man, formidable representative of moralizing ignorance, once the fall has taken place. Los is a smith, forging forms, and Orc a fiery rebel, but the fallen Tharmas is a raging chaos, for as the element of unity he loses all coherence when things fall apart.

The reader about to start *The Four Zoas*, assuming that he has read Blake's sequence of minor poems with the enjoyment of comprehension and exuberant response, may well be tempted to the question: why ought there to be difficulties for me before I can begin reading a long poem? Ought not an epic, as the most ambitious of poems, to begin and end in the reader's delight, in his joy at a good story well told? The answer is surely "Yes, it ought to," and *The Four Zoas* does. There will be conceptual difficulties as we proceed, but they are unimportant, and no further mythic identifications need detain us now. The wrong way to read Blake is to translate every action of each being into its supposed symbolic value. Blake's complexities exist, because Blake's mind is as powerful and original in the poet's supreme act of *invention* as Dante's was, or Milton's. But all the complexities resolve themselves in the continuity of *The Four Zoas* as of *Milton* after it (*Jerusalem* is a more difficult *kind* of poem, as we shall see). Blake does not need anybody to elucidate his ideas for the alert reader. What a critic can do for that reader is to increase his alertness, to help him recognize much that is left implicit. Writing to a clergyman who had criticized the artist's fancy as seeming to be "in the other world, or the World of Spirits," Blake boldly defended his mythmaking and its claim to an audience:

> You say that I want somebody to Elucidate my Ideas. But you ought to know that What is Grand is necessarily obscure to Weak men. That which can be made Explicit to the Idiot is not worth my care. The wisest of the Ancients consider'd what is not too Explicit as the fittest for Instruction, because it rouzes the faculties to act.[2]

The aroused reader is what *The Four Zoas* demands, a spectator who will attempt to enter into Blake's images by means of his own

poetic powers, on the fiery chariot of creativity that every man's con-
templative strength potentially constitutes. Blake provides the best introduction for any reader in his own commentary on his lost painting, A Vision of the Last Judgment:

> If the Spectator could Enter into these Images in his Imagina-
> tion, approaching them on the Fiery Chariot of his Contempla-
> tive Thought, if he could Enter into Noah's Rainbow or into
> his bosom, or could make a Friend & Companion of one of these
> Images of wonder, which always intreats him to leave mor-
> tal things (as he must know), then would he arise from his
> Grave. . . .[3]

That attitude of receptivity, the willingness to make friends and
companions of Blake's images of wonder, is what can be hoped for
from a common reader who loves or likes poetry. The critic of Blake
who asks the common reader to study Neoplatonism, Gnosticism, or
whatever, or to attend the critic while *he* studies it, has mistaken his
poet, and misleads or repels Blake's kind of reader.

In what follows I will introduce Blake's myth into the commentary
only where the poem introduces it. The beauty of *The Four Zoas*
is finally a function of the radiant adequacy of its form, of Blake's
skill in execution. Nothing infuriated Blake more than to be told that
as painter or poet he could invent, but failed in execution. For him,
"Execution is only the result of Invention," and "Ideas cannot be
Given but in their minutely Appropriate Words."[4] An unfortunate
effect of much Blake criticism has been to name his major poems
"the Prophetic Books" as if they were something other than poems,
to be read as the imperfect records of some fearsome revelation.
Throughout the first part of this book I have tried to emphasize that
Blake's poems are primarily poems, literary works that will yield their
meaning and beauty to any reader who will go to them as he might
go to Milton or Yeats. Blake does excel all other poets in the strength
and originality of his conceptual powers, but he ought not to suffer
for that uniqueness. There have been great poets whose conceptual
powers were not extraordinary (Spenser and Tennyson among these)
and poets greater than Blake who were content to derive much of

the conceptual basis of their art from tradition (Dante and Milton are the supreme examples). Blake is, of course, not completely alone in thus combining intellectual inventiveness and individuality of vision. The generations of major poets directly after him—Wordsworth and Coleridge and then Keats and Shelley—exhibit something of this remarkable imaginative autonomy, a freedom from outworn conceptualizations of reality. Like Blake, they showed more enterprise in walking naked, in casting off eighteenth century ideas of order. The useful analogues to *The Four Zoas* are not in esoteric religious traditions, but in English Romantic poetry, and some of them will be invoked in the discussion that follows.

Creation-Fall: Night I, Fall of Tharmas

Blake divides the poem into nine parts called "Nights," partially in imitation of Edward Young's *Night Thoughts*, for which he had just completed a magnificent series of illustrations, and partially because the original *Vala* was to have been a dream-poem, like *Europe*. As with *The Book of Los*, the poem begins as a "Song of the Aged Mother," first called Eno in Blake's manuscript, with the name then changed to Vala, a prime villainess of the work. The opening lines return Blake to the easy power of his most characteristic line, the fourteener, in which all of *The Four Zoas*, *Milton*, and *Jerusalem* are written:

> The Song of the Aged Mother which shook the
> heavens with wrath,
> Hearing the march of long resounding strong
> heroic Verse
> Marshall'd in order for the day of
> Intellectual Battle.

Intellectual battle is the subject matter of Blake's epic, the staple of its action. The basis for battle is stated first in terms of its lost contrary, the unsundered brotherhood of Eden or Eternity:

> Four Mighty Ones are in every Man: a Perfect
>   Unity
> Cannot Exist but from the Universal Brother-
>   hood of Eden
> The Universal Man, to Whom be Glory Evermore.
>   Amen.

The Brotherhood, the Man, and God are one, Albion, but he will be inactive in the poem, merely a victim to be saved from the deathly consequences of his own errors. The immediate epic hero, for whom Blake now invokes a very unclassical Muse, is Los the artificer:

> Los was the fourth immortal starry one, & in
>   the Earth
> Of a bright Universe Empery attended day &
>   night,
> Days & nights of revolving joy. Urthona was
>   his name
> In Eden; in the Auricular Nerves of Human Life
> Which is the Earth of Eden, he his Emanations
>   propagated,
> Fairies of Albion, afterwards Gods of the
>   Heathen.
>   Daughter of Beulah, sing
> His fall into Division & his Resurrection to
>   Unity:
> His fall into the Generation of decay &
>   death & his
> Regeneration by the Resurrection from the
>   dead.

This invocation deliberately introduces some basic elements in the story of the poem. In the reference to Los as the fourth, and the special emphasis placed upon him, there is an allusion to the story of the three Israelites put into a furnace by Nebuchadnezzar (Blake's emblem of the natural man, or fallen Albion) in the Book of Daniel.

Walking with the three in the fire there appears a fourth "like the Son of God," whom Blake takes to be Los, at home in the human furnace of the creative heart.

In the unfallen world Los lived in the earth, and his eternal name, Urthona, may be a play on earth-owner. *Then* the revolving of earth was a movement from joy to joy, for the earth of Eden was the same as the unfallen Man's sense of hearing, the apocalyptic sense of poetry and music. In that earth of song, Urthona bred "his Emanations," the first time we have encountered what will be one of Blake's important notions. An emanation is literally what comes into being from a process of creation in which a series of effluxes flow from a creator. As a created form an emanation can be male or female or both; either way it is opposed to the Spectre or shadow, a baffled creation or residue of self that has failed to emanate, to reach an outer but connected existence. The emanations of Los are his "Sons & Daughters," forming first the poetic mythology of Eden (Fairies of Albion) and then the pagan Gods after the fall of Los, when forms of worship are abstracted from poetic tales.

Blake's Muse is a daughter of Beulah, his new name for Innocence, based on the vision of a "married land" in Isaiah and Bunyan. As such, she is a daughter of Inspiration as opposed to the classical daughters of Memory whose absence Blake had gently mocked in his early lyric *To the Muses*. The Earth Mother is to sing the fall of Urthona, the imaginative principle, into the world of Experience, now called Generation after the life cycle enacted within it. Los can become Urthona again, the earth of Experience can be restored to the eternal sense of hearing, only by the regeneration of the body's resurrection from a universe of division and death.

Blake commands his Muse to rush into the midst of the Fall's events by beginning with the fall of Tharmas, instinctual unity, referred to as "Parent pow'er, dark'ning in the West." The West, from *Tiriel* on, has been the domain of the body in Blake, and the cosmic body is slipping into chaos. Since he is the parent power of the other faculties, the fall of Tharmas—who is the body's instinctual energy, which can comprehend and hold together the rival energies of intellect, imagination, and emotion—must necessarily bring all the rest down with him.

We are not told, at this point, what is bringing Tharmas down, and what therefore is tearing the human integral apart. But Tharmas himself is already separated from his emanations, the forms he has created and loved. The chief of them, Enion, is an earth-mother like the Eno of *The Book of Los*. Torments of love and jealousy prey on Tharmas and Enion alike. The principal emanation of Albion, the unified man, is Jerusalem or Liberty, city and woman, symbolizing man's spiritual freedom from all conventions and limitations. By an act of what he claims to have been pity, but appears to be love, Tharmas has taken Enitharmon to himself, thus embracing the creation of Urthona, and disturbing the union of Eternity. The act in itself is not culpable, but its consequence is the jealous flight and self-concealment of Enion. Physically this means that Tharmas has grown indefinite, as Enion is his outermost form or expanding horizon of prolific delight. In this indefiniteness he has "hidden Jerusalem in silent Contrition," and so lost sight of his freedom. The poem's action begins with the bitter recriminations and terrible nostalgias of Tharmas and Enion. Having "found Sin" in her beloved's "Dark recesses," she claims that she cannot return. His reply is the first of the poem's great passages:

> Why wilt thou Examine every little fibre of
>   my soul,
> Spreading them out before the sun like stalks
>   of flax to dry?
> The infant joy is beautiful, but its anatomy
> Horrible, Ghast & Deadly; nought shalt thou
>   find in it
> But Death, Despair & Everlasting brooding
>   Melancholy.
> Thou wilt go mad with horror if thou dost
>   Examine thus
> Every moment of my secret hours. Yea, I know
> That I have sinn'd, & that my Emanations are
>   become harlots.
> I am already distracted at their deeds, & if
>   I look
> Upon them more, Despair will bring self-murder
>   on my soul.

O Enion, thou art thyself a root growing in
hell,
Tho' thus heavenly beautiful to draw me to
destruction.

Enion murders to dissect, for her examination too-literally naturalizes the soul. To anatomize is to slay joy; a living being can be
described but not analyzed. Tharmas is desperately protesting against
his reduction, but he is trapped by antithetical emotions, including
the masochism of apprehending Enion's hellish and destructive
beauty as a heavenly quality. He understands that he is being destroyed because he is confronted by a separate Female Will, a part
of himself now become a hostile natural force. In the repose of
Eternity, which was the Innocence of Beulah, the voluntary self-
surrender of the Female Will made possible the continuation of creative life, for no object completely separate from a form-giving subject
could come into being. With a major part of his world now refusing
him, Tharmas is compelled to sink into chaos:

So saying, he sunk down into the sea, a pale
white corse.
In torment he sunk down & flow'd among her
filmy Woof,
His spectre issuing from his feet in flames
of fire,
In gnawing pain drawn out by her lov'd
fingers: every nerve
She counted, every vein & lacteal, threading
them among
Her woof of terror. Terrified & drinking
tears of woe
Shudd'ring she wove nine days & nights,
sleepless; her food was tears.

The woof of Enion, woven into the shape of nine days and nights,
is the Circle of Destiny, the cycle of organic existence, a veil of material illusion. Everything in Tharmas that is not spectral is woven

into this veil of external Nature, and his shadowy remnant is only
the isolated self's will towards death. If the instinctual unity or sense
of organic wholeness in man is rent apart, the shreds of that instinct
can long only for the negative unity of death. This entry of death
into their world horrifies Blake's Muses, who are the guardians of
instinctual Innocence:

There is from Great Eternity a mild &
      pleasant rest
Nam'd Beulah, a soft Moony Universe,
      feminine, lovely,
Pure, mild & Gentle, given in Mercy to
      those who sleep,
Eternally created by the Lamb of God around,
On all sides, within & without the Universal
      Man.
The daughters of Beulah follow sleepers in
      all their Dreams,
Creating spaces, lest they fall into Eternal
      Death.
The Circle of Destiny complete, they gave to
      it a space,
And nam'd the space Ulro, & brooded over it
      in care & love.
They said: "The Spectre is in every man
      insane & most
Deform'd. Thro' the three heavens descending
      in fury & fire,
We meet it with our songs & loving blandish-
      ments, & give
To it a form of vegetation. But this Spectre
      of Tharmas
Is Eternal Death. What shall we do? O God,
      pity & help!"
So spoke they, & clos'd the Gate of the
      Tongue in trembling fear.

The whole of this passage has about it that subtle and beautiful irony we have encountered in the *Songs of Innocence* and *The Book of Thel*. Beulah is a benevolent state, and its daughters are guided by kindly impulses, yet its dangers are not less evident than its rewards, and the actions of its daughters can be destructive, as indeed they are here. Beulah is a passive state, lit by the moon of pitying affection, not by the sun of active passion. It is a dreamworld, in that its Innocence is too disorganized to withstand the generative pressures of Experience. The function of the daughters of Beulah is to create spaces that keep the mind's sleep from becoming death. Beulah is the slough of Eternity; it provides as much relaxation for the creative spirit as the spirit can afford. The world of unconditioned Imagination has definite form without fixed time or space. Time and space enter into Beulah as a relieving world of temporal appearances, a rest from the strenuous makings and unmakings of imaginative passion. The spaces of Beulah are momentary acts of indulgence, that even the most vigorous of artists must grant himself; a provisional universe of illusory appearances, even of beliefs. But these forms do not insist upon themselves as realities, for they are only the wavering shadows in the water of Thel's existence, mutable visions of Innocence. The health of the creative life, for Blake, lies in the willingness of these forms and extra-artistic beliefs to sacrifice themselves so as to revive the mind's power to visualize fresh appearances.

Confronted by the Circle of Destiny, the phenomenal residue of Tharmas, the daughters of Beulah lose their courage and create a self-aggrandizing form, the state of Ulro. Ulro's name is possibly a play on "unrule" or "unruly." It is a chaotic existence, characterized by the kind of brooding isolation and self-adulation we have seen vividly embodied in *The Book of Urizen*. Something of a shudder can be felt in Blake's picture of his Muses as brooding over Ulro "in care & love." The space of Ulro is genuinely diabolic, and not in the Blakean sense, for this is a self-enclosing mental space that insists upon being taken as phenomenal finality, and so menaces man with true madness. Ulro, insofar as it gets within a man, is his Spectre, "insane & most deform'd." The daughters of Beulah attempt to meet the Spectre "with our songs & loving blandishments" and so to confine it by a variety of naturalization: "give to it a form of vegetation." But the Spectre of Tharmas is the precise negation of Beulah or Innocence: he is emblematic of the horrors of sundered life, the breaking-apart of the organic continuity of man and nature, man and woman, man and man. In their terror, the daughters complete the fall of Tharmas by closing the Gate of the Tongue, and so splitting off the fourth or sexual sense of man into its two components of taste and touch. Taste goes down into the welter of the abyss, soon to be joined by the ears of Urthona, the eyes of Urizen, and the sensitive nostrils of Luvah. Touch, isolated and truncated, will remain as the last gate partially open to the human potential.

The warfare between Spectre and Emanation, Tharmas and Enion, now succeeds their mutual rejections and transformations. Enion repents of her weavings, but the Spectre will not forgive, and desires to justify his sufferings by abstracting them into an idea of the Holy. The fallen tongue of Tharmas, once the gate to the Innocence of communion, has become the tongue of the Accuser of sin, which stings with venom. Unobtrusively Blake has presented a fine insight into the account in Genesis of the fall from Innocence. The serpent or tempter was an attribute of Adam himself, the tongue of man turned from a perfect tasting of everything he touched to a stinging rejection of the life outside him that ought to have been one with the life within.

Enion was once the joy that life took in its own power to create more life. As a separate being, confronting the Spectre of life, she is only a state of sick dismay. Yet, though Tharmas is now "wrath embodied in Deceit," and she a shadowy survival of her true self, they are attracted to one another, even as Adam and Eve lust for each other after the Fall in *Paradise Lost*. The contention of Tharmas and Enion becomes a sexual coupling, and Enion wanders away to bear Los and Enitharmon, a radical departure from the myth of *The Book of Urizen*, where Enitharmon sprang from Los as Eve did from Adam.

Of the four Zoas or primal beings of Blake's present myth, only Urthona does not fall, but is engendered in the fallen world as a child of the decayed parent powers of Innocence. Enion is the mother of the *Songs of Experience*, the Earth crying out in *Earth's Answer*. Los and Enitharmon are the little boy and little girl lost of Experience; their trials represent the bafflement of the imagination in a state that cannot fulfill it, and which therefore must try to destroy it. Nature works in them destructively from the beginning. They scorn their mother, cruelly driving her away, and are no kinder to one another:

> Alternate Love & Hate his breast; hers Scorn
> & Jealousy
> In embryon passions; they kiss'd not nor
> embrac'd for shame & fear.
> His head beam'd light & in his vigorous voice
> was prophecy.
> He could controll the times & seasons & the
> days & years;
> She could controll the spaces, regions, desart,
> flood & forest,
> But had no power to weave the Veil of covering
> for her sins.

The prophetic boy controls time, and his sister dominates space, for they are all that is left of their parents, who embodied the sensory powers of man. Even the ungenerated Enitharmon, when she was an implicit aspect of the Urthona of Imagination in Eternity, had something of the sinister about her, for the passion of Tharmas towards her led to his fall. Blake has held the symbolic meaning of that fall in abeyance, but now it is revealed. Tharmas forgot his unifying function and sought the outer delight of the perceptive or imaginative faculty, and found it all too ironically, for in becoming his it has incarnated itself as his daughter and replaced him in existence. By seeking to become more of man, Tharmas has become much less, and dwindled to "spaces, regions, desart, flood & forest." Enitharmon is the presiding deity of these wastes, but her power is limited. Unlike Enion or the goddess Vala (about to be introduced) she cannot weave a veil of illusion.

She celebrates Vala's ability to do so (Vala's name may be based on the word "veil") in a Song of Death that further explains the fall of Tharmas, this time by reference to the fall of Albion, or Man Himself. Albion sleeps, and his intellectual component Urizen sleeps as well. The regents of the emotional life, Luvah and Vala, rise up from the heart into the sleeping brain. Vala seduces Albion, and Luvah emulates the pattern of the myth of Phaethon in Ovid. He "siez'd the Horses of Light & rose into the Chariot of the Day," thus usurping Urizen's place. We are already familiar with some of the fallen combats of Urizen and Luvah, under Luvah's temporal or "diabolic" name of Orc, but those conflicts have little to do with this mythic displacement. Luvah and Vala are the inner and outer principles of the emotional life. When they rise into the brain of man they are out of their place, and Blake is no more attached to "sex in the head" than Lawrence was. The turning of Albion to Vala is a disaster because it creates an *idea* of sex as separate from an implicit sexuality firmly distributed as an implicit element in all being. The idea of sex, like the Urizenic idea of the holy, is a violation of the harmony of genuinely human existence, for everything that lives is both equally holy and equally sexual. When Albion becomes Vala's lover, he exalts a part of creation over the unity of it, and becomes an idolator of an aspect of his own self. As this aspect is both outer (because emanative) and also only partial, Albion is doomed to collapse, and all his powers with him.

Los takes Enitharmon's Song of Death as a challenge of the Female Will, "once born for the sport & amusement of Man, now born to drink up all his Powers?" He strikes his sister down, and warns her that Luvah's own fate was terrible, lost in the bloody beams of a false morning. Albion lies in a deadly sleep as a mighty achievement of Female power, but Los and Enitharmon have been generated to reintegrate the Divine Image and so awaken Albion:

> Refusing to behold the Divine Image which all
>   behold
> And live thereby, he is sunk down into a
>   deadly sleep.
> But we, immortal in our own strength, survive
>   by stern debate
> Till we have drawn the Lamb of God into a
>   mortal form.
> And that he must be born is certain, for One
>   must be All

And comprehend within himself all things both
    small & great.
We therefore, for whose sake all things
    aspire to be & live,
Will so recieve the Divine Image that amongst
    the Reprobate
He may be devoted to destruction from his
    mother's womb.

This is the first statement of Blake's version of the story of Christ's Incarnation that we have encountered since the birth of Orc as Christ-child in *Europe*. The "Reprobate" are the visionaries or outcast prophets, called "Devils" in *The Marriage of Heaven and Hell*. Los is prophesying that the fallen Luvah or man of passion will reappear in the generative world as a redeeming Lamb of God.

In scorn of this hope Enitharmon calls down Urizen who descends in character, gloomily declaring that he is now God from Eternity to Eternity. He offers Los dominion over the sinful Luvah and Vala, even as Satan offers Jesus power over the fallen world in *Paradise Regained*. Behind his offer is a grim and solipsistic faith in the selfhood:

Why should the Divine Vision compell the sons
    of Eden
To forego each his own delight, to war against
    his spectre?
The Spectre is the Man. The rest is only
    delusion & fancy.

The potential contest between Urizen and Los is averted by the prophet's pity for Enitharmon, his repentance for his temporal blow against the spatial illusion. Pity divides his soul, and he falls in love with his dangerous sister, in a failure of the imagination. They eat of the fleshly bread and drink the nervous wine of earthly existence, and by this parody of the communion ritual they accept the bondage of Experience. They soon find mutual discontent and scorn again, but their marriage feast is nevertheless celebrated, a ceremony that drowns Innocence in the watery chaos of mingled time and space.

The occasion of the feast provides Blake with an opportunity for one
of his great Hebraic chants, the hymn of triumphant Experience that
ends in a prophecy of the "fierce Terror," Orc, and of the even
more fearful "Spectre of Urthona," one of the crucial figures in *The
Four Zoas*:

> There is no City nor Cornfield nor Orchard!
>   all is Rock & Sand.
> There is no Sun nor Moon nor Star, but
>   rugged wintry rocks
> Justling together in the void, suspended by
>   inward fires.
> Impatience now no longer can endure.
>   Distracted Luvah,
> Bursting forth from the loins of Enitharmon,
>   Thou fierce Terror,
> Go howl in vain! Smite, smite his fetters!
>   smite, O wintry hammers!
> Smite, Spectre of Urthona! mock the fiend who
>   drew us down
> From heavens of joy into this deep. Now
>   rage, but rage in vain.
>
> Thus sang the demons of the deep; the Clarions
>   of war blew loud.

In the world of Ulro, which is a generative existence collapsed
into rock and sand, the exasperated emotional life is manifested as
the impatience of Orc, or Luvah born from Enitharmon, as in
Europe. But this Orc inherits Luvah's culpability for the Fall; he who
seeks to raise us is blamed for having drawn us down to this deep.
The psuedo-Los who bound him with the chain of Jealousy in *The
Book of Urizen* is now identified as a third component of Urthona,
besides Los proper and Enitharmon. In the fallen world the prophet
has a dark double or negation; the selfish ego within him shadows
his every act. This ego or fearful selfhood is the element in every
poet that seeks to constrict his power of vision. This Spectre of
Urthona haunts Romantic poetry. He is the Ruin that haunts Love

as a shadow in *Prometheus Unbound,* and appears again as the First Spirit in Shelley's most beautiful lyric, *The Two Spirits: An Allegory.* In Wordsworth he is the "hope unwilling to be fed," the nameless fears of *Resolution and Independence.* In Coleridge he triumphs, driving the poet into discursive expression. In Blake, he fights a long war with Los, and is not defeated until the wonderful and definitive ninety-first plate of *Jerusalem,* as we will see. The sound of his wintry hammers ends the vengeful "Song sung at the Feast of Los and Enitharmon," for the song and the marriage it celebrates are among the Spectre's great triumphs.

At a distance from the Feast, Enion, blind and age-bent, weeps upon the desolate wind, uttering Earth's lamentation for the consummation of the marriage of limitations in Experience:

> Why does the Raven cry aloud and no eye
> pities her?
> Why fall the Sparrow & the Robin in the
> foodless winter?
> Faint! shivering they sit on leafless bush,
> or frozen stone.

Enion's lament is a protest against Experience's answer to the beautiful but deluded questioning of *The Lamb* in *Songs of Innocence.* Enion's own questions are unanswerable in the only contexts she knows, the contrary states of Innocence and Experience, for no imaginatively satisfying theodicy can be fashioned from that opposition. The effect of Enion's song upon Eternity is to bring forth an answering groan, for she has presented vividly "the image of Eternal Death." Even Urizen, sitting in ostensible triumph at the Feast of Los and Enitharmon, had sighed with a sense of his faded radiance:

> forgetful of the flowing wine
> And of Ahania, his Pure Bride; but she was
> distant far.

In this atmosphere of terrible regret, a saving group of Eternals meet to consider the condition of Albion. It is a weakness of Blake's myth in *The Four Zoas* that he gives us no way of accounting for the

continued existence of a saving remnant in Eternity when all the Zoas
are in the process of falling. He visualizes this remnant because his
fable needs them, but his fable has no room for them. They are an
afterthought, and are never in *The Four Zoas* integrated into the
myth's structure. To this Council of God, which meets as One Man
in the Image of Christ, there come messengers of Beulah saying
"Shiloh is in ruins." The reference to Shiloh is probably not to the
place of the Tabernacle and Ark (Joshua 18:1) but to the puzzling
"The sceptre shall not depart from Judah, nor a lawgiver from between his feet, until Shiloh come" (Genesis 49:10). Blake seems to
follow the tradition of taking "Shiloh" as a name for Christ, meaning "the bringer of Peace." That this Shiloh is in ruins accounts
for the contentions in war between Luvah and Urizen. The messengers of Beulah kneel in Beth Peor, the burial place of Moses, clearly
a spot of ambiguous value for Blake. Their account of the revolt of
Luvah clarifies the story we have heard from Enitharmon, for it demonstrates that Urizen is equally culpable. In a parody of Satan's plot
with Beelzebub in *Paradise Lost* V 673–93, Urizen proposes to
Luvah that they act together to usurp Albion. Yet Luvah has already
decided to abandon his proper place in the cosmos of Eternity, to
smite Albion and then try his strength with Urizen. Discord begins
between these Titans of love and intellect, and the tumult affects
the innocent faculties as well:

> Beside his anvil stood Urthona dark; a mass
>   of iron
> Glow'd furious on the anvil prepar'd for
>   spades & coulters. All
> His sons fled from his side to join the
>   conflict; pale he heard
> The Eternal voice; he stood, the sweat chill'd
>   on his mighty limbs.
> He drop'd his hammer: dividing from his aking
>   bosom fled
> A portion of his life; shrieking upon the wind
>   she fled,
> And Tharmas took her in, pitying.

The flight of Urthona's emanation from him is the imagination's loss of joy in itself when it hears the Eternal voice lamenting the breaking asunder of the fourfold human unity. In the story we have come round the grim circle to the start of Night I again; the pity of Tharmas for Enitharmon, and the jealous rage of Enion.

Night I ends with the remnant of the Family Divine drawing up the tent of Eternity, and so consolidating the phenomenal world, as they did in the *Book of Urizen*. But this time there is a difference, for they do not altogether abandon fallen humanity:

> Then they Elected Seven, called
> the Seven
> Eyes of God & the Seven Lamps of the Almighty.
> The Seven are one within the other; the Seventh
> is named Jesus,
> The Lamb of God, blessed for ever, & he
> follow'd the Man
> Who wander'd in mount Ephraim seeking a
> Sepulcher,
> His inward eyes closing from the Divine vision,
> & all
> His children wandering outside, from his
> bosom fleeing away.

These Seven Eyes of God are also seven Orc cycles, "one within the other," the seventh starting with the birth of Jesus, a symbolism tentatively presented in *Europe*.[5] The prophet Zechariah (4:10) speaks of seven "eyes of the Lord, which run to and fro through the whole earth." Zechariah calls them seven Lamps also, and as such they reappear in Revelation.[6] As the Seventh Eye, Jesus protectively follows the wandering Albion who seeks only a Sepulchre, abandoned as he is by his sustaining children. To wander "in mount Ephraim" is to be in the kingdom of Tirzah, the mother of our mortal part, for Ephraim is used by the Prophets as a name for the Northern Kingdom of Israel, of which Tirzah was the capital. Ephraim is also mentioned in John 11:54 as the place where Jesus went after raising Lazarus from the dead. Blake's use of the Bible here is typical of his mature attempt to write "the Bible of Hell."

Albion is wandering in the realm of mortality, where man's long home is finally the Sepulchre, but that same realm is also identified with the ultimate regeneration of being raised from the dead.

In the additional lines scrawled by Blake after the end of his second draft of this Night I, he gives us a vision of struggle between the Daughters of Beulah and Enitharmon over the safeguarding of Albion's abandoned Emanation, Jerusalem, the city and woman whom apocalypse must seek to recover. Jerusalem, the spiritual liberty of all men, their freedom from the inner restraints of institutional hierarchies, could be set free through the gate of imagination but for the natural barrier established by Enitharmon:

> The Emanation stood before the Gates of
>   Enitharmon,
> Weeping; the Daughters of Beulah silent in
>   the Porches
> Spread her a couch unknown to Enitharmon;
>   here repos'd
> Jerusalem in slumbers soft, lull'd into silent
>   rest.
>
> Terrific rag'd the Eternal wheels of intellect,
>   terrific rag'd
> The living creatures of the wheels in the
>   Wars of Eternal life.
> But perverse roll'd the wheels of Urizen &
>   Luvah, back revers'd
> Downwards & outwards, consuming in the wars
>   of Eternal Death.

The repose of Jerusalem is the latency of our own freedom, the slumber of creative autonomy in the mind of every man. The Wars of Eternal life were the progressing clashes of contraries in Eden, where the whole soul of man was brought into being in a strenuous balance of opposing vision. But the wheels and their living creatures, Ezekiel's chariot and the cherubim convoying it, have been replaced by a demonic parody. The opposing principles of Urizen and Luvah, the mind and the affections attempting to absorb one another, cause the chariot, which is at once God's body and Man's, to reverse its motion, and fall downwards and outwards, into the night of time and the desert of space. The first section of Blake's epic ends as it should, with a retrospect showing the pattern of fall against a background of the upper world so wantonly and absurdly laid waste.

This account of Night I of *The Four Zoas* has emphasized intellectual symbolism, mostly by explicit translation. Yet as one reads on in the poem, or rereads Night I, one feels less and less the necessity for such translation. *The Four Zoas* does not reduce to a structure of ideas; indeed the poem is primarily a series of dramatic scenes or dialectical encounters, illustrating "the torments of Love & Jealousy" that brought about and continue to maintain the suffering condition of mankind. But since these encounters are utterly *within the self*, Blake does insist upon the reader's firm grasp of the poem's argument. The proper balance between the rival claims made on the reader depends upon individual experience in dealing with the poem; clearly Blake hopes for a certain exuberance in the reader, to carry him past many details that may for some time be understood only imperfectly.

Night I has described the fall of Tharmas, or catastrophe as seen from the perspective of the lost power of Innocence, the lost ability to move instantly from desire to realization. Night II changes this perspective to the self-induced ruin of desire itself. The loss of Eden is followed by the darkening of the next age of Man, the agony of passion deprived of every generous impulse once primal to it. Night II of *The Four Zoas* was originally Night I of V*ala*, and contains more poetry of the highest order than the present Night I does. Yet Blake was correct in creating the new first book of his poem, though he sacrificed rhetorical immediacy in doing so. The fall of Tharmas is fundamental for everything that comes after it, and the comparative abstractness of much in Night I allows the subsequent parts of the poem to concentrate their energies on a vividness and directness in presentation that could not otherwise be achieved.

Night II, Fall of Luvah

The poem V*ala* began with the present Night II of *The Four Zoas*. As Blake first wrote it, V*ala* opened with marvelous swiftness:

Man calld Urizen & said: "Behold these
    sickning Spheres.
Take thou possession! take this Scepter!
    go forth in my might
For I am weary & must sleep in the dark
    sleep of Death."

In the revision into the opening of Night II of *The Four Zoas*,
these lines lost one kind of aesthetic force but gained another:

Rising upon his Couch of death Albion beheld
    his Sons.
Turning his Eyes outward to Self, losing the
    Divine Vision,
Albion call'd Urizen & said: "Behold these
    sick'ning Spheres,
Whence is this voice of Enion that soundeth
    in my Porches?
Take thou possession! take this Scepter! go
    forth in my might
For I am weary & must sleep in the dark sleep
    of Death.
Thy brother Luvah hath smitten me, but pity
    thou his youth
Tho' thou hast not piti'd my Age, O Urizen,
    Prince of Light."

Something of Blake's austere clairvoyance has departed, but the
richness and complexity gained count for more than the loss. Man
is in the sleep of nature, the phenomenal life that is vacant and vain
compared to his abandoned life in Eternity. The revolt of Urizen
against him has been relatively secret, but the onslaught of Luvah
was overt. Outraged by the treachery of his affective part, Albion
turns his eyes outward to his own Self or Spectre, and the lapsed
Urizen is prepared to assume the role of Spectre of Albion. The sick-
ening spheres are the whirling wheels, rushing downwards and outwards, that now constitute the Circle of Destiny, the same dull round

or mill of meaninglessness prophesied by Blake's early tracts. In the porches of Albion, once his ears, watched over by Urthona, but now merely passive receptors, the lament of Enion is heard, crying out against the darkening of the Innocent Vision. In his weariness Man abdicates to Urizen, though in the consciousness that Urizen has been treacherous also. But a horror of the emotions, and the affliction of guilt at his own "sin" with Vala, now cause Albion to choose Urizen as a regent.

With his unequalled (and so little praised) sense of cosmic drama, Blake depicts a Urizen greater and more self-divided than the hideous protagonist of *The Book of Urizen*:

> Urizen rose from the bright Feast like a star
>   thro' the evening sky
> Exulting at the voice that call'd him from
>   the Feast of envy.
> First he beheld the body of Man, pale, cold;
>   the horrors of death
> Beneath his feet shot thro' him as he stood in
>   the Human Brain
> And all its golden porches grew pale with
>   his sickening light,
> No more Exulting, for he saw Eternal Death
>   beneath.
> Pale, he beheld futurity; pale, he beheld
>   the Abyss
> Where Enion, blind & age bent, wept in
>   direful hunger craving
> All rav'ning like the hungry worm & like
>   the silent grave.
> Mighty was the draught of Voidness to draw
>   Existence in.

The irony of Urizen's position derives from the baffling of his expectation. As in *The Book of Urizen*, he fears futurity; in his essence he opposes any sense of possible sublimity. He has desired supremacy, but the world he inherits for his rule is a dangerous ruin, haunted by the ghostly Enion, who, from being the joy of Innocence, has become the sorrow of the Void, the terrifying song of the Abyss. Urizen, like Milton's Satan, does not lack courage. He becomes "the great Work master" or demiurge, commanding his children to the immense labor of building a fallen world, a "Mundane Shell around the Rock of Albion." This new creation is another fearful episode in the Fall of the human integral:

> The tygers of wrath called the horses of
>   instruction from their mangers,
> They unloos'd them & put on the harness of
>   gold & silver & ivory,
> In human forms distinct they stood round
>   Urizen, prince of Light,
> Petrifying all the Human Imagination into
>   rock & sand.
> Groans ran along Tyburn's brook and along
>   the River of Oxford
> Among the Druid Temples. Albion groan'd on
>   Tyburn's brook;
> Albion gave his loud death groan. The
>   Atlantic Mountains trembled.
> Aloft the Moon fled with a cry; the Sun with
>   streams of blood.
> From Albion's Loins fled all Peoples and
>   Nations of the Earth,
> Fled with the noise of Slaughter & the
>   stars of heaven fled.
> Jerusalem came down in a dire ruin over all
>   this Earth.

Urizen thinks he is establishing a merciful limit beyond which reality cannot contract, but he deceives himself and directs the building of Ulro, the reductive state of abstract brooding on the self that at last petrifies the human imagination into the rock and sand of the material world. The tygers of wrath are wiser than the horses of instruction, but wisdom is abdicated here, and the sacrificial nature worship Blake calls Druidism is manifest alike in the gallows at Tyburn and at the university. The Atlantic mountains come down to sink beneath the sea, and the nations flee from the engendering power of their common father. Man's Christian Liberty comes down in a dire ruin over all the earth, to be replaced by covenanted institutions.

In a symbolism that one suspects is very late in Blake's work, and probably imported back into the *Zoas* manuscript from *Jerusalem*, Blake brilliantly identifies Albion with Jacob, and natural or Adamic man with Jacob's sons Reuben and Levi:

> Their eyes, their ears, nostrils & tongues roll
> outward; they behold
> What is within now seen without; they are raw
> to the hungry wind.
> They become Nations far remote, in a little &
> dark Land.

This is the cavern-existence of Deistic man, doomed to be hunted down "before the hounds of Nimrod," Milton's figure of fallen tyranny and natural bondage. One might expect Urizen to be triumphant in these mighty works of his all-miscreant brain, but instead he has a vision of woe and fear. Luvah, cast into the furnaces of affliction that are the mills or intellectual systems of Urizen, is tortured by his former emanation Vala. As Luvah is becoming an Orc figure, a dying god of the vegetative cycle like Tammuz or Adonis, Vala has become the beauty and cruelty of that form of natural religion. She is a vegetation goddess demanding sexual sacrifices. Contemplating this savage alteration of love into sadism, Urizen has an intimation of his vulnerability, which will lead to his own fall in Night III.

From the furnaces of Urizen the voice of Luvah is raised, dignified but desperate, and lamentably mistaken, as all the tragic creatures in this poem are mistaken. Blake is so skilled at dramatizing self-delusion that we are too ready to give Luvah our undivided sympathy as he cries out against Vala:

> I loved her, I gave her all my soul & my
> delight,
> I hid her in soft gardens & in secret
> bowers of summer,

Weaving mazes of delight along the sunny
      paradise,
Inextricable labyrinths. She bore me sons
      & daughters,
And they have taken her away & hid her from
      my sight.
They have surrounded me with walls of iron
      & brass. O Lamb
Of God clothed in Luvah's garments! little
      knowest thou
Of death Eternal, that we all go to Eternal
      Death,
To our Primeval Chaos in fortuitous concourse
      of incoherent
Discordant principles of Love & Hate. I
      suffer affliction
Because I love, for I was love, but hatred
      awakes in me,
And Urizen, who was Faith & certainty, is
      chang'd to Doubt;
The hand of Urizen is upon me because I
      blotted out
That Human delusion, to deliver all the sons
      of God
From bondage of the Human form. O first born
      Son of Light,
O Urizen my enemy, I weep for thy stern
      ambition,
But weep in vain. O when will you return,
      Vala the Wanderer?

In the earlier lines of this complaint, Luvah gives the remarkable
history of how he created and nurtured the deceiving beauty of his
lost Emanation, in a cycle of transformations from Earth-worm to
scaled Serpent to Dragon to a human infant. Out of earth comes
a natural dread, which becomes a Dragon of mortality, only to yield
to a human image of regeneration. But the beloved child, in the
passage quoted just above, becomes the temptress of natural appear-

ance. What Luvah cannot see is that the responsibility is his own; the fault is Love's. The possessiveness of Luvah, expressed in the covert places of secret bowers, mazes, inextricable labyrinths, leads to the dark secret love that destroys life. Addressing the Savior who will come clothed in Love's garments, Luvah despairingly warns of the necessity of eternal death.

In his chaotic vision Luvah gets everything wrong: the creative contraries of eternal life now seem only a "fortuitous concourse of incoherent discordant principles," and he believes that affliction is his only because he still loves, not through his attempt to capture the function of reason, to bring down the head into the loins. Amidst these delusions his primal gift of affection allows him some last insights. He shifts his tense and realizes that he *was* love but is becoming hatred; that Urizen was intellectual faith and certainty, but has become doubt and the fear of futurity. Blake is too good a poet to leave the fallen Luvah in this much clarity. The confused being concludes by defending his cleaving asunder of the human image as a blotting-out of the "Human delusion." Blake's angriest kind of oblique irony appears in this ostensible Deliverer's claim that he has released mankind "from bondage of the Human form." Luvah has become rather like D. H. Lawrence in his more inauthentic moments, "reasoning from the loins in the unreal forms of Ulro's night."

After the Divine Love has been "quite melted with woe," the outward form of that Love in the Eternal world falls also. Vala becomes a heap of ashes, and mankind in the generative world is cut off from the hiding places of its emotional power. Blake bitterly observes the variety of experiential responses to this ruin. Some men see visions and seek brotherhood again, but the most do not:

> But many stood silent, & busied in their families.
> And many said, "We see no Visions in the
>   darksom air.
> Measure the course of that sulphur orb that
>   lights the darksom day,
> Set stations on this breeding Earth & let
>   us buy & sell."
> Others arose & schools erected, forming
>   Instruments

> To measure out the course of heaven. Stern
>   Urizen beheld
> In woe his brethren & his sons, in dark'ning
>   woe lamenting
> Upon the winds, in clouds involv'd, Uttering
>   his voice in thunders,
> Commanding all the work with care & power
>   & severity.

The complexity of Urizen's reaction here was prefigured in *The Book of Urizen* (Chap. VIII, section 3), when the Demiurge "sicken'd to see" his creations appear. The measurers Urizen beholds are his true servants, but he will retain just enough of the Eternal vision, until his downfall in Night III, so that meanwhile his followers dismay him.

As the creation of the Mundane Shell goes forward, one sees that Blake's description of the process is a powerful mockery of all the philosophers and theologians, Plato included, who have brought out number, weight, and measure to calculate the dearth of fallen creation:

> Then rose the Builders; First the Architect
>   divine his plan
> Unfolds. The wondrous scaffold rear'd all
>   round the infinite,
> Quadrangular the building rose, the heavens
>   squared by a line,
> Trigons & cubes divide the elements in
>   finite bonds.
> Multitudes without number work incessant: the
>   hewn stone
> Is plac'd in beds of mortar mingled with the
>   ashes of Vala.
> Severe the labour; female slaves the mortar
>   trod oppressed.

This passage begins as satire, and ends as moral protest, a typical progression for Blake. Those who would square the heavens by a line are the same as those who exploit human labor, mixing their mortar with the ashes of the world's beauty.

When he seeks repose from directing these dark labors, Urizen turns to his emanation Ahania, who is a wisdom goddess like the classical Athena. The downfall of Urizen, still to come, is hinted in the alienation that now becomes evident:

> When Urizen return'd from his immense
>   labours & travels,
> Descending, she repos'd beside him, folding
>   him around
> In her bright skirts. Astonish'd & Con-
>   founded, he beheld
> Her shadowy form now separate; he shudder'd
>   & was silent
> Till her caresses & her tears reviv'd him to
>   life & joy.
> Two wills they had, two intellects, & not as
>   in times of old.
> This Urizen perciev'd, & silent brooded in
>   dark'ning Clouds.
> To him his Labour was but Sorrow & his
>   Kingdom was Repentance.
> He drave the Male Spirits all away from
>   Ahania,
> And she drave all the Females from him away.

The self-seeking intellect has found itself, and the separation involved in such discovery is an intimation of mortality. To find another in the self, to externalize it, to grow jealously possessive of it; the dreary cycle is never-ending in Blake's reading of solipsistic psychic existence. The sorrow of Urizen attracts Los and Enitharmon, the fierce children of Experience introduced in Night I. They arrive, to extract a sadistic pleasure from the woes of Urizen, and the more intense sufferings of Luvah and Vala. As befits such pleasure, these children are prompted to accuse one another of sexual sin, and their contentions serve to re-create the strife of their elders. As she tastes her augmenting powers to hurt, Enitharmon begins to mature into the courtly love Queen of Heaven we have seen her as in *Europe*. She sings an exquisitely wrought hymn of woman's dominion over man that is as sinister as any expression of the Female Will in Blake:

> The joy of woman is the death of her most
>   best beloved
> Who dies for Love of her
> In torments of fierce jealousy & pangs of
>   adoration.
> The Lovers' night bears on my song
> And the nine spheres rejoice beneath my
>   powerful controll.
>
> They sing unceasing to the notes of my
>   immortal hand.
> The solemn, silent moon
> Reverberates the living harmony upon my
>   limbs;
> The birds & beasts rejoice & play,
> And every one seeks for his mate to prove
>   his inmost joy.
>
> Furious & terrible they sport & red the
>   nether deep;
> The deep lifts up his rugged head,
> And lost in infinite hum[m]ing wings
>   vanishes with a cry.
> The fading cry is ever dying;
> The living voice is ever living in its
>   inmost joy.

Yeats praised this poem as reminding him of many ancient hymns, yet felt regret that its singer was not Freya or some similar goddess of a traditional mythology.[7] No inherited European mythology, not even the Norse, would have been uninhibited enough to give us a song so explicit as this in its deliberate association of ritual female chastity with the sexual perversion of sadism. Enitharmon rejoices in the pain of love, and only then does she countenance the fury of blood and mire seeking its fulfillment in the nether deep, bringing about what Yeats was to term, in Enitharmon's savage spirit, "the uncontrollable mystery on the bestial floor."[8]

Enitharmon's song kindles delusive sexual hopes in Los, who is abandoned by her in the shadows as she flees "outstretch'd upon the immense like a bright rainbow, weeping & smiling & fading." The rainbow, an orthodox emblem of covenant, here represents the deceptiveness of nature, as it will in Shelley's last poem, *The Triumph of Life*. By living in pursuit of this light, Los drives Enion further and further into non-existence, for only he can recover the vision of Innocence, and he cannot do that without re-creating fallen nature. The further away Enion is driven, the more certain it is that Ahania, the delight of natural wisdom, must also be drawn into the abyss. Night II ends with a song of Enion that is one of Blake's greatest lyrics, equal to the prophetic chants in Zechariah and Job that it echoes:[9]

> I am made to sow the thistle for wheat; the
>   nettle for a nourishing dainty.
> I have planted a false oath in the earth,
>   it has brought forth a poison tree.
> I have chosen the serpent for a councellor
>   & the dog
> For a schoolmaster to my children.
> I have blotted out from light & living the
>   dove & nightingale
> And I have caused the earth worm to beg
>   from door to door.
>
> I have taught the thief a secret path into
>   the house of the just.
> I have taught pale artifice to spread his
>   nets upon the morning.
> My heavens are brass, my earth is iron, my
>   moon a clod of clay.
> My sun a pestilence burning at noon & a
>   vapour of death in night.

What is the price of Experience? do men
     buy it for a song?
Or wisdom for a dance in the street? No,
     it is bought with the price
Of all that a man hath, his house, his wife, his
     children.
Wisdom is sold in the desolate market where
     none come to buy,
And in the wither'd field where the farmer
     plows for bread in vain.

This is a song of extremest Experience, at that furthest verge of the
generative existence where one either falls into the unorganized chaos
of solipsism or breaks through to a second and higher Innocence,
the Organized Innocence that can live with knowledge, not the
Innocence that is also ignorance. Enion desires to pass into that state,
but she lacks the actualizing power of Tharmas, who has been reduced to a shadow of his capability. She now understands the price
of Experience, because she has so overwhelmingly paid it. The terrible
poignance of her song is in its absolute universality of reference, as
well as in its direct relevance to Blake's own life. Wisdom can be sold
only where none come to buy, and the farmer vainly plows even as
the painter and poet vainly engraves.

Job, in his bitterness, had cried out a similar sorrow:

> But where shall wisdom be found? and
> where is the place of understanding?
>
> Man knoweth not the price thereof;
> neither is it found in the land of the
> living.   28:12–13.

So far Enion's song is no more than a modification of Biblical
poetry. Suddenly the image of the withered field suggests the central
moral paradox of Experience, already presented in *The Human Abstract*. Our joys and our virtues are founded upon the sufferings of
others:

It is an easy thing to triumph in the
    summer's sun
And in the vintage & to sing on the waggon
    loaded with corn.
It is an easy thing to talk of patience to
    the afflicted,
To speak the laws of prudence to the houseless
    wanderer,
To listen to the hungry raven's cry in
    wintry season
When the red blood is fill'd with wine &
    with the marrow of lambs.

It is an easy thing to laugh at wrathful
    elements,
To hear the dog howl at the wintry door,
    the ox in the slaughter house moan;
To see a god on every wind & a blessing on
    every blast;
To hear sounds of love in the thunder storm
    that destroys our enemies' house;
To rejoice in the blight that covers his
    field, & the sickness that cuts off
    his children,
While our olive & vine sing & laugh round
    our door, & our children bring fruits
    & flowers.

Then the groan & the dolor are quite forgotten,
    & the slave grinding at the mill,
And the captive in chains & the poor in the
    prison, & the soldier in the field
When the shatter'd bone hath laid him
    groaning among the happier dead.

It is an easy thing to rejoice in the tents
    of prosperity;
Thus could I sing & thus rejoice, but it is
    not so with me.

This is the winter vision, and truer than its contrary so long as we live in Experience. Blake is thrusting directly at everything in us that seeks to protect us from the deranging consequences of a full consciousness of human suffering. If, at any given moment, we allowed ourselves to apprehend the total reality of the pain and poverty abroad in the world, we would either sicken of our own sensitivity, or fall a little more into the sleep of death that depends upon our evasions of consciousness.[10] Enion, having been cast into the void, now has absolute awareness, and insists upon either deliverance from this knowledge or else destruction. Her lamentation ends Night II by awakening Ahania from Urizen's couch. Once the wisdom goddess has gone to the margin of Chaos to behold the spectrous form of Enion, she can rest no more with Urizen, and the fall of the eternal Intellect is made inevitable. Even an intellectual vision of human suffering is enough to turn the mind's delight from its sense of well-being to an inability to accept an existence grounded on the victimization of instinctive impulses. The vivid image of the tormented goddess unifies the end of Night II and the swift disasters that are to come.

Night III, Fall of Urizen

There are only two events in Night III, the fall of Urizen and the return to power of the Spectre of Tharmas. Both epic incidents are of the highest importance to Blake, for the crashing down in ruin of the Arch-rationalist, and the desperate reassumption of authority by the remnants of bodily life are crucial in the poet's reading of the psychic history of late eighteenth-century England. Both events lead to the mission of Los in Night IV, and the quest of Los in Blake's own enterprise, the heroic effort to make of his poetry a hammer without a master, a shaping spirit that will compel reality to appear, and at last even force history to its apocalyptic climax.

Night III opens as it must, with Urizen's suicidal rejection of his emanation. Ahania is like the Wisdom of Jehovah that played before him in the Book of Proverbs, and helped inspire him to his Creation, and also like the Sapience of Spenser in the *Hymne of Heavenly Love*. But Urizen insists on treating her as if she were Sin to his Satan in *Paradise Lost,* and we remember again that Blake's Urizen and Milton's Satan had much in common in the marvelous poem *Europe.*

Ahania begins by gently reproving Urizen for the fearful doubts that have begun to oppress him: "Why wilt thou look upon futurity, dark'ning present joy?" His answer relates to the archetype of the Zeus of Aeschylus or the Jupiter of Shelley fearing the child who is to displace him. He fears "that prophetic boy," Orc, the reborn Luvah of *America* and *Europe.* As Ahania meditates the cause of this killing fright, she comes to understand Urizen's error, and tries to persuade him of it:

> O Prince, the Eternal One hath set thee
>   leader of his hosts,
> Leave all futurity to him. Resume thy
>   fields of Light.
> Why didst thou listen to the voice of Luvah
>   that dread morn
> To give the immortal steeds of light to his
>   deceitful hands?
> No longer now obedient to thy will, thou
>   art compell'd
> To forge the curbs of iron & brass, to build
>   the iron mangers,
> To feed them with intoxication from the wine
>   presses of Luvah
> Till the Divine Vision & Fruition is quite
>   obliterated.
> They call thy lions to the fields of blood,
>   they rouze thy tygers
> Out of the halls of justice, till these dens
>   thy wisdom fram'd
> Golden & beautiful but O how unlike those
>   sweet fields of bliss
> Where liberty was justice & eternal science
>   was mercy.

This eloquent appeal breathes the visionary nostalgia that Blake
excels at expressing. The fields of Light have been forsaken, yet the
mind has only to desire them, and they will be repossessed. Ahania
is a faithful but misled wife in assuming that Urizen must have been
seduced by Luvah, but as readers we have learned better. But she
understands magnificently what we find so difficult to comprehend,
the greatness of Urizen even in Blake's eyes, the extent to which
Urizen is a being of splendor. It is too easy to underestimate Blake.
Urizen is after all the Jehovah of orthodoxy, whether Jewish or
Christian. The awe and reverence that believers feel for Jehovah is
properly due to Urizen also. Indeed Blake now shows us how Man
came to so revere Urizen as God:

> Then Man ascended mourning into the splendors
> of his palace,
> Above him rose a Shadow from his wearied
> intellect
> Of living gold, pure, perfect, holy; in white
> linen pure he hover'd,
> A sweet entrancing self delusion, a wat'ry
> vision of Man
> Soft exulting in existence, all the Man
> absorbing.

The numinous dream of guilty Man became the spectral embodiment of the exhausted intellect, the passive projection of greatness
into an abstract idea of the Holy. This vision is watery because it is
unorganized, chaotic, a wilful consequence of the ignorance that
attends the desperate longings by which we seek to escape Experience. The "Slumberous Man," seeking to evade the confrontation of
himself, resigned all of his values to Urizen, the broken head of his
former unity.

This could not be borne by the anguished emotions, the spectral
Luvah who wrestled with Albion above the corpse of Eternity. All
this is in the past, for Nights I and II are now being retold from
Ahania's perspective. To Albion, Luvah seemed like the Satan of the
Book of Job, for Albion, like Job, was left "cover'd with boils from
head to foot." In anger, Man put forth Luvah from his presence,

and so began the orthodox tradition of associating emotional energy
with Satan, a tradition vigorously assaulted in *The Marriage of
Heaven and Hell*, as we have seen.

Ahania ends her recital of dire events past by an ambiguous account
of the subsequent fall of Luvah and Vala, the passional life of mankind.

> "They heard the Voice & fled swift as the
>   winter's setting sun.
> And now the Human Blood foam'd high. I saw
>   that Luvah & Vala
> Went down the Human Heart where Paradise &
>   its joys abounded,
> In jealous fears, in fury & rage, & flames
>   roll'd round their fervid feet,
> And the vast form of Nature like a Serpent
>   play'd before them;
> And as they went in folding fires & thunders
>   of the deep,
> Vala shrunk in like the dark sea that leaves
>   its slimy banks,
> And from her bosom Luvah fell far as the
>   east & west
> And the vast form of Nature like a Serpent
>   roll'd between.
> Whether this is Jerusalem or Babylon we know
>   not.
> All is Confusion. All is tumult, & we alone
>   are escaped."
> She ended, for his wrathful throne burst
>   forth the black hail storm.

The dramatic fervor of this passage is justified by its *rightness*;
these are the exact tones in which the merciful element in the mind
would react to the collapse of love into organic cycle, of creative
passion into the Serpent of Nature. The final lines carry the vital
question. Ahania is in Urizen's realm, but is that state the Jerusalem
of Man's outer being in the full freedom that once was his, or is it

the Babylon of the fallen tyrannies of this world? Urizen cannot abide the question, and replies with the hatred of the wrathful sky-gods for any hint of opposition:

> "Am I not God?" said Urizen, "Who is Equal to me?
>   Do I not stretch the heavens abroad, or fold
>   them up like a garment?"
> He spoke, mustering his heavy clouds around
>   him, black, opake.
> Then thunders roll'd around & lightnings darted
>   to & fro;
> His visage chang'd to darkness, & his strong
>   right hand came forth
> To cast Ahania to the Earth. He siez'd her by
>   the hair
> And threw her from the steps of ice that froze
>   around his throne,
> Saying: "Art thou also become like Vala? thus
>   I cast thee out!
> Shall the feminine indolent bliss, the
>   indulgent self of weariness,
> The passive idle sleep, the enormous night &
>   darkness of Death
> Set herself up to give her laws to the active
>   masculine virtue?"

In this passage Urizen determines his own fall, for to so completely reject the total form of everything one has loved is to guarantee the onset of self-destruction. The blindness of Urizen leads him to cast out the pleasures of meditation, and he cannot sustain the barrenness that must result. Urizen thinks that he is defending activity against passivity, the male against the female, and light against darkness, but this is the illusion of every intellectual system whatsoever. He has heard the truth about himself, but he avoids it by the conviction that what blackens the image of self is only "a wat'ry image/Reflecting all my indolence, my weakness & my death." Milton's Satan told Beelzebub that to be weak was miserable, doing or suffering, and Blake's Urizen is inverting that genuinely demonic lesson. What makes one miserable must be weakness and not conscience, and needs to be cast out, even if it has the form of our most intense desires. Urizen fears that Ahania is becoming another destructive Vala, but he cannot realize that if destructive sexual beauty has a male counterpart it is himself, the whirlpool of pride that is self-congratulatory intellect.

He has not long to wait for the personal consequences of his sanctimoniousness. With a tremendous crash the mathematic heavens so laboriously formed in Night II come hurling down, and the instinctual chaos of Night I is restored. In the wreck of Urizen the Spectre of Tharmas or Circle of Destiny rises again, as the shattered unity moves woefully to recover what little can be recovered:

> Tharmas rear'd up his hands & stood on the
>   affrighted Ocean.
> The dead rear'd up his Voice & stood on the
>   resounding shore,
>
> Crying: "Fury in my limbs! destruction in my
>   bones & marrow!
> My skull riven into filaments, my eyes into
>   sea jellies
> Floating upon the tide wander bubbling &
>   bubbling,
> Uttering my lamentations & begetting little
>   monsters
> Who sit mocking upon the little pebbles of
>   the tide
> In all my rivers & on dried shells that the
>   fish
> Have quite forsaken. O fool! fool! to lose
>   my sweetest bliss.
> Where art thou, Enion? ah too near to
>   cunning, too far off
> And yet too near. Dash'd down I send thee into
>   distant darkness
> Far as my strength can hurl thee; wander there
>   & laugh & play

Among the frozen arrows; they will tear thy
    tender flesh.
Fall off afar from Tharmas, come not too near
    my strong fury.
Scream & fall off & laugh at Tharmas, lovely
    summer beauty,
Till winter rends thee into Shivers as thou
    hast rended me."

This is poetry of so high an order that it renders one apologetic
to point out its excellence. But so little has been said to the purpose
about Blake's epic style that even obvious felicities are worth evidencing. Tharmas is dead or lost Innocence, the state of being fully
integrated Man, the power of harmony that we toil vainly all our
lives to find again. Tharmas is like Melville in the most memorable
of his poems, *After the Pleasure Party*, asking the most important of
questions:

What Cosmic jest or Anarch blunder
The human integral clove asunder
And shied the fractions through life's gate?

At the close of Night III Tharmas is the ghost of that human
integral, and his voice is the voice of chaos itself. In the passage
under discussion, chaos finds a voice unmatched in poetry before or
since, a bellowing, thundering, sobbing, bursting voice, to use Blake's
own adjectives for it. Tharmas has become the old man of the sea, or
the Demogorgon of the abyss, without shape or form. There is certainly an ironic humor in Blake's dramatization of this watery voice,
for not only the images of these lines but their passions as well are
altogether antithetical. Tharmas is conscious of the grotesque horror
of his metamorphosis: his filament-riven skull, his sea-jelly eyes. With
a shock we realize that this is *our* skull, these bulging protuberances
are *our* eyes, for we are Tharmas. And his pitiful attempts to overcome his hatred for Enion, his crippling desire for revenge; these are
our hesitations in love and forgiveness. Our emanation of lost Innocence seems "too near to cunning, too far off and yet too near."
    The fall of Urizen has restored nothing, for what has been liber-

ated is the indecisiveness that cannot take us out of the fallen world. Tharmas once was the power to realize desire; now he cannot even maintain himself in a desire. Enion hears hatred in his voice, and to escape plunges into the cold billows, a watery existence that withers her away into Entuthon Benithon, Blake's rather cumbersome name for "the forests of the night," or wilderness of Experience. Tharmas repents, too late, and finds she has become "Substanceless, voiceless, weeping, vanish'd, nothing but tears." Night III ends with Ahania taking Enion's wandering place on the edge of the Abyss. If she too falls over, then the joy of intellect, the mind's desire to be led on from delight to delight, will vanish. Poised on this verge of further cyclic calamity, the poem begins a new movement, exploring the consequences of the triple fall that has formed it, and seeking a gate to renewal.

Struggles of Contraries: Night IV, The Mission of Los

Tharmas, riding over his dark Abyss, sees Los and Enitharmon rise from it, and turns to them with apparently loving hope, for they are what remains of human possibility. Yet, being what he now is, the hope of Tharmas is not necessarily very admirable, any more than Los and Enitharmon now seem a very likely pair to bring about a salvation. When we last encountered them (towards the end of Night II) they were thoroughly Urizenic, and they seem to have been carried down in Urizen's descent. In the Abyss of instinct ruled by Tharmas, they long for the banished world built by "the Architect divine," Urizen. Tharmas vengefully divides them, and from this separation the most enigmatic of Blake's mythic beings is born:

> A shadow blue, obscure & dismal; like a
>   statue of lead
> Bent by its fall from a high tower, the
>   dolorous shadow rose.

These brilliant lines vividly present the Spectre of Urthona, the fearful ordinary ego or selfhood of fallen man, a shadow of the imaginative power man once possessed. Los has yet to mature into

the artist-prophet or capable imagination he is to become, but the
Spectre, who is the burden of self in every artist, is already a finished
being, leaden and twisted and paradoxically cloudy. A dialogue between the Spectre of Urthona and the stricken Tharmas serves to
review the events of the fall from Albion's unity. Tharmas turns from
the Spectre to charge the reluctant Los with his mission:

> Take thou the hammer of Urthona. Rebuild
>   these furnaces.
> Dost thou refuse? mind I the sparks that
>   issue from thy hair?
> I will compell thee to rebuild by these my
>   furious waves.

In orthodox mythic history, this is chaos come again, and a demonic being is forcing man's shaping power to do its work. From
Blake's Bible-of-Hell perspective, a false creation has yielded to a
genuine chaos, and for the better, since Los, however painfully, will
do eventually a more imaginative job of creating than Urizen could
do.

The central part of Night IV, Los's attempt to hammer the fallen
Urizen into definite form, is essentially a revision of the similar activity in *The Book of Urizen* and *The Book of Los*. Only the motive
of Los's fierce labors has changed. In the earlier poems Los sought
to set some limit to the changes of Urizen; to find some boundary
for the dissolving mind. Here, in *The Four Zoas*, Tharmas seeks,
through Los, a universe to rule over, even though it be one of death
and decay. Baffled instinctual forces will destroy what is being
renewed, yet they hope to find in renewal some little semblance of
the unsundered world that has been lost. Tharmas has no benevolent
intentions, but he believes that Enion may reappear, however fit-
fully, if some order other than rational can be imposed upon the
cosmos.

As Los works in his furnaces, raging against Tharmas, he creates
the divisions of time, the seven ages of man. In doing so he re-
fashions the mind in the image of Adamic man, the only image the
sundered prophet can visualize. But the vision of redemption, though
Los cannot see it at this point, enters again once the creation is

finished. Though Blake's myth still leaves a saving remnant of Eternity quite unaccountable, nevertheless the Savior who is to come in Luvah's robes now sets limits beyond which Albion and his components cannot fall. Albion will contract no further than Adam, and will reach his limit of Opacity or dead materiality in Satan, which is Urizen's name in time just as Los is Urthona's name in the fallen dimension.

A violent irony follows, as is customary in Blake. Los misunderstands this providential setting-of-limits, and drops his hammer in despair. "He became what he was doing: he was himself transform'd." After these many stages of fall we have come at last to what hurt Blake the most; the fall of the mortal poet's imagination, the darkening of creative vision in this world. As Night IV closes Los begins a terrible dance of transformation that will submit the poetic genius of man to the organic rigors of history.

Night V, The Orc Cycle Begins

Infected, Mad, he danc'd on his mountains
        high & dark as heaven,
Now fix'd into one stedfast bulk his features
        stonify,
From his mouth curses & from his eyes sparks
        of blighting,
Beside the anvil cold he danc'd with the
        hammer of Urthona,
Terrific, pale. Enitharmon stretched on the
        dreary earth
Felt her immortal limbs freeze, stiffning,
        pale, inflexible.
His feet shrink with'ring from the deep,
        shrinking & withering,
And Enitharmon shrunk up, all their fibres
        with'ring beneath,
As plants wither'd by winter, leaves &
        stems & roots decaying
Melt into thin air, while the seed driv'n
        by the furious wind,

Rests on the distant Mountain's top. So
    Los & Enitharmon,
Shrunk into fixed space stood trembling on
    a Rocky cliff,
Yet mighty bulk & majesty & beauty remain'd,
    but unexpansive.
As far as highest Zenith from the lowest
    Nadir, so far shrunk
Los from the furnaces a space immense, &
    left the cold
Prince of Light bound in chains of intellect
    among the furnaces;
But all the furnaces were out & the bellows
    had ceast to blow.

With this tremendous intensity, the fifth Night draws us into its frightening theme, the cycle of ironic repetitions that confines a merely organic energy, a desire that will not rise above the natural. In these lines Los's metamorphosis into our time becomes complete. Blake's passion is so black and majestic an emotion that most of his critics falsify it by evasion. The mountains are as dark and high as heaven, and as stonily deceptive. This is the existence of man, and man indeed at his imaginative best; an infected, mad dance into confinement, a withering up of our potential. Los dances brandishing the masterless hammer of Urthona, but he wields it vainly, for his anvil of creativity is cold. The effect of this wonderful passage is like the phenomenal effect of great cliff formations; inhuman, yet testifying to the fallen greatness of man, for to Blake these craggy barrennesses are the remnants of a human face, an apocalyptic Man seen afar, but dwindled into the gray particulars of isolated selves, of meaningless rock formations. In the furious wind of time Los shrinks away from his furnaces, and Urizen is left a cold monster bound in chains of intellect, waiting for a vivifying fire.

The night blows cold, and Enitharmon clings round the prophet's knees, shrieking in the dismal wind. There, in this ultimate badness, she brings forth a fresh life. The terrible scene around her shows Blake in his descriptive greatness:

> But from the caves of deepest night
> ascending in clouds of mist,
> The winter spread his wide black wings
> across from pole to pole;
> Grim frost beneath & terrible snow link'd
> in a marriage chain
> Began a dismal dance. The winds around on
> pointed rocks
> Settled like bats innumerable ready to fly
> abroad.
> The groans of Enitharmon shake the skies,
> the lab'ring Earth,
> Till from her heart rending his way a
> terrible child sprang forth
> In thunder, smoke & sullen flames & howlings
> & fury & blood.

This is the best of Blake's births of Orc, of unbounded energy breaking out of the zones of death and time, seeking its own freedom. Red Orc comes again, and after fourteen summers embraces his mother, as he did in the "Preludium" to *America*. The chain of jealousy, devouring, forms on the bosom of Los, and at last he yields to it, and nails Orc down upon a mountaintop, as in *The Book of Urizen*.

But Orc grows amid his chains, for life cannot be restrained. And even fallen Imagination learns, for Los repents, but too late. He comes, with Enitharmon, to free his son, but cannot:

> But when they came to the dark rock & to
> the spectrous cave,
> Lo, the young limbs had strucken root into
> the rock, & strong
> Fibres had from the Chain of Jealousy inwove
> themselves
> In a swift vegetation round the rock &
> round the Cave
> And over the immortal limbs of the terrible
> fiery boy.

In vain they strove now to unchain. In vain
    with bitter tears
To melt the chain of Jealousy; not Enitharmon's
    death,
Nor the Consummation of Los could ever melt
    the chain
Nor unroot the infernal fibres from their
    rocky bed,
Nor all Urthona's strength, nor all the
    power of Luvah's Bulls,
Tho' they each morning drag the unwilling
    Sun out of the deep,
Could uproot the infernal chain, for it had
    taken root
Into the iron rock & grew a chain beneath
    the Earth
Even to the Center, wrapping round the Center;
    & the limbs
Of Orc entering with fibres became one with
    him, a living Chain
Sustained by the Demon's life. Despair &
    Terror & Woe & Rage
Inwrap the Parents in cold clouds as they
    bend howling over
The terrible boy, till fainting by his side,
    the Parents fell.

In these lines, one of the darkest of Blake's themes finds its full expression. The torments of jealousy, so vividly set forth in *Visions of the Daughters of Albion* and the Notebook poems, achieve their masterpiece in this irreparable binding of Orc. Primal energy, the libido that springs ever upward, is permanently associated with Jealousy, and desire acquires forever its dark double, the ruin that shadows love. The Chain of Jealousy has become a swift *vegetation*; and once naturalized it is not to be rooted out but will grow into the Tree of Mystery. Los cannot know it as yet, but he has established what Northrop Frye so usefully termed "the Orc Cycle," the ironic myth by which Orc must be born only to grow and age into Urizen, the process described definitively in Blake's manuscript ballad, *The Mental Traveller*.

As in *The Book of Urizen* the voice of the bound Orc awakens Urizen from his deathly sleep; the mind comes to consciousness again in the most fallen of its forms when it is stung by the menace of rising bodily energy. In contemplating his own condition, Urizen nearly wins our sympathy by his beautiful lament that ends Night V. His song is built on the poignant contrast between his present state and his position in Eternity, a contrast that recalls the situation of Milton's Satan:

> I call'd the stars around my feet in the night
> of councils dark;
> The stars threw down their spears & fled
> naked away.
> We fell.

The reminder of *The Tyger* here is a clear association of that lyric with the fall of Urizen. The Bard of Experience, frightening himself into religious apprehensions, unconsciously satirized himself, for his Urizenic hymn had a hidden reference to Urizen's failure. Overcome by a consciousness of his loss Urizen resolves to explore the dens of the world in which he has awakened. He seeks to "find that deep pulsation that shakes my cavern with strong shudders," for the pulsation of Orc's energy is a threat to the bounded mind. With this unholy resolution to a sinister quest, Night V uneasily ends.

Night VI, The Dens of Urizen

To understand the heroic but negative activity of Urizen in Night VI, we need to review our knowledge of him until this time. Urizen began as the Prince of Light, the Zoa who had in his care the intellectual sun of Eternity, the human reason that was transcendent light, the head of the unfallen Albion. After his revolt against Man, Urizen altered, but did not immediately fall. The brain, for a while, survived the impairment of the body's instincts and the loins' affections. At this stage Urizen was a demiurge or mock-creator (as Blake took the Jehovah of Genesis to be). The faded Morning Star had light enough to design and build a model of the original cosmos, but this fallen creation could not last. When Urizen cast out Ahania he provided for his own fall as well, and his artifice of Eternity came crashing down with him. In the ensuing welter (Blake's parallel to the age of Noah's flood) the fallen Tharmas reassumed control, but with severely reduced power and with total loss of his vision of Innocence. Out of this second chaos Los, compelled by Tharmas, has rebuilt Urizen in mortal form, and has begun the cycles of history by fathering Orc on Enitharmon. It is at just this point that Urizen comes to consciousness again, but as a demoniac and emasculated mental force, determined to submit all of remaining reality to a parody of the intellectual faith that has been lost.

The doctrine of Urizen *is* the Christianity of all the churches, of every institutional and historical form of Christianity, so far as Blake is concerned (though one would hardly realize that from reading many of Blake's commentators). Urizen, stung to life again, explores his dens as Satan explored chaos in *Paradise Lost*, Book II. Satan sought an escape from Hell, and an entrance into Adam's realm. Urizen seeks only to know the dimensions of the fallen world, that he may consolidate it as his own domain. As he has lost much of his intellectual power, he will rely (like Milton's Satan) on cunning, and on the subtler artifice of Mystery, the element in orthodox religion Blake hated most passionately.

As he begins to explore his dens, Urizen suddenly is confronted by three unknown women, "who would not suffer him to approach, but drove him back with storms." This incident is based on Satan's meeting with his daughter, Sin, in *Paradise Lost*, Book II. Though a trinity suggesting the three Norns, these women are Urizen's unrecognized daughters, and represent the human body in its natural, given condition, the body fated to die. Blake had essayed just such an encounter in Tiriel's cursing of his children, particularly of his daughter Hela, a symbolic action later developed in *The Book of Urizen* VIII:3. The daughters prevent Urizen from satisfying his thirst at the river they guard, for they worship Tharmas, the watery god of chaotic nature. The eldest of them perpetually fills an urn and pours water from it, with "sighs & care," and seems to represent the sorrow of natural sexuality, the loins condemned to the meaning-lessness of mere repetition. She has a name written on her forehead, which suggests the apocalyptic Whore named Mystery in Revelation. The second, clad in blue, evidently is the fallen heart, for her power "draws all into a fountain at the rock of thy attraction." The blue color is an ironic reference to the Virgin's color in Catholic tradition, for this is clearly the deceptive and destructive female heart that Blake portrays. The third and youngest woman, clad in shining green, divides the river into four. She may represent the fallen mind, veg-etated and sundering, transforming the organic sense of primal Man into the four fallen senses. Whatever their precise meaning, these three daughters together embody the tyranny of nature over man.

As they and Urizen prepare for battle, there is mutual recognition. Urizen is horrified to see that these are indeed his daughters, for in Eternity they were visions of potential in the loins, heart, and mind of Man, and now they have withered into grotesque mate-rializations of those glorious conceptions. Unable to acknowledge his responsibility for these creatures, Urizen dismisses them with a curse.

The curse summons Tharmas, who arrives to offer Urizen a suicide pact, in one of Blake's grimmest incidents:

> For death to me is better far than life;
>   death my desire
> That I in vain in various paths have sought,
>   but still I live.
> The Body of Man is given to me. I seek in
>   vain to destroy,
> For still it surges forth in fish & monsters
>   of the deeps,
> And in these monstrous forms I Live in an
>   Eternal woe,
> And thou, O Urizen, art fall'n, never to be
>   deliver'd.
> Withhold thy light from me for ever & I
>   will withhold
> From thee thy food; so shall we cease to be,
>   & all our sorrows

> End, & the Eternal Man no more renew beneath
>   our power.
> If thou refusest, in eternal flight thy beams
>   in vain
> Shall pursue Tharmas, & in vain shalt crave
>   for food. I will
> Pour down my flight thro' dark immensity
>   Eternal falling.
> Thou shalt pursue me but in vain, till
>   starv'd upon the void
> Thou hang'st, a dried skin, shrunk up, weak
>   wailing in the wind.

The poetic greatness of these lines harbors in Blake's gift for vital-izing conceptual allegory. The reader needs to remember that this horrible offer is made by a ruined life-force to an intellect that can only murder to dissect, but the meaning of the passage cannot be reduced to such a translation. The meaning is very largely a func-tion of the marvelously rendered nervous diction of Tharmas, the despairing rhythms of an impulsive consciousness disgusted by the outward forms it is compelled to assume. Tharmas is immortal life ironically desiring only death, vainly seeking to destroy its indestruct-ible self. Sundered Innocence cannot bear its own disorganization, and reacts only with revulsion to every organizing propulsion put forth by its own evolutionary nature. Tharmas has become a polypus, a chaotic cluster that "surges forth in fish & monsters of the deeps." He knows that only total darkness can destroy "these monstrous forms," and such darkness can result only from a voluntary dimming of whatever light of intellect is left to the spinning chaos of our world. That intellect, such as it is, must feed upon the life that only Tharmas can provide. But Urizen does not even bother to reply to Tharmas, for the excellent reason that what Tharmas offers is no different from what Tharmas threatens. Even as before, Tharmas is too confused a being to express himself with consistency. The god who both entreated and threatened Enion, in mindless simultane-ity, now offers to withhold food from Urizen, and then threatens to do just that if Urizen refuses.

The pragmatic heroism of Urizen is expressed in his disdainful silence. He knows already that life will flee his analytical light, and he knows also how desperately he must forage for nourishment in the world of space and time. He explores his dens, resolutely making a path "toward the dark world of Urthona," that is, the fallen remnants of the quarter of the cosmos occupied by Urthona in Eternity, but now abandoned. Urizen seeks imaginative materials, but for a binding rather than a making function.

As Urizen journeys, he beholds the terrors of the Abyss, the ruined spirits of humanity. What he sees is our world:

> Scar'd at the sound of their own sigh that
> seems to shake the immense
> They wander Moping, in their heart a sun,
> a dreary moon,
> A Universe of fiery constellations in their
> brain;
> An earth of wintry woe beneath their feet,
> & round their loins
> Waters or winds or clouds or brooding
> lightnings & pestilential plagues.
> Beyond the bounds of their own self their
> senses cannot penetrate:
> As the tree knows not what is outside of
> its leaves & bark
> And yet it drinks the summer joy & fears
> the winter sorrow,
> So in the regions of the grave none
> knows his dark compeer
> Tho' he partakes of his dire woes & mutual
> returns the pang,
> The throb, the dolor, the convulsion, in
> soul-sickening woes.

The inner and the outer, once intimately connected, have drawn apart and the mind fevers at its own false creation. Blake describes here what he takes to be the primordial condition of fallen man, a state haunted by the consciousness of lost mythic connections, between man and nature, man and man, man and time, and man

and his own body. The passage describes, more brilliantly than any
I know in literature, the onset of phenomenological disorder, the
first signs of man's sick consciousness.

Horrors multiply, for what Urizen sees is the hell of unredeemed
nature, as Blake thought it to be. Even a catalog of these visions
is overwhelmingly dismal: torture chambers, marching armies of
Female Wills, "the forms of tygers & of Lions, dishumaniz'd men."
Just as the Bard of Experience dishumanized Man by seeing the
Urizenic vision of a Tyger of Wrath, so now Urizen himself is
affrighted by the multitudes of his own dishumanized forms.
Desperately he tries to confront these forms in organizing dialogue,
but the confrontations of Innocence are not so readily renewed:

> Oft would he stand & question a fierce
>   scorpion glowing with gold;
> In vain; the terror heard not. Then a
>   lion he would sieze
> By the fierce mane, staying his howling
>   course. In vain the voice
> Of Urizen, in vain the Eloquent tongue.
>   A Rock, a Cloud, a Mountain,
> Were now not Vocal as in Climes of happy
>   Eternity
> Where the lamb replies to the infant voice
>   & the lion to the man of years
> Giving them sweet instructions; where the
>   Cloud, the River & the Field
> Talk with the husbandman & shepherd. But
>   these attack'd him sore,
> Siezing upon his feet & rending the sinews;
>   that in Caves
> He hid, to recure his obstructed powers with
>   rest & oblivion.

Blake is condensing into a few lines what is at the same time
one of his central themes and major procedures. In Eternity life
confronted life, and nothing could dwindle to an object-status, for
every rock, cloud and mountain was like a man seen afar, and

seemed a man again when met face to face. Blake's Eternity is like Wordsworth's apocalyptic vision of the Simplon Pass in *The Prelude*, Book VI, where every crag speaks as if a voice were in it. The difference is that Wordsworth's Eternity is renewed by experiences in which nature overcomes nature, but Blake's Eternity cannot be renewed within natural experience at all.

Unable to re-establish a world of relationship, Urizen flees in terror from this ruined South (which had been his own quarter in Eternity). He cannot calm these elemental objects "because himself was subject"; he must alter his own ego, and he will not as yet attempt such a transformation. He turns instead towards the East, which had been the realm of Luvah.

But the heart of fallen reality has become a "dismal void," and so Urizen falls into "the Eastern vacuity, the empty world of Luvah." Urizen falls as far as the previously ordained Limit of Contraction, the dimensions of Adamic Man that Los has been forced to create. In this vacuous environment, within the limits of his fresh incarnation, Urizen turns to his most characteristic activities, the creation of Newtonian conceptions of space. He forms Vortexes, and these cause the living wheels of heaven to shrink away within, withering away. The Vortex, more fully developed in Blake's *Milton*, is another phenomenon indicating the world to be fallen, for the vision of Eternity is content with the infinite flat plain that reality offers to the healthy imagination. The vision of whirling immensities, the fallen imagination of space, is created by Urizen so as to fix reality "into another world better suited to obey his will."

As Urizen weeps hypocritically over what he is doing to mankind, he proceeds to become the Jehovah or aged sky-god of orthodoxy. His tears condense into the spider's Web of Religion, a net to catch all human aspiration. In frozen holiness, he moves into the world that was Urthona's, but is now the region where Los has confined the fresh passions of Orc. Urizen hears the howling of the child more and more distinctly, and redoubles his efforts when suddenly:

> full before his path,
> Striding across the narrow vale, the
> Shadow of Urthona

A Spectre Vast appear'd, whose feet & legs
    with iron scaled,
Stamp'd the hard rocks expectant of the
    unknown wanderer
Whom he had seen wandring his nether world
    when distant far,
And watch'd his swift approach; collected,
    dark, the Spectre stood.
Beside him Tharmas stay'd his flight &
    stood in stern defiance,
Communing with the Spectre who rejoic'd
    along the vale.

The Spectre of Urthona and Tharmas ally themselves against
Urizen, and in defense of Orc. In a previous book I have analyzed
this dramatic opposition as a parallel to a momentary alliance of the
ego and the id in protection of the libido against the wily arts of
the superego.[11] As a rough bringing-together of Blake and Freud
this had some suggestive value, but it now seems to me another
unnecessary reduction of Blake's poetic mythology into mental figures
less imaginative than Blake's own very subtle ones. Tharmas, like
the id, is the regent of bodily appetite, and Luvah-Orc is a life-force
rising from bodily appetite. But Freud located reason in the ego,
separating it from the moralizing function of the superego. Blake
assigns both reason and social morality to Urizen, and splits up the
ego into Los and the Spectre of Urthona, the "I" as potential creator and the "I" as selfhood, fearful and time-obsessed. Blake allows
therefore for two very different ideas of conflict in an individual
consciousness, one between id and restraining ego against superego,
the other between active and passive aspects of the true self.

The movement of Tharmas to bar Urizen from Orc is a turning
point in The Four Zoas, for by such a gesture Tharmas again affirms
the will to live. That the Spectre of Urthona should join in such
a movement is more of a surprise, and even more of an apocalyptic
portent. The buried life in Man is being threatened by a censorious
conformity, and the Spectre, though an insane and deformed
version of the creative impulse, cannot abide the threat. Yet, at this

point in Blake's epic, Urizen is powerful enough to offer battle to both chaotic space and chaotic time, as they seem to his limited vision:

> Then Urizen arose upon the wind, back many a
>   mile
> Retiring into his dire Web, scattering
>   fleecy snows
> As he ascended, howling loud; the Web
>   vibrated strong,
> From heaven to heaven, from globe to globe.
>   In vast excentric paths
> Compulsive roll'd the Comets at his dread
>   command, the dreary way
> Falling with wheel impetuous down among
>   Urthona's vales
> And round red Orc; returning back to Urizen
>   gorg'd with blood.
> Slow roll the massy Globes at his command,
>   & slow o'erwheel
> The dismal squadrons of Urthona; weaving the
>   dire Web
> In their progressions & preparing Urizen's
>   path before him.

The Web of Religion prepares Urizen's way before him, and from it the Spectre of Urthona and Tharmas flee. The Web is reality as seen through the hypocritical veil of religious mystery. Tharmas fears the Web because the finite vision of a cosmos that it imposes is a direct menace to his most vulnerable quality, his inability to renew all the stuff of life in an exclusively human form. The Spectre cannot withstand the Web because the Spectre *is*, in a sense, our fear of bodily death, of time's stop, and the Web fits our death into a pattern of inevitability. Tharmas and the Spectre of Urthona do not care enough for Orc to free him, but they understand that his continuance insures them against Urizen, the debased apprehension that would reduce them to components of the Web.

The struggles of Nights IV through VI resulted in Urizen's effort to rule as the god of the fallen world. Blake came at the close of Night VI to a crisis of his own imagination, though only a structural rather than a spiritual one, in my judgment. The crisis is not resolved adequately in *The Four Zoas*, which may have been a cause of Blake's decision to abandon the poem. To understand Blake's difficulties, the reader needs to examine carefully the sequence of events in the later sections of *The Four Zoas*, for the difficulties Blake encounters there are central to the modern imagination, and prophetic of the difficulties so often met and so infrequently mastered in the major poetry of our own time.

Threshold of Recovery:
Night VII, First Version. Crisis

It is customary to speak of Blake's two attempts at Night VII as two "versions," but the word is misleading if it is taken to mean that one is a revision of the other. They are rather alternate versions of a crucial section of the poem, and might better be called rival visions. On internal evidence the one beginning "Then Urizen arose" is the later of the two, and was probably written to replace the one now to be discussed. This first attempt was much revised by Blake, who clearly was unhappy with it, and who finally so scrambled the sequence of passages within it that a reader cannot be sure what the best and definitive sequence is.

As this first Night VII opens (to follow Blake's revised ordering) Urizen sits on the Rock of his covenant and proclaims his triumph. He has explored his dens, and is confident of mastery. Of his possible competitors, Los is at this point little more than a baffled prophet of carnage, a primitive poet whose expressiveness is confined to heroic battle hymns. Tharmas is a vengeful chaos, dimly aware that his "crystal form" of Innocence can return to him only if life can be fostered, but so chaotic and murderous in his own consciousness that he cannot retain his benevolent impulses more than momentarily. Luvah has vanished from the world, but Urizen will soon show a dim and troubled awareness that the imprisoned fresh vegetative life of Orc is a renovation of the absent Zoa of affection. There is no Spectre of Urthona in this first Night VII, so that we can surmise that he is a later conception of Blake, and appeared in Night VI only after the second Night VII was written.

Enitharmon has survived also, but like Los she represents a creativity degenerated into a lust for war, which in her appears as the Female Will to sexual dominion, just as it did in *Europe*. As such, Enitharmon is allied to Urizen.

After Urizen displays his confidence and Los, Tharmas, and Enitharmon are revealed in their ruin, the next movement in the first Night VII begins. Vala, now become Urizen's harlot, stands before the bound Orc, in a scene strongly resembling the "Preludium" to *America*. He breaks loose, but this time *after* she embraces his fire. He is defeated by Urizen's forces, and suffers a crucifixion, nailed to Urizen's Tree of Mystery. In his agony he becomes the Serpent form he previously inhabited in Urizen's orthodox vision of him, and his human form is lost. The Christ of each Orc cycle goes up the Tree of Mystery and becomes in time another Jehovah-Urizen, an Odin slain as a sacrifice to Odin, a perpetuating process by which God avoids a humanizing vision of himself.

The remainder of the first Night VII deals with an encounter between the Shadowy Female Vala and Tharmas still searching for his Enion. Each shows some evidence of understanding that they must admit love back into their universe, but neither has any apprehension of how their deliverance is to be accomplished. In the closing lines of this plainly unsatisfactory sequence of compulsions and faint hopes, an aggregate of Spectrous terror begins to solidify in the world and is named Satan, the Selfhood proper or Death, to be distinguished from the sick self-will of the creature we have met as the Spectre of Urthona, or spirit of temporal anxieties. The desire to clarify this difficult distinction, as Middleton Murry and Frye have in their separate ways surmised, was probably the cause of Blake's putting aside of this first Night VII, and his writing of the second and finer version.[12] There are some remarkable moments in the original Night VII, but the reader ought to neglect it for the definitive later version, which allows the poem to recover its coherence and the psychic immediacy of its theme. The crisis Blake had to master by discarding the earlier version was precisely that he had failed to bring the poem's story to a crisis; he discovered that he was inventing too exuberantly, and was not shaping Night VII to a point

of decision. That point comes, with power and clarity, in the later
Night VII, when Los and the Spectre of Urthona embrace, and
then are able to turn to Enitharmon as a unity. From this first reunion, the ultimate regenerations of a Last Judgement come to be
generated in turn, till Man is again made one.

Night VII, Later Version. Culmination

Until now, Blake's epic has lacked a true hero, quite deliberately,
for in fallen worlds where all action is equivocal, no hero can exist.
The principal protagonist of most of *The Four Zoas* has been
Urizen, just as Satan dominates the earlier books of *Paradise Lost*.
Blake's problem in his later version of Night VII and in Night VIII
is to define a hero and his antagonists, and so prepare for the
revelation of Night IX or "The Last Judgment."

The later version of Night VII opens with Urizen's triumph over
Tharmas and the Spectre of Urthona:

> Then Urizen arose. The Spectre fled &
>   Tharmas fled;
> The dark'ning Spectre of Urthona hid
>   beneath a rock.
> Tharmas threw his impetuous flight thro' the
>   deeps of immensity
> Revolving round in whirlpools fierce, all
>   round the cavern'd worlds.

Urizen does not pursue them but descends silently to the Caves
of Orc, where the red child suffers Promethean torments. Urizen
does not approach too close to this ferocious being, but seats himself on a rock and ranges his books of morality around him for protection, while he broods enviously over the energetic life of the child.
The envy of Urizen infects his subordinate Los, in a remarkably
fused passage:

> Los felt the Envy in his limbs like to a
>   blighted tree,

For Urizen fix'd in envy sat brooding &
    cover'd with snow;
His book of iron on his knees, he trac'd the
    dreadful letters
While his snows fell & his storms beat to
    cool the flames of Orc
Age after Age, till underneath his heel a
    deadly root
Struck thro' the rock, the root of Mystery
    accursed shooting up
Branches into the heaven of Los; they,
    pipe form'd, bending down
Take root again whereever they touch,
    again branching forth
In intricate labyrinths o'erspreading
    many a grizly deep.

Here rock and sky are joined together by the mysterious envy of
vegetative intellect for human energy, in a symbolism we have already examined in *The Human Abstract* of Experience. Urizen's
hatred of Orc is the hatred of youth by age, revolt by reaction, the
lively by the deadness of convention. But Blake does not simplify
the hatred into any pattern; the "intricate labyrinths" of envy take
root wherever they touch, and have as many sources as they have
victims. Moreover they blight the envious, and even Urizen is amazed
and discomfited by the sudden growth of a Tree of Mystery. The
Tree's growth Blake had described vividly in *The Book of Ahania*,
where he had associated its name with the Mystery of Revelation
17:5, "Babylon the Great, the mother of harlots and abominations of
the earth," or Blake's Vala in her later career. The tree, as many
Blake scholars have evidenced, has a literary source in *Paradise Lost*,
IX, 1101–10, where it is the banyan from which Adam and Eve take
fig leaves to cover their nakedness, after they have attained knowledge of good and of evil. To Blake the banyan and the Tree of
Knowledge were the same Tree of Mystery, and belonged to Urizen,
the god of repressive morality.

With great pain Urizen drags his books of wisdom "out of the
dismal shade," but he cannot disentangle "the book of iron," a clear

association of the oppressive mysteries of morality and warfare. Free to ponder on Orc again, Urizen finally dares a direct address to his contrary principle:

> Pity for thee mov'd me to break my dark
>   & long repose,
> And to reveal myself before thee in a form
>   of wisdom.
> Yet thou dost laugh at all these tortures
>   & this horrible place;
> Yet throw thy limbs these fires abroad that
>   back return upon thee
> While thou reposest, throwing rage on rage,
>   feeding thyself
> With visions of sweet bliss far other than
>   this burning clime.
> Sure thou art bath'd in rivers of delight,
>   on verdant fields
> Walking in joy, in bright Expanses sleeping
>   on bright clouds
> With visions of delight so lovely that they
>   urge thy rage
> Tenfold with fierce desire to rend thy chain
>   & howl in fury
> And dim oblivion of all woe & desperate repose.
> Or is thy joy founded on torment which others
>   bear for thee?

Two mythic analogues are in the background of this situation: the story of Prometheus and the confrontations of Satan and the young Christ in Milton's *Paradise Regained*. Neither is an exact parallel, but each contributes an element of meaning to Blake's vision of dialogue between a Prince of the powers of the air and an earth-bound Titan who must suffer for his passionate desires. Just as Satan wishes to confirm his suspicion that Christ is indeed the Son of God, so Urizen seeks to know with certainty whether the bound figure before him is a rebirth of his heavenly rival, Luvah. Just as Zeus desired to convert Prometheus to his own cause, moved by fears of futurity, so the doubting Urizen wishes to make Orc into himself, lest Orc prove his destroyer.

The hypocrisy of Urizen is paradoxically an honest one; he does feel pity but his tears solidify into the Web of Religion, for his are the negative virtues of the Human Abstract, of a bound that must find a center of energy to enclose. He cannot understand Orc's terrible laughter, the mocking scorn of pain, and so he asks the properly Satanic question: "Or is thy joy founded on torment which others bear for thee?" Urizen has gotten the truth just the wrong way round; what he fears is that Orc's torment should prove vicarious, a suffering for the salvation of others.

Orc's reply is what we might expect, knowing that vehement spirit from *America:*

> Thy Pity I contemn. Scatter thy snows
>   elsewhere.
> I rage in the deep, for Lo, my feet &
>   hands are nail'd to the burning rock,
> Yet my fierce fires are better than thy
>   snows. Shudd'ring thou sittest.
> Thou art not chain'd. Why shouldst thou
>   sit cold grovelling, demon of woe,
> In tortures of dire coldness? now a Lake
>   of waters deep
> Sweeps over thee freezing to solid; still
>   thou sit'st clos'd up
> In that transparent rock as if in joy of
>   thy bright prison,
> Till, overburden'd with its own weight
>   drawn out thro' immensity,
> With a crash breaking across, the horrible
>   mass comes down
> Thund'ring, & hail & frozen iron hail'd from
>   the Element
> Rends thy white hair; yet thou dost, fix'd
>   obdurate, brooding sit
> Writing thy books. Anon a cloud fill'd
>   with a waste of snows

> Covers thee, still obdurate, still resolv'd
>   & writing still;
> Tho' rocks roll o'er thee, tho' floods pour,
>   tho' winds black as the sea
> Cut thee in gashes, tho' the blood pours
>   down around thy ankles,
> Freezing thy feet to the hard rock, still
>   thy pen obdurate
> Traces the wonders of Futurity in horrible
>   fear of the future.

This begins as Promethean defiance and rapidly becomes a sustained recognition of Urizen's true state, closed up in the rock of ultimate error, self-regarding contemplation. The emblems of Urizen's condition, barren rock and vaporous cloud, are also presages of his dire future, to be lost in the indefinite, bound into chaos. Urizen's reply is to summon his three daughters, whom he had cursed when exploring his dens. Now they are compelled by him to labor at kneading Orc's bread, the fruit of the Tree of Mystery, as we learn in Night VIII. The bread of Orc, as is proper for the material sustenance of that raging energy, is sexual in origin, but morbidly so, for Orc is made by Urizen to feed upon frustrations. Urizen's daughters represent the vision of the fallen body as a triple prison, the head, heart, and sexual organs turned into confinements. Orc listens to their despairing songs, "hung'ring on the cold wind that swagg'd heavy with the accursed dough." As they labor upon Urizen's rock, their now genuinely Satanic father reads them a sermon from his book of brass. All the force of Blake's prophetic indignation, rendered more effective by the irony of the presentation, is gathered together in this masterpiece of Urizenic counsel:

> Compell the poor to live upon a Crust of
>   bread, by soft mild arts.
> Smile when they frown, frown when they smile;
>   & when a man looks pale
> With labour & abstinence, say he looks healthy
>   & happy;

And when his children sicken, let them die;
    there are enough
Born, even too many, & our Earth will be overrun
Without these arts. If you would make the
    poor live with temper,
With pomp give every crust of bread you give;
    with gracious cunning
Magnify small gifts; reduce the man to want a
    gift & then give with pomp.
Say he smiles if you hear him sigh. If pale,
    say he is ruddy.
Preach temperance: say he is overgorg'd &
    drowns his wit
In strong drink, tho' you know that bread &
    water are all
He can afford. Flatter his wife, pity his
    children, till we can
Reduce all to our will, as spaniels are taught
    with art.

Mark Schorer comments usefully on this passage that "not only does it caricature the eighteenth-century concept of benevolence, but it attacks the Malthusian theory of population" as well.[18] Blake attributes to Urizen what he most hated in the supposed moral wisdom of his time, rationalizations that tried to justify or explain away the sufferings of the exploited poor in England. The wisdom of Urizenic intellectuals like Malthus, as Blake sees in a flash of insight, is a kind of Pavlovian conditioning that will reduce the poor to the status of spaniels.

This is Blake at his most direct. The rest of Urizen's sermon is not less effective for being mythic in expression. He is confident that the song of Moral Duty as sung by his daughters will serve to draw down Enitharmon beneath the Tree of Mystery, where she will be given to the Spectre of Urthona, whom Los will then have to serve in jealous fury. If the perceptive powers of man are thus given over to his fearful and time-harried will, if the positive side of his ego is to yield to the negative, then the fallen state will never be overturned.

Though Orc rages against the "cold hypocrite," he realizes that
he has begun to weaken. In desperation, Orc reveals his true identity:

> Art thou the cold attractive power that holds
>   me in this chain?
> I well remember how I stole thy light & it
>   became fire
> Consuming. Thou Know'st me now O Urizen
>   Prince of Light,
> And I know thee; is this the triumph, this
>   the Godlike State?

Orc is both Phaethon and Prometheus, and shares in their errors,
but as Luvah he has reminded Urizen of how mutual the responsibility for the Fall is. Urizen is terrified, yet he has triumphed, for
now the Orc cycle completes itself, as Orc "began to organize a
Serpent body." The strength of organic energy has not been enough
to resist the cunning of Urizen, and Orc is compelled in serpent
form to "stretch out & up the mysterious tree," a crucified god of
death to be worshipped as the son of Jehovah-Urizen. The equivocal
vision of Blake's minor poems has reached its own destruction; Orc
is not a liberator but only a sacrifice of life to death. Political revolution is just that, revolution, the revolving of another cycle of
revolt aging into repression, Orc dying into Urizen's religion, the
French Revolution passing into the despotism of Napoleon.

With Orc's transformation complete, Night VII starts a new movement, in which Los for the first time assumes a semblance of the
heroic role he will take on so fully in *Jerusalem*. Yet one can hardly
believe at first that this deluded being is capable of more than
passive suffering or of some malforming directed by a superior intellect or will. We see Los once again as a victim of jealousy, tormented by the vengeful Enitharmon. He sings a beautiful lament
for his withdrawn emanation, yet it avails him nothing, for she has
entered upon the final stages of her fall. As the Shadow of Enitharmon (deftly translated by Frye as "yardstick space") she descends
down the Tree of Mystery to embrace the Spectre of Urthona
(named by Frye, in this context, as "clock time").[14] What we have
in this encounter is the meeting of a decayed imaginative will, the

day-to-day life of even a poet like Blake, with the decayed joy of imagination that any poet's beloved is likely to become. Shelley, who understood this dialectic of love and creativity as well as Blake did, spoke of it in *Prometheus Unbound* as the ruin or desolation that shadows love, the dark double of any creative impulse. I have noted before that the Spectre of Urthona appears in Shelley as the First Spirit in the great (and neglected) lyric, *The Two Spirits: An Allegory*. Like Blake, Shelley was counting the cost of vision, and finding that its price was all that a poet was.

The dialogue between the Spectre of Urthona and the Shadow of Enitharmon is altogether sinister, and its very accents are made to testify to a sickness of spirit, the exhaustion of imagination. The Shadow of Enitharmon, like Eve in *Paradise Lost*, is "intoxicated with the fruit of this delightful tree," and so is prepared to embrace the Spectre, though she finds him a horrible form. She shows her passion for the Spectre by giving him her own account of Albion's fall. In this version, Albion is again spoken of as having taken Vala for his beloved, and so preparing the circumstances that will lead to his fall. But a new event is inserted into the story; Urizen was born as an altogether separate being from that unfortunate union, so that his motive for rebellion against Albion now takes on an Oedipal element.

The Spectre replies with a speech that hovers on the edge of imaginative understanding, showing us the inadequacy of the fallen will, bemused by its own fear of temporal decay:

> Thou knowest that the Spectre is in Every
>   Man insane, brutish,
> Deform'd; that I am thus a ravening devouring
>   lust, continually
> Craving & devouring; but my Eyes are always
>   upon thee, O lovely
> Delusion, & I cannot crave for any thing but
>   thee; & till
> I have thee in my arms & am again united to Los
> To be one body & One spirit with him. Not so
> The Spectres of the Dead, for I am as the
>   Spectre of the Living.

All that is lacking from this declaration is the Spectre's realization that it is capable of the breakthrough to Eternity that it so desires. Lacking this, the Spectre prematurely embraces the Shadow of Enitharmon in the act of love, engendering a "wonder horrible" that is to consolidate as an ultimate form of error in Night VIII as a freshly incarnated Vala. Time and Space, Will and Female Will, have been brought together to breed a monster that will culminate the rough bestiality of Experience. The pathetic irony is that the Spectre of Urthona knows that the Female world he embraces is only a "lovely Delusion," but his desperate impatience betrays him.

Sharp upon this climax Blake moves to a contrary mingling:

> But then the Spectre enter'd Los's bosom.
> Every sigh & groan
> Of Enitharmon bore Urthona's Spectre on
> its wings.
> Obdurate Los felt Pity. Enitharmon told
> the tale
> Of Urthona. Los embrac'd the Spectre,
> first as a brother,
> Then as another Self, astonish'd, humanizing
> & in tears,
> In Self abasement Giving up his Domineering
> lust.

In this moment, necessarily both in and out of time, fallen man's will and imagination are joined again, and the humanizing process at last begins. The Spectre, for all its fear of daily hazards, can utter fundamental truth to Los. By this astonishing revelation Los learns the necessity of "Self annihilation," the overcoming of the impulse to appropriate for oneself, and by sharing reaches reality. Yet salvation is not to be achieved so easily; Enitharmon flees from her reunited lovers to the shade of Urizen's tree. Though abandoned by her, Los and the Spectre of Urthona commence the building of Blake's New Jerusalem, a spiritual London like Spenser's Cleopolis, named Golgonooza (perhaps New Golgotha, as Foster Damon and Margoliouth have surmised).

Though the rebuilding of Eternity through art has begun, Los

cannot prevail in his new realization of truth. Like Milton's Adam
he is too much attached to his beloved, and he joins Enitharmon
in eating of the fruit of Urizen's Tree of Mystery, though like Adam
he knows better. As in Milton, the fruit is the knowledge of the
negations of moral good and moral evil, a denial of existential contraries, a divorce between the Heaven of intellect and the Hell of
passion. Los plucks the fruit, eats of it, and sits down in despair, to
be comforted by "Urthona's spectre in part mingling with him,"
so that time begins to serve as a consoler and redeemer for the
despondent imagination.

One of Blake's most moving myths now emerges out of the co-
operation of Los and his brotherly Spectre. The Spectre weeps in
contrition, blaming himself for the dreadful state of separation,
which is true enough, as he can be equated with that element in
Urthona that caused the Divine Smith to drop his hammer and suffer
a failure of nerve at the end of Night I. The Spectre of Urthona can
be saved, as he now realizes, because he has a "counterpart" in Los,
an impulse that can be merged with him to produce a creative will,
to put an integrating power into time. But what of the other Spectres
of human existence, doomed to a sleep of death without such "counterparts?" The conceptual image here turns upon the necessity of
saving a world without poetry by merging poetry with it; to make
imaginative counterparts for the mass of men.

Los answers his Spectre by urging upon him the inward vision
of the archetypal counterpart, Christ, named here as "the Lamb of
God clothed in Luvah's robes of blood descending to redeem."
The Spectre responds to this vision, but Enitharmon does not.
Despite her refusal to participate, Los feels the imaginative desire
to "fabricate embodied semblances," artifices of eternity, in which
the dead can live again, to form a world "to comfort Orc in his dire
sufferings." The desire of Los is the desire of Blake, and *The Four
Zoas* is such a world. In this aesthetic resolve Los suddenly recaptures
the fire of Urthona, the creative strength of God or eternal Man:

> look! my fires enlume afresh
> Before my face ascending with delight as
> in ancient times!

Moved by this renewal of Los's inspiration, Enitharmon comes at last to encourage him in his labors. His creations appear first as his sons, Rintrah and Palamabron, Hebraic prophet of wrath and Greek oracle of compassion, spirits of fathering civilization. What remains of Orc is comforted by their appearance, as is Tharmas, who in these signs of fresh life reads a presage of the return of Enion. Even Urizen is sundered by this resurgence of art; the creative remnant in him is reborn in Rintrah, but his Spectre will not allow itself to be drawn away, and will appear as the Satan-Urizen of Night VIII. As Night VII ends Los is astonished to find that he loves what in Urizen can be saved:

> Startled was Los; he found his Enemy Urizen now
> In his hands; he wonder'd that he felt love
>   & not hate.
> His whole soul loved him; he beheld him an
>   infant
> Lovely breath'd from Enitharmon; he trembled
>   within himself.

Night VII, in this revised version, has given birth to dual transformations of psychic potential. The first has left us with a shadowy female, Vala, the delusive beauty of nature, and with a Satanic Urizen, the concentration of everything deathly in the fallen intellect. The second has given us a Los reformed into a poet-prophet like Blake himself, capable of loving everything that is most opposed to him. From the conflict of these two principles, that toward natural death and that toward imaginative life, the antimonies of Night VIII will be formed.

Night VIII, The Ashes of Mystery

As Albion lies upon the oozy Rock of nature, trapped in the horrible dreams that have constituted the first seven Nights of Blake's poem, the remnant of Eternity meet as "one Man, Even Jesus" to fix again the Adamic limit of Contraction, the point beyond which the human can never fall. With this limit set, Albion begins to stir in his sleep, "to wake upon the Couch of Death." Like the Shunammite's son in II Kings 4:35, Albion's sign of reviving life is that "he sneezed seven times." Touched by Elisha the prophet's staff, the Shunammite's child "sneezed seven times, and the child opened his eyes." Blake's homely metaphor based upon this implies that Albion must rasp through seven Orc cycles before the final opening of his eyes into the light of Eternity.

The stirring of Albion awakens the evidences of love in his children. Los beholds the Divine Vision through the broken gates of Enitharmon's heart, for the natural heart now begins to be overcome by imaginative promptings. In a wonderful transformation Enitharmon, who has symbolized the female will toward dominion, now turns to a benefactress:

> Then Enitharmon erected Looms in
>   Luban's Gate
> And call'd the Looms Cathedron; in these Looms
>   she wove the Spectres
> Bodies of Vegetation, singing lulling Cadences
>   to drive away
> Despair from the poor wondering spectres, and
>   Los loved them
> With a parental love, for the Divine hand was
>   upon him
> And upon Enitharmon, & the Divine Countenance
>   shone
> In Golgonooza. Looking down, the Daughters
>   of Beulah saw
> With joy the bright Light, & in it a Human form,
> And knew he was the Saviour, Even Jesus &
>   they worshipped.

Luban is perhaps an alternate name for Mount Ararat, where the Ark of Noah came to rest.[15] As a gate of the New Golgotha that is Blake's City of Art, Luban symbolizes a rest for the spectres of men from the tormented flood of Experience. The Looms of Enitharmon, called Cathedron (why, I am uncertain) are a generative artifice of mercy, the use of natural existence for the purpose of imaginative redemption.[16] The furnaces of Los in his City of Art constitute a similar artifice of eternity, by which natural substances are hammered into enduring forms. Enitharmon has become the providence of space and Los the redeeming power of time; once the movement to apocalypse begins death is changed into sleep, and the sleeping forms of space and time can be transmuted into the human forms of art. The human form finally rendered by art is, for Blake, the human form divine of Jesus, and now becomes evident as the last temporal appearance of the fallen Zoa of the power of love.

When the Spectre of Urizen sees this appearance, he is perplexed and terrified, for he sees at once this new Luvah or passional man and also the old Luvah or Orc, whom he has metamorphized into a Serpent of Mystery. In desperation, the spectral Urizen emulates Milton's Satan and invents engines of war "to undermine the World of Los & tear bright Enitharmon to the four winds." But this assault upon futurity is misdirected:

> Terrified & astonish'd, Urizen beheld the
> battle take a form
> Which he intended not; a Shadowy
> hermaphrodite, black & opake;
> The soldiers nam'd it Satan, but he was yet
> unform'd & vast.
> Hermaphroditic it at length became, hiding
> the Male
> Within as in a Tabernacle, Abominable, Deadly.

Blake's Satan is a shadowy Hermaphrodite because he embodies the self-congratulatory state of Ulro, the chaotic condition in which a brooding subject endeavors to contemplate all reality as being drawn up into itself. In this absorption of the object-world into a solipsistic consciousness, the emanative or created world vanishes, and the spectral brooder is alone with himself. In the Eden that was Eternity, the subject was a creator and the object-world his creation. In the Beulah of human sexuality at its most liberating, the subject is male and his objective counterpart a woman. In generative Experience subject and object are separated, but maintain the integrity of independent existence. Blake's Satan is an Hermaphrodite be-cause, as Frye remarks, he represents a sterile fusion of male subject and female object "into an indivisible abstract or spectral world."[17]

Vala, the Shadowy Female of natural attractiveness, judges the descending savior to be "the murderer of my Luvah, cloth'd in robes of blood." She is Isis, mother and mistress of Osiris, properly seeing in Jesus a final replacement for the cyclic vegetative god of natural religion, and calling to Satan-Urizen for revenge against the new revelation.

As this revenge prepares itself, Los and Enitharmon re-create Jerusalem, the spiritual liberty of mankind, and the lost emanation of Albion. Against this liberty, celebrated in an Edenic song of thanksgiving, are now set the forces of despotic hatred. Satan and Vala we know already, but two other females also appear with Satan, Tirzah and Rahab. Tirzah is the Mother Nature of *Songs of Experience*, the mother of man's mortality, the molder of the cruelty of the natural heart. Rahab, a redeemed harlot in the Book of Joshua and in Dante, is identified directly by Blake with the un-redeemable harlot of Babylon, the Mystery of the book of Revelation. Blake departs quite deliberately from the figurative or typological reading of Rahab in the Bible of Heaven, and presents us with his Bible of Hell's most sinister female. For Rahab is an orthodox type of the Church, identified by traditional commentary (and Dante) with the bride of the Song of Songs. Erich Auerbach, interpreting Dante's Rahab, can explain for us the basis of Blake's powerful and intense reversal of orthodox vision:

> Concerning Rahab, all ancient commentators consider her as a type of the church; her house alone, with all its in-habitants, escapes perdition, just as the church of the faithful will alone be saved when Christ appears for the last judgment; she found freedom from the fornication of the world by way of the window of confession, to which she bound the scarlet rope, the sign of Christ's blood, *sanguinis Christi signum*. Thus she is *figura Ecclesiae*, and the scarlet rope, like the posts struck with the blood of the Lamb in Exodus, becomes the figure of Christ's redeeming sacrifice.[18]

As an interpretation of Joshua 2, this kind of typology plainly would have infuriated Blake. For him Rahab is indeed the Church, all the Churches, but she is unceasing in her whoredoms, and no one is to be saved through her. Blake identifies the Rahab of Jericho with the other Rahab of the Old Testament, the sea monster associated with Egypt and Babylon in the Psalms and Isaiah, and therefore a type of Job's Leviathan. This Rahab Blake identifies also with the Covering Cherub of Ezekiel, once an inhabitant of Eden, but now a demon blocking man's way back to Paradise. If the reader will forgive all this complexity of Biblical reference, he ought by now to have a good notion of what Blake's Rahab is. She is the emblem of earthly political tyranny (Egypt, Babylon, the English state church) and of spiritual tyranny as well, any supposedly Christian church's claim to exclusive salvation. Such a claim is a Covering Cherub or Leviathan straddling nature and separating mankind and imaginative redemption. Blake, in *Milton*, calls Rahab "Religion hid in War," a profound description of the treacherous (and all but canonized) whore of Jericho, the woman who was Egypt, Babylon, and Rome, and who for Blake was London and Canterbury in his own time.

Rahab appears by Satan's side when he calls together "twelve rocky unshap'd forms" in Amalek, a land hostile to Israel, and therefore to Albion. They are a deadly jury to try the Lamb of God, to number him among the transgressors against Urizenic law. Amidst them beamed:

> A False Feminine Counterpart Lovely of
>   Delusive Beauty,
> Dividing & Uniting at will in the Cruelties
>   of Holiness,
> Vala, drawn down into a Vegetated body,
>   now triumphant.
> The Synagogue of Satan Clothed her with
>   Scarlet robes & Gems,
> And on her forehead was her name written in
>   blood, "Mystery."
> When view'd remote, she is One; when view'd
>   near she divides

To multitude, as it is in Eden, so permitted
    because
It was the best possible in the State called
    Satan, to save
From Death Eternal & to put off Satan
    Eternally.
The Synagogue Created her from Fruit of
    Urizen's tree
By devilish arts abominable, unlawful,
    unutterable,
Perpetually vegetating in detestable births
Of female forms, beautiful thro' poisons
    hidden in secret
Which give a tincture to false beauty; there
    was hidden within
The bosom of Satan The false Female, as in
    an ark & veil
Which Christ must rend & her reveal. Her
    daughters are call'd
Tirzah; She is named Rahab; their various
    divisions are call'd
The daughters of Amalek, Canaan & Moab
    binding on the stones
Their victims, & with knives tormenting them,
    singing with tears
Over their victims.

The New Testament rhetoric of "Satan's Synagogue" is part of
Blake's attack on the churches; in his vision as the Jewish Church
was then, so is the Church of England in his own time. Vala, the
delusion of beauty, but a genuine delusion in that she is all too
lovely, in this passage merges into the identity of Rahab or the
visible church. The stone altars and knives of sacrifice are Druidic,
transferred here to the heathen nations. The sacrifice of the last incarnation of Luvah, bound upon the stems of the vegetative universe,
is followed by an epiphany of Rahab. She stands before Los in her
pride among the furnaces of poetic creation, but he confronts her
with tenderness, seeking to win her away from Satan:

> Los wip'd the sweat from his red brow &
>   thus began
> To the delusive female forms shining among
>   his furnaces:
> "I am that shadowy Prophet who six thousand
>   years ago
> Fell from my station in the Eternal bosom.
>   I divided
> To multitude, & my multitudes are children
>   of Care & Labour.
> O Rahab, I behold thee. I was once like
>   thee, a Son
> Of Pride, and I also have pierc'd the Lamb
>   of God in pride & wrath."

The times are close to completion as Los recounts his generations, and defines the "State nam'd Satan" as one that cannot be redeemed. He presents the vision of the Seven Eyes of God, and urges Rahab to set Jerusalem free, but:

> Rahab, burning with pride & revenge, departed
>   from Los.
> Los drop'd a tear at her departure, but he
>   wip'd it away in hope.
> She went to Urizen in pride; the Prince of
>   Light beheld
> Reveal'd before the face of heaven his
>   secret holiness.
>
> Darkness & sorrow cover'd all flesh.
>   Eternity was darken'd.

Even the Spectral Urizen has just enough of the human left in him to feel banefully the presence of Rahab, his secret pride of holiness utterly revealed for what it is, the female death, a dull and numbing stupor. Like the Lucifer of Dante or the Satan of Milton

he becomes a supine being, "and his immense tail lash'd the Abyss."
His embrace of Rahab makes him the great Dragon of the Revelation of John the Divine, rising in the form of the serpentine Orc
of Mystery.

As Urizen "forgets his wisdom in the abyss," Tharmas and Urthona
give their power to Los for the approaching contest. If Error is about
to fully reveal itself, the same revelation may serve to uncover reality,
as Tharmas and Urthona are dimly aware.

The voices of the outcasts, Ahania and Enion, now rise again,
presaging apocalypse. The chant of Ahania is a pure lament, for
the mind's eye cannot see what is about to come, but the great song
of Eternity returns once more in the instinctual suppressed joy of
Innocence as Enion cries aloud:

> The Lamb of God has rent the Veil of Mystery,
>   soon to return
> In Clouds & Fires around the rock & the
>   Mysterious tree.
> And as the seed waits Eagerly watching for
>   its flower & fruit,
> Anxious its little soul looks out into the
>   clear expanse
> To see if hungry winds are abroad with their
>   invisible array,
> So Man looks out in tree & herb & fish &
>   bird & beast,
> Collecting up the scatter'd portions of his
>   immortal body
> Into the Elemental forms of every thing that
>   grows.

This is the faith of organized Innocence, the wisdom born of
sundering, the hand that inflicted the wound now learning to heal
it. The scattered components of man in nature are now collected
up by man into everything that grows, in preparation for a great
harvest and vintage of the nations. Whatever grows, whatever passes
through generation, is now a stage towards redemption:

And in the cries of birth & in the groans of
    death his voice
Is heard throughout the Universe. Whereever a
    grass grows
Or a leaf buds, The Eternal Man is seen, is
    heard, is felt,
And all his sorrows, till he reassumes his
    ancient bliss.

Even as these portents mount, Rahab mounts also to her triumph:

Rahab triumphs over all. She took Jerusalem
Captive, a Willing Captive, by delusive arts
    impell'd
To worship Urizen's Dragon form, to offer
    her own Children
Upon the bloody Altar. John saw these things
    Reveal'd in Heaven
On Patmos Isle, & heard the souls cry out to
    be deliver'd.
He saw the Harlot of the Kings of Earth, &
    saw her Cup
Of fornication, food of Orc & Satan, press'd
    from the fruit of Mystery.

Here Blake not only follows the Revelation of John, but seeks to make his vision and John's a momentary identity. The "food of Orc & Satan, press'd from the fruit of Mystery" by Urizen's unhappy daughters, becomes one with the "abominations and filthiness" of the Whore of Babylon's fornications with the rulers of the darkness of this world.

Blake's Rahab is subtler than John's Scarlet Woman, for the eighteenth century has a subtler spirit of evil in heavenly things than times past, in Blake's view. Rahab hears the song of Enion and "no more spirit remain'd in her." She begins to waver, and the crisis within her produces the Deism of Blake's age, as he wished to name it. Satan divides against Satan, and determines to consume Rahab or Mystery so as to bring another Mystery, Phoenixlike, from her ashes:

To burn Mystery with fire & form another from
    her ashes,
For God put it into their heart to fulfill
    all his will.

The Ashes of Mystery began to animate; they
    call'd it Deism
And Natural Religion; as of old, so now
    anew began
Babylon again in Infancy, call'd Natural
    Religion.

These lines, which end Night VIII, present in very condensed
form Blake's sardonic analysis of "the Ashes of Mystery," or eighteenth-century natural religion. Deism tries to prove "Christianity Not
Mysterious," replacing supernatural revelation by natural reason. But
the Deists replace the Mystery of revelation with the Mystery of
nature, and their trinity of reason, nature, and society is to Blake
another triple-headed manifestation of Female Will. The fire of Critical Deism burns up Mystery, and then the spectral reasonings of
Constructive Deism form another Rahab from her ashes, a new Babylon in its infancy. Blake's imagination could no more accept the
universe of Newton than it could the god of the churches. Blake's
god was human in the clear light of creative vision, and so was
Blake's cosmos, if the eye would only see everything it was capable of seeing. What makes this polemic so sardonic is the Blakean
conviction that Deism is providential: "For God put it into their
heart to fulfill all his will." Deism, to Blake, is absolute Error; the
ultimate negation of the truth. Such negation, to Blake, must
compel a vision of the Last Judgment:

The Last Judgment [will be] when all those are Cast away
who trouble Religion with Questions concerning Good & Evil
or Eating of the Tree of those Knowledges or Reasonings
which hinder the Vision of God turning all into a Consuming Fire. When Imagination, Art & Science & all Intellectual
Gifts, all the Gifts of the Holy Ghost, are [despis'd] look'd
upon as of no use & only Contention remains to Man, then
the Last Judgment begins, & its Vision is seen by the Imaginative Eye of Every one according to the situation he holds.[19]

Night IX, The Last Judgment

Then will happen such things as may well be called prodigies.
The Wolf FENRIS will devour the Sun. . . . Another monster will carry off the Moon . . . the Stars shall fly away and
vanish from the heavens: the earth and the mountains shall
be seen violently agitated; the trees torn up from the earth
by the roots; the tottering hills to tumble headlong from their
foundations; all the chains and irons of the prisoners to be
broken and dashed in pieces. Then is the Wolf Fenris let loose;
the sea rushes impetuously over the earth, because the great
Serpent, changed into a Spectre, gains the shore. . . . The great
Ash Tree of Ydrasil is shaken; nor is any thing in heaven or earth
exempt from fear and danger.

Northern Antiquities, "Of the
Twilight of the Gods"[20]

Blake's most exuberant and inventive poetry, probabiy the most
energetic and awesome in the language, is to be found in Night
IX of *The Four Zoas.* In his visualization of apocalypse Blake is
most strikingly original, owing little to Revelation, and only a little
more to *Northern Antiquities,* his likely source for Norse mythology.
Blake wrote greater (and quieter) poetry than Night IX, in *Milton*
and in *Jerusalem,* where his inventiveness is subtler and more internalized. But he never equalled the Orc-like liberation of creative
power that he accomplished in this most primordial of his myths,
most vital of his projections of imaginative desire.

Night IX begins with the despair of the regenerating Los and
Enitharmon, who labor at building the new Jerusalem (at once city
and woman, art and Albion's bride). They labor in tears, for their
vegetative eyes appear to see the murdered Luvah-Jesus as being
still in his Sepulcher. Jesus stands beside them, but they are not
aware of his presence. Unable to believe in the resurrection of the
body, Los and Enitharmon begin the apocalypse by Los's uncompre-
hending but imaginatively correct attack upon nature. Los does the
right thing for the wrong reason:

Terrified at Non Existence,
For such they deem'd the death of the body,
        Los his vegetable hands
Outstretch'd; his right hand branching out
        in fibrous strength
Siez'd the Sun; His left hand like dark
        roots cover'd the Moon,
And tore them down cracking the heavens across
        from immense to immense.

With this gigantic image of natural destruction, a poetic thrust
at the deadness of the cosmos, the Last Judgment begins:

Then fell the fires of Eternity with loud
        & shrill
Sound of Loud Trumpet thundering along from
        heaven to heaven
A mighty sound articulate. "Awake, ye dead,
        & come
To Judgment from the four winds! Awake &
        Come away!"
Folding like scrolls of the Enormous volume
        of Heaven & Earth,
With thunderous noise & dreadful shakings,
        racking to & fro,
The heavens are shaken & the Earth removed
        from its place,
The foundations of the Eternal hills discover'd.
The thrones of Kings are shaken, they have lost
        their robes & crowns;
The poor smite their oppressors, they awake up
        to the harvest;
The naked warriors rush together down to the
        sea shore
Trembling before the multitudes of slaves now
        set at liberty.

> They are become like wintry flocks, like forests
>   strip'd of leaves;
> The oppressed pursue like the wind; there is no
>   room for escape.

In this passage the political vision of Blake reaches its wishful climax and passes away, to be absorbed into the more strenuous themes of human integration.

The cracking apart of the heavens lets loose the Spectre of Enitharmon on the troubled deep, for she has presided over Deist or Newtonian space. The Spectre of Urthona, whose will has controlled the clock-time of nature, receives her in a pathetic last embrace, vividly described:

> The Spectre of Enitharmon let loose on the
>   troubled deep
> Wail'd shrill in the confusion & the Spectre
>   of Urthona
> Reciev'd her in the darkening south; their
>   bodies lost, they stood
> Trembling & weak, a faint embrace, a fierce
>   desire, as when
> Two shadows mingle on a wall; they wail &
>   shadowy tears
> Fell down & shadowy forms of joy mix'd with
>   despair & grief;
> Their bodies buried in the ruins of the
>   Universe
> Mingled with the confusion. Who shall call
>   them from the Grave?

Space and time have become two shadows mingling on a crumbling wall, and even the shadows are lost when the wall of nature falls down. In the flames the voices of Rahab and Tirzah are heard wailing, until "they give up themselves to Consummation." The codes of Urizen unroll in the serpentine flames of Orc, as Urizen's southern quarter of fallen intellect comes down and all nature is reduced to its true chaos. Animals find human voices, and human fears, to advise one another to flee from the wrath of an exploding Mystery:

> The tree of Mystery went up in folding
>   flames.
> Blood issu'd out in mighty volumes, pouring
>   in whirlpools fierce
> From out the flood gates of the Sky. The Gates
>   are burst; down pour
> The torrents black upon the Earth; the blood
>   pours down incessant.
> Kings in their palaces lie drown'd. Shepherds,
>   their flocks, their tents,
> Roll down the mountains in black torrents.
>   Cities, Villages,
> High spires & Castles drown'd in the black
>   deluge; shoal on shoal
> Float the dead carcases of Men & Beasts, driven
>   to & fro on waves
> Of foaming blood beneath the black incessant
>   sky, till all
> Mystery's tyrants are cut off & not one left
>   on Earth.

Raising himself from his rocky slumbers, Albion now begins the process of human integration. He summons Urizen:

> Come forth from slumbers of thy cold
>   abstraction! Come forth,
> Arise to Eternal births! Shake off thy
>   cold repose,
> Schoolmaster of souls, great opposer of
>   change, arise!

But Urizen, having become the prone Lucifer of Dante or Milton, is a stony form of death, a dragon of the deeps, and does not reply. He is shocked into repentance by a tremendous threat from the now thoroughly aroused Albion:

> My anger against thee is greater than against
>   this Luvah,
> For war is energy Enslav'd, but thy
>   religion,
> The first author of this war & the distracting
>   of honest minds
> Into confused perturbation & strife & honour
>   & pride,
> Is a deceit so detestable that I will cast
>   thee out
> If thou repentest not, & leave thee as a rotten
>   branch to be burn'd
> With Mystery the Harlot & with Satan for Ever
>   & Ever.
> Error can never be redeemed in all Eternity,
> But Sin, Even Rahab, is redeem'd in blood &
>   fury & jealousy—
> That line of blood that stretch'd across the
>   windows of the morning—
> Redeem'd from Error's power. Wake, thou
>   dragon of the deeps!

War is a sexual perversion, an enslavement of organic energy, but Luvah, who is that energy, is less culpable than the enslaver, Urizen, whose idea of selfish holiness engendered the war within Albion's members, the civil strife of the psyche. The Harlot Mystery is Error and must be cast out beyond the balance of contraries, but Rahab or nature can be separated from Mystery, for Sin, unlike Error, can be redeemed. The "line of blood that stretch'd across the windows of the morning" is the "line of scarlet thread in the window" (Joshua 2:18) by which the harlot Rahab was to be recognized and so spared the destruction visited upon the rest of Jericho. In orthodox typology the scarlet rope was "the sign of Christ's blood," but again Blake inverts the orthodox figure. Rahab's line of blood, the Church's appropriation to itself of Christ's sacrifice, blocked the clear windows of the morning, the apocalyptic hopefulness announced in the very first lines of Blake's *Poetical Sketches*, his first work. The line of blood has been withdrawn, and Urizen is warned to separate his Sin from Satan's Error, lest he perish forever with Satan and Mystery.

Very movingly, considering what he has been, Urizen weeps in the darkness, "anxious his scaly form to reassume the human." He understands now that the pleasures of Eternity are in this moment, that the powers of infinity are in the here and now. He casts forth his fears of futurity, for "futurity is in this moment." Liberated from self, he shakes off his snowy limbs and becomes a radiant youth again, a true Prince of Light.

Since, for Blake, the nature of sin is that it is a state of remaining *with* oneself, the casting-out of sin by Urizen prepares him for reunion with Ahania. But it is like Urizen to show intellectual impatience, and his attempt to embrace Ahania again is premature. The mind's pleasure in its own powers must wait upon the mind's reintegration with the human faculties of affection, instinct, imagination. Ahania is watched over by the three daughters of Urizen (for the first time performing a beneficent action) while the uncovering of reality goes forward.

Albion comforts Urizen by promising him Ahania's renovation when Jerusalem, "a City, yet a Woman" descends from the reconstituted heavens, like the bride of the Lamb in Revelation. Urizen accepts, conscious of his error, and the work of destruction to prepare for a re-creation goes on. The vision of cherubim in Ezekiel and Revelation comes again as a portent of the Four Zoas moving as one Man, but this time both Albion and Urizen are premature in their attempt to enter the Consummation:

> Fourfold each in the other reflected; they
> are named Life's in Eternity.
> Four Starry Universes going forward from
> Eternity to Eternity.
> And the Fall'n Man who was arisen upon the
> Rock of Ages
> Beheld the Vision of God & he arose up from
> the Rock
> And Urizen arose up with him, walking thro'
> the flames

> To meet the Lord coming to Judgment; but the
> flames repell'd them
> Still to the Rock; in vain they strove to
> Enter the Consummation
> Together, for the Redeem'd Man could
> not enter the Consummation.

Before even redeemed Man can enter into his own unity again, the whole cosmos must be delivered by a great harvest and vintage, as in Revelation. But Blake's is the most active of revelations, and the Zoas or living principles of humanity must themselves work the process of rejuvenation. In a series of magnificent passages, the human cycle of regeneration is carried through. The Sons of Urizen plow up the universe, and Urizen himself, again the immortal sower with a lap full of seed, sows the souls who will be resurrected in "the human harvest springing up." Only after Urizen has exercised his powers in this activity that unites intellect and earth does Ahania finally return to him:

> A time they give to sweet repose till all
> the harvest is ripe.
> And Lo, like the harvest Moon, Ahania cast
> off her death clothes;
> She folded them up in care, in silence, &
> her bright'ning limbs
> Bath'd in the clear spring of the rock;
> then from her darksome cave
> Issu'd in majesty divine. Urizen rose up
> from his couch
> On wings of tenfold joy, clapping his hands,
> his feet, his radiant wings
> In the immense: as when the Sun dances upon
> the mountains
> A shout of jubilee in lovely notes responding
> from daughter to daughter,
> From son to son; as if the stars beaming
> innumerable

Thro' night should sing soft warbling,
    filling earth & heaven;
And bright Ahania took her seat by Urizen
    in songs & joy.

Here the moon-goddess of primordial religion is redeemed into the passionate joy of consciousness at the energetic employment of its own creative powers.

As the fires of nature have burned on, they have consumed the serpentine Orc of Satan-Urizen's natural religion. The consummated Orc separates again into Luvah and Vala, and these scorched beings submit to Albion's judgment and forgiveness, expressed in a passage that summarizes the central themes of *The Four Zoas:*

Luvah & Vala, henceforth you are Servants;
    obey & live.
You shall forget your former state; return
    O Love in peace,
Into your place, the place of seed; not in
    the brain or heart.
If Gods combine against Man, setting their
    dominion above
The Human form Divine, Thrown down from their
    high station
In the Eternal heavens of Human
    Imagination: buried beneath
In dark Oblivion with incessant pangs, ages
    on ages,
In enmity & war first weaken'd, then in stern
    repentance
They must renew their brightness & their
    disorganiz'd functions
Again reorganize, till they resume the image
    of the human,
Cooperating in the bliss of Man, obeying
    his Will,
Servants to the infinite & Eternal of the
    Human form.

The return of Luvah and Vala into the loins establishes the brain
as Urizen's again, and prepares the heart for the reception of a reconstituted Tharmas. The image of the human is now resumed, and
Luvah and Vala are reborn into Beulah, the Garden of Innocence.
They represent the return into being of the lost children of the *Songs
of Innocence*. Blake's imagery of Innocence, with its precarious
beauty and wavering intensity, now returns to his poetry, but expressed with a new confidence, a firmness based upon definite organization:

> Rise up, O Sun, most glorious minister &
>   light of day.
> Flow on, ye gentle airs, & bear the voice
>   of my rejoicing.
> Wave freshly, clear waters flowing around
>   the tender grass;
> And thou, sweet smelling ground, put forth
>   thy life in fruits & flowers.
> Follow me, O my flocks, & hear me sing my
>   rapturous song.
> I will cause my voice to be heard on the
>   clouds that glitter in the sun.
> I will call & who shall answer me? I will
>   sing; who shall reply?
> For from my pleasant hills behold the living,
>   living springs,
> Running among my green pastures, delighting
>   among my trees.
> I am not here alone: my flocks, you are my
>   brethren;
> And you birds that sing & adorn the sky,
>   you are my sisters.
> I sing, & you reply to my song; I rejoice,
>   & you are glad.
> Follow me, O my flocks; we will now descend
>   into the valley.

This is the triumph of Blake's pastoral vision, balancing the deliberate failure of that vision in its thematically "unorganized" form, in the *Songs of Innocence* and *The Book of Thel*. The revival of Innocence brings about the resurrection of the primal spirits of Innocence, its loving mother and father, Enion and Tharmas the Shepherd. Blake handles this resurrection with exquisite skill. The regenerate Vala leads her flocks to a riverbank, and there sees a vision that is the redeeming contrary to her earlier narcissism:

> She stood in the river & view'd herself
>   within the wat'ry glass,
> And her bright hair was wet with the waters;
>   she rose up from the river,
> And as she rose her eyes were open'd to the
>   world of waters.
> She saw Tharmas sitting upon the rocks beside
>   the wavy Sea.
> He strok'd the water from his beard & mourn'd
>   faint thro' the summer vales.

She hears the voice of a chaos willing to surrender itself; Tharmas cries out: "Lo, I have calm'd my seas." The gentlest of all Blake's ironies follows. Vala returns to her pleasant house in the lower paradise:

> And saw in the door way beneath the trees two
>   little children playing.
> She drew near to her house & her flocks
>   follow'd her footsteps.
> Their children clung around her knees; she
>   embrac'd them & wept over them.

These apocalyptic children are Tharmas and Enion, reborn into the world that once they presided over, but now must learn anew. The return of Innocence has meant that Tharmas must be born again, in the hope that the Experience of sundering, once surmounted, will protect him forever from a second fall.

With the unity of Man, his power to convert desire into fulfill-

ment, once again growing to maturity, Urizen is able to begin the
Great Harvest. A powerful passage conveys the joy attending "the
Furious forms of Tharmas humanizing":

> The roots shoot thick thro' the solid rocks,
>   bursting their way
> They cry out in joys of existence; the broad
>   stems
> Rear on the mountains stem after stem; the
>   scaly newt creeps
> From the stone, & the armed fly springs from
>   the rocky crevice;
> The spider, The bat burst from the harden'd
>   slime, crying
> To one another: "What are we, & whence is our
>   joy & delight?
> Lo, the little moss begins to spring, & the
>   tender weed
> Creeps round our secret nest." Flocks brighten
>   the Mountains,
> Herds throng up the Valley, wild beasts fill
>   the forests.

With this awakening all about them, Albion and his sons sit down
to a great feast, a humanistic communion in which the bread and
wine are the body and blood of a resurgent nature become an integral human. After the harvest festival, the vintage begins, symbolizing the ultimate transformations of reality:

> The morning dawn'd. Urizen rose, & in his
>   hand the Flail
> Sounds on the Floor, heard terrible by all
>   beneath the heavens.
> Dismal loud redounding, the nether floor
>   shakes with the sound,
> And all Nations were threshed out, & the
>   stars thresh'd from their husks.

Then Tharmas took the Winnowing fan; the
    winnowing wind furious
Above, veer'd round by the violent whirlwind,
    driven west & south,
Tossed the Nations like chaff into the seas
    of Tharmas.

The perspective here is that of Eternity; from our fallen and temporal perspective enormous wars and calamities of nature are raging. In the midst of these liberating combats, Blake inserts a moving little song by an African Black that replaces the deceived vision of *The Little Black Boy* of Innocence, and leaves him free with "limbs renew'd." This interlude is a pause before the great chant that concludes Night IX, that goes from line 692 to the end, and is dominated by the resurrected Luvah, who stamps out the grapes of wrath and bears away the families of Earth. The glowing diction of this chant surpasses everything previous in Blake, and exhibits perfectly Blake's "beautiful laughing speech":

"Attempting to be more than Man We become
    less," said Luvah
As he arose from the bright feast drunk
    with the wine of ages.
His crown of thorns fell from his head, he
    hung his living Lyre
Behind the seat of the Eternal Man & took
    his way
Sounding the Song of Los, descending to the
    Vineyards bright.
His sons arising from the feast with golden
    baskets follow,
A fiery train, as when the Sun sings in the
    ripe vineyards.
Then Luvah stood before the Wine press; all
    his fiery sons
Brought up the loaded Waggons with shoutings;
    ramping tygers play

> In the jingling traces; furious lions sound
>   the song of joy
> To the golden wheels circling upon the pave-
>   ment of heaven & all
> The Villages of Luvah ring; the golden tiles
>   of the villages
> Reply to violins & tabors, to the pipe, flute,
>   lyre & cymbal.

Luvah is transformed here from Jesus-as-dying-god to the wine-god of a Dionysiac rebirth. The wine press is both fallen warfare and redeemed wars of love, the creative strife of Eternity. The worship of Luvah in the fallen world, whether in the mystery-religions of a vegetation god or the mystery-religion of Jesus, is of course a mistaken worship, and substitutes sacrifice and corporeal war for the intellectual combats of unfallen Man:

> How red the Sons & Daughters of Luvah! how
>   they tread the Grapes!
> Laughing & shouting, drunk with odors, many
>   fall o'erwearied:
> Drown'd in the wine is many a youth & maiden;
>   those around
> Lay them on skins of tygers or the spotted
>   Leopard or wild Ass
> Till they revive, or bury them in cool Grots
>   making lamentation.
>
> But in the Wine Presses the Human Grapes
>   sing not nor dance,
> They howl & writhe in shouts of torment, in
>   fierce flames consuming,
> In chains of iron & in dungeons circled with
>   ceaseless fires,
> In pits & dens & shades of death, in shapes
>   of torment & woe;
> The Plates, the Screws & Racks & Saws & cords
>   & fires & floods,

The cruel joy of Luvah's daughters, lacerating
   with knives
And whips their Victims, & the deadly sport
   of Luvah's sons.

The frenzy described here has an indisputable sexual element, for both war and sacrificial religion are founded upon the perversion of sexual energies. Listening to these torments, Albion calls upon both Tharmas and Urthona to arise, to end these torments by a fully capable imaginative making of human blood into apocalyptic wine:

Then Tharmas & Urthona rose from the Golden
   feast satiated
With Mirth & Joy: Urthona, limping from his
   fall, on Tharmas lean'd,
In his right hand his hammer. Tharmas held
   his Shepherd's crook
Beset with gold, gold were the ornaments form'd
   by sons of Urizen.
Then Enion & Ahania & Vala & the wife of dark
   Urthona
Rose from the feast, in joy ascending to their
   Golden Looms.

Urthona is the partially crippled smith of mythological tradition, like Vulcan, but he compensates for his limping by leaning on Tharmas. As Urthona is the figure of the artist-poet, Blake is tacitly admitting that human creative power has been hurt, but the reliance for support on the strength of Tharmas suggests the artist's salvation from his crippling. The power to create more life, to extend the unitary instincts of Innocence into the imagined world of desire, will serve to relieve the artist as he recovers from his fall into division.

As the wives of the Zoas work at weaving the woof of a new nature, Tharmas and Urthona gather the vintage that Urizen sowed and harvested, and Luvah so ambiguously pressed out:

Tharmas went down to the Wine presses &
   beheld the sons & daughters
Of Luvah quite exhausted with the labour
   & quite fill'd
With new wine, that they began to torment
   one another and to tread
The weak. Luvah & Vala slept on the floor,
   o'erwearied.
Urthona call'd his sons around him: Tharmas
   call'd his sons
Num'rous; they took the wine, they separated
   the Lees,
And Luvah was put for dung on the ground by
   the Sons of Tharmas & Urthona.
They formed heavens of sweetest wood, of
   gold & silver & ivory,
Of glass & precious stones. They loaded all
   the waggons of heaven
And took away the wine of ages with solemn
   songs & joy.

No poet but Blake could have written this, and few poets have
written better. It is difficult to believe that only a specially instructed
reader can read these lines and know their excitement and beauty.
These lines are profound, absolutely relevant to the life of every
man, and phrased inevitably and economically. The worshippers
of the dying god of vegetative nature, Bacchic celebrants of the
sexual mysteries of the individual and of society, are at last exhausted
even by their own cruelties, and yet cannot stop their tormentings.
Filled with the new wine, the perpetually renewed sexual cycle, they
turn upon one another. On the floor of the Wine-presses the god
and the goddess of this orgy sleep in the weariness of satiety. Adonis
has died and been reborn once too often; Osiris has been rent apart
and come together with Isis again for a last time. Now the vegetative
mysteries are over; the dying gods are dead, and only the human is
to remain. The wine of life is separated from the lees of the deathly,
and the dying-god aspect of man's emotional being is "put for dung
on the ground," to fertilize the new birth of a nature that will cease

to be cyclic. The wine of ages, the waters of a more abundant life, are carried off in a harvest festival of rejoicing by everything in man that is most creative.

A last winter comes upon the ruined remnants of the fallen world, and nature groans in darkness, in the night of Time. But the new age comes, and with it a promise of an end to the great winter of the world:

> The Sun has left his blackness & has found a
>   fresher morning,
> And the mild moon rejoices in the clear &
>   cloudless night,
> And Man walks forth from midst of the fires:
>   the evil is all consum'd.
> His eyes behold the Angelic spheres arising
>   night & day;
> The stars consum'd like a lamp blown out, &
>   in their stead behold
> The Expanding Eyes of Man beholds the depths
>   of wondrous worlds!

This is our sun, our moon, our eyes, but our eyes expanding, breaking out of the confines of our perceptual caverns. And sun, and moon, the universe entire, are as we are, that we may be as they are, both of us the human released from every limitation and therefore both of us the divine. Like Keats's intelligences which are atoms of perception, we too know, and we see, and we are god:

> One Earth, one sea beneath; nor Erring
>   Globes wander, but Stars
> Of fire rise up nightly from the Ocean
>   & one Sun
> Each morning like a New born Man issues
>   with songs & joy
> Calling the Plowman to his Labour & the
>   Shepherd to his rest.
> He walks upon the Eternal Mountains, raising
>   his heavenly voice,

> Conversing with the Animal forms of wisdom
>   night & day,
> That, risen from the Sea of fire, renew'd
>   walk o'er the Earth.

The restoration to Eden nears completion, and the limbs of the maimed smith, Urthona, are renewed. The Tygers that roamed in the forests of the night are gone, their place taken by the Lions of Urthona, royal emblems of poetic power, that "in evening sport upon the plains." They raise their faces from the Earth, conversing with Albion:

> How is it we have walk'd thro' fires & yet
>   are not consum'd?
> How is it that all things are chang'd even
>   as in ancient times?

They have been through an agony of flame, like the children of Israel in Nebuchadnezzar's furnaces, yet the flame has not singed a sleeve. All things are changed, but only to what they were in the beginning. In a profound breath of peace Blake sings the completion of this first of his major poems, his heroic efforts at speaking a word that is his word only, and yet can speak also to the generality of men awake enough to seek more life:

> The Sun arises from his dewy bed & the
>   fresh airs
> Play in his smiling beams giving the seeds
>   of life to grow,
> And the fresh Earth beams forth ten thousand
>   thousand springs of life.
> Urthona is arisen in his strength, no longer
>   now
> Divided from Enitharmon, no longer the Spectre
>   Los.
> Where is the Spectre of Prophecy? where the
>   delusive Phantom?
> Departed. & Urthona rises from the ruinous
>   Walls

In all his ancient strength to form the
golden armour of science
For intellectual War. The war of swords
departed now.
The dark Religions are departed & sweet
Science reigns.

The Science that reigns here is the complete knowledge or human consciousness of art at its most coherent and comprehensive, and the intellectual war is the strife of contraries that enlivens Blake's heaven, and forbids it to become static.

Why did Blake abandon this magnificent poem, with its gigantic and meaningful myths, and its surpassing wealth of language and incident? We can only speculate at this point, though *The Four Zoas* ought to seem a more problematic work than it does now, when we look back upon it after a consideration of the more lucid and orderly *Milton* and the subtler and still more profound *Jerusalem*. Northrop Frye has suggested that Blake may have realized that nothing in the poem accounted for the origins of its marvelous apocalypse, a shudder in the dark that urged Blake onwards to a vision that became the greatest of wish-fulfillments.[21] We can supplement this speculation, perhaps, by observing that *Milton* and *Jerusalem* are more personal poems than *The Four Zoas*, more directly reflective of Blake's own life and sufferings.

In *Milton* and *Jerusalem* the figure of Los becomes central, replacing Urizen and Luvah-Orc as the chief protagonist of Blake's myth. The myth itself is radically simplified in *Milton*, and then becomes very complex again in *Jerusalem*, but there the complexity is more acutely psychological and even analytical than it is in *The Four Zoas*. In some ways Blake's transition from his first to his later epics is very like Shelley's movement from *Prometheus Unbound* to *The Triumph of Life*, and Keats's remarkably condensed poetic development between *Hyperion* and *The Fall of Hyperion*. In all three poets an attempt at a relatively impersonal myth of fall and redemption is followed and transcended by a deliberate turn to the subjective, a heightening of self-examination at the expense of a larger accounting for the fall of a world. *The Four Zoas* has not only given us an inexplicable apocalypse (as *Prometheus Unbound* did also) but it has failed to justify the sense in which Los and his City of Art constitute an agency of salvation for man. Like *The Triumph of Life* and *The Fall of Hyperion* (and Wordsworth's *Prelude* also), the brief epic *Milton* deals primarily with the story of a poet's incarnation. In Blake this is the renewal and clarification of Milton's vision, or the poetic vision proper, by William Blake. Shelley and Keats did not survive to write the great epics of their maturity, and Wordsworth decayed into the celebrator of the Urizenic labyrinths of moral virtue who so disfigures *The Excursion*. Of the great Romantics only Blake kept his full powers into a magnificent maturity, and so was able to write *Jerusalem*, probably the most original and certainly the least read and studied of the greater long poems in the English language.

The Four Zoas is a vital poem, for all its interleavings and unresolved revisions, but Blake could not stop with it, and would not even acknowledge it as a poetic success, for he did not engrave it. He ought to have done so, and to have made a definitive version of it, but even without such polishings the poem remains, burning with an energy that nothing else in English has in such intensity. Blake was so prodigal of his genius in his late thirties and early forties that the Prolific in him overflowed, and threatened to drown out the Devourer in an excess of delights, by an inventing imagination so fecund as to be without real parallel since Dante. But Blake was more than a young Orc, and did not forget that he wished to attain a marriage of his Bible of Hell to the Bible of Heaven. He gave up *The Four Zoas* because it explained, too well and in too many ways, how the world had reached the darkness of his own times, but explained hardly at all what that darkness was, and how it was to be enlightened.

CHAPTER TEN

Later Poems from the Notebook and the Pickering Manuscript

My Spectre around me night & day . . .

Between 1800 and 1803, Blake began to use his Notebook for more ambitious shorter poems than he had scribbled in it earlier. About 1803, he made a fair copy of some of these poems, with some others, known today as the Pickering Manuscript (after one of its Victorian owners). These later lyrics and fragments, some of them among Blake's finest, can be considered as Blake's most important abandoned work besides *The Four Zoas*. In the best of them, he gives gnomic and simple expression to the titanic themes and visionary intensities more complexly explored in his epics.

The Spectre and Emanation figures of *The Four Zoas* are set forth in a microcosm of the Tharmas-Enion or Urizen-Ahania struggle in a singularly powerful lyric:

> My Spectre around me night & day
> Like a Wild beast guards my way.
> My Emanation far within
> Weeps incessantly for my Sin.

The Spectre here is a protective shadow whose "guarding" has become an ambiguous menace, for it keep others from the Self. The Emanation has failed to emanate, but keeps itself within the psyche, weeping incessantly for the speaker's undefined Sin. The function of the Emanation is to become what Shelley called "a soul out of my soul," a creative achievement, the form of what a man loves through creation. If this creation does not take place, the restrained creator is trapped in the state of Ulro:

> A Fathomless & boundless deep,
> There we wander, there we weep;
> On the hungry craving wind
> My Spectre follows thee behind.

This world is chaos, and the shadow stalks the grieving wanderers, caught like them in a craving that is unwilling to be fed. The speaker strives desperately to dissociate himself from his Spectre, urging his beloved to return, so as to liberate his Emanation, but this quarrel of lovers is too deadly to be so easily reconciled. As in the earlier Notebook, Blake is crying out against the jealous possessiveness of Female Will, whether it be present in one wife or in all of nature:

> Dost thou not in Pride & scorn
> Fill with tempests all my morn,
> And with jealousies & fears
> Fill my pleasant nights with tears?

She has slain twenty-eight of his loves, a lunar cycle of what might have been his imaginative achievements. Nevertheless he begs her to return, to join him in mutual forgiveness. The reply, delivered with stunning dramatic force, is the authentic voice of female jealousy:

> Never, Never I return:
> Still for Victory I burn.
> Living, thee alone I'll have
> And when dead I'll be thy Grave.

> Thro' the Heaven & Earth & Hell
> Thou shalt never never quell:
> I will fly & thou pursue,
> Night & Morn the flight renew.

This is the voice also of Enitharmon in *Europe,* seeking dominion for woman over man through the bondage of history, burning for victory at the expense even of love. Utterly Blakean is the sinister transition from the female possessiveness of "thee alone I'll have" to the apotheosis of the female in a sepulchral nature: "I'll be thy Grave."

Faced with this doom of a perpetual cycle of flight and pursuit, the speaker asserts his freedom from natural bondage:

> Till I turn from Female Love,
> And root up the Infernal Grove,
> I shall never worthy be
> To Step into Eternity.

This of course does not mean that the speaker is going to be either ascetic or homosexual, but only that he is going to give up love as the Female Will understands it. The Infernal Grove grows Trees of Mystery, of natural deceptiveness, and from these forests of the night no man steps forth into the sexual wholeness of Eternity. The speaker (clearly Blake himself) vows another fate:

> And, to end thy cruel mocks,
> Annihilate thee on the rocks,
> And another form create
> To be subservient to my Fate.

The rocks are the gray particulars of Ulro, individual but indefinite. Blake urges the creation of minute particulars into another form, a vision of love that serves the human, rather than seeks to sunder it. Hopelessly, Blake makes a last plea:

> Let us agree to give up Love,
> And root up the infernal grove;
> Then shall we return & see
> The worlds of happy Eternity.

To find a love that does not seek to drink the other lover up was the desire of Oothoon, and she failed. Blake ends in the noble but lost gesture; to return in love by giving up the religion of love. He heard his own voice only; all response was wanting, and in this hope he could prophesy for no man, not even himself.

The Golden Net

This poem, from the Pickering Manuscript, is a masterpiece of bitter economy and restraint. At the break of day, in a quest towards the emancipation symbolized by a risen morning, a young man encounters three weeping Virgins who question his journey and seek to hold him by their grief. All of them embody Love and Beauty, but in the passive modes of restraint and suffering. For these, despite the enticements of their piteous disguise, are Blake's Fatal Sisters, a Triple Female representing three attracting aspects of the confining natural world. They provoke pity, which divides the soul, and keeps the quester from the imagined land of the poet's desire:

> The one was Cloth'd in flames of fire,
> The other Cloth'd in iron wire,
> The other Cloth'd in tears & sighs
> Dazling bright before my Eyes.
> They bore a Net of Golden twine
> To hang upon the Branches fine.

The first Virgin is tormented by desire itself, as symbolized by the flames. The second, a stage beyond, suffers from the frustration of sexual impulse, the frustrating barrier being the iron wire. The third has reached the last stage in this natural cycle of desire, repression and grief. They bear together the Net of natural religion, to hang upon the branches fine of the Tree named Mystery. The "golden" suggests a deceptive exterior; the twine hints at the weaving of the three Fates. When the Young Man's soul is melted away in pity, he and his quest are lost:

> Whey they saw my Tears, A Smile
> That did Heaven itself beguile,
> Bore the Golden Net aloft
> As on downy Pinions soft
> Over the Morning of my day.
> Underneath the Net I stray,
> Now intreating Burning Fire,
> Now intreating Iron Wire,
> Now intreating Tears & Sighs.
> O when will the morning rise?

If there is an answer to that question, it must be: when you will, but not through your willing. The defeated quester is left in his natural prison, still unable to repudiate the pity that has divided his soul.

The Mental Traveller

Blake's later manuscript poems handle the outlines of his myths with an assured freedom that allows him a unique measure of poetic spontaneity. A critic who translates a poem like *The Mental Traveller* or *The Crystal Cabinet* back into the more technical vocabulary of *The Four Zoas* does Blake the disservice of concealing the kind of popular art or higher simplicity that Blake labored to attain. What counts most about *The Mental Traveller* is its openness and vigor; the marching rhythms and easy diction suggest that Blake is attempting his own kind of lyrical ballad, and consciously wants to give the reader a story so direct and passionate in its grim ironies that the quite overt moral will ring out unmistakably in the poem's last line: "And all is done as I have told." The Orc cycle, the withering of desire into restraint, is the theme of *The Mental Traveller* as it was of much of *The Four Zoas*, but to say that *The Mental Traveller* is "about" the Orc cycle is to schematize too quickly. A descriptive account of the poem ought to emphasize the large movements of its drama; the symbolic vision will emerge of itself, for that is the poem's greatness. The reader is compelled by the

poem's very starkness to solve the relationship between the poem's
events and the pattern of similar ironic repetitiveness in the reader's
own life.

The poem's title clearly refers to the "I" who chants its events, and
whose wondering observation of the cycle of natural life determines
the poem's fresh and startled tone. The poem is a report of a strange
and distorted planet given by a being who has stumbled upon it and
cannot altogether believe the horrors he has seen. His nervous vi-
brancy is felt in every stanza, as he strives to communicate to us,
the poem's implied audience, the grim marvels of an existence that,
by the poem's largest irony, is already our own:

> I travel'd thro' a Land of Men,
> A Land of Men & Women too,
> And heard & saw such dreadful things
> As cold Earth wanderers never knew.

This Traveller, who is presumably one of Blake's unfallen Eternals, moves mentally through our world, expecting that a Land of
Men will yield him human images. But he sees that the human image
is already divided; the Sexes have sprung from shame and pride, and
it is a Land of Men and Women too. He hears, sees and also *knows*
what the cold wanderers of Earth hear and see also, but cannot
apprehend as knowledge, which is one of the poem's major points.
If you cannot learn from experience, then you must suffer it over
and over again. In the next stanza the Mental Traveller contrasts
the fallen process of birth with the Eternal progression reached
through the liberating strife of contraries:

> For there the Babe is born in joy
> That was begotten in dire woe;
> Just as we Reap in joy the fruit
> Which we in bitter tears did sow.

The sexual meeting of fallen man and woman seems a "dire woe"
to this being, who compares it to the intellectual warfare of Eternity. The fruit of Eternity is a liberated creation, but the fruit of

earthly intercourse is a Babe who suffers the fate of the Norse Titan Loki, of Jesus, and of Prometheus, three incarnations of Luvah as a suffering Orc, or simply three dying man-gods:

> And if the Babe is born a Boy
> He's given to a Woman Old,
> Who nails him down upon a rock,
> Catches his shrieks in cups of gold.
>
> She binds iron thorns around his head,
> She pierces both his hands & feet,
> She cuts his heart out at his side
> To make it feel both cold & heat.

Loki, punished for his part in the slaying of Balder, suffered precisely as the Babe does in the first of these stanzas, and the allusions to Jesus and Prometheus are unmistakable in the second. But, more directly, this is *any* new human child, and *every* new human impulse, idea, creation, fresh life of all kinds. An old woman, a nurse or foster mother, nature itself, receives this new imaginative force, and nails him down to the rock of material existence, the fallen body and its limitations. The Babe's shrieks are precious to her, as Loki's were to the gods, for they are evidences of her continued dominion over man. She makes a martyr lest she have to contend with a fully human antagonist. The iron thorns are not only an allusion to Jesus, but also to Blake's ironclad Spectre of Urthona, the crippled, anxiety-ridden temporal will of man. The pierced hands and feet betoken the impairment of man by nature, and the exposed heart is the depraved natural heart, bereft of the affective powers of Eternity. For death feeds upon life, nature on the human, the Old Woman on the Babe:

> Her fingers number every Nerve,
> Just as a Miser counts his gold;
> She lives upon his shrieks & cries,
> And she grows young as he grows old.

This is horror, the genuine obscenity of a vampire will, natural and female, nourishing itself on the only wealth we have, the substance of our hope, the possibility manifested in a human child. But the horror is ours; the poem's speaker maintains his grimly level tone, as he continues to describe a world so different from his own.

It begins to be clear that the poem has two cycles moving in it, in opposite directions, and out of phase with one another. The female or natural cycle is moving backwards, the male or human cycle forward: "And she grows young as he grows old." At mid-phase they meet, and enact a scene akin to the "Preludium" of *America*, where Orc rends up his manacles and possesses the nameless female who had cared for him:

> Till he becomes a bleeding youth,
> And she becomes a Virgin bright;
> Then he rends up his Manacles
> And binds her down for his delight.
>
> He plants himself in all her Nerves,
> Just as a Husbandman his mould;
> And she becomes his dwelling place
> And Garden fruitful seventy fold.

She has numbered his nerves; now he plants himself in all of hers. One remembers the outcry of Tharmas against Enion in Night I of *The Four Zoas*, warning against the examining of every little fibre of his soul, the ghastly post-reflective anatomy of the infant joy. The known has become the knower; the used the user. The marriage between the human and the natural that is Beulah (celebrated also by Wordsworth in his *Recluse* fragment) is parodied by the youth's exploitation of the female, his seventyfold yield from nature. This second phase passes to a third, as he ages and she merges with his environment, to disappear for a time:

> An aged Shadow, soon he fades,
> Wand'ring round an Earthly Cot,
> Full filled all with gems & gold
> Which he by industry had got.

And these are the gems of the Human Soul,
The rubies & pearls of a lovesick eye,
The countless gold of the akeing heart,
The martyr's groan & the lover's sigh.

They are his meat, they are his drink;
He feeds the Beggar & the Poor
And the wayfaring Traveller:
For ever open is his door.

His wealth is the proper equivalent of his aging into spectral form, for it consists of the morbid secretions of human suffering, particularly sexual repression based on courtly love convention. He feeds on this and so clearly he is now a Urizenic figure. He extends this cannibal fare as charity, in an exemplification of the morality taught in *The Human Abstract*. When new life enters this dead world, it comes as delusion, with the reappearance of the female as an infant changeling on the hearth:

His grief is their eternal joy;
They make the roofs & walls to ring;
Till from the fire on the hearth
A little Female Babe does spring.

And she is all of solid fire
And gems & gold, that none his hand
Dare stretch to touch her Baby form,
Or wrap her in his swaddling-band.

We age, and nature is born anew, a mocking solid fire that we dare not touch. The joy of others is the grief of the aged; from the revelry one cannot share, the hearth-fire that warms others, springs the illusion of a daughter, an absolute otherness. Her fire is not creative fire, but allied to the gems and gold of repression. She is a nature that cannot be humanized by our touch, swaddled by our control. And she grows all too quickly:

> But She comes to the Man she loves,
> If young or old, or rich or poor;
> They soon drive out the aged Host,
> A Beggar at another's door.

The third phase ends. We have moved from cruel nurse and infant
to sadistic lover and mistress to vicious changeling and frustrate
father. Nature has been Tirzah, Vala, Rahab, in that sequence; man
has aged from an infant Orc to a beggared Urizen. Now something new has entered the poem, sardonically and destructively. The
female, growing forward in cycle, secures a human in an earlier phase
than the unhappy Host. All the males in the poem are one man,
humanity, men and women together. All the females are nature,
the confinements of the human. Blake's irony is at its most fearful;
we are driven out into our wildernesses by a love-alliance of nature
and our own earlier self. Blake is striking at memory and its torments;
for the human and the imaginative are one, and the poem now
becomes quite evidently a history of the fate of our imagination in
the context of natural existence. What can we do when afflicted by
imaginative senility?

> He wanders weeping far away,
> Untill some other take him in;
> Oft blind & age-bent, sore distrest,
> Untill he can a Maiden win.
>
> And to allay his freezing Age
> The Poor Man takes her in his arms;
> The Cottage fades before his sight,
> The Garden & its lovely Charms.

The cycles are reversed again, as the aged man takes on another
form of nature to serve as Abishag to his David. But he is deliberately choosing delusion, and his experiential world is thereby
converted into an Ulro:

> The Guests are scatter'd thro' the land,
> For the Eye altering alters all;
> The Senses roll themselves in fear,
> And the flat Earth becomes a Ball;

> The stars, sun, Moon, all shrink away,
> A desart vast without a bound,
> And nothing left to eat or drink,
> And a dark desart all around.

Our sense of other selves vanishes, and the flat earth Blake associated with ordinary imaginative possibility is replaced by the spectral ball of universes seen through the wrong or dwarfing end of vision, the inverted vortex of Newtonian observation. Until at last man and his delusive hope of nature are left alone together in the desert of the isolated self. The fourth phase or love-and-war game of Spectre and Emanation now moves to its climax:

> The honey of her Infant lips,
> The bread & wine of her sweet smile,
> The wild game of her roving Eye,
> Does him to Infancy beguile;
>
> For as he eats & drinks he grows
> Younger & younger every day;
> And on the desart wild they both
> Wander in terror & dismay.
>
> Like the wild Stag she flees away,
> Her fear plants many a thicket wild;
> While he pursues her night & day,
> By various arts of Love beguil'd,
>
> By various arts of Love & Hate,
> Till the wide desart planted o'er
> With Labyrinths of wayward Love,
> Where roams the Lion, Wolf & Boar,
>
> Till he becomes a wayward Babe,
> And she a weeping Woman Old.

As the courtly elaboration of enticement and chase proceeds, the desert becomes as labyrinthine as the natural heart. The old man, beguiled to second childhood, has grown backwards, in the natural not the human manner, as this poem would insist. His attempt at humanizing nature has failed; she has acquired only the human character of aging. When he is finally a *wayward* Babe, and she a *weeping* Woman Old, they are each only a step away from the confined Babe and the cannibalistic Old Woman of the poem's early stanzas. Just before they reach that point, and so close the cycle again, we are given one hope of breaking through these ironies, of freeing the human from the natural:

> Then many a Lover wanders here;
> The Sun & Stars are nearer roll'd.
>
> The trees bring forth sweet Extacy
> To all who in the desart roam;
> Till many a City there is Built,
> And many a pleasant Shepherd's home.

Here and here alone we have a choice; we can cancel the cycles of futurity through the civilizing vision of art. Just before the Babe sinks into his swaddling bands again, the liberating impulse of human love brings the sun and stars nearer to man, promises to restore man's primal context. We roam in the desert, the Ulro to which we have reduced our context, but in that desert we can breathe the sweet ecstasy wafted to us by the vegetative life of Generation. If we expand our senses, stung by those odors of life, then we can build again the cities of Eden and find our way back to the pleasant shepherd's home of Beulah. If we do not, then the imaginative life in us passes from the wayward to the frowning Babe, and we wither the life in others:

> But when they find the frowning Babe,
> Terror strikes thro' the region wide:
> They cry "The Babe! the Babe is Born!"
> And flee away on Every side.
>
> For who dare touch the frowning form,
> His arm is wither'd to its root;
> Lions, Boars, Wolves, all howling flee,
> And every Tree does shed its fruit.

This is closer to the birth of Orc in *The Four Zoas* than it is to the peaceful birth in *Europe* or at the opening of *The Mental Traveller*. Orc comes as a child of terror, Christ the Tyger rather than Christ the Lamb, a revelation like that presented by Yeats in *The Second Coming*.[1] This child carries both the threat and the promise of apocalypse, but the weeping Woman Old is now a grimly capable nature, and the poem ends by completing its now hopeless cycle:

> And none can touch that frowning form,
> Except it be a Woman Old;
> She nails him down upon the Rock,
> And all is done as I have told.

The Babe of the opening could be given to the Old Woman; now none can touch the frowning Babe but his crucifying foster mother. The only change is slight but baleful; the cycle has become more dreadful. In the final line the Mental Traveller refuses to go further in his narration; he dismisses what is to come as mere organic repetition. He has seen a world unable or unwilling to rescue itself from a mere round of organic repetitions, a Urizenic mill of meaningless wheels.[2]

Like other poems in the Pickering Manuscript, *The Mental Traveller* testifies to a gathering bitterness in Blake, an increasing puzzlement as to how the imagination is to attain an uncovering of reality, a rending of nature's veil.

The Crystal Cabinet

To understand the complexity of Blake's attitude towards the beauty of the external world, we need to begin by discarding any simplistic theory that would explain away that attitude as a supposed development in time. On this reading (still widely held) the younger Blake was an almost Wordsworthian celebrant of nature, but the mature Blake turned away from any hope for the natural man or his environment and desired instead a conflagration of man and nature, burning both away until a supernatural and mystical order of reality might be compelled to appear. There are in fact passionate celebrations of the beauty of nature as late as passages in the millenarian epic *Milton,* and profound dissatisfactions with nature as early as the *Poetical Sketches,* so clearly neither half of the developmental theory will serve. Nor is there much point in ascribing this kind of reader's confusion to Blake himself, who felt that what could be made explicit to the idiot was not worth his care. Blake's poetry, from first to last, is for the reader patient and intelligent enough to make imaginative distinctions, and to enjoy the subtler shadings of the playful light of intellect.

Nature, in Blake as in so many Renaissance poets and thinkers, admits of two views—hard and soft. In the hard vision primacy is assigned to the extent to which nature is fallen; in the soft, to that limited but genuine extent that nature remains paradisal, however decayed. As Blake developed, he emphasized more and more his version of the hard view; the attractions of Beulah began to be eclipsed by its dangers. The poems of the Pickering Manuscript, especially *The Mental Traveller* and even more so *The Crystal Cabinet,* tend to exhibit this hardening in Blake. I suspect that these poems may even have been written after *Milton* though before *Jerusalem,* for they share *Jerusalem's* harshness.

The Crystal Cabinet is one of the most perfect of Blake's shorter poems. It opens with the directness that only a poetic master achieves:

> The Maiden caught me in the Wild,
> Where I was dancing merrily;
> She put me into her Cabinet
> And Lock'd me up with a golden Key.

The youth dancing merrily in the Wild is caught by the Maiden in the midst of his dance; there is no suggestion that he seeks to evade capture, or to resist her. To be put into her Cabinet, and locked up with a golden key, is a fairly unequivocal statement of sexual intercourse, in which the Maiden is relatively the active partner. The Cabinet is its own world, described in the imagery of Blake's Beulah:

> This Cabinet is Form'd of Gold
> And Pearl & Crystal shining bright,
> And within it opens into a World
> And a little lovely Moony Night.

From what follows in the poem (and from the title) one can surmise that the crystal dominates the Cabinet walls. The gold and pearl are presumably related to the morbid secretions (due to sexual repression) that pass as wealth in *The Mental Traveller*. Within the Cabinet, another World opens before the youth, like the one he has left, but a little lovely Moony Night rather than a glad day. The triple adjective is faintly ironic, for the Night of Beulah, lit ambiguously by the moon of female love, has a certain fragility in its beauty, a flaw in its reality. Yet, for a moment, it seems to grant a heightened vision of the mundane:

> Another England there I saw,
> Another London with its Tower,
> Another Thames & other Hills,
> And another pleasant Surrey Bower,
>
> Another Maiden like herself,
> Translucent, lovely, shining clear,
> Threefold each in the other clos'd—
> O, what a pleasant trembling fear!

In this movement towards the center of vision the youth ends with another Maiden *like* the one he has entered, but not the same, for this one has the properties of her Cabinet-substances: translucent, lovely, shining clear. More crucially, this is a Maiden who appears as either a kind of Chinese-box effect, three females each of whom is outlined within the other, or more likely three reflected images or mirror-outlines enclosed within one another. The next stanza does more towards resolving this visual complication:

> O, what a smile! a threefold Smile
> Fill'd me, that like a flame I burn'd;
> I bent to Kiss the lovely Maid,
> And found a Threefold Kiss return'd.

It may be that the youth is in a looking-glass world, a carnival of mirrors in which reflections from three sides only partially converge in the midst, producing a troubled and evasive image. The sight of the threefold Maiden provokes both desire and fear, the trembling of anticipatory pleasure. The triple smile fills the youth (presumably his answering smile will appear triple as well), and he burns *like* a flame, a similitude but not an actualization of desire. He meets the frustrating return of a threefold kiss, and strives to seize what seems to him the palpable Maiden, inmost of the three forms. But he seizes destruction, for the nature of Beulah is that only its substances are eternal. Its forms are transient, and the inmost form does not belong to it:

> I strove to sieze the inmost Form
> With ardor fierce & hands of flame,
> But burst the Crystal Cabinet,
> And like a Weeping Babe became—
>
> A weeping Babe upon the wild,
> And Weeping Woman pale reclin'd,
> And in the outward air again
> I fill'd with woes the passing Wind.

The crystalline structure cannot sustain the youth's exuberance; the sexual encounter does not yield an achieved knowledge or final reality. The youth, baffled in his ambition to find an apocalypse in sexual satisfaction, enters the second infancy or Ulro that sundered Innocence is likely to engender. From a dancer in the Wild, at one with it, he has become a weeper upon it. The Maiden's ardor of the poem's opening is now transmuted into the ambiguity attending a "Weeping Woman pale reclin'd." The outward air that was freedom is now only a medium upon which to project a lamentation.

Blake developed the symbolic situation of *The Crystal Cabinet* in *Jerusalem* 70:17–31, where the Maiden becomes Rahab and the youth all that is consumed by her threefold kiss. In the manuscript lyric the identification is fortunately not so specific; if the Maiden's beauty is delusive she is nevertheless not accountable for the poem's disaster. In the aspiration of sexual response, seeing the universe with the intensity imparted by desire, the youth attempts to move directly from the threefold world of Beulah to the fourfold finality of Eden.[3] But love and art cannot so quickly be compounded, and an increase in sensual fulfillment within nature is only the start of a revelation, not its liberating completion. The poem's beauty is to have implied all this, while keeping within its own ambiguous properties, its troubled and treacherous surfaces.

Auguries of Innocence

The theme of apocalypse receives more positive expression in this quatrain and its following stream of couplets, which are not really a single or unified poem but rather a loose sequence of aphorisms. The quatrain is one of Blake's most famous admonitions:

> To see a World in a Grain of Sand
> And a Heaven in a Wild Flower,
> Hold Infinity in the palm of your hand
> And Eternity in an hour.

Usually this is interpreted as mysticism or at least some extraordinary mode of vision, but in actuality it is a simpler yet more drastic way of seeing what are literally "auguries of Innocence," omens of human renovation. The grain of sand is an emblem of dehumanization, yet once it was part of a human world. The wild flower is an organic growth, natural and not human, yet unlike the sun-flower of Experience the wild flower can be a portent of a human and active heaven. The "how" is explicit; this can be done by overcoming the fallen categories of space and time, by seeing what Wordsworth called a "spot of time," a vision of the eternal here and now, not there and when. But Wordsworth had his vision through the mediation of memory; Blake sees what can be seen in an immediacy. Blake's quatrain is urgent, for if the infinite and the eternal are not to be participated in by the poet's vision here and now, then they are never to exist at all.

The couplets begin with a series of warnings that relate the wounding of any part of the organic creation to a larger marring of nature.

If everything that lives is holy, then the impairment of one life lessens all. This humanitarian intensity leads to a Hebraic denunciation of social injustice:

> The Beggar's Rags, fluttering in Air,
> Does to Rags the Heavens tear.
> The Soldier, arm'd with Sword & Gun,
> Palsied strikes the Summer's Sun.
> The poor Man's Farthing is worth more
> Than all the Gold on Afric's Shore.
> One Mite wrung from the Labrer's hands
> Shall buy & sell the Miser's Lands:
> Or, if protected from on high,
> Does that whole Nation sell & buy.

The prophetic passion climaxes the poem by a chant based on the Book of Jonah:

> We are led to Believe a Lie
> When we see With not Thro' the Eye
> Which was Born in a Night to perish in a Night
> When the Soul Slept in Beams of Light.
> God Appears & God is Light
> To those poor Souls who dwell in Night,
> But does a Human Form Display
> To those who Dwell in Realms of day.

Jonah, angry that his prophecy against Nineveh had not been fulfilled, went out of the city, to rest under the shadow of a gourd that the Lord made to come up over him. When God's worm "smote the gourd that it withered," Jonah was made angry again, to be taught the lesson of the true uses of prophecy:

> Then said the Lord, Thou hast had pity on the gourd, for the which thou hast not labored, neither madest it grow; which came up in a night, and perished in a night:

> And should I not spare Nineveh, that great city? . . . 4:10–11

The irony here is directed both against a mistaken notion of prophecy (that it foretells an inevitable future, rather than the decisive power of the eternal now) and against the desire for destruction that wills a premature apocalypse, without waiting upon the fulfillment of time. In the passage that ends Blake's *Auguries* the bodily eye is identified with the shadowing gourd, born in the night of our fall to perish in the night of our destruction. Blake's irony is at its subtlest as he plays with the equivocal beams of light that blind us in our wilful darkness. The eye of our corporeal existence, a narrow opening in our material cavern, was born when our soul slept in the heavenly light. If our soul had kept awake in that light, we would not have fallen, and would now have an eye to see *with*, rather than one we must see *through*, if we are to see our own relation to what we were. But like Jonah we are poor souls dwelling within the mental cavern or whale's belly of the night, the dark forest in which the Bard of Experience saw his Tyger.

As God taught Jonah the humane view of apocalypse, so now Blake seeks to teach it to himself. God appears as a light shining into our darkness if we insist upon dwelling in darkness. But if we see through the eye, then we see auguries of a second Innocence, and dwell in the clear realms of day, where the Tygers of Wrath are anything but fearful, and where God displays the form of the human.

This lesson of the *Auguries* is Blake's own prelude to his brief epic *Milton*, a majestic poem centering on the necessity for the poet's own clearing of his bodily eye, the purging from his own consciousness of everything that is not imaginative. In *Milton* we meet a greater Blake than we have encountered previously, a more profound poet, chastened in rhetoric, and thoroughly in control of his subject.

CHAPTER ELEVEN

Prelude to Apocalypse: *Milton*

Book I, Milton's Descent

Blake's *Milton* is a poem in two books, together comprising a brief epic of about two thousand lines, on the probable model of Milton's *Paradise Regained*, a poem of similar length in four books. Like *Paradise Regained*, *Milton* takes the Book of Job as its ultimate model. All three works center on the dual themes of theodicy and self-recognition, God's justice and man's realization of that justice in his relation to God. Blake's title page bears the Miltonic motto: "To Justify the Ways of God to Men," but the God of *Milton* is not the God of *Paradise Lost* and *Paradise Regained*. Blake's God is referred to in the eighth line of the poem by the resounding title of the "Eternal Great Humanity Divine," and the development of Milton in Blake's poem is from the Puritan to this Blakean idea of God.

Blake begins with a "Preface" that echoes the anti-classical bias of Milton's Jesus in *Paradise Regained* (IV, 331–364), a polemic that prefers the Sublime of the Bible to the imitative art of the Greeks and Romans. One can feel the intensity with which Blake must have responded to Milton's Hebraic passion as the earlier poet attacked classical poetry:

> Remove thir swelling Epithets thick laid
> As varnish on a Harlot's cheek, the rest,
> Thin sown with aught of profit or delight,
> Will far be found unworthy to compare
> With *Sion's* songs, to all true tastes excelling.

Blake goes back to his own satirical *To The Muses* of *Poetical Sketches* as he predicts that in the New Age he heralds "the Daughters of Memory shall become the Daughters of Inspiration," the classical Muses the Daughters of Beulah, the Hebraic married land. As he cries out against those "who would, if they could, forever depress Mental & prolong Corporeal War," Blake is suddenly moved to a plain expression of his theme in marching quatrains:

> And did those feet in ancient time
> Walk upon England's mountains green?
> And was the holy Lamb of God
> On England's pleasant pastures seen?
>
> And did the Countenance Divine
> Shine forth upon our clouded hills?
> And was Jerusalem builded here
> Among these dark Satanic Mills?

These feet walked England's mountains and pastures because Albion as Divine Man was originally one with Jesus. The second stanza contrasts the clouded hills of Blake's England with the human radiance that was replaced by landscape. The dark Satanic Mills have nothing to do with industrialism, but are at one with the vision of the second series of the 1788 tracts, *There Is No Natural Religion:*

> The bounded is loathed by its possessor. The same dull round, even of a universe, would soon become a mill with complicated wheels.

This mill reappeared in the last "Memorable Fancy" of *The Marriage of Heaven and Hell*. In *Milton* the Mills of Satan are spoken of as grinding down creation, transforming the world of Generation into the reductive abstractions of Ulro. This process has gone so far that the first two stanzas of Blake's dedicatory hymn are not just rhetorical questions. Blake has the faith that Jerusalem *was* once built in England, but the Satanic Mills seem to be at work providing objective evidence that this could not have been.

To meet this challenge Blake now states his own defiant and heroic quest as a poet:

Bring me my Bow of burning gold:
Bring me my Arrows of desire:
Bring me my Spear: O clouds unfold!
Bring me my Chariot of fire.

I will not cease from Mental Fight,
Nor shall my Sword sleep in my hand
Till we have built Jerusalem
In England's green & pleasant Land.

The bow of burning gold is a deliberate contrast to the black bow of Urizen in *The Book of Ahania*, which will reappear as the black bow of Satan in *Jerusalem*. The clouds are Urizenic; the Chariot is Miltonic, in the tradition of Ezekiel's Enthroned Man. Gray, in *The Progress of Poesy*, had spoken of Milton as one "that rode sublime/Upon the seraph-wings of Extasy," directly associating Milton with "the living Throne, the saphire-blaze" of Ezekiel's chariot. Blake enters that chariot now in *Milton*, to fight sword in hand the mental wars of the eternal world until the enduring City is built again in the pastoral land of his own childhood.

To justify his assumption of the Miltonic role of poet-prophet, Blake ends his "Preface" with a motto from the Book of Numbers: "Would to God that all the Lord's people were Prophets" (11:29). The speaker is Moses, who is "redeemed" in *Milton* as the mythic figure Palamabron, identified also with Blake himself, as we are about to see. In *Milton* two of the Lord's people, Milton and Blake, join as one to create mutually the vision of an English prophet, and so prepare the way for the prophecy of *Jerusalem*, that supreme attempt on the part of an honest man to tell his nation that if it went on so, the result would be so, the yielding of creation to Satan the Miller of Eternity, the reductive fallacy incarnate.

Milton proper opens fittingly with a great invocation to the Daughters of Inspiration, patronesses of sexual fulfillment:

Daughters of Beulah! Muses who inspire the
    Poet's Song,
Record the journey of immortal Milton thro'
    your Realms

Of terror & mild moony lustre in soft sexual
    delusions
Of varied beauty to delight the wanderer
    and repose
His burning thirst & freezing hunger! Come
    into my hand,
By your mild power descending down the Nerves
    of my right arm
From out the Portals of my Brain, where by
    your ministry
The Eternal Great Humanity Divine planted
    his Paradise.

The realms of Beulah are described equivocally, here as elsewhere
in Blake, but Milton himself will overcome their soft delusions and
win his way through them back to our harsher generative world.
Blake invokes the Daughters, but carefully limits their inspiring function. Their mild power descends down the nerves of *his* creating
right arm from out the portals of his own brain, where a poet's
paradise was planted by God the Human Imagination. The Daughters aided in that planting; they now lend their power also to Blake's
hand, but in both cases they are ministers only, not mastering
forces. Blake has invoked his Muses, but believes that too many
Muses, including those of the historical Milton, have turned out
to be so many Female Wills in the past. He commands the Daughters therefore to admit their own errors, to "tell also of the False
Tongue! vegetated/Beneath your land of shadows." The False
Tongue is the fallen Tharmas, the human taste of Innocence that
turned into the poisonous tongue of the Serpent of Satan, when
Tharmas began his fall in Beulah.

With the Muses thus both invoked and chastised, Blake asks them
to move into the midst of events in his epic story:

Say first! what mov'd Milton, who walk'd
    about in Eternity
One hundred years, pond'ring the intricate
    mazes of Providence,

> Unhappy tho' in heav'n—he obey'd; he murmur'd
>   not; he was silent
> Viewing his Sixfold Emanation scatter'd thro'
>   the deep
> In torment—To go into the deep her to redeem
>   & himself perish?

Milton had died in 1674. One hundred years later the young Blake began to write poems in Milton's tradition worthy of the master. The Eternity Milton has found is the heaven he visualized in *Paradise Lost*, but being there he is unhappy though uncomplaining. He ponders "the intricate mazes of Providence," ironically recalling the demons of his Hell who:

> reason'd high
> Of Providence, Foreknowledge, Will, and Fate,
> Fixt Fate, free will, foreknowledge absolute,
> And found no end, in wand'ring mazes lost.

What moves Milton is in the first place his realization that his own vision needs to be reseen. He has left behind him in the torment of unredeemed nature his Emanation, Sixfold presumably because he had three wives and three daughters. But his Emanation is primarily the world he created or helped create, not just his marriages and family but also his poems and their prophecy. As Milton looks down he sees the world of Blake's time, the tyranny portrayed in Night VIII of *The Four Zoas*. What he sees bears a complex relation of responsibility to what he has made, though *his* creation is in torment because scattered through *the* creation. The Miltonic division between heat and light, the casting out of desire by reason, has in Blake's reading of history a prime responsibility for the natural religion of eighteenth-century culture, its rejection of imagination and embrace of abstract reasoning in the religious sphere.

Yet Blake has progressed beyond this kind of criticism of Milton, which in any case had been developed as far as it could go in *The Marriage of Heaven and Hell*. The poem *Milton* is not written to correct *Paradise Lost* so much as to invoke Milton as a savior for Blake and for England, and therefore for mankind. Milton must descend in order to redeem his creations, and this redemption has a vicarious element in it. Milton's selfhood must perish: the Spectre must vanish if the Emanation is to reveal herself. The Spectre in Milton is everything that impeded his lifelong quest to achieve a societal and artistic form that would unify man in the image of God. The Spectre is therefore every impulse towards dualism, which must include the impulse that shaped the God and Satan of *Paradise Lost* as antithetical beings, and then assigned so much of human energy and desire to Satan.

If the departure from Milton's mind of a kind of Puritan censor is then the theme of Blake's poem, we would expect Blake to develop an alternative reading of cosmic history and human character to that offered in Milton's Puritan epic. Blake seems to have contemplated a longer and more self-contained *Milton* than the one he wrote, but the poem as it was engraved assumes a good deal of this alternative cosmic and psychological argument as being already evident to the reader. This is not the difficulty it might seem, for what *Milton* draws upon is a reading knowledge of the abandoned *Four Zoas*. Armed with our memories of that ambitious poem, we can understand the Bard's Song that immediately moved Milton to his determination of seeking our world again:

> What cause at length mov'd Milton to this
> unexampled deed?
> A Bard's prophetic Song! for sitting at
> eternal tables,
> Terrific among the Sons of Albion, in chorus
> solemn & loud
> A Bard broke forth: all sat attentive to the
> awful man.

The Bard's Song introduces the reader of Blake to an apparent difficulty that will be even more evident in *Jerusalem*: the poet's supposed indecision as to his poem's sequence, his alternative orderings of the engraved plates. The point of Blake's experimentation with continuity, here and in *Jerusalem*, is that the sequence of these poems is frequently not temporal, certain crucial events being both simultaneous with one another and also existent in the continual present of Eternity. Thus, the Bard's Song heard by Milton is sung in Eternity, yet deals with psychic and cosmic events that have taken place where the temporal and eternal dimensions meet, and continue into the historical present of Blake's sojourn (1800–03) at the village of Felpham in Sussex under the patronage of William Hayley, friend and biographer of the poet Cowper, and temporal friend but spiritual and eternal enemy of the poet Blake.

In the following account of the Bard's Song I will follow what seems to be Blake's final ordering of the plates, though I agree with Frye that his possible order of the "C" copy (2, 7, 4, 6, 3, 8 ff., omitting 5) gives the reader a clearer narrative progression.[1] Yet, as Frye himself has observed, the Bard's Song is not the story of a sequence of events, but rather "a series of lifting backdrops," a brilliant experiment in the shifting of visionary perspectives.[2] In this experiment, especially in its final ordering, many contexts meet to suggest how a dispute between a true poet and a poetic impostor widens into a theory of psychological types, and becomes at last a major step towards imaginative emancipation on the poet's part.

The Bard begins by telling us that there are three classes of men, created by the shaping hammer of Los and then woven into their outer garment or bodily form by the looms of Enitharmon. These classes are fallen divisions, for they were made "when Albion was slain upon his Mountains." The three classes are the two Contraries, the Reprobate and the Redeemed, and the Reasoning Negative, the Elect. Blake is refining further the ironic vocabulary of *The Marriage of Heaven and Hell*, with its simpler distinction between Reprobate Devils and Elect Angels. The Redeemed is a class between prophetic Devils and restraining Angels, and includes the larger psychic part of every poet, and indeed of every man. For all three classes are in every man, but one class or another is dominant at one particular time or stage of his development.

The names of Blake's three classes are in part clearly a mockery of Calvinist terminology, for the Elect are to Blake those who worship Satan or the Spectre, while the Reprobate are Elijah or John the Baptist figures, avatars of prophetic tradition. The Redeemed are also named ironically, for the whole point about them is that they are struggling, usually blindly, for redemption. They are a cultural battleground on which the prophets and the upholders of a repressive society meet in combat. If the Redeemed embrace the Reprobate, then contraries meet, and progression takes place, for the Redeemed are now identified with the Devourer of *The Marriage of Heaven and Hell*. The Redeemed of the Bard's Song is the Son of Los named Palamabron, whom we met in *Europe* as a spirit of emergent civilization. The Reprobate of the Song is another Son of Los, Rintrah, who in the "Argument" of *The Marriage of Heaven and Hell* and in *Europe* represented prophetic tradition.

A third Son of Los, though here the sonship is highly equivocal, is Satan or the Elect. If Palamabron embraces Satan then he allies himself with a negation, not a contrary, and no cultural progression is possible. Palamabron's strife of love with Rintrah is society's creative struggle with its prophets, but his acceptance of Satan is a rejection of the civilizing possibilities of prophecy, and finally a dismissal of public honesty.

All this is involved in the Bard's distinction between the Three Classes, but the Bard takes us further back into mythic origins before he adumbrates his categories. He begins with the creation of definite form out of the fallen Urizen by a terrified Los, drawing directly upon Blake's earlier accounts of this creation in *The Book of Urizen* and *The Four Zoas*. Once again we see the seven ages of creation, the creation-fall of man into our present limited body. Again, the major personages of the myth experience their painful births. The natural heart sinks into the Deep of our world, and Los broods over it in dangerous pangs that fever to a false creation:

> He hover'd over it trembling & weeping;
> suspended it shook
> The nether Abyss; in tremblings he wept
> over it, he cherish'd it
> In deadly, sickening pain, till separated
> into a Female pale
> As the cloud that brings the snow; all the
> while from his Back
> A blue fluid exuded in Sinews, hardening
> in the Abyss
> Till it separated into a Male Form howling
> in Jealousy.

The pale Female is Enitharmon, and her sinister pallor is at once the dubious purity attendant upon a Queen of Heaven, and the cloudy presage of the snow of restrained desire. The Male Form is the Spectre of Urthona; the hardening, sinewy blue fluid a strange metaphor for the constituent element in nervous, temporal, wilful fear, a negation of the red blood of life. The remainder of the creation myth here is greatly simplified from its earlier appearances; now all the other beings appear in the fallen world as children of Los and Enitharmon, for nothing comes into even mortal being without an imaginative making. The last-born is Urizen's Spectre, now definitely identified as Satan:

> At last Enitharmon brought forth Satan.
>   Refusing Form in vain,
> The Miller of Eternity made subservient to
>   the Great Harvest
> That he may go to his own Place, Prince of
>   the Starry Wheels
> Beneath the Plow of Rintrah & the Harrow of
>   the Almighty
> In the hands of Palamabron, Where the Starry
>   Mills of Satan
> Are built beneath the Earth & Waters of the
>   Mundane Shell.

The stars in their fixed courses were Urizen's; now in a daring metaphor they are one with Satan's mills in the fallen world. Rintrah is a Plowman, Palamabron a Harrower, Satan a Miller; the activities are brilliantly chosen. Rintrah's prophetic wrath plows up nature, making possible a new planting of more human life. Palamabron's civilizing pity (of a kind that need not divide the soul) levels the plowed land, breaking up the resistant clods of reluctant nature, completing the work of the prophet. But to be harrowed is to be tormented or distressed, and this darker aspect of the word will be relevant to Palamabron. Satan grinds down created life; his mills must be made subservient to the apocalyptic Harvest, for they seek their own reductive and meaningless ends.

Suddenly the Bard rushes us into the midst of the dispute that is the main subject of his Song. We hear Los chastising Satan, and identifying him as the turner of the starry wheels of heaven, at once mills and constellations. By virtue of this function Satan is "Newton's Pantocrator, weaving the Woof of Locke," that is, the ruler and creator of the universe explained by Newton's cosmology and Locke's epistemology, a universe that to Blake is "Druidic" and "Deistic," for reasons explained before. Satan has sought to usurp the Harrow of Shaddai (Hebrew name for "the Almighty," as in the Book of Job), which would mean that the humane ethic formulated by Palamabron out of Rintrah's cleansing wrath would be transformed into "a Scheme of Human conduct invisible & incomprehensible." Palamabron then is the humane element in Moses and other codifiers of religion, while Satan is the Accuser who insinuates himself into all such codification. Yet Satan relies on his amorphousness to escape detection in his infiltrations, which is why he is spoken of in a passage quoted above as "Refusing Form in vain," and why he goes off weeping when he is compelled to obey the angry command of Los.

At the end of the fourth plate, Blake's Bard suddenly shifts perspective, to give the reader a vision of the opposition between Human Proportion, "displaying Naked Beauty, with Flute & Harp & Song" and "Druidical Mathematical Proportion of Length, Bredth, Highth." The first is the art molded by the Redeemed out of Reprobate perception; the second is the Lockean way of putting the world together, accomplished by the Redeemed under the tutelage of the Elect. Satan's attempt to assume the harrow of Palamabron is an attack upon inspired art, with results immediately evident at the beginning of the poem's fifth plate:

> Palamabron with the fiery Harrow in
>   morning returning
> From breathing fields, Satan fainted
>   beneath the artillery.

We have been given another detail of the quarrel between Palamabron and Satan (biographically, between Blake and his Elect patron, Hayley). The associations of the detail are beautifully expressed, and only immediately difficult, for they link up to the anger of Los we have just encountered. Palamabron returns with his fiery Harrow, having broken up nature into a greater wealth of life, leaving behind him "breathing fields." So Blake would have returned to daily social life with Hayley, after a night of labor at *Milton*. And so Hayley-Satan, trying to assume control of the harrow of poetry, would have "fainted beneath the artillery," artillery in its sense of weapons of war, here the flaming arrows thrown off by the harrow. In a startling referential leap, Satan's inability to bear the heat of a creative desire is equated to the Christian doctrine of the Saviour's assumption of sin in his incarnation. Satan is unable to bear the creative fire because he has not sacrificed self.

Again delaying a full account of the dispute with Satan, the Bard commences a majestic chant that continues through most of the fifth and sixth plates. Most of the subject matter is familiar to us. We hear again the mocking pity of the Female Will enumerating human limitations, but there is now an answering sound, the beating hammer of Los, regulating the classes of men, until at last the hitherto fragmented story is given us with powerful directness. Satan, with an altogether sinister and "incomparable mildness," softly entreated Los for Palamabron's station. Lest Satan accuse his brother of ingratitude, he is allowed his way, but returns "terrified, overlaboured & astonish'd." We need not fall back upon Blake's biography to follow what now happens in the poem, but it is instructive to do so, if only to see how greatly Blake transforms his own experience when he uses it in the poem.

The story of Blake's sojourn at Felpham is a pathetic one, and can be derived largely from Blake's own letters. Blake was forty-three when he set out for Felpham, and by any worldly test a sad failure, though he had written some of the finest poems in the language, painted some of the most vital pictures done by an Englishman, and singlehandedly made a comprehensive mythology, an achievement still unique among poets, though many have attempted it since Blake. But the poems and the myth remained unknown, and the pictures almost so. Blake earned what living he could get as an engraver, and by the late summer of 1800 he could get little work in that profession. He had a faithful patron, Thomas Butts, but badly needed another, and thought he had found one in the genial William Hayley, who had been William Cowper's friend and supporter, and who was then starting the only work we remember him by, *The Life of Cowper*.[3]

Cowper, like Blake, sought to revive Miltonic poetry, though not on Blake's scale or with Blake's intensity. The early *Mad Song*, in *Poetical Sketches*, may be taken as an ironic paralleling of Cowper's fate, seeking refuge from sensibility in madness. Years after the Felpham interlude, when the embittered Blake scrawled his poem on Cowper in his Notebook, he had come to suspect Hayley's patronage of Miltonic poets as a Satanic tendency to oppress visionaries, so as to enforce the Urizenic lesson:

> And 'tis most wicked in a Christian Nation
> For any Man to pretend to Inspiration.[4]

As late as 1819, Blake returned to the case of Cowper, when annotating a book on insanity. Called mad so often (critics who ought to know better still mutter about Blake's paranoia) he seems to have investigated the book in an ironical spirit, for his note has Cowper desiring true insanity and saying of Blake: "You retain health and yet are as mad as any of us all—over us all—mad as a refuge from unbelief—from Bacon, Newton and Locke."[5] At Felpham Blake nearly went "mad" in this special sense as a refuge from Hayley and the world of polite disparagement that Hayley represented. Blake's triumph over this madness is in one sense the biographical foundation of *Milton*, for Blake saved himself by Milton's help, as the poem will make clear.

Hayley could make nothing of *The Four Zoas*, which Blake seems to have shown him, and for Blake's own worldly good tried to persuade an epic poet to abandon his vocation. To understand Blake's shock we need to realize that Hayley *was* kindly, and moreover that Hayley was a good representative of Elect taste. Blake had begun with great expectations of Hayley and Felpham, hoping he might have found a haven in which to write a great English epic. On September 23, 1800, soon after arriving at Felpham, Blake wrote to Butts:

Work will go on here with God speed.—A roller & two har-
rows lie before my window. I met a plow on my first going out
at my gate the first morning after my arrival, & the Plowboy
said to the Plowman, "Father, The Gate is Open."[6]

There are the plow of Rintrah and the harrow of Palamabron,
but the glorious expectation of the gate open to eternal vision was
not fulfilled without torment. The mills of Satan (on one level,
Hayley's provision of silly but financially necessary commissions for
engraving) might have been suggested to Blake by Cowper's gently
ironic poem *The Flatting Mill,* if he had happened to see it among
Hayley's Cowper papers:

> Alas for the poet! who dares undertake
>   To urge reformation of national ill—
> His head and his heart are both likely to ache
>   With the double employment of mallet and mill.

The flatting mill of Hayley's employment was at last too much
for Blake. His letters to Butts from Felpham record his growing
consciousness that he was betraying his gifts by association with
Hayley, and his resolution to enlarge and confirm his "Enthusiasm,"
in spite of the Hayleys of this mundane existence. Blake came to
learn that Hayley was his corporeal friend but spiritual enemy. In a
letter to his brother, James Blake, he bluntly stated of Hayley: "The
truth is, As a Poet he is frighten'd at me & as a Painter his views
& mine are opposite."[7] Whatever Hayley consciously wished for
Blake (and all the evidence indicates Hayley's intentions were be-
nign), Blake finally suspected that the Spectre or Satan in Hayley
wished him nothing but destruction.

The episode with the soldier, Scholfield, which led to Blake's
trial for seditious utterance, will be recounted when we consider
Jerusalem, for which it provides the kind of biographical *materia
poetica* that the dispute with Hayley gives to *Milton.* What is relevant
here is that the corporeal Hayley behaved very well towards Blake
in everything concerned with the trial, and helped secure Blake's
acquittal. But Blake, back in London, never got over the uneasy

suspicion that something in Hayley wanted the prophetic voice stilled in England, by one means or another.

This long biographical excursus ought to have prepared for a return to the poem. We left Satan overcome and astonished after a day's labor with the usurped harrow of Palamabron. The poem resumes:

> Next morning Palamabron rose: the horses of
>   the Harrow
> Were madden'd with tormenting fury, & the
>   servants of the Harrow,
> The Gnomes, accus'd Satan with indignation,
>   fury and fire.
> Then Palamabron, reddening like the Moon in
>   an eclipse,
> Spoke, saying: "You know Satan's mildness
>   and his self-imposition,
> Seeming a brother, being a tyrant, even
>   thinking himself a brother
> While he is murdering the just: prophetic I
>   behold
> His future course thro' darkness and despair
>   to eternal death.
> But we must not be tyrants also: he hath
>   assum'd my place
> For one whole day under pretence of pity and
>   love to me.
> My horses hath he madden'd and my fellow
>   servants injur'd.
> How should he, he, know the duties of another?
>   O foolish forbearance!"

Blake had allowed Hayley to usurp the poet's function, while Blake ground down his own inspiration at Hayley's command. But the harrow's horses and serving Gnomes (earth spirits subservient to Urthona, the unfallen Los) cannot tolerate Satanic mastery; the implement of art suddenly is drawn by Horses of Wrath, rebelling against a mock-poet. What is most relevant to *Milton's* central meanings here is that Palamabron-Blake judges against himself for "foolish forbearance," for having suffered a fool gladly.

Palamabron summons Los and Satan, with a call "loud as the wind of Beulah that unroots the rocks & hills." The wind of Beulah is Blake's equivalent of Wordsworth's "correspondent breeze" and Shelley's West Wind, for the breath of inspiration is both creative of art and destructive of the natural order.[8] So Palamabron's movement towards a confrontation with Satan is itself the act of writing a poem.

Los appears before his two sons as a god of the imagination, asked to judge between them, to assign responsibility for a state in which the horses of the harrow "rag'd with thick flames redundant," a tempest of energy vexing its own creation. Satan weeps, "and mildly cursing Palamabron, him accus'd of crimes" Satan himself had wrought. The "*mildly* cursing" is a grimly humorous observation on the benignity of the officious Hayley. The entire scene of the quarrel is now surveyed in a brilliant expansion of comic vision:

> But Satan, returning to his Mills (for Palamabron
>   had serv'd
> The Mills of Satan as the easier task) found
>   all confusion,
> And back return'd to Los, not fill'd with
>   vengeance but with tears.
> Himself convinc'd of Palamabron's turpitude,
>   Los beheld
> The servants of the Mills drunken with wine
>   and dancing wild
> With shouts and Palamabron's songs rending
>   the forests green
> With ecchoing confusion, tho' the Sun was
>   risen on high.

Satan-Hayley has ended with the very Elect conviction of his own righteousness, confirmed by his indignation at the Blakean joyousness into which his Mills have been momentarily transformed. Los is unable to render judgment, because he knows that Palamabron forsook his station, moved by false pity that "divides the soul and

man unmans" and by "officious brotherhood." Contention therefore continues, with strife between Rintrah and Satan expanding
into associations of Rintrah and Michael, the opponent of Satan in
Revelation. The strife is judged by an Assembly of Eden, called down
by Palamabron. In the midst of the Assembly, Palamabron utters
Blake's most bitter prayer:

> O God, protect me from my friends, that they
>   have not power over me.
> Thou hast giv'n me power to protect myself
>   from my bitterest enemies.

The prayer is dreadfully prophetic, for the judgment goes against
Rintrah, though in a complex way:

> Then rose the Two Witnesses, Rintrah &
>   Palamabron:
> And Palamabron appeal'd to all Eden and
>   reciev'd
> Judgment: and Lo! it fell on Rintrah and
>   his rage,
> Which now flam'd high & furious in Satan
>   against Palamabron
> Till it became a proverb in Eden: Satan is
>   among the Reprobate.

The wrath of Rintrah, when it appears in Rintrah himself or in
Palamabron (for their role as "Witnesses" see Revelation 11:3) is
a cleansing emotion, and clarifies the division between art and nature, eternal life and mundane death. The same wrath, when it
appears in Satan, is only a deathly hatred. But the Assembly is unable to make this distinction; the rage of Rintrah, evident in Satan's
going over to him (Hayley's loss of his usually trimphant temper,
as Frye wittily puts it) is condemned by the monstrously misleading
proverb: "Satan is among the Reprobate." In reaction to this, Los
goes over to Rintrah also, and so the opposition between Los and
Satan, poetry and its demonic parody, is at last sharpened. This
sharpening compels Satan to appear in his true form, as Ezekiel's

Covering Cherub, the Accuser's Tongue, or fallen Tharmas. The first of the following passages is *Milton* 9:30–35; the second is Ezekiel 28:14–16:

> Thus Satan rag'd amidst the Assembly, and
>   his bosom grew
> Opake against the Divine Vision; the paved
>   terraces of
> His bosom inwards shone with fires, but the
>   stones becoming opake
> Hid him from sight in an extreme blackness
>   and darkness.
> And there a World of deeper Ulro was open'd
>   in the midst
> Of the Assembly In Satan's bosom, a vast
>   unfathomable Abyss.

Thou art the anointed cherub that covereth; and I have set thee so: thou wast upon the holy mountain of God; thou hast walked up and down in the midst of the stones of fire.

Thou wast perfect in thy ways from the day that thou wast created, till iniquity was found in thee.

. . . and I will destroy thee, O covering cherub, from the midst of the stones of fire.

Confronted by this manifestation of Satan as error incarnate, the misled Assembly is held in an awful silence. But Los and Enitharmon recognize Satan as their old foe Urizen, and Los rejects the jealous morality of Satan as an imposture. He cries out against the emanations of Rintrah and Palamabron, Ocalythron and Elynittria respectively, sun goddess and moon goddess, whom we have previously seen in *Europe*. Elynittria in particular, as a Diana-figure, is condemned as one who "darkenest every Internal light with the arrows of thy quiver," arrows that ought to be of desire, but now are "bound up in the horns of Jealousy to a deadly fading Moon."

This emphasis on Female Jealousy leads into the last section of the Bard's Song, a lament of Satan's emanation Leutha, again introduced to us in *Europe*. It seems clear that *Europe*, with its deliberate Miltonic parodies and its ironic apotheosis of the nightmare of history, is the inevitable prelude to and best introduction for *Milton*. Leutha is clearly modeled upon Satan's daughter and mistress, Sin, in Book II of *Paradise Lost*. But Blake's Sin, unlike Milton's, is repentant. Leutha completes the Bard's story of the Palamabron-Satan dispute by giving us the fullest and most internalized account of Satan's unsurpation of the Harrow. As an analysis of the mingled love and hate that Blake saw Hayley as bearing towards him, it could scarcely be bettered. But it is more than that; its mythic dimensions expand until it is a paradigm of society's love-hate relationship towards inspired art.

Satan's emanative portion, his repressed creativity, loved Palamabron and sought to approach him, but was repelled by Elynittria, more beautiful than Leutha precisely because Palamabron is an artist, a maker of civilizations. Unable to proceed openly, Leutha engendered in Satan "his soft delusory love to Palamabron, admiration joined with envy." The Elect advance upon the Redeemed, offering love and assistance, but harboring the murderous lust of possessiveness. The age will accept Blake as an artist, but only if he will become a Hayley, not a reborn Milton.

The Bard's Song concludes with a sudden sweep of vision, outward from the dispute of Elect and Redeemed into the central Blakean myth familiar to us from *The Four Zoas*. The Limits of Opacity (Satan) and Contraction (Adam) are fixed; the seven Eyes of God or Orc cycles are appointed; the Lamb of God suffers for man, that Albion may be awakened.

When the Bard ceases, a loud murmur against his song is heard in Eternity, for "Pity and Love are too venerable for the imputation of Guilt." Pity and Love are what Satan supposedly possessed in abundance, and in any case the Pity of Palamabron and the Love of Leutha are certainly the culprits of the Bard's story. In all of Eternity, only Milton knows better; he alone is ready to cast out Pity and to root up the infernal grove of Female possessiveness called love. In a moment of overwhelming decision, Milton "took off the robe of the promise & ungirded himself from the oath of God." He is throwing off his own Puritanism, and leaving the Elect so as to become one of the Reprobate and then descend to struggle in behalf of the Redeemed. He has awakened, and sees his heaven as an illusion, a premature rest:

> What do I here before the Judgment? without
>   my Emanation?
> With the daughters of memory & not with the
>   daughters of inspiration?
> I in my Selfhood am that Satan. I am that
>   Evil One.
> He is my Spectre: in my obedience to loose
>   him from my Hells,
> To claim the Hells, my Furnaces, I go to
>   Eternal Death.

"That Satan" is both the Elect being of the Bard's Song, and the great rebel of *Paradise Lost*. Milton chooses to go to Eternal Death (ironically, our life) to loose Satan from the Hells Milton himself created. The Hells are Milton's unrealized creations, now to be made into his Los-like Furnaces. Yet this is only the smaller part of Blake's meaning. Milton's responsibility for the culture Blake insists upon regarding as "Deist" is very great in Blake's view, for Milton was the last English prophet (before Blake) but he was a prophet who had not subdued his own Spectre. Not that Blake is judging thus from any supposedly superior position; far from it. *Milton* does not exist to convert John Milton into being a Blakean; Blake's part in the poem rises out of *his* desperate need for Milton's strength. Blake knew better than any man how hard it is to fight off the Spectre; that indeed is what much of *Jerusalem* is about. What Milton accomplishes on the great forty-first plate of this poem, "Self-annihilation and the grandeur of Inspiration," is not claimed by Blake for himself until the even greater ninety-first plate of *Jerusalem*, which is, to me, the most exalted and moving passage in all Blake's poetry. Milton *was* a true poet, *the* true poet, as far as Blake was concerned, and only his Spectre belonged to the Elect. Certainly, according to Blake, the Spectre wrote a good part of all of

Milton's poetry, but Blake knew the high cost, aesthetic and moral, of constantly struggling to keep the Spectre out of a poem.

From this point on, *Milton* becomes a majestic and relatively simple poem, overwhelmingly rewarding the reader who has been patient with the necessary complexities of the Bard's Song. The remainder of Book I falls into a series of inevitable divisions. The descent of Milton to our world (14:33 to 18:50) is followed by the crucial wrestling between Milton and Urizen and its consequences (18:51 to 20:42). The Eternals' reactions to Milton's descent are culminated (20:43 to 21:44), after which Milton's emanation Ololon resolves to descend also (21:45 to 22:3). Blake and Los merge in preparation for meeting Milton (22:4 to 22:26), after which we hear a dialogue between Los and his sons on the meaning of Milton's descent (22:27 to 24:43). This expands to a description of the world of Los or Blake's vision of "the labour of six thousand years" of fallen history, which takes us to the end of the twenty-ninth plate and concludes Book I of the poem.

Milton's descent from Eden begins with a pause "on the verge of Beulah," where he beholds his own Shadow, the spectral or Satanic form he must first reassume and then annihilate. This Shadow is hermaphroditic, for reasons explained earlier in the discussion of the Satanic hermaphrodite in *The Four Zoas* (see p. 258). The confusion between subject and object in Beulah is the beginning of a "dread shadow twenty-seven fold" that reaches through the vegetative world of Generation "to the depths of direst Hell" (a real Hell) in Ulro. The twenty-seven foldness of the Spectre associates itself in Blake's numerical symbolism with the twenty-seven "churches" into which the cycle of history or Seven Eyes of God are divided, and also with the relations between Satan, Rahab, and Tirzah as a multiple of error, a symbolism most clearly described by Frye.[9]

The Seven Eyes protect Milton in the form of Seven Angels of the Presence who enter the shadow-worlds with him. One of the aspects of the poem *Milton* that is most surprising is the power of an individuality to exist simultaneously in several different states of being. Even as Milton descends and "to himself he seem'd a wanderer lost in dreary night," his real and immortal Self sleeps in Eden. Later, his generative form will wrestle steadily with Urizen in a match that goes on through much of the poem while other aspects of his being move to join Blake and Los.

The startling transformations of our spatial concepts reach a height as Milton comes down like a comet:

> The nature of infinity is this: That every
> thing has its
> Own Vortex; and when once a traveller thro'
> Eternity
> Has pass'd that Vortex, he percieves it roll
> backward behind
> His path, into a globe itself infolding, like
> a sun,
> Or like a moon, or like a universe of starry
> majesty,
> While he keeps onwards in his wondrous
> journey on the earth;
> Or like a human form, a friend with
> whom he liv'd benevolent.
> As the eye of man views both the east &
> west encompassing
> Its vortex, and the north & south with all
> their starry host,
> Also the rising sun & setting moon he views,
> surrounding
> His corn-fields and his valleys of five
> hundred acres square,
> Thus is the earth one infinite plane, and
> not as apparent
> To the weak traveller confin'd beneath the
> moony shade.
> Thus is the heaven a vortex pass'd already,
> and the earth
> A vortex not yet pass'd by the traveller
> thro' Eternity.

This is one of Blake's great passages, based on a psychology that is necessarily a cosmology (as indeed all psychologies may be). *The Mental Traveller* introduced us to this cosmology, and *Milton* relies upon it. What needs to be grasped at once is that there is nothing esoteric about this passage, for Blake's account of the Vortex is descriptive, and indeed only a prophecy of the phenomenological approach to psychology so common in our time.

A vortex is usually defined as a massy fluid in circular motion, with a vacuum in its midst, formed by the motion which tends to draw towards that vacuum whatever it can affect; most simply then, a whirlpool drawing existence in. Frye remarks on the serpentine form of Blake's vortex,[10] and clearly it is intended as a description of phenomenal existence, associated with Orc, the natural man, who is in all of us. To pass *through* a vortex in this sense is to see an object from the object's own point of view, as both Frye and Hazard Adams have noted in regard to this passage.[11] If, like Milton, you are entering an object-world from a higher world where subject and object are creator and creation, then every object you encounter comes to enclose your vision; in seeing it as first separate, and then entering it, you pass from the outer ring of the whirlpool it extends towards you to the vacuum at its center. If you look behind you once you are past that center, the eddy is circular, and at last an enclosed globe, once you are altogether clear of the object. Yet the object need *not* be that fixed density or infolded globe, and here Blake most directly anticipates the phenomenological psychiatrists. It can be "like a human form, a friend with whom he liv'd benevolent." In the presence of a beloved person, the object-world is very close and can be seen as friendly and humanized. In a hostile presence, or in solitude, it can roll far away, and englobe itself into the universe of mocking spheres Blake associated with Newtonian vision. For the eye so to look upon the object-world is indeed to see east and west both together, for the eye recognizes everything, and so all directions enter into the eye: they are at home in it, and its vortex is truly encompassed. Such an eye sees the earth of imagination as "one infinite plane," unlike the weak, corporeal traveller who is confined beneath the world of Beulah in generative bondage.

This image of the vortex is illuminated in the subtle and central passage that follows:

First Milton saw Albion upon the Rock of
    Ages,
Deadly pale outstretch'd and snowy cold,
    storm cover'd,
A Giant form of perfect beauty outstretch'd
    on the rock
In solemn death: the Sea of Time & Space
    thunder'd aloud
Against the rock, which was inwrapped with
    the weeds of death.
Hovering over the cold bosom in its vortex
    Milton bent down
To the bosom of death: what was underneath
    soon seem'd above:
A cloudy heaven mingled with stormy seas in
    loudest ruin;
But as a wintry globe descends precipitant,
    thro' Beulah bursting
With thunders loud and terrible, so Milton's
    shadow fell
Precipitant, loud thund'ring, into the Sea
    of Time & Space.

The vast breach of Milton's descent has taken him through the ruined heart of the deathly Albion. Milton enters the whirlpool of the fallen, natural heart, passing through until the underneath becomes the above, and discovering that the human heart has become only "a cloudy heaven mingled with stormy seas in loudest ruin," which means that it is dominated by Urizen, cloudy sky-god, and Tharmas, chaotic instinct become the god of tormented waters. Once Milton has passed through Albion's heart, the vortex he has penetrated rolls behind him in the form of a wintry globe thundering through the lower heavens. So, as the poet returns to our world, he seems a falling star like his own Satan:

Then first I saw him in the Zenith as a
    falling star
Descending perpendicular, swift as the
    swallow or swift:
And on my left foot falling, on the tarsus,
    enter'd there:
But from my left foot a black cloud redounding
    spread over Europe.

This begins Milton's union with Blake, but the significance of this extraordinary metaphor remains ambiguous for a time. The black cloud is ominous, yet Milton begins to attain illumination. He sees that he must reconcile himself with his sixfold emanation, the three wives and three daughters whom Blake names "Rahab and Tirzah, & Milcah & Malah & Noah & Hoglah." Rahab is added by Blake to make up the six, but the other five, including Tirzah, are identified in Numbers 26:33 as the daughters of Zelophehad, who was sonless, like the aged Milton. These daughters caused Moses to legislate the validity of a separate female inheritance, which to Blake symbolized a triumph of the Female Will. Their number, five, he took as an indication that they were associated with the senses of fallen man. In regard to Milton, they represent his sensual bondage (with Rahab as regent of the senses) and his mistaken struggle with the Female Will, mistaken because he did not strive to humanize it. In a brilliant (though historically distorted) vision, Blake sees the wives and daughters of Milton sitting ranged round him like so many rocks, writing in Urizenic thunder at his dictate. When he dictated thus "his body was the Rock Sinai," like the rock of Urizen that slew Fuzon in *The Book of Ahania.*

Part of the redeemed Milton has begun to enter Blake, but part journeys "above the rocky masses of the Mundane Shell," our present universe, which only a Rintrah can plough, and only a Palamabron harrow. As Milton journeys, he repeats the course of two earlier wanderers in the wilderness, Moses among the Midianites, and Jesus in the Temptation.

The reactions to Milton's descent are treated with Blake's customary irony. Since he appears to be a falling star, he is confused

with Satan, so that Los is appalled at his approach, while the Shadowy
Female welcomes it for the wrong reasons.

One being, the spectral or stony fallen Urizen, knows exactly
what the return of Milton means, and he emerges to engage Milton
in a wrestling match as dramatic and powerful as anything in Blake,
a struggle that calls on Milton to be at once a Samson, a Jacob, and
a new Moses for his people:

> Urizen emerged from his Rocky Form & from
>   his Snows,
> And he also darken'd his brows, freezing dark
>   rocks between
> The footsteps and infixing deep the feet in
>   marble beds,
> That Milton labour'd with his journey & his
>   feet bled sore
> Upon the clay now chang'd to marble; also
>   Urizen rose
> And met him on the shores of Arnon & by the
>   streams of the brooks.
>
> Silent they met and silent strove among the
>   streams of Arnon
> Even to Mahanaim; when with cold hand Urizen
>   stoop'd down
> And took up water from the river Jordan,
>   pouring on
> To Milton's brain the icy fluid from his
>   broad cold palm.
> But Milton took of the red clay of Succoth,
>   moulding it with care
> Between his palms and filling up the furrows
>   of many years,
> Beginning at the feet of Urizen, and on the
>   bones
> Creating new flesh on the Demon cold and
>   building him
> As with new clay, a Human form in the Valley
>   of Beth Peor.

This magnificent passage does assume the reader's knowledge of some crucial Biblical references. The Arnon is a river flowing westward into the Dead Sea, and dividing off the Trans-Jordan lands of the Israelites from Moab. Numbers 21:14 associates the Arnon and the Red Sea, by which the Israelites escaped the deathly bondage of Egypt. The Arnon in Blake has the same significance, as Milton Percival observes, for through it one passes from the body of death into the generative body, from Urizenic law to the sacrifice of Luvah for man.[12] Mahanaim (Genesis 32:2) is where Jacob wrestled with God until he had secured a blessing and the name of Israel. Succoth is where Jacob went afterwards, to build a house and booths (Genesis 33:17), the booths giving the place its name, and associating the story with the harvest festival, where four plants represent four classes of men uniting as one man in worship. Beth Peor is the burial place of Moses in the land of Moab. Drawing all this together and applying it to Blake's passage, we suddenly behold the audacity and clarity with which Blake has molded his sources.

Urizen fears that Milton is coming to overturn his laws, for Milton began by taking off the robe and ungirding himself from the oath of Urizen-Jehovah's convenant with Moses. So Urizen goes forth to battle, turning the warm clay Milton walks upon to freezing and purgatorial marble. They meet and wrestle, two silent and mighty champions, on the shores of Arnon, the body of law striving with the human form divine. Their struggle is like the wrestling of Jehovah and Jacob, except that Milton will not repeat Israel's mistake; he wants to re-form God, and not merely to extract a blessing for himself.

As the battle continues, Urizen attempts an icy intellectual baptism of Milton with Jordan water, but Milton fights back by taking the Adamic red clay of Succoth, emblem of a human harvest, and sculpturing the bare bones of the cold Urizen until he has made him into a Human form in the same valley where the body of Moses or Urizenic law is forever buried. Milton's activity is artistic, and gives the sculptor's gift of life, of red flesh to cold marble, making God into a Man, Urizen into Adam.

The justification of Blake's method in *Milton* is that the referential scaffolding, once learned, can be thrown aside. What remains

is the kind of passage just described, fifteen lines that state with
dramatic economy and inevitable phrasing a conflict that other
poets could not express so adequately at many times the length.

Milton and Urizen, "the Man and Demon, strove many periods."
As the wrestling continues, Rahab and Tirzah send forth temptations
"in all their beauty to entice Milton across the river." Like the living
Moses (not the dead Moses of the Law) Milton must resist this
temptation, and must refuse to cross the Jordan and enter the land
that is to be Israel. If Milton did cross, he would become only
another "King of Canaan" and a High Priest of Natural Religion.
The historical Milton, Blake believed, made the mistake of trying
to cross, as a champion of the Puritan Revolution and a servant
of Cromwell. But Blake's Milton has learned that lesson; he does
not desire to be the founder of yet another church.

Milton does not allow the siren voices to distract him from his
great task. He labors on at sculpturing Urizen, with the result that
"now Albion's sleeping Humanity began to turn upon his couch,"
warmed by the flame of Milton's descent. But though Albion stirs
towards life, Los has till now opposed Milton's passage. At last, almost in despair, he remembers "an old Prophecy in Eden recorded":

> That Milton of the Land of Albion should up
>   ascend
> Forwards from Ulro from the Vale of Felpham,
>   and set free
> Orc from his Chain of Jealousy.

Felpham is where Blake dwells, in an Ulro presided over by a
"mild" and weeping Satan, his natural man or Orc bound down
by the devouring Chain of Jealousy, the selfish possessiveness of
Satan. Moved by his recollection of the prophecy, Los descends down
to the mundane world, to view Satan sleeping in Udan-Adan, the
watery illusion or fallen lake of the indefinite universe. With Los
present, Blake attains to a moment of humanistic illumination, as
Milton joins him and the later poet accepts the union. The passage
climaxes in one of Blake's (or any poet's) greatest metaphors:

But Milton entering my Foot, I saw in the
    nether
Regions of the Imagination—also all men on
    Earth
And all in Heaven saw in the nether regions
    of the Imagination
In Ulro beneath Beulah—the vast breach of
    Milton's descent.
But I knew not that it was Milton, for man
    cannot know
What passes in his members till periods of
    Space & Time
Reveal the secrets of Eternity: for more
    extensive
Than any other earthly things are Man's
    earthly lineaments.
And all this Vegetable World appear'd on my
    left Foot
As a bright sandal form'd immortal of precious
    stones & gold.
I stooped down & bound it on to walk forward
    thro' Eternity.

The Reprobate prophet has become one with the Redeemed poet, and the consequence is a heightened power of vision. Milton enters Blake by the foot because that is the part of the human body associated with Urthona, the Eternal form of Los, and it is the Los or poet in Blake in whom Milton lives again. In the Eternal world the imagination made its home in the earth of Eden, the auricular nerves of Urthona, as the opening lines of *The Four Zoas* put it. In the fallen world the nether regions of the imagination are in the labyrinths of Ulro beneath the gardens of Beulah, but now they have been opened up by the vast breach of Milton's descent through Albion's heart. Though Blake does not yet know it is Milton who has come to him, he is aware of an increase in prophetic power. With a new confidence he sees all of nature as one bright sandal on his own foot, symbolizing the possibility of a redeemed beauty in nature as a consequence of a prophetic stance. With a beautiful gesture of acceptance, Blake receives this hope of a new world, and prepares to walk forward through Eternity.

Blake's acceptance of his mission leads to a similar resolution by Ololon, the Redeemed composite form in Eden of Milton's emanation. In Eden she is "a sweet River of milk & liquid pearl," akin to the "pure river of water of life, clear as crystal" of Revelation 22:1. Her name is evidently based on a Greek word for the lamentation of women to the gods, and her function is the ironic reversal of such a meaning, for though she laments over Milton, she shares in his resolving courage, and emulates him by voluntarily abandoning Eden for the perilous struggles of earth. Blake's response to her inspiring resolution is to complete the incarnation of the Poetical Character within himself:

> While Los heard indistinct in fear, what
>   time I bound my sandals
> On to walk forward thro' Eternity, Los
>   descended to me;
> And Los behind me stood, a terrible flaming
>   Sun, just close
> Behind my back. I turned round in terror,
>   and behold!
> Los stood in that fierce glowing fire; & he
>   also stoop'd down
> And bound my sandals on in Udan-Adan;
>   trembling I stood
> Exceedingly with fear & terror, standing in
>   the Vale
> Of Lambeth; but he kissed me and wish'd me
>   health,
> And I became One Man with him arising in my
>   strength.
> 'Twas too late now to recede: Los had
>   enter'd into my soul:
> His terrors now possess'd me whole! I arose
>   in fury & strength.

The union with Milton had begun the redemption of Generation, the bright vegetative world. The union with Los begins the clarification of Ulro, the indefinite world of abstractions; Los binds on Blake's sandals in Udan-Adan, the lake of illusion. Blake identifies his own trembling here with the district of Lambeth in London, where most of his earlier poetry was created, as if to say that the earlier uncertainties of his myth are now to be dispelled.

Los, having entered into Blake's soul, states his relation to time, for he is its redemptive aspect:

> I am that Shadowy Prophet who Six Thousand
> Years ago
> Fell from my station in the Eternal bosom.
> Six Thousand Years
> Are finish'd. I return! both Time & Space
> obey my will.
> I in Six Thousand Years walk up and down;
> for not one Moment
> Of Time is lost, nor one Event of Space
> unpermanent;
> But all remain: every fabric of Six Thousand
> Years
> Remains permanent, tho' on the Earth where
> Satan
> Fell and was cut off, all things vanish &
> are seen no more,
> They vanish not from me & mine; we guard
> them first & last.
> The generations of men run on in the tide of
> Time,
> But leave their destin'd lineaments permanent
> for ever & ever.

The six thousand years of our fallen history are one eternal moment to Los, for whom nothing human has ever been or ever can be lost. Some Blake scholars seem unable to mention Shelley without a snort of disapproval (Bronowski is a notable example) but Los is a very Shelleyan being, and the best exposition I know of the function of Los is in Shelley's magnificent (and now undervalued) essay, A *Defence of Poetry*, which remains the most profound discourse on poetry in the language. Considering the great poets of the past, Shelley says of them that "they have been washed in the blood of the mediator and redeemer, Time." Their Spectres or Elect parts vanish; their redeemed imaginations survive, to mediate for us.

Blake goes with Los to the gate of the city of Golgonooza, but does not enter, for the sons of Los, Rintrah and Palamabron, brood fearfully at the Gate, anguished at Milton's descent, which they believe to be a triumph for Satan. One point of this incident is to show us that Blake is now distinct from Palamabron, since the distinction could not be made in the Bard's Song. More important is the mistaken identification the sons of Los make, confusing the Milton of the descent with the historical Milton, whose Puritan religion they blame, most persuasively, for the triumph of Mystery. Their complaint allows Blake to summarize his view of religion in his own time. He attacks through their outcry the legacy of Puritanism, the Deism of Voltaire and Rousseau, and the falling-away from vision of Swedenborg. But he praises the revivalism of Whitefield and Wesley, and takes those evangelists as trumpets of judgment, forerunners of his own more strenuous prophecy, signs of Albion's awakening.

In reply to his sons' protests, Los proclaims Milton as "the Signal that the Last Vintage now approaches." But neither they nor any other being but Blake will believe him, which prompts Blake to a tremendous description of the world of Los. This description, one of Blake's most elaborate set-pieces, continues until the end of Book I of the poem. It is, as Frye observes, an attempt to see the whole objective world as a creation of Los,[13] an act of vision so prodigious as to strain even Blake's inventiveness. The three hundred lines of this chant are uneven, but they include some of Blake's finest poetry, and move us more effectively to a possible recovery of human potential than anything in *The Four Zoas* does. Middleton Murry finely emphasized the triumphant refrain of "These are the Sons of Los" that rises from Blake's chant, remarking on the splendor of meaning involved in that simple statement when encountered in its full context:[14]

Thou seest the Constellations in the deep &
    wondrous Night:
They rise in order and continue their
    immortal courses
Upon the mountains & in vales with harp &
    heavenly song,
With flute & clarion, with cups & measures
    fill'd with foaming wine.
Glitt'ring the streams reflect the Vision
    of beautitude,
And the calm Ocean joys beneath & smooths
    his awful waves:

These are the Sons of Los, & these the
    Labourers of the Vintage.
Thou seest the gorgeous clothed Flies that
    dance & sport in summer
Upon the sunny brooks & meadows: every one
    the dance
Knows in its intricate mazes of delight
    artful to weave:
Each one to sound his instruments of music
    in the dance,
To touch each other & recede, to cross &
    change & return:
These are the Children of Los. Thou seest
    the Trees on mountains,
The wind blows heavy, loud they thunder
    thro' the darksom sky,
Uttering prophecies & speaking instructive
    words to the sons
Of men: These are the Sons of Los: These
    the Visions of Eternity,
But we see only as it were the hem of their
    garments
When with our vegetable eyes we view these
    wondrous Visions.

The greatness of this, and of similar passages in *Milton* and *Jerusalem*, is as much beyond the minor poems of Blake as parts of *Paradise Lost* are beyond *Comus* and *Lycidas*. The largest context of this vision is in Blake's "rejection" of the natural world, which is again revealed as being from the first only a dialectical or provisional rejection. Nature, viewed from the perspective of Los, can after all be seen as imagination itself, for the poet's eyes can give even "to airy nothing a name and a habitation delightful," as Blake's deliberate borrowing from Shakespeare's Theseus claims. So even the Constellations, the Starry Wheels of Urizen-Satan, regain their ancient order a.1d music; the awful Ocean of Tharmas "joys beneath," and both stars and waves have become the Sons of Los, laborers in the Vintage that is to yield the wine of salvation. The butterflies of summer are humanized, for they too are the children of Los; and the trees become aeolian harps through the work of instructive winds, an uncharacteristic metaphor for Blake, but inevitable in this vision of all nature as existent under the fatherhood of Los. The other term of Blake's dialectic, the expansive imagination that phenomenal nature cannot comprehend, enters inevitably at the passage's close, to remind us that even the awakened vision of nature gives us only the hem of the imaginative garment.

As the chant of the world of Los continues, a good portion of the anatomy of Blake's mature myth is revealed. What Blake is showing us here is *how* Los rescues us from the sleep of death, for:

> He is the Spirit of Prophecy, the ever
>   apparent Elias.
> Time is the mercy of Eternity; without Time's
>   swiftness,
> Which is the swiftest of all things, all
>   were eternal torment.

The ever apparent Elias (New Testament name for Elijah) is the type of John the Baptist, and it is only the prophetic element in us that makes time a swift mercy, rather than the crippled time of the dark brother of Los, the clock-ridden Spectre of Urthona. The world of Los comprises everything in the state of Experience that progresses through the action of contraries and that is built up as a guard against chaos, but only in a continual sense, since such constructs are never to be valued for their own sakes, but constantly to be created and destroyed by the imagination. Los is therefore an artificer, and everything he builds is only an artifice of Eternity, a sculpture that the fire of fresher vision will burn down.

This work of Los is carried out in three visionary places with the exuberant names of Golgonooza, Allamanda, and Bowlahoola. I have had students who protested that these names inescapably suggested exotic cheeses or football cheers, but they are delightfully arbitrary names that have the immense advantage of eliminating irrelevant ideological associations. Blake had a boisterous sense of humor (to which that splendid poem *When Klopstock England Defied* bears immortal witness) and he chose his new names with ironic care. Golgonooza may have a Golconda or a Golgotha association (as remarked earlier) and Allamanda does suggest the alimentary canal and Bowlahoola the bowels. As Golgonooza is the City of Los, the artifice of Jerusalem, so Allamanda "call'd on Earth Commerce, is the Cultivated land around the City of Golgonooza," reclaimed by the Sons of Los from the forests of the night, the wilderness of error Blake calls Entuthon. This visionary commerce or humanized work has the same function in society that the alimentary canal has in the body, and is necessary to fill out Blake's anthropomorphic myth. Similarly the irreducible or physiological laws of man (as opposed to the Urizenic ones) are called Bowlahoola, and underlie the world of Los, working "in the basement of the imagination," as Frye puts it.[15] The golden Dome of Cathedron, Enitharmon's workshop for weaving outward natural coverings, we have met before in *The Four Zoas*. The sum of these few necessary identifications comes out in *Milton's* more deliberately prosaic passages:

> And every Generated Body in its inward form
> Is a garden of delight & a building of
>   magnificence
> Built by the Sons of Los in Bowlahoola &
>   Allamanda:
> And the herbs & flowers & furniture & beds
>   & chambers

Continually woven in the Looms of
 Enitharmon's Daughters,
In bright Cathedron's golden Dome with
 care & love & tears.
For the various Classes of Men are all
 mark'd out determinate
In Bowlahoola, & as the Spectres choose
 their affinities,
So they are born on Earth: & every Class is
 determinate.

 It can be protested that such passages are not poetry, and in a sense they clearly are only expositional, but long poems have their flats and resting places, and the reader need only learn to use them properly. They are no more frequent in *Milton* and *Jerusalem* than in *The Faerie Queene* and *Paradise Lost*, or any romance or epic whatsoever. Like Spenser and Milton, Blake developed his own versions of high, middle, and low styles, or as Blake phrased it in his preface to *Jerusalem:* "the terrific numbers are reserved for the terrific parts, the mild & gentle for the mild & gentle parts, and the prosaic for inferior parts; all are necessary to each other."

 Book I ends with the vision of time and space as those categories are remade by Los. One of Blake's justly famous passages gives a definitive statement of poetic time:

Every Time less than a pulsation of the
 artery
Is equal in its period & value to Six
 Thousand Years.
For in this Period the Poet's Work is Done,
 and all the Great
Events of Time start forth & are conciev'd
 in such a Period,
Within a Moment, a Pulsation of the Artery.

 This prepares for the more extended vision of the space created by the Sons of Los:

The Sky is an immortal Tent built by the
    Sons of Los:
And every Space that a Man views around his
    dwelling-place
Standing on his own roof or in his garden
    on a mount
Of twenty-five cubits in height, such space
    is his Universe.
And on its verge the Sun rises & sets, the
    Clouds bow
To meet the flat Earth & the Sea in such an
    order'd Space:
The Starry heavens reach no further, but here
    bend and set
On all sides, & the two Poles turn on their
    valves of gold;
And if he move his dwelling-place, his heavens
    also move
Where'er he goes, & all his neighbourhood
    bewail his loss.
Such are the Spaces called Earth & such its
    dimension.
As to that false appearance which appears to
    the reasoner
As of a Globe rolling thro' Voidness, it is
    a delusion of Ulro.
The Microscope knows not of this nor the
    Telescope: they alter
The ratio of the Spectator's Organs but
    leave Objects untouch'd.
For every Space larger than a red Globule
    of Man's blood
Is visionary, and is created by the Hammer
    of Los:
And every Space smaller than a Globule of
    Man's blood opens
Into Eternity of which this vegetable Earth
    is but a shadow.

The red Globule is the unwearied Sun by Los
created
To measure Time and Space to mortal Men
every morning.

A reader who has made the minimal effort necessary to understand Blake ought to find his aesthetic reward in passages like this. The sky is a tent because it is a provisional artifice; like the tents of the wandering Israelites it can be moved at the inspired will of man. The universe is seen by each man according to the position that he holds, and what he sees is not delusion, for the starry heavens are not an infinite abyss but a phenomenon made for and by man. Our heavens move where we go, and the loss of a man diminishes the skies. The delusions of Ulro make a man a point on a globe rolling through voidness, but this globe is nonexistent, not to be seen as such even through a scientific instrument. For every space, being visionary, is made within a pulsation of the artery by the poet's art, except for the little globes of man's blood, the irreducible units of the human existence, and visions still smaller. These last open into Eternity, escaping time more definitively than all the artifices of Los do. The red Globule beating within us is the inward sun, the pure flame by which we live, microcosm of the daily outward center of the creation.

If we stand back from Blake's presentation of the world of Los at the close of Book I of *Milton*, we can see that he has given us something altogether new in his poetry. For the first (and sadly the last) time he has shown the generative world, life as we ordinarily see it, under the aspect of the human. Not that this is an immediately optimistic view of nature, for the progression involved includes the Wine-press of war on earth, in a passage derived from the *Zoas* manuscript, but it has in it the particular hopefulness of the prophet who believes that his world is at the turning and who believes in the decisive power of this moment. That, as I understand it, is the meaning of Blake's magnificent attempt at reclaiming the state of Experience at the end of Book I of *Milton*. We have passed from Palamabron-Blake in the Bard's Song, victimized by his own pity and love, to Milton-Blake in the vision of Los, creating a more human universe by correcting rather than abolishing the natural one.

Milton's descent has saved Blake for the life of prophecy, has confirmed Blake in his vocation of an honest man who is also a poet and who speaks his mind. Nothing is left to be said on this side of the poem, and what Milton could do for Blake he has done. What remains is to recover Innocence as a complement to a revived Experience, and to this subtler recovery Book II is dedicated. In it Milton does for himself what Blake judged him not to have done in history, and so brings both the active world of Generation and the passive, receptive life of Beulah or Innocence to the threshold of more psychic abundance, of undying life.

Book II, Milton's Purgation

Blake seems to have foreshortened Book II, which is not quite half the length of Book I, and which moves through its relative complexities with startling (and effective) abruptness. Evidently Blake wished us to understand that very nearly all the *action* of his poem is concentrated in a few moments of decision in Book I. The events of Book II are few, but each is central to the fulfillment of the themes announced earlier in the poem.

Book II begins with the descent of Ololon into Beulah, a state described more fully here than anywhere else in Blake. The ambiguities of Beulah were first explored by Blake in *Songs of Innocence* and *The Book of Thel*; in *Milton* they are totally exposed. Blake is not attempting a breakthrough into the Eden of finality in this poem. The inmost form is grasped in *Jerusalem*, which is Blake's testament or total statement. The recovery in *Milton* is a restoration of Innocence in its second or "organized" sense, and is therefore associated with sexual union, with Blake's version of the Divine Marriage in the tradition initiated by the Song of Solomon and Isaiah. Milton must purge himself of selfhood and Ololon of any remnant of the Female Will. The two achievements taken together will bring about a balance of creating and created forces, a balance exemplified by that state "where no dispute can come" because in it "Contrarieties are equally true." This "married land," Beulah, has many beautiful presentations in literature, but none so significant as Blake's:

Beulah is evermore Created around Eternity,
        appearing
To the Inhabitants of Eden around them on
        all sides.
But Beulah to its Inhabitants appears within
        each district
As the beloved infant in his mother's bosom,
        round incircled
With arms of love & pity & sweet compassion.
        But to
The Sons of Eden the moony habitations of
        Beulah
Are from Great Eternity a mild & pleasant Rest.

Beulah is the emanative world of Eden, the innocent vision of
nature as perfectly loving mother. Yet it is not what Eden's creation
would have been if unrestrained, but rather a refuge from "the great
Wars of Eternity, in fury of Poetic Inspiration." The emanations that
could not bear to live the life of unbounded Man, the fury of perpetual creation of mental forms, begged a habitation, lest they be consumed when "his joy became terrible to them." They were the
gentler graces of the primordial Man, his outward loves and pities,
and desired only to subsist in themselves. The place they won for
themselves was meant to serve for others:

Into this pleasant Shadow all the weak &
        weary
Like Women & Children were taken away as
        on wings
Of dovelike softness, & shadowy habitations
        prepared for them.
But every Man return'd & went, still going
        forward thro'
The Bosom of the Father in Eternity on Eternity,
Neither did any lack or fall into Error without
A shadow to repose in all the Days of happy
        Eternity.

As a garden of delight Beulah is only a relaxation from the energies of creativity, but it clearly has a therapeutic value even for Eden. What is found wanting or mistaken in the eternal world can sleep in Beulah until it is strong enough to enter again into the fires of Eden. But Ololon does not descend into it for that reason, and the mystery of her coming, together with her lamentation for Milton, causes all Beulah to weep. The visible glory of Ololon as she comes down is associated with the radiance of the Lord himself, or Man. This falling light, misunderstood on the earth as an advent of disaster, is in one sense the glory that Milton created in the heavens, especially in the great invocation to light that opens Book III of *Paradise Lost*.

As the earth trembles below, and Beulah weeps above, Blake exquisitely sets against this weeping his own "Vision of the lamentation of Beulah over Ololon":

> Thou hearest the Nightingale begin the Song
> of Spring.
> The Lark sitting upon his earthy bed, just
> as the morn
> Appears, listens silent; then springing from
> the waving Cornfield, loud
> He leads the Choir of Day: trill, trill, trill,
> trill,
> Mounting upon the wings of light into the
> Great Expanse,
> Reecchoing against the lovely blue & shining
> heavenly Shell.
> His little throat labours with inspiration;
> every feather
> On throat & breast & wings vibrates with the
> effluence Divine.
> All Nature listens silent to him, & the awful
> Sun
> Stands still upon the Mountain looking on
> this little Bird
> With eyes of soft humility & wonder, love
> & awe.

> Then loud from their green covert all the
>   Birds begin their Song:
> The Thrush, the Linnet & the Goldfinch, Robin
>   & the Wren
> Awake the Sun from his sweet reverie upon the
>   Mountain.
> The Nightingale again assays his song, & thro'
>   the day
> And thro' the night warbles luxuriant, every
>   Bird of Song
> Attending his loud harmony with admiration &
>   love.
> This is a Vision of the lamentation of Beulah
>   over Ololon.

From Eden, the lamentation of Beulah may seem an expression of grief, but from our world of Generation any song of Beulah is a song of Spring, the natural world expressing itself at its most delightful. With great skill Blake introduces in this and the next passage the two messengers of Los, the natural signs that his visions are at hand, the lark's song, and the dance, color, and odor of the wild thyme. They are chosen for their leadership of the songs and dances of the new day. The nightingale begins the song, but the lark leads the choir of day. The special reverence paid the nightingale throughout this passage is the most gracious of tributes to the blind Milton, who in the invocation to Book III of *Paradise Lost* compared his nightly labors on the poem to the nightingale's song, composing even:

> as the wakeful Bird
> Sings darkling, and in shadiest Covert hid
> Tunes her nocturnal Note.

Blake's return to Innocence is even more triumphant as he sees the wild thyme lead the dance of flowers:

> Thou percievest the Flowers put forth their
>   precious Odours,

And none can tell how from so small a center
    comes such sweets,
Forgetting that within that Center Eternity
    expands
Its ever during doors that Og & Anak fiercely
    guard.
First, e'er the morning breaks, joy opens in
    the flowery bosoms,
Joy even to tears, which the Sun rising dries:
    first the Wild Thyme
And Meadow-sweet, downy & soft waving among
    the reeds,
Light springing on the air, lead the sweet
    Dance: they wake
The Honeysuckle sleeping on the Oak; the
    flaunting beauty
Revels along upon the wind; the White-thorn,
    lovely May,
Opens her many lovely eyes listening; the
    Rose still sleeps,
None dare to wake her; soon she bursts her
    crimson curtain'd bed
And comes forth in the majesty of beauty;
    every Flower,
The Pink, the Jessamine, the Wall-flower,
    the Carnation,
The Jonquil, the mild Lilly, opes her heavens;
    every Tree
And Flower & Herb soon fill the air with an
    innumerable Dance,
Yet all in order sweet & lovely. Men are
    sick with Love.
Such is a Vision of the lamentation of Beulah
    over Ololon.

Og was a giant king defeated and slain by Moses (Numbers
21:33–35), while Anak was the ancestor of a race of giants who
affrighted the Israelites (Numbers 13:33). Throughout *Milton* these

sinister beings and their cohorts Sihon (also destroyed by Moses) and Satan are workers at the dark Satanic Mills, murderous and Elect Accusers of sin. But they have their providential function, though they perform it unwillingly. We are told later, in *Jerusalem* 49:54–59, that these beings are the arches of Albion's Tomb, Guards of the Body of Divine Analogy. Most simply, they are a barrier between the mundane and imaginative worlds, or as Foster Damon succinctly states their function: "they guard jointly the gates of the heart and the brain in nature as well as in man."[16]

In this surpassingly beautiful passage the reference to Og and Anak is a triumphant irony, for the central emphasis of these lines is on the imaginative vision re-creating nature. With the previous passage, these lines are the answering chorus to the vision of the world of Los at the end of Book I. The pungent odor of the wild thyme, coming first to Blake's sense in the morning even as the lark's song first reaches him, is a defiance of the small center from which it comes, even as the lark's song is astonishing in coming from so small a throat. But Eternity expands from the Center in Blake's redeemed world, where inward and upward are the same direction, just as outward and downward together form the contrary direction. Og and Anak as Millers of Eternity would like to grind the Center down, but must fiercely guard it instead. Out of that Center, as out of the lark's throat, comes an "order sweet & lovely," for nature at its best, to Blake, is an imitation of the human art of the eternal world. Center, one feels compelled to add, is not a concept out of any esoteric doctrine or mysticism here, but simply means "center," a point of organization within every part of the creation around which that part coheres and so constitutes an individuality or Minute Particular, against which the grindings-down of Satanic Millers cannot prevail.

No commentator on these two passages that form Blake's "Vision of the lamentation of Beulah over Ololon" can leave them without the uneasy feeling that he may have intruded unnecessarily on some of the most beautiful lines in English poetry. No poet who could write like this is to be assumed incapable of creating the effect of sensuous beauty in verse whenever and however he wished:

> . . . the flaunting beauty
> Revels along upon the wind; the White-thorn,
>   lovely May,
> Opens her many lovely eyes listening; the
>   Rose still sleeps . . .

Most readers who think they prefer Blake's minor to his major poems (without having read the latter) do so on the assumption that he lost the ability to write as he did in the *Songs of Innocence* or *The Book of Thel.* Blake never wrote a line without trying to clarify its relation to a larger context, and he was too great a verbal artist not to seek the appropriate style for each context. He did not abide in the vision of Innocence; no poet can without enfeebling his art. The greatness of Keats is his breaking with that vision in the Great Odes and *The Fall of Hyperion,* just as the relative failure of Tennyson was his inability either to find a mature context for his poetry or to form a style suitable for a harsher context than the imitative harmony of sensuous delight. Much in *Milton* and even more in *Jerusalem* is stark and harsh, but the poetry is always there, firmly articulate and coherent, and rising into rhapsodic eloquence when the theme demands it.

The lamentation of Beulah is interrupted by a dialogue in Eden between Milton's immortal form and his seven guardian Angels. Milton, in a daring appropriation of the manuscript poem on Spectre and Emanation, is now heard declaring his repudiation of his own heavens:

> I have turned my back upon these Heavens
>   builded on cruelty;
> My Spectre still wandering thro' them follows
>   my Emanation,
> He hunts her footsteps thro' the snow & the
>   wintry hail & rain.
> The idiot Reasoner laughs at the Man of
>   Imagination,
> And from laughter proceeds to murder by
>   undervaluing calumny.

The ruinous cycle of strife between Spectre and Emanation is likened to the Spectre Accuser or idiot Reasoner's murderous calumny of genius. Both instances are "natural," in the sense of a nature not re-formed by Los and his children. The Seven Angels, led by Lucifer, the light-bearing unfallen Satan (identified with Hillel by Blake's apparently deliberate misreading of a Hebrew phrase in Isaiah 14:12) instruct Milton in the saving contrary to what he has repudiated. They summarize Blake's doctrine of States:

> Distinguish therefore States from Individuals
> in those States.
> States Change, but Individual Identities
> never change nor cease.
> You cannot go to Eternal Death in that which
> can never Die.
> Satan & Adam are States Created into Twenty-
> seven Churches,
> And thou, O Milton, art a State about to be
> Created,
> Called Eternal Annihilation, that none but
> the Living shall
> Dare to enter, & they shall enter triumphant
> over Death
> And Hell & the Grave: States that are not,
> but ah! Seem to be.
>
> Judge then of thy Own Self: thy Eternal
> Lineaments explore,
> What is Eternal & what Changeable, & what
> Annihilable.
> The Imagination is not a State: it is the
> Human Existence itself.

Satan is the limit beyond which materiality or opaqueness cannot go; Adam is the limit beyond which the human powers of sense cannot contract. The twenty-seven Churches are that many demonic cycles of fallen history, named Churches after the institutionalized spiritual errors of each age. The State of Milton, which is about to be created by the poet's self-purgation, is a state of self-annihilation, in which the Spectre is cast off by the awakened humanity in a man. To enter that state is to cast off also everything that can die, every mortal encrustation, for the Imagination cannot pass away, being not a state but the Human Existence itself. We verge for the first time in Blake on what will be the burden of *Jerusalem*, the distinction between mortality as the self's prison and immortality as the imagination's freedom.

The dialogue of Milton and the Seven Angels ends with the same image of Christ's death clothes thrown aside as began *The Marriage of Heaven and Hell*. With an effective juxtaposition, Blake begins a new plate (33) in which the Divine Voice of awakened Man is heard amidst the Songs of Beulah, echoing Isaiah and Solomon's Song:

> When I first Married you, I gave you all my
>   whole Soul;
> I thought that you would love my loves & joy
>   in my delights,
> Seeking for pleasures in my pleasures, O
>   Daughter of Babylon.
> Then thou wast lovely, mild & gentle; now
>   thou art terrible
> In jealousy & unlovely in my sight, because
>   thou hast cruelly
> Cut off my loves in fury till I have no love
>   left for thee.

Blake is modifying the myth of the married land, which in Isaiah and his commentators is essentially a parable of faith, into an image of free love, free of the possessive jealousy that characterizes Female Love. The Daughter of Babylon here is not yet the harlot Rahab, but any Daughter of Beulah who seeks to be the sepulchre or permanent monument of a human love. By extension, she is also what Ololon might have become had she not chosen to follow Milton in his descent.

As Ololon goes down through Beulah its singers hail her as the repentant cause for the descent of Milton and his Seven Angels (together "the Eight Immortal Starry-Ones") from Eden to Ulro.

Ololon looks down into the ironically named Heavens of Ulro, seeing in them the two fountains of the River of Life in Eternity, intellectual War and Hunting, now become "Fountains of bitter Death & of corroding Hell." Ololon's descent, despite this frightening vision, opens a wide road from Generation to Eden, in contrast to the broad way from Hell to fallen earth opened by Sin and Death in *Paradise Lost*. The moment of Ololon's arrival in our world, the generative universe of Los and Enitharmon, is celebrated by Blake with a kind of wondering joy:

> There is a Moment in each Day that Satan
>   cannot find,
> Nor can his Watch Fiends find it; but the
>   Industrious find
> This Moment & it multiply: & when it once
>   is found
> It renovates every Moment of the Day if
>   rightly placed.

This moment is the pulsation of the artery, in which the poet's work is done, and the emblems of the moment, the Wild Thyme and the Lark, re-enter the poem:

> Just in this Moment, when the morning odours
>   rise abroad
> And first from the Wild Thyme, stands a
>   Fountain in a rock
> Of crystal, flowing into two Streams: one
>   flows thro' Golgonooza
> And thro' Beulah to Eden beneath Los's
>   western Wall:
> The other flows thro' the Aerial Void & all
>   the Churches,
> Meeting again in Golgonooza beyond Satan's
>   Seat.
>
> The Wild Thyme is Los's Messenger to Eden,
>   a mighty Demon,

Terrible, deadly & poisonous his presence in
    Ulro dark;
Therefore he appears only a small Root
    creeping in grass
Covering over the Rock of Odours his bright
    purple mantle
Beside the Fount above the Lark's nest in
    Golgonooza.
Luvah slept here in death & here in Luvah's
    empty Tomb.
Ololon sat beside this Fountain on the Rock
    of Odours.

The streams are like the single pure river of water of life of
Revelation 22:1, their division being the interesting feature. One
flows through artistic creation on to the recovered paradise and then
on to Eternity, the western Wall of Los undoubtedly standing here
for the human body. The other, more deviously, survives the chaos
of space and the dogmas of the historical Churches to flow at last
beyond Satan's seat into Golgonooza, whence it can pursue the course
of its brother-stream. Blake's point is that nothing can be lost from
the moment of creation, for the Fountain of life stands *in* this
moment, and whatever is diverted into the void of dogmatic belief
will find its way home again. The Wild Thyme's odor is a response
of earth to the poet's moment, and this response becomes a "Mes-
senger to Eden," a mighty Demon only if its presence is felt by
a dweller in Ulro, like the Urizen who was stung to life again by
the odors of Generation. In its restrained appearance, in our world,
the Wild Thyme covers the Rock of nature with a bright purple
mantle, purple flowers being a traditional emblem for mourning the
death of a young man or a god. Here the dying man-god is Luvah-
Jesus, and the Rock of Odours or revived nature is his empty
tomb, signifying his resurrection. Ololon, waiting for Milton to come
to her, sits beside the redeemed tomb and the life-giving fountain,
taking on the function of the rescued heroine of romance.

Meanwhile the Lark mounts up and enters the Heaven or illusive
abode of the Church Blake calls Luther, the last of the twenty-seven
Churches or Orc cycles. The Lark is met by another Lark, and a

succession is set up, until twenty-seven immortal moments have
served to traverse the twenty-seven illusions of orthodoxy. The twenty-
eighth Lark reaches the earth again to inaugurate the twenty-eighth
Church which is no church but the imaginative freedom that is
Blake's version of Milton's Christian Liberty. As this means that
redemption is at hand, "the Twenty-eighth bright Lark met the
Female Ololon descending into my garden," the garden of Blake's
cottage at Felpham (charmingly shown in the design on plate 36):

> And as One Female Ololon and all its mighty
> Hosts
> Appear'd, a Virgin of twelve years: nor
> time nor space was
> To the perception of the Virgin Ololon; but
> as the
> Flash of lightning, but more quick, the Virgin
> in my Garden
> Before my Cottage stood; for the Satanic Space
> is delusion.

Ololon in her descent is a multitude, the mighty hosts associated
with the glory of the Savior, but she appears in Blake's garden as
a "Virgin of twelve years," the female on the threshold of her sexual
nature, poised between the choices of Oothoon and Thel, to seek
love or run shrieking from its consequences. Her appearance in Blake's
garden is the destruction of the Satanic delusions of time and space.
Milton has sought her in vain, but *her* quest is realized; the emanation is within us, and can appear where and when it will.

Blake now enters into the dignity of his final role in the poem,
to be the seer of the Miltonic Great Marriage:

> For when Los join'd with me he took me in
> his fi'ry whirlwind:
> My Vegetated portion was hurried from
> Lambeth's shades;
> He set me down in Felpham's Vale & prepar'd
> a beautiful

Cottage for me, that in three years I might
    write all these Visions
To display Nature's cruel holiness, the
    deceits of Natural Religion.
Walking in my Cottage Garden, sudden I
    beheld
The Virgin Ololon & address'd her as a
    Daughter of Beulah:

The "cruel holiness" of nature exists in Ololon only as her virginity, which is Blake's most ironic reversal of Milton, whose *Comus* with its virgin heroine is the most un-Blakean of major English poems. The dialogue between Ololon and Blake is worthy of the occasion. The prophet asks Ololon to comfort his wife, and she confesses her terror at her own Act in Great Eternity which separated her from Milton in her own selfish chastity and holiness. The rest of the poem is a witness to the consequences of Ololon's readiness to put off the selfish virtues of the orthodox heavens.

In answer to Ololon's search, Milton now descends into Blake's garden. Blake sees in Milton what in *Jerusalem* he will find in himself, a concentration of error, a Spectre that must be subdued. In the Miltonic Shadow there appear the gods of the heathen, from Baal and Ashtaroth to Saturn, Jove, and Rhea, and the twenty-seven Churches from Adam to Luther. For Milton in his orthodoxy had been one with the Covering Cherub, a guardian of the sacred become a barrier between man and his salvation. Now the great Puritan comes down to Blake's cottage garden, to confront the form of his most beloved creation:

And Milton collecting all his fibres into
    impregnable strength
Descended down a Paved work of all kinds
    of precious stones
Out from the eastern sky; descending down
    into my Cottage
Garden, clothed in black, severe & silent
    he descended.

Against the possibility that this greatest of the Sons of Los may cast him out forever, Satan manifests himself on the chaotic sea:

> The Spectre of Satan stood upon the roaring
> sea & beheld
> Milton within his sleeping Humanity; trembling
> & shudd'ring
> He stood upon the waves a Twenty-seven fold
> mighty Demon
> Gorgeous & beautiful; loud roll his thunders
> against Milton.
> Loud Satan thunder'd, loud & dark upon mild
> Felpham shore
> Not daring to touch one fibre he howl'd round
> upon the Sea.

Satan is not only the history of religion incarnate; his is the genuine attraction or sinister beauty, the singular persuasiveness of that history. There is in Blake not only a fear of this Satan, but a mature realization that he like all men is capable of standing in Satan's bosom:

> I also stood in Satan's bosom & beheld its
> desolations:
> A ruin'd Man, a ruin'd building of God, not
> made with hands:
> Its plains of burning sand, its mountains
> of marble terrible:
> Its pits & declivities flowing with molten
> ore & fountains
> Of pitch & nitre: its ruin'd palaces &
> cities & mighty works:
> Its furnaces of affliction in which his
> Angels & Emanations
> Labour with blacken'd visages among its
> stupendous ruins;
> Arches & pyramids & porches, colonades &
> domes,

In which dwells Mystery, Babylon; here is
    her secret place;
From hence she comes forth on the Churches
    in delight;
Here is her Cup fill'd with its poisons in
    these horrid vales,
And here her scarlet Veil woven in
    pestilence & war;
Here is Jerusalem bound in chains in the
    Dens of Babylon.

The greatness of this is not just in Blake's rhetoric, powerfully concentrated as that is in this passage. What makes these lines so very moving is concentrated in "A ruin'd Man, a ruin'd building of God, not made with hands." For the Spectre ought to be Man, but is ruined; the Spectre in all its ruin remains a building that even the hands of Los cannot make from whatever exuberance of creative desire. Milton sculpts human form unto Urizen, but this is a remaking, not an original creation. The vision of desolation that Blake sees in Satan's bosom is terrible because those plains of burning sand were once the human form divine, and those domes of Babylon were once the City of God.

Facing Satan, Milton states both his knowledge of Satan's nature, and his own refusal to be a twenty-eighth fallen Church, a greater than Satan in Satan's place:

Thy purpose & the purpose of thy Priests
    & of thy Churches
Is to impress on men the fear of death, to
    teach
Trembling & fear, terror, constriction,
    abject selfishness.
Mine is to teach Men to despise death & to
    go on
In fearless majesty annihilating Self,
    laughing to scorn
Thy Laws & terrors, shaking down thy
    Synagogues as webs.

Satan's reply is a desperate assertion of his Godhood, but he is
already defeated. The Starry Seven Angels of the Presence signal
this defeat by suddenly appearing around Milton on Blake's path.
They sound the trumpets of apocalypse, bidding Albion awake from
his slumbers of six thousand years. Satan is allowed a final manifestation in the shape of a demonic parody of the God of Ezekiel's
chariot, and then Albion begins to stir. In a remarkable passage the
whole of England is seen as an anthropomorphic projection, struggling to rise up, like Milton's own vision of an awakening English
nation in his *Areopagitica:*

> His head bends over London; he sees his
>   embodied Spectre
> Trembling before him with exceeding great
>   trembling & fear.
> He views Jerusalem & Babylon; his tears flow
>   down.
> He mov'd his right foot to Cornwall, his
>   left to the Rocks of Bognor.
> He strove to rise to walk into the Deep, but
>   strength failing
> Forbad, & down with dreadful groans he sunk
>   upon his Couch
> In moony Beulah. Los, his strong Guard,
>   walks round beneath the Moon.

In this immense effort, Albion has failed, and his final awakening
is left for *Jerusalem.* But he has striven to rise, and his continued
rest in Beulah is providential, guarded by Los who encircles the
reigning Moon that regulates Beulah. Albion's effort is a prophecy
of complete awakening, and it is enough to cause Urizen to faint
in terror among the Brooks of Arnon, where still he strives with
the indomitable Milton, in a struggle that will not terminate until
apocalypse.

At last Milton and Ololon meet, to find the love of contraries and,
through one another, the divine form of the human. Ololon has
seen Milton "strive upon the Brook of Arnon," and she has seen
also enough of the world of Blake's time to identify herself with

the "impossible absurdity" of natural religion, outrageous in its foolishness because it seeks to justify the wretchedness of this world. The heavens she has abandoned were the allegorical abode worshipped by this world, and she was the principal ornament of those heavens. When she rejects herself, she causes a manifestation of Satan's dreaded emanative portion, Rahab the Whore of Babylon:

> No sooner she had spoke but Rahab Babylon
>   appear'd
> Eastward upon the Paved work across Europe
>   & Asia,
> Glorious as the midday Sun in Satan's
>   bosom glowing,
> A Female hidden in a Male, Religion hidden
>   in War,
> Nam'd Moral Virtue, cruel two-fold Monster
>   shining bright,
> A Dragon red & hidden Harlot which John in
>   Patmos saw.

Rahab is the Female Will to the exclusive possession of holiness hiding within the Male Will to murderous conquest, and so truly she is "Religion hidden in War." She is state religion, and the moral virtue in the name of which societies exploit and murder, at all times and in every place. But once she has been exposed for what she is, she vanishes from this poem, for a complete epiphany of the Antichrist is what *Milton* on its negative side has sought to achieve. It will be for *Jerusalem* to destroy this evident error, once *Milton* has exposed Rahab and Satan in all their delusiveness.

What remains in *Milton* are the poem's finest passages, in a subtly organized conclusion. Milton turns towards Ololon in terrible majesty, urging her to obey his inspired counsel towards self-annihilation. The Negation of moral virtue, symbolized by Ololon's virginity, must be destroyed if the creative Contraries of Milton and Ololon are to be redeemed. The climax is in Milton's great chant of prophetic dedication on the forty-first plate:

To bathe in the Waters of Life, to wash off
    the Not Human,
I come in Self-annihilation & the grandeur
    of Inspiration,
To cast off Rational Demonstration by Faith
    in the Saviour,
To cast off the rotten rags of Memory by
    Inspiration,
To cast off Bacon, Locke & Newton from
    Albion's covering,
To take off his filthy garments & clothe
    him with Imagination,
To cast aside from Poetry all that is not
    Inspiration,
That it no longer shall dare to mock with
    the aspersion of Madness
Cast on the Inspired by the tame high finisher
    of paltry Blots
Indefinite, or paltry Rhymes, or paltry
    Harmonies,
Who creeps into State Government like a
    catterpiller to destroy;
To cast off the idiot Questioner who is
    always questioning
But never capable of answering, who sits
    with a sly grin
Silent plotting when to question, like a thief
    in a cave.

The central image here is of the contrasting garments, Memory and Imagination. If there is a single central image in *Milton*, it is the garment, from the weavings of Enitharmon's looms that cover the three classes of men through Milton's taking off the robe of the promise on to the appearance of Jesus in the apocalyptic "Garment dipped in blood" that emerges from the dispelled clouds of Ololon on the forty-second plate. The whole of Milton's heroic testimony is concentrated in this multiple image, for the garment that must be put off is revealed as only an "Incrustation over my Immortal Spirit," to be cleansed from every human face by self-examination. To cast off the false garment is to become free of "the idiot Questioner," the brooder who squats in Ulro and whose doubtings ruin poets. "The idiot Questioner" is one with the doubts that Wordsworth overcomes in *Resolution and Independence*, and with the Remorse cast out by Yeats in A *Dialogue of Self and Soul*. He is the shadow haunting every body, the Covering Cherub acting as barrier between creative desire and artistic completion.

The reply of Ololon to Milton's declaration is the last crisis of the poem:

> Is this our Feminine Portion, the Six-fold Miltonic
>   Female?
> Terribly this Portion trembles before thee, O
>   awful Man.
> Altho' our Human Power can sustain the severe
>   contentions
> Of Friendship, our Sexual cannot, but flies into
>   the Ulro.
> Hence arose all our terrors in Eternity, & now
>   remembrance
> Returns upon us. Are we Contraries, O Milton,
>   Thou & I?

The "our" of the first line here indicates that the struggle is over; Ololon desires to be one with Milton. Beulah must surrender to Eden, and the sexual threefold must become the human fourfold. The spectral garment is one with Ololon's virginity, the will of an element in the Feminine Portion to remain mocking, outward and elusive. The wars of Eden can be sustained by the human, but these "severe contentions of friendship" are too much for the sexual nature, which takes refuge in the Ulro. Blake does not mean that Milton and Ololon are giving up sexual love, but rather that like the speaker in *My Spectre around me night & day* . . . they resolve to give up Female Love, the sexual conventions of society and religion. They are truly to be Contraries:

So saying, the Virgin divided Six-fold, & with
    a shriek
Dolorous that ran thro' all Creation, a
    Double Six-fold Wonder
Away from Ololon she divided & fled into the
    depths
Of Milton's Shadow, as a Dove upon the stormy
    Sea.

As her virginal Spectre leaves Ololon, with a death-shriek that is
the contrary of Thel's final shriek as she fled back to Beulah, Blake's
imagery suggests the story of Noah's flood and its subsiding. Chaos
is ending, and so the virginal self flies off as the dove at last departed.
As an image of salvation, a Moony Ark at once an emblem of Beulah
and another reminiscence of Noah's salvation, Ololon now descends
again into Felpham's Vale. Her clouds are now the "Garment dipped
in blood" of Jesus, who is himself "the Starry Eight" become "One
Man." With this manifestation at hand, Blake has a vision of the
prelude to apocalypse:

And I beheld the Twenty-four Cities of Albion
Arise upon their Thrones to Judge the Nations
    of the Earth;
And the Immortal Four in whom the Twenty-four
    appear Four-fold
Arose around Albion's body. Jesus wept &
    walked forth
From Felpham's Vale clothed in Clouds of blood,
    to enter into
Albion's Bosom, the bosom of death, & the Four
    surrounded him
In the Column of Fire in Felpham's Vale; then
    to their mouths the Four
Applied their Four Trumpets & them sounded to
    the Four winds.

The Immortal Four are the redeemed Zoas sounding the trumpets
of judgment. Shattered by that immortal sound, Blake is momentarily overcome:

Terror struck in the Vale I stood at that
    immortal sound.
My bones trembled, I fell outstretch'd upon
    the path
A moment, & my Soul return'd into its mortal
    state
To Resurrection & Judgment in the Vegetable
    Body;
And my sweet Shadow of Delight stood trembling
    by my side.

Commentators seeking to find a mystic in Blake swoop at this passage with happy avidity, and mis-read as usual in doing so. The passage is dramatic, and deliberately naturalistic; its naturalism is indeed its entire point. Blake is telling us that he cannot get beyond the laws of the body here; the trumpet of a prophecy fells him for a moment, until he revives to await "Resurrection & Judgment" in the mortal or vegetative body. Milton himself was a mortalist, believing that body and soul died together, and would be resurrected together. Blake more than Milton knows that body and soul cannot be divided.

With Blake and his wife observing from their Felpham garden, the presages of apocalypse gather together:

Immediately the Lark mounted with a loud trill
    from Felpham's Vale,
And the Wild Thyme from Wimbleton's green &
    impurpled Hills.
And Los & Enitharmon rose over the Hills of
    Surrey:
Their clouds roll over London with a south
    wind; soft Oothoon
Pants in the Vales of Lambeth, weeping o'er her
    Human Harvest.
Los listens to the cry of the Poor Man; his
    Cloud
Over London in volume terrific low bended in
    anger.

There is exact poetic justice in Oothoon's entry upon this scene, for she now receives the Human Harvest she deserved, and which nothing in the world of *Visions of the Daughters of Albion* could give her. The poor man's cry is the prophet's impetus, and the angry cloud of Los over London hints at a prophetic destruction of all exploiting tyrannies. As *Milton* reaches its closing lines, Blake brings us back to the universe of the Bard's Song, but with a completing difference. The Mills of Satan are gone; the Plow of Rintrah and the Harrow of Palamabron have done their work, and life is prepared for its deciding climax:

> Rintrah & Palamabron view the Human Harvest
> beneath.
> Their Wine-presses & Barns stand open, the
> Ovens are prepar'd,
> The Waggons ready; terrific Lions & Tygers
> sport & play.
> All Animals upon the Earth are prepar'd in
> all their strength
>
>
> To go forth to the Great Harvest & Vintage
> of the Nations.

Like the Book of Job and *Paradise Regained*, Blake's *Milton* is a study in gathering self-awareness. Job and Milton's Son of God come to recognize themselves in their true relation to God. Blake's Milton recognizes himself as God or imaginative Man and proceeds to purge from himself everything opposed to that recognition. But where the Book of Job and *Paradise Regained* identify sonship to God with obedience to Him, Blake's *Milton* urges us to "seek not thy heavenly father then beyond the skies" but rather "obey thou the Words of the Inspired Man." Job and Milton's Son of God overcome their temptations, which in Job are deeply involved with inner conflicts. Blake's Milton is close to Job in that he must rid himself of the conviction of his own righteousness before he can resolve the conflict within his own self.

The clearest link between the Book of Job, *Paradise Regained*, and *Milton* is that the protagonist of each work must overcome Satan, or a condition brought on by Satan's activity. Here *Milton* occupies a kind of middle position with respect to both the earlier works. Like Job, Blake's Milton must overcome his Satanic situation or inwardness, rather than Satan himself. But like the Son of God, Blake's Milton must resist overt Satanic temptations as well. Blake's Milton is both a suffering man, like Job, and a Son of God, very like Milton's Christ.

Something of the beauty of *Milton's* form ought to be evident by now, and I would make the claim that it is a poem worthy of a place beside the Book of Job and *Paradise Regained*. One question remains: is it a theodicy in as clear a sense as they are? Does it earn its Miltonic motto: "To Justify the Ways of God to Men?" It does, if one remembers exactly how the Bard's Song, that extraordinary transfiguration of a biographical incident, finds its place in the poem. Just as *Paradise Regained* afforded Milton the opportunity to explore the Jobean problem within himself, so Blake's *Milton* allows the later poet to advance his personal solution to the problem of evil as it confronted him in his own life. The historical Milton indeed became a Rintrah in the wilderness, and a lonely prophet is an excellent prospect for Satan. *Paradise Regained* concludes with the Son of God returning to his mother's house, to wait again upon the will of God. So John Milton, at the end, learned to wait, comforted by a paradise within himself, happier far than the outer one he had failed to bring about in his England. Blake's temptation, in the Bard's Song, is an instructive contrast to this pattern of painfully acquired patience and prophetic hope. Under the "mild" self-imposition of a subtler Satan than the ones who tried Job and Christ, Blake is tempted to forsake prophecy altogether. He has ranged against him not only the desert silence where he should have auditors, but all the subtle pressures of conformity, the persuasiveness of Moral Virtue. Rescued by Milton's descent, and realizing that he is the reincarnation of Milton, Blake is strengthened to the spiritual audacity by which he transvalues the entire notion of theodicy. What justifies the ways of God to men in *Milton* is finally just and only this: that certain men have the courage to cast out what is not human in them, and so become Man, and to become Man is to have become God.

The ways of God can be justified to men only insofar as men can and do put themselves beyond the "cloven fiction" that creates the initial problem of theodicy. To Job man and God were radically divided, one from the other, and to the historical Milton this otherness was bridged only by a historical Incarnation. To Blake all dualities are spectral, and Christ and the human imagination in the freedom of its power are as one. The greatness of Blake's *Milton* is a poetic greatness; the poem excels in design and execution, and yields to few other poems in its rhetorical art. Yet the greatness of Blake's argument counts for much also, and the lasting beauty of *Milton* is partly due to the moving passion with which Blake believed in the truth of the awakened imagination, and the holiness of the affections of the altogether human as opposed to merely natural heart. Even if, with Keats, we have more faith in the natural heart than Blake did, we can feel the critical force of so energetic and human a prophecy.

CHAPTER TWELVE

Blake's Epic: *Jerusalem*

Of the Sleep of Albion, Chapter I

Jerusalem is Blake's personal word or poetic argument in its achieved form. A lifetime of experimentation with new poetic forms and with a new articulation of mythic structure reached its climax in *Jerusalem*, which seems to me the only rival to Wordsworth's *The Prelude* as the supreme long poem in English since Milton.

We know that Blake began *Jerusalem* at least as early as 1804, the date he placed on his title page, but we cannot know with any precision when he may be said to have finished the poem. *Jerusalem* is about as long as the complete manuscript of *The Four Zoas*, and twice the length of *Milton*, which serves it as a kind of thematic prelude. Blake divides the hundred plates of *Jerusalem* into four "chapters," each with its prose preface and introductory rhymed lyric. The poem's title refers, as it did earlier in Blake, to a being at once city and woman, described in the subtitle as "the Emanation of the Giant Albion."

The poem *Milton*, like *The Prelude*, concerned itself directly with a personal and creative crisis in the poet's life. *Jerusalem*, like *Paradise Lost*, is a retrospective poem of a different kind, a long Song of Experience that attempts a cosmic survey of the fallen condition. *Jerusalem* was certainly conceived in its present form after the crisis at Felpham was over. Blake had been tried severely, and had emerged whole and resolute, but with a new hardness in his prophetic attitude. There is no equivalent in *Jerusalem* to the wonderful vision of a natural world being redeemed by the work of Los that we are given in the closing plates of the first book of *Milton*. Instead the first chapter of *Jerusalem* is largely concerned with the contrary vision. We are shown not the world of Los but the world of Albion, nature viewed not as Generation but as the delusive nightmare-world of the Ulro.

Blake, in the preface to Chapter I of *Jerusalem*, refers to the poem as a "more consolidated & extended Work" than he has attempted previously. The consolidation of its structure is indeed the most striking feature of *Jerusalem* as compared to either *The Four Zoas* or *Milton*. It is a very orderly poem, much more so than the comments of many of Blake's critics would lead us to expect. Yet its order is unusual, for Blake's model is no longer *Paradise Lost* as it was in *The Four Zoas* or *Paradise Regained* as in *Milton*. The continuity of *Jerusalem* is strikingly like the organization of the book of Ezekiel, and it is not accidental that *Jerusalem* is the most biblical of Blake's works, both in its allusions and in its tone. Each of *Jerusalem's* four chapters founds its structure upon a gradually sharpening antithesis between two contrary forces. In the first chapter these are Albion and Los, respectively the tendency towards mental chaos in the English people, and the organizing and creative component within that people, particularly as existent in a single poet who has become the inheritor (as he believes) of what is most vital in English poetic tradition. In the second chapter this antithesis evolves into the process by which Los seeks to form an image of salvation from the repetitive cycle of nature and history that Albion has become. This process, in the third chapter, culminates in an opposition between "Deism" and Blake's interpretation of Jesus. From this opposition there emerges, in the fourth and last chapter, a clarifying confrontation of error and truth, which causes a Last Judgment to begin.

As a general principle of organization, a series of gradually sharpening antitheses leading to a necessity for moral choice, this resembles the pattern of the major prophetic books of the Bible. Blake calls himself "a true Orator" in the preface to Chapter 1, and true orators are precisely what the Hebrew prophets attempted to be. The books of Ezekiel and the other prophets are essentially collections of public oratory, poems of admonition delivered to a wavering people. The poems are interspersed in chronicles that deliberately mix history and vision, the way events were and the way the prophet fears they will turn out to be if they continue as they are going, or hopes they will emerge if the people will realize that they are at the turning and can control events by a change in spirit.

Like Isaiah and Ezekiel, Blake believed that he had the decisive power of the eternal moment of human choice as a direct gift and trust from the Divine, and he seems to have imitated the organization of their books even as he believed his election as prophet was in direct succession to their own. Isaiah and Ezekiel, like Amos before them, renewed the vision of Elijah. Blake had seen himself as renewing the vision of the English Elijah or Rintrah, Milton. With Milton firmly within him, Blake turns in *Jerusalem* to the re-creation in English terms of the work of Hebraic prophecy. In the form he chooses for his poem he now goes beyond Milton, who modified but largely retained the form of the classical epic for the content of Hebraic inspiration. Blake seeks a more radical unity in *Jerusalem*, and writes what would be a new kind of poem in English if the King James books of the prophets did not so magnificently exist. A great deal of the trouble critics have had with *Jerusalem* is simply the result of irrelevant formal expectations on their part. The principles of form that guide Blake, and which he develops with enormous skill, are the literary principles implicit in Ezekiel and the other prophetic books of the Bible. *Jerusalem* will seem much less of a poetic sport if read in their company.

The prefatory lyric to Chapter 1 directly claims that the God who spoke to Moses, presumably a humanizing rather than Urizenic Jehovah, now "speaks in thunder and in fire" through Blake. This speech is clearly not Urizenic, for it is identified as "thunder of Thought & flames of fierce desire." Nor does Blake hear God externally, but from "the depths of Hell" or human desire and "within the unfathom'd caverns of my Ear." Hearing is the sense associated with Urthona, and the Blake of *Milton* became one with Los, Urthona's temporal form; fallen, hence the caverns, but with infinite potential, and so "unfathom'd."

Blake begins by a condensed statement of his poem's theme:

> Of the Sleep of Ulro! and of the passage
>   through
> Eternal Death! and of the awaking to
>   Eternal Life.

The Sleep of Ulro into which Albion has sunk is the abyss in which the poem will begin. Eternal Death, as in *Milton*, means the generative existence or Experience, and Eternal Life is the state in which art is created, eternal because by it each moment is hallowed. Remembering Milton's invocations in Books III, VII, and IX of *Paradise Lost*, Blake also portrays himself as visiting "Sion and the flow'ry Brooks beneath" at night:

> This theme calls me in sleep night after
>   night, & ev'ry morn
> Awakes me at sun-rise, then I see the
>   Saviour over me
> Spreading his beams of love, & dictating
>   the words of this mild song.

Jerusalem is anything but a "mild song," and clearly this dictating refers only to the gentle lines that follow, in which the Saviour, who is one with the Imagination, awakens Blake out of the sleep of Beulah but fails to stir Albion out of the dogmatic slumbers of his jealous fears. The sleepers are called on not only to wake but to "expand," for they cannot be saved but by increased perception:

> Awake! awake O sleeper of the land of
>   shadows, wake! expand!
> I am in you and you in me, mutual in love
>   divine:
> Fibres of love from man to man thro' Albion's
>   pleasant land.
> In all the dark Atlantic vale down from the
>   hills of Surrey
> A black water accumulates, return Albion!
>   return!

Thy brethren call thee, and thy fathers, and
    thy sons,
Thy nurses and thy mothers, thy sisters and
    thy daughters
Weep at thy soul's disease, and the Divine
    Vision is darken'd:
Thy Emanation that was wont to play before
    thy face,
Beaming forth with her daughters into the
    Divine bosom,
Where hast thou hidden thy Emanation
    lovely Jerusalem
From the vision and fruition of the Holy-one?
I am not a God afar off, I am a brother
    and friend;
Within your bosoms I reside, and you reside
    in me:
Lo! we are One, forgiving all Evil; Not
    seeking recompense;
Ye are my members O ye sleepers of Beulah,
    land of shades!

All the themes of *Jerusalem* are sounded in these intense lines, from the identity of God and awakened man in their mutuality of love through the imaginative fibres that must bind man to man if England is to be liberated from the vegetative fibres that form the chains of selfhood and jealousy. The black water that accumulates as history rises to its climax is at once the spilled blood of Albion and the Atlantic Ocean that has washed over the unfallen vale of Atlantis to make it a dark vale or chaotic sea of formless error. The Divine Vision or emanative world is darkened, the poignant allusion being to the outcry of forsaken wisdom in Proverbs 8:22–30, "when there were no depths" and when "I was daily his delight, rejoicing always before him." That wisdom, Jerusalem, man's liberty from constricting codes, has been hidden by man himself, in the delusion that his God is a heavenly father beyond the skies. Though the true God urges the forgiveness of evil, and repudiates all notion of recompense, the sick-unto-death Albion is not thus to be persuaded:

But the perturbed Man away turns down the
    valleys dark;
Saying, we are not One: we are Many, thou
    most simulative
Phantom of the over heated brain! shadow
    of immortality!
Seeking to keep my soul a victim to thy
    Love! which binds
Man the enemy of man into deceitful
    friendships:
Jerusalem is not! her daughters are
    indefinite;
By demonstration man alone can live, and
    not by faith.
My mountains are my own, and I will keep
    them to myself.

The denial of unity here is also a denial of the reality of vision,
and turns a hope of concord between man and man into the false
honesty of preferring open hostility to deceitful friendship.[1] If the
daughters of Jerusalem are indefinite, then human liberty has no firm
outline, and Jerusalem indeed is not. To live by demonstration is to
be imprisoned by Experience, by the self-aggrandisement that ends
in the self-enclosure of solipsism. These jealous fears that preclude
the giving away of oneself find their fullest expression in Albion's
"hiding his Emanation upon the Thames and Medway, rivers of
Beulah." Spenser, whose Gardens of Adonis are the most beautiful
presentation in English of the state Blake called Beulah, had pictured
the marriage of the Thames and Medway rivers as an ultimate image
of concord in the natural world. Now Blake reverses that image,
and the married land becomes a hiding place for the outcast form of
Albion's love.

Albion's despairing choice of the worst provokes Blake to the first
of Jerusalem's great chants of sorrow. The England Blake loved is
clouded over by this wilful rejection of the saving beams of love. The
capital and university cities "are driven among the starry Wheels,

rent away and dissipated," given over to the Satanic mills that find their heavenly manifestation in the Zodiac. As the coherence of earth is scattered into Urizen's heaven it is "enlarg'd without dimension," and so loses its human lineaments. The human perfection of natural objects, the extent to which they still formed a portion of man's proper home, becomes "small & wither'd & darken'd." Against this shrinking away of man Blake sets his poetic activity:

> Trembling I sit day and night, my friends are
> > astonish'd at me,
> Yet they forgive my wanderings, I rest not
> > from my great task!
> To open the Eternal Worlds, to open the
> > immortal Eyes
> Of Man inwards into the Worlds of Thought:
> > into Eternity
> Ever expanding in the Bosom of God, the
> > Human Imagination.
> O Saviour pour upon me thy Spirit of meekness
> > and love:
> Annihilate the Selfhood in me: be thou all
> > my life!

Without the context of *Milton*, we might be mistaken as to what Blake means. With it there is no excuse for thinking a passage like this to be conventionally pietistic or in any way mystical. To annihilate the Selfhood is to emulate Blake's Milton by washing off the Not Human, to cast off the rotten rags of every covenanted religion, and indeed to liberate the spirit from every convention of belief, every shred of institutional or historical Christianity. Many of Blake's best and most devoted critics have sought to mitigate the completeness of Blake's rejection here, but they ought to remain on their Beulah-couches without seeking to have their master join them in that soft repose. If Blake is a Christian (and he insisted always that he was) then the vast majority of Christians are not. Such a declaration may appear highhanded or facetious, but it is made humbly and seriously. Blake identified the fully liberated Imagination with the Holy Ghost; such an identification makes Isaiah or

Shelley or Yeats or any man set free into his full creative potential a Christian, whether he thinks himself one or not. Blake was a great poet, and his rhetorical transvaluations and persuasive definitions are justified by their liveliness and the aesthetic uses to which he put them. But it hardly seems right that his expositors should claim his creative freedom at redefinition of accepted terms. If the theologians of the different Christian orthodoxies are true Christians, then Blake is not, and it seems more accurate to name him an apocalyptic humanist than a Christian, little as he would have liked such a classification.

As Blake sets to his harsh task of describing Albion's torments, he begins with a list of demonic beings, twelve fallen Sons of Albion and their even more sinister Emanations. Together these "war to destroy the Furnaces" of Los, and so "to desolate Golgonooza, and to devour the Sleeping Humanity of Albion in rage & hunger." As all but three of the Sons of Albion bear names derived from men associated with Blake's trial for alleged seditious utterances at Felpham, we are compelled momentarily to consider the impingement of Blake's life upon *Jerusalem*, much as we did with the Bard's Song in *Milton*.

Two troopers, Schofield and Cock, perjured themselves by swearing a warrant against Blake "for an assault & Seditious words" after the poet had turned Schofield out of his Felpham cottage garden and pushed the cursing soldier some fifty yards to where he was quartered. With much help from the mildly Satanic Hayley, spiritual enemy but corporeal friend, Blake was acquitted at his trial, but the experience was a nightmare, and understandably so. Blake's life was not in jeopardy but his freedom was, in an England fearful of Napoleonic invasion. Fortunately, as David Erdman puts it, Blake's "neighbors were less loyal to the code of Urizen than to its victim."[2] But Schofield and Cock, and the judges Quantock, Peachey, and Brereton, and four other men with names like Kotope, Bowen, Hutton, and Slayd (they may have been troopers or court officials or simply malicious neighbors) won the dubious immortality of entering as villains into Blake's major poem. Only Scholfield (Blake spells his name in different ways) is of individual importance in *Jerusalem*, together with the three Sons named "Hand & Hyle & Coban." The twelve Sons together form a Starry Wheel or Zodiacal jury of Urizenic Accusers, and are associated by Blake with Job's comforters, the accusers of Socrates, and the accusers at Faithful's trial in Bunyan's *Pilgrim's Progress*.[3] Hand, Hyle, and Coban are the triple accuser of man in *Jerusalem*, with Hand usually serving as the representative of the twelve Sons in the aggregate, and filling the role of Satan or the Spectre of Urizen.

The twelve Emanations of these Sons bear names from early British history, and are united into the two beings we have encountered before, Tirzah and Rahab. Together the Sons and their Emanations reduce Jerusalem to a Urizenic "pillar of a cloud," scattering the spiritual liberty of man until she wanders away "into the Chaotic Void." The poem's first crisis takes place on its sixth through eleventh plates as Los, weeping for Jerusalem and seeking to reclaim her, and clearly one with Blake since their union in *Milton*, struggles with his own selfhood, the embittered Spectre of Urthona.

The poetry of these plates is among Blake's most poignant, for the struggle here is his most painful one, as it concerns a combative encounter with his own Selfhood. Blake was not only a neglected prophet during the years *Jerusalem* was written; he was also a failed artist in that no audience for his work existed. His Spectre of Urthona had much with which to reproach his Los, "bitterly cursing him for his friendship to Albion."

Within the myth, what the Spectre of Urthona protests is his creative brother's refusal to despair. The provocation for despair is evident: Hand the Urizenic Accuser (based on the Hunt brothers whose magazine had attacked Blake) and Hyle (the name suggests both Hayley and the Greek for "matter") are becoming great in the world. They represent fallen reason and nature respectively, and the anxiety-ridden temporal will is moved to hatred and indignation by them, passions that must yield to an accommodation with the world Hand and Hyle dominate. The third Son of Albion, Coban (perhaps an anagram of Bacon) has become the father of Nimrod, prototype of all murderous tyrants and hunters of men. Schofield has risen as a newly created Adam, coming out of Edom as a demonic parody of salvation. This Schofield, the Spectre of Urthona warns, is coming to reign over Los, to punish him in his body even as Satan punished Job.

Against this fearful prospect the heroic Los stands unmoved, even venturing upon a wry humor at the start of his reply:

Los answer'd: Altho' I know not this, I
    know far worse than this:
I know that Albion hath divided me, and
    that thou O my Spectre,
Hast just cause to be irritated; but look
    stedfastly upon me;
Comfort thyself in my strength; the time
    will arrive
When all Albion's injuries shall cease,
    and when we shall
Embrace him, tenfold bright, rising from
    his tomb in immortality.

What Los offers his own spectral part is a hope based on the redemptive power of time, which can make the harsh state of Experience into "holy Generation, Image of regeneration." If the spirit
of clock-time cannot accept this hope, then it must submit unwillingly to assist Los in his terrible labors. The Spectre pretends obedience, but hungers and thirsts for the poet's life, "watching his time
with glowing eyes to leap upon his prey." So Blake must have worked
on, warily, knowing his imagination was threatened by his daily
cares, by the spectral being whom society could starve, nature could
slay, reason could despise, and mystery could corrupt. The greatness
of Los's oration to his threatening Spectre is the greatness of Blake's
own insight into everything within himself that threatened the
emergence of his own poetry in an uncrippled and authentic form:

Thou art my Pride & Self-righteousness:
    I have found thee out:
Thou art reveal'd before me in all thy
    magnitude & power:
Thy Uncircumcised pretences to Chastity must
    be cut in sunder:
Thy holy wrath & deep deceit cannot avail
    against me,
Nor shalt thou ever assume the triple-form
    of Albion's Spectre,

For I am one of the living: dare not to mock
    my inspired fury.
If thou wast cast forth from my life, if I
    was dead upon the mountains
Thou mightest be pitied & lov'd; but now I
    am living: unless
Thou abstain ravening I will create an eternal
    Hell for thee.
Take thou this Hammer & in patience heave
    the thundering Bellows,
Take thou these Tongs: strike thou alternate
    with me: labour obedient.

This is poetry of the highest order because every syllable in it bears
the almost intolerable pressure of an inward torment that the poet
is not content to express as such but insists on transvaluing into a
universality of artistic process. Christopher Smart in the frequent
self-reference of his moving *Jubilate Agno* and William Collins at
least once, in his turbulent *Ode on the Poetical Character*, are
Blake's nearest ancestors here, but neither attained to the power
of Blake's self-knowledge and both went mad in their despairing
efforts to express the burden of their struggle with the Spectre within
them. That Blake should ever have been considered insane is one
of the genuine ironies of literary history, for no poet has ever understood so well what there was within him that might threaten his
sanity, and no poet has ever struggled so powerfully to overcome
his own morbidity.

What Los denounces in his Spectre is his own "Pride & Self-
righteousness." Once revealed in their magnitude of error, these
qualities can be circumcised, and their "holy wrath" exposed for the
"deep deceit" it is. The anger of the Spectre is a mockery or demonic parody of the prophet's "inspired fury"; we have encountered
this travesty before in the Bard's Song in *Milton*, when Satan went
over to Rintrah and provoked the ironic proverb: "Satan is among
the Reprobate." Los has become too wise for such deception; the
ravening Spectre is compelled to labor obediently at the furnaces
of art. Yet even this labor brings no immediate joy, for the themes
of apocalyptic poetry are fearful:

I labour day and night. I behold the soft
  affections
Condense beneath my hammer into forms of
  cruelty,
But still I labour in hope, tho' still my
  tears flow down,
That he who will not defend Truth, may be
  compell'd to defend
A Lie, that he may be snared and caught
  and snared and taken:
That Enthusiasm and Life may not cease:
  arise Spectre arise!

Los is repeating the lines from *Milton* (8:46–48) in which Palama-bron called down an assembly to judge between Satan and himself. If the defenders of a Lie can be exposed as such, then they can be snared and taken and so cease from troubling. Against the defenders of a Lie the poet and his groaning Spectre now create a barrier against chaos called the Spaces of Erin. As Erin or Ireland is a geographical buffer for England against the Atlantic, so Blake's Erin is a protection for Albion against the stormy waves of space and time, and against the abstract negation of moral law that the Sons of Albion have fashioned from the Contraries of desire and restraint. In the night of history, standing in London, building the city of inspired art, Los is moved to express the guiding principle of Blake's poetry:

I must Create a System, or be enslav'd by
  another Man's.
I will not Reason & Compare: my business
  is to Create.

Jerusalem is a system to free us from systems; Blake knows that if he were to be reasonable and comparative, he would find much that is imaginative mingled with the spectral aspect of Bacon or Newton, but he is a poet, not a historian of culture. His business is to create, and he believes that the Baconian and Newtonian systems enslave the imagination and so impede creation.

In ironic answer to this noble declaration his Spectre attacks Los where he is weakest, his potential bitterness towards the betrayals of Female Love, the possessive Sin of Enitharmon. Blake was too honest and too bedevilled in his own past to evade this point, and Los attempts no direct answer to it. The poor Spectre, in a speech of deliberate pathos, identifies itself with a sickness unto death:

> O that I could cease to be! Despair! I
> am Despair
> Created to be the great example of horror
> & agony; also my
> Prayer is vain. I called for compassion:
> compassion mock'd;
> Mercy & pity threw the grave stone over
> me, & with lead
> And iron, bound it over me for ever: Life
> lives on my
> Consuming, & the Almighty hath made me his
> Contrary,
> To be all evil, all reversed & for ever
> dead: knowing
> And seeing life, yet living not; how can I
> then behold
> And not tremble? how can I be beheld & not
> abhorr'd?

To this horror of the process of mere repetition, Los can offer no consolation, but nevertheless works on, "striving with Systems to deliver Individuals from those Systems." The saving forces of the world of Los come forth from his furnaces: Erin, the Daughters of Beulah, and the Sons and Daughters of Los. Together, these "Labourers in the Furnaces" utter a prophetic lament for Jerusalem, which expands first into a vision of the city of Los; and next into a gloriously vivid but very grim vision of the world of Albion, a sad contrast to the vision of the world of Los at the climax of Book I of *Milton*. We have now to consider in sequence the remainder of Chapter 1 of *Jerusalem*: first this lament and subsequent visions; then a description of how Albion's fall took place; next a dialogue of the

fallen Albion and his Emanation; and finally a lament of the land of
Beulah over Albion that ends the chapter.

The lamentations of Los and his children center in two crucial
matters. The first is the transference of Albion's emanative life from
Jerusalem to her Shadow, Vala, the veil of natural appearance that
conceals man's freedom from natural limitation. The other is Los's
own realization that his Spectre's accusation is in part true. Albion
is dead, because his Emanation is divided from him. Los is alive, yet
he feels his Emanation also dividing from him. We are now deep
enough in Blake so that direct translation of the myth may well be
an intrusion, but Blake's art is so vital here that commentary is a
temptation.

The outer world of man ought to be what he both creates and
loves, and the authenticity of that world is the guarantee of man's
freedom, called Jerusalem or Liberty in Blake's myth. When Man
comes to love what he has already made, and neglects the potential
of further creation, then he substitutes Vala, or the possessive love
of a fixed natural order, for Jerusalem. This is Fall, and only the
divided and endangered Imagination can work to restore man to what
he was. But the Imagination in the Fall divides two ways. The
simpler we have seen; a conflict between the self and the creative
principle in every poet. The more difficult is between the creative
principle and its own emanative portion, already sketched for us in
the manuscript lyric *My Spectre around me night & day*. The paradox
of the Imagination, to Blake, is that it survives these wars of love
that have already slain the wholeness of man. It survives because it is
one with the Holy Ghost; it is what remains of divinity in man.

Kept from despair by this realization, Los leads his fellow-
laborers in the building of a New Jerusalem. As they work they
see one of the greatest of Blake's visions, the chant that details first
the walls of Golgonooza and then the world of fallen Albion. This
description is one of Blake's most complex, and involves a comparison of England and Palestine, and of Albion and Jacob (called
Israel) and their respective sons.

The frequently homely imagery of the Hebrew prophets: the
potter's wheel of Jeremiah, the iron pan and barber's razor and
boiling pot and measuring reed of Ezekiel, the plumbline and bas-
ket of summer fruit of Amos; these are the precedents for Blake's

minute particulars of vision as he describes the building of Los's City. The remarkable attempt to particularize the outer forms of the City on plates 12 and 13 is evidently based on the example of Ezekiel, where the book from its fortieth chapter on is devoted to giving "the measures of the city," the house of God which is to be rebuilt, and also on the twenty-first chapter of Revelation, which imitates Ezekiel.

Blake's account of Los's city begins with a great passage describing its building:

> What are those golden builders doing? where
>   was the burying-place
> Of soft Ethinthus? near Tyburn's fatal Tree?
>   is that
> Mild Zion's hills, most ancient promontory,
>   near mournful
> Ever weeping Paddington? is that Calvary and
>   Golgotha
> Becoming a building of pity and compassion?
>   Lo!
> The stones are pity, and the bricks, well
>   wrought affections
> Enamel'd with love & kindness, & the tiles
>   engraven gold,
> Labour of merciful hands: the beams & rafters
>   are forgiveness:
> The mortar & cement of the work, tears of
>   honesty: the nails
> And the screws & iron braces are well wrought
>   blandishments
> And well contrived words, firm fixing, never
>   forgotten,
> Always comforting the remembrance: the floors,
>   humility:
> The cielings, devotion: the hearths, thanks-
>   giving.
> Prepare the furniture, O Lambeth, in thy
>   pitying looms,

The curtains, woven tears & sighs wrought
    into lovely forms
For comfort; there the secret furniture of
    Jerusalem's chamber
Is wrought: Lambeth! the Bride, the Lamb's
    Wife, loveth thee:
Thou art one with her & knowest not of self
    in thy supreme joy.
Go on, builders in hope, tho' Jerusalem
    wanders far away
Without the gate of Los, among the dark
    Satanic wheels.

Blake's images here recall George Herbert's *The Church Floore*, where the stones are patience and humility and "the sweet cement" is charity. The virtues in Blake's lines are rather more humanistic and inclusive, for the golden builders are building a New Jerusalem that is a city of art. Ethinthus appeared in *Europe* as one of Enitharmon's daughters, a "queen of waters" who rejected the call of the earth-worm and left him in human solitude while she enjoyed her night of holy shadows. She is therefore *The Sick Rose* of Experience, and her burying-place was at Tyburn, the London gallows Blake identifies with Golgotha, for her death was due to Druidic religion, and the "self-enjoyings of self-denial." In the building of New Golgatha or Golgonooza her burial spot is transfigured, and the dismal natural cycle of *The Sick Rose* comes to an end. Lambeth, where Blake first formed his myth, is remembered for its inspiring function, as Blake goes on to follow Ezekiel and John of Patmos in a comprehensive description of a fourfold spiritual London.

Of the description of Golgonooza (from 12:45 to 13:29) and of certain other catalogues in *Jerusalem* one is tempted to the comment that the Rabbis of the Talmud made on similar passages in Ezekiel's chapters on the New City: only the prophet Elijah, heralding the ultimate redemption, will elucidate these difficulties. S. Foster Damon has been the Rabbi Chanina ben Hezekiah of these matters, and beyond him I cannot go. I think the reader is well advised to enjoy

them for their color and rhetoric, once he has grasped their function
in the poem. A passage like the following emphasizes the *otherness* of this city, its difficulty of access, for like Yeats's Byzantium it
is a city where only forms abide, and these forms are as startling as
similar images in Ezekiel, Revelation, and Dante:

> The Western Gate fourfold is clos'd, having
>   four Cherubim
> Its guards, living, the work of elemental
>   hands, laborious task,
> Like Men hermaphroditic, each winged with
>   eight wings.
> That towards Generation, iron: that toward
>   Beulah, stone:
> That toward Ulro, clay: that toward Eden, metals:
> But all clos'd up till the last day, when the
>   graves shall yield their dead.

The Cherubim are associated with the unfallen Urizen, and the
Western Gate belongs to the human body throughout Blake's symbolism. The other associations of the passage can be worked out from
The Four Zoas, but what is crucial is that this gate, like all the others,
is terrible to the eye of fallen man, and that the cherubim, presumably identical with those who guard the Tree of Life against us,
prevent us also from bursting the gate and so breaking out of the
body's limitations. Blake was, I think, very nearly the subtlest of
poets, and one can suspect (with Damon) that Golgonooza is not a
vision of perfection, unlike the cities of Ezekiel and Revelation.[4]
Blake is hinting that everything in art that is not clearly human im-
pedes our way back into the City of God, and there seems to be a
good deal in Los's vision that is not immediately as human as Blake
(and we) might wish. Aspects of the city are fearful because it is
surrounded by our world, "a Land of pain and misery and despair
and ever brooding melancholy." On all sides, as Los walks the walls
of his city, he sees the shapes of menace, the nightmare of incoher-
ence that would reduce his hard-won forms to the abyss:

There is the Cave, the Rock, the Tree, the
    Lake of Udan Adan,
The Forest and the Marsh and the Pits of
    bitumen deadly,
The Rocks of solid fire, the Ice valleys,
    the Plains
Of burning sand; the rivers, cataract &
    Lakes of Fire,
The Islands of the fiery Lakes, the Trees
    of Malice, Revenge
And black Anxiety, and the Cities of the
    Salamandrine men:

. . . .
The land of darkness flamed, but no light
    & no repose:
The land of snows of trembling & of iron
    hail incessant:
The land of earthquakes, and the land of
    woven labyrinths:
The land of snares & traps & wheels &
    pit-falls & dire mills.

No poet surpasses Blake in such catalogues of dread, but even he
has no other sustained recital of the winter vision as the one he now
suffers. Los views in succession all the ruin set forth in *The Four
Zoas:* the Covering Cherub, the Serpent Orc, the Dragon Urizen,
Tharmas the Devouring Tongue, and the isolated emanations. His
impingement on this world of sorrows comes to an end with the close
of the fourteenth plate, where he sets against such a world the hope
of his children: "every one a translucent Wonder, a Universe
within." He is poised before the open question of whether such
artifices of eternity can restore Jerusalem from the pale cloud she
has become to the promise she once held.

The next plate is identified by Blake as his own "awful Vision."
It begins with the image of "Hand & Hyle rooted into Jerusalem"
and of Skofeld, the new Adam, "Vegetated by Reuben's Gate in
every Nation of the Earth." Blake's age, according to his myth, is
moving towards the conclusion of the sixth Eye of God, the Jehovah

cycle that has reached its last phase in the twenty-seventh church, called Luther. Jehovah made a covenant with Jacob, thereafter called Israel, who is Blake's fallen Albion and like Jacob has twelve sons of whom Hand is the oldest. Israel's oldest son was Reuben, notorious for his instability. Hand and Reuben are therefore respectively the Spectre of the natural man and the natural or ordinary man proper in *Jerusalem*. This becomes much clearer in Chapter 2 of the poem; all that need be realized here, in Blake's lament on plate 15, is that the natural man in Blake's contemporary world is in danger of being taken over by Hand and Skofield, Satanic Accusers. The long and cold repose of Albion has led to endless intellectual error; to the "iron scourges" of Bacon and Newton. The very power of scientific thought is what Blake fears, knowing that it may replace imagination even in him. "Reasonings like vast Serpents," he revealingly cries out, "Infold around my limbs, bruising my minute articulations." Natural science fits too well as the intellectual garment of the natural man, and the serpentine Orc within Blake may suffer the fate of becoming one with the systems Blake strives to overcome. For Blake is one prophet against an entire age:

> I turn my eyes to the Schools & Universities
> of Europe
> And there behold the Loom of Locke, whose
> Woof rages dire,
> Wash'd by the Water-wheels of Newton: black
> the cloth
> In heavy wreathes folds over every Nation:
> cruel Works
> Of many Wheels I view, wheel without wheel,
> with cogs tyrannic
> Moving by compulsion each other: not as
> those in Eden, which
> Wheel within Wheel in freedom revolve in
> harmony & peace.

The satiric brilliance of Blake's imagery here is in its juxtaposition of three areas of reference: industrial, apocalyptic (from Ezekiel), and personally mythic. The Satanic mills of education weave the black

cloth of what Blake believes to be intellectual error; Newton's physics
and cosmology provide the motive power, and they are Water-wheels
because water is a Blakean symbol for the delusion of materiality and
the wheels are the spinning heavens. Wheel within wheel, the Edenic
movement, typified Ezekiel's vision of the wheels and their work, the
Enthroned Man riding the cherubim. Wheel without wheel is the
counter movement, and the spinning effect is like Blake's whirlpool
image of the vortex in *Milton*: a movement seen with the corporeal,
not the creative eye.

What Blake views is two contrary movements, art against nature,
the sons of Los opposing the vegetating sons of Albion. The sons
of Los are at work "cutting the Fibres from Albion's hills," while
the spectral sons are involved in Reuben's enrooting of his brethren,
a process stretching from Noah to Abram. Abram's flight from
Chaldea to become Abraham the patriarch of the Israelites constitutes a refuge for the natural man, a movement towards imaginative
salvation.

Contemplating the struggle of contraries in history, Blake sees
the confluence of Biblical and English religion as the work of a Divine
mercy, which sets "the Furnaces of Los in the Valley of the Son
of Hinnom." That valley is the origin of Gehenna, Moloch's place
of sacrifice, and if the furnaces of Los can reclaim reality there, where
men had to pass through or over the fire, then nothing need cause
us to despair. The work of Los's furnaces dominates plate 16 of the
poem, which is mostly a mere catalogue of the bringing-together of
the British counties under the rule of various sons of Jacob. No defence on poetic grounds of such a list is possible, but a great poet
can be pardoned his few descents into excessive literal-mindedness.
The Bible has its genealogies, Spenser his pageants of British mon-
archs, Milton his fondness for listing geographical place names, and
Blake his elaborate over-ingenuity at mythic cartography: all these are
offences against literary tact that we endure for the sake of the sublimity that exists side-by-side with them. Perhaps creative psychology
requires these mundane cataloguings as ballast for intensely visionary
passages; *Jerusalem* in any case has fewer of them than its detractors
lead one to believe.

Blake's immediate use of having divided up Britain between the
sons of Jacob is a rather effective one, as it prepares the way towards

stating a belief in literary archetypes. Every fundamental story exists already in the great code of art that is the Bible, and so the activities of Albion's sons repeat the pattern set by the sons of Israel. For:

> All things acted on Earth are seen in the
>   bright Sculptures of
> Los's Halls, & every Age renews its powers
>   from these Works
> With every pathetic story possible to happen
>   from Hate or
> Wayward Love; & every sorrow & distress is
>   carved here,
> Every Affinity of Parents, Marriages &
>   Friendships are here
> In all their various combinations wrought
>   with wondrous Art,
> All that can happen to Man in his pilgrimage
>   of seventy years.
> Such is the Divine Written Law of Horeb &
>   Sinai,
> And such the Holy Gospel of Mount Olivet &
>   Calvary.

This is so profound a statement of the relation, for Blake, between art and reality, that one does well to read in it the relation to typical events that *Jerusalem* itself has for Blake. Like Yeats's sages who stand in God's holy fire, as in the gold mosaic of a wall, so all that can happen to man stands in Los's imaginative fire, as in the bright sculptures of a hall. Blake's point is complex: not only can all earthly actions be seen in Los's sculptures, but the power that moves them depends on the sculptures for its renewal. This function of Los's archetypes is akin to his mediating service as redemptive time. Because Los carves his forms, because the poet can do his work, fresh human life pulsates through nature. Nothing can be further from Platonism than this doctrine of the utter dependence of nature upon art for its energies, as the ultimate forms are made by Los, the imaginative principle in man, and do not exist apart from man's creativity.

That creativity is turned by Los as a fury against the sons of Albion on the next plate, a fury that compels the Spectre of Urthona to divide into a laboring force within the four elements. One of Blake's most difficult passages deals with Los's use of his Spectre to frighten the temptresses who are Albion's daughters:

> But Los himself against Albion's Sons his
>   fury bends, for he
> Dare not approach the Daughters openly
>   lest he be consumed
> In the fires of their beauty & perfection
>   & be Vegetated beneath
> Their Looms in a Generation of death &
>   resurrection to forgetfulness.
> They wooe Los continually to subdue his
>   strength; he continually
> Shews them his Spectre, sending him abroad
>   over the four points of heaven
> In the fierce desires of beauty & in the
>   tortures of repulse. He is
> The Spectre of the Living pursuing the
>   Emanations of the Dead
> Shudd'ring they flee: they hide in the
>   Druid Temples in cold chastity,
> Subdued by the Spectre of the Living &
>   terrified by undisguis'd desire.

On a primary level this relates to the necessity of the imagination's resisting the attractions of nature; Los himself dare not be exposed to the delusive but overpowering beauty of the daughters, lest he be naturalized out of his mission into the pleasures and terrors of mundane life. Los practices concealment; the poet hides in the man's crippled will, and the spectral form causes nature to shudder. The entire process is summarized in the fine irony of the ugly Spectre yet being "of the living" Los, while the beautiful Emanations belong to the death-in-life state or Ulro of the sons of Albion. The Spectre of Urthona, turned loose, is a grotesque version of "undisguised desire," a parody of the more human Los. Certainly on the secondary level Blake is criticizing himself in this little mythic episode; he fights nature by indirection because he is not strong enough to overcome nature by nature at this point.

The remainder of plate 17 is devoted to Los's predicament, caught between a Spectre that wishes to negate him and an Emanation desiring to dominate him. Though this may be fairly direct spiritual biography on Blake's part, its force and value reside in its accuracy as a presentation of the permanent dilemmas of an artist who has not achieved a full integration of the world within himself.

The agony of Los is expressed in an uncharacteristic threat of hatred towards Skofield and Hand that ends plate 17. The rhetorical shock of this hatred carries the poem through its abrupt transition to the plangent myth of Albion, Vala, and Jerusalem that occupies the remainder of its first chapter. The twelve sons of Albion appear as three immense Wheels or a triple Accuser uttering a howl of execration against Albion, "father now no more." They accuse Jerusalem of harlotry, in the manner but not the substance of Jeremiah, and they proclaim their intention "to build Babylon the City of Vala, the Goddess Virgin-Mother." Vala in this context is emblematic of phenomenal nature, as she was in *The Four Zoas*, and the worship of a virginal nature combines for Blake the worst aspects of the Female Will with asceticism. Coupled with the accusation of harlotry against Jerusalem, this gives us an incarnate body of error, exhibiting Moral Virtue and materialism combined in a single form.

As the accusations go on, Albion declines into a catastrophic winter, in which his affections become separated from him and "now appear withoutside," including the ravening Spectres of his children. His fall brings on "the dark incessant sky," like "the black incessant sky" that was cut off with all Mystery's tyrants in Night IX of *The Four Zoas*.

In his fall Albion collapses first "into the Night of Beulah, and the Moon of Beulah rose clouded with storms." What follows is a scene of sinister beauty:

He found Jerusalem upon the River of his
    City soft repos'd
In the arms of Vala, assimilating in one
    with Vala,
The Lilly of Havilah; and they sang soft
    thro' Lambeth's vales
In a sweet moony night & silence that they
    had created
With a blue sky spread over with wings and
    a mild moon,
Dividing & uniting into many female forms:
    Jerusalem
Trembling; then in one comingling in eternal
    tears,
Sighing to melt his Giant beauty on the
    moony river.

Havilah is mentioned in Genesis (2:11) as a land of gold surrounded by one of the four rivers of paradise. Later in Genesis (10:6–10) Havilah is identified as a son of Ham's son Cush, and thus a brother to the dreadful Nimrod, hunter of men and founder of Babel. For Blake every identity of names in the Bible was significant and so his Havilah partakes of both sources: a portion of the earthly paradise, and a brother to Nimrod. As the "Lilly of Havilah" Vala is both a paradisal nature goddess and a sinister partaker in Nimrod's legacy of earthly tyranny. For Jerusalem to be "assimilating in one with Vala" is a disaster, a mistaken mingling of man's freedom with his bondage. The soft song they sing together is a temptation to melt Albion's unfallen beauty on the moony river of Beulah's ambiguous forms.

The torments of love and jealousy unfolded on plates 20 through 24 are as complexly stated as such matters are likely to seem to their protagonists, but they are simple enough in their cause. Albion meets both Jerusalem and Vala with reproaches, blaming them for his disease of shame that covers him, Job-like, with the boils of sin. Yet clearly the culpability for his plight is entirely his own, as was foreshadowed in the earlier account of his murderous love for Vala, in *The Four Zoas*, VII, 239–54. He has put aside the full humanity of Jerusalem to take unto himself the affective life of one of his aspects, Luvah the Zoa of passion. By tearing off the veil of Vala and entering into possession of her, he gave himself over to a selfish exaltation of one element in the human unity over all the others, and slew the inmost life of that element in the process (he speaks of himself as having placed Luvah into his sepulchre).

As a psychic allegory we investigated this fall in discussing *The Four Zoas*. In *Jerusalem* Blake cares only for the consequences of this story: can the protagonists learn to forgive one another? Jerusalem herself certainly can, but Albion is too given over to a masochistic self-absorption with his sin, and Vala battens on remorse. When Albion laments the fall of his children into natural religion, Vala exults in the lying confusion that the Nimrod of the new Adam Skofield is "the mighty Huntsman Jehovah" himself. She mockingly repeats the lamenting rejection of Tharmas by Enion in Night I of *The Four Zoas*, a deliberate self-parody on Blake's part, for Vala is hardly a spirit of Innocence. The parody continues, but in deadly earnest, with Jerusalem directing to Albion the protesting reply of Tharmas to Enion: "Why wilt thou number every little fibre of my Soul?" Blake does not plagiarize from himself without a purpose, and the purpose here is to give a darkly demonic travesty of the fall from Innocence in Night I of *The Four Zoas*.

Albion's despair becomes total when he wishes the forgiving Jerusalem into the void, and masochistically offers himself to the Druidic sacrificial knife of Vala. To Jerusalem's offer of forgiveness in place of punishment he reacts with destructive remorse, and dies into mortal life with a curse against the divinity of his own Manhood. He is like a Job who might have been had he obeyed the counsel to despair of his finely laconic and sardonic wife: "Dost thou still retain thine integrity? curse God, and die." Albion does not retain his integrity, curses the God in Man, and is shattered into innumerable fragments as he dies.

The whole of plate 24 is given to the agony of Albion's death-lament, which includes a Blakean history of religion in miniature, from Druidic worship to the founding of Babylon as a parody of Jerusalem on to the Crucifixion. This last event seems a final delusion to the hysterical Albion, who quite properly blames himself for "these smitings of Luvah."

As he falls from Beulah into the sleep of Ulro, the veil of Vala, or illusion of materiality, "rushes from his hand, Vegetating Knot by Knot, Day by Day, Night by Night." The great Atlantic rolls its waves, and the chaos of nature asserts itself, "turning up the bottoms of the deeps."

The first chapter of *Jerusalem* ends with a great lamenting in Beulah, deploring the oaken groves of Druidic religion and the dragon temples of war. The mourning song ends with a prayer to the Lamb of God to descend and create "States" so as to deliver individuals from the imputation of sin. We have seen the meaning of this doctrine as developed in *Milton*, where the States called Satan and Rahab can be rejected, freeing the individuals momentarily ensnared in such conditions.

With all its complications the first chapter of *Jerusalem* is quite clear in its structure, which is a deliberate circle, starting with Albion in the sleep of Ulro and then explaining gradually how he came to fall into that state of existence. We are left with the contraries of the sleeping Albion and his guard, the creating Los, and their negation in the sons of Albion and Vala their goddess. In the second chapter Los renews his struggle, seeking to form out of the historical cycles of man in nature a new image of the human, lest time never move to its judging climax and man be left scattered in the deep.

The Terrible Separation, Chapter II

The initial problem in considering this chapter is one we encountered on a smaller scale in the Bard's Song of *Milton*; the alternate ordering of the plates by Blake himself. In this commentary I will follow Blake's revised order, not the one used in the editions of Sloss and Wallis and of Keynes, but available in the facsimile of *Jerusalem* published for the Blake Trust. A reader with an edition using the earlier order need only read the poem's hundred plates in the sequence 1–28, 33–41, 43–46, 42, 29–32, 47–100, to achieve the revised text I follow here. It will be noted from this list that all the rearrangement is in the second chapter (plates 28–50). My references to plates will give the revised number first and the earlier one after it in parentheses.

Both of Blake's sequences *work*; the structure of *Jerusalem*, particularly of its second chapter, is not that of continuous narrative but of thematic juxtaposition, of enforcing an opposition by a progressive sharpening of spiritual conflict. This sharpening seems to me more skillfully rendered in the revised sequence, but there is a certain abrupt power in some of the transitions in the earlier order that Blake had to sacrifice in attaining the subtler effects of the second version.

Chapter II of *Jerusalem* begins with a prose address "To the Jews." Blake insists that Britain was the seat of the ancestral religion of the Jews, for Abraham and Noah were Druids. This is not to be taken literally, although Blake undoubtedly derived the notion from antiquarians who held it quite seriously. Blake means essentially that all natural religions are one, and also that all inspired religions are one. All paganism, to Blake, is Druidism, even in its sophisticated form of Deism. All true religion is the imaginative faith of Blake's Jesus. When Blake says that Jerusalem was "the Emanation of the Giant Albion," meaning the actual Jewish city as well as *his* Jerusalem, he is not involving himself in the nonsense of Anglo-Israelite speculations, any more than his reference to the cabalistic tradition "that Man anciently contain'd in his mighty limbs all things in Heaven & Earth" means that he is a devotee of the Christian Cabala. Blake is taking widely scattered material and molding it for his own imaginative purposes. The first chapter of *Jerusalem*, presenting the basic characters and problem of the poem, was dedicated to the Public in general. The second is offered to the Jews because it will show the endeavor of Los to make temporal succession into poetic progression, history into vision. As the people of the Bible, the Jews are intimately involved in that struggle, though their rejection of Jesus is taken by Blake as a failure to complete their visionary quest.

Here, as in the late *Everlasting Gospel*, Blake shows a sadly conventional reading of the relation between the Old Testament and the New. Though he caught the prophetic spirit of Amos and Isaiah so precisely in most respects, he was incapable of freeing himself from the traditional Christian misinterpretations of Pharisaic religion, and adopted the absurd and simplistic dialectic which opposes the supposed legalism of the Jews to the presumably greater spirituality of their offspring and rivals. I labor this point not out of Jewish rancor against Blake but as part of the critic's genuine function. I agree with Northrop Frye that to understand *Jerusalem* we need to know how Blake read the Bible, but I don't believe that Blake's reading of the Bible was as imaginatively liberated as Frye takes it to have been.[5] No English poet had so perfect an intuitive grasp of the prophetic tradition as Blake had, yet Blake made a costly imaginative error in directly identifying prophecy and apocalypse. The first certainly includes the second, but the essence of Hebrew prophecy is not apocalypse but the kind of ethical decisiveness that turns the mundane into the hallowed existence without consuming the natural man. Blake, as I understand him, was not a mystic, but he had the mystic's impatience. If he had been less insistently apocalyptic, his greatest poem, *Jerusalem*, would have a less difficult greatness. But to say even so much against Blake is to be forced to remember what he faced: an age of tyranny and war in which the inherited assumptions of his culture quite properly seemed to him altogether Satanic, and in which he alone seemed to be keeping faith with imagination and religious humanism.

The address to the Jews includes one of Blake's finest ballads, the stanzas beginning with "The fields from Islington to Marybone," in which Jerusalem and London are most appealingly identified. Profoundly moving as the entire poem is, it rises to a particular poignance in its two final stanzas:

> A man's worst enemies are those
> Of his own house & family;
> And he who makes his law a curse,
> By his own law shall surely die.
>
> In my Exchanges every Land
> Shall walk, & mine in every Land,
> Mutual, shall build Jerusalem;
> Both heart in heart & hand in hand.

The first of these stanzas is not so bitter as it may seem. His own house and family are enemies to a man only in the sense that they reinforce his own Spectre, for they compel him to do the Spectre's work by being his hostages to fortune. The universality of the second stanza is central to *Jerusalem*, and to William Blake.

The second chapter proper begins with the fallen Albion transforming the perfection of his former life into "an envied horror, and a remembrance of jealousy." Everything he now sees appears to him as an accursed witness of sin. He reacts against this hated object-world by reducing it to the gray particular of his own self, "into solid rocks, stedfast." It takes only a moment to realize that we have met a figure like this before in Blake. Cold snows drift round him, ice covers his loins, a Tree of Mystery shoots up underneath his heel. He is Urizen or very nearly so, preacher of Moral Virtue, promulgator of "the Law of God who dwells in Chaos hidden from the human sight."

His Spectre, Satan, approves his attitude, and his Emanation, now Vala, appears to him with a glance that enrobes him in a garment of death. Los, at his Anvil, hears Vala's claim that she alone is beauty and love, and cries out against Albion's creation of a Female Will. The prophet does more than cry out; he defies Hand, the eldest spectral son of Albion, by first identifying him with Jacob's eldest son Reuben enrooting himself into Bashan (the land of Og, given to Reuben's descendants by Moses in Numbers 32:33) and then seeking to part Reuben from Hand by sending him over the Jordan. This is a fairly complex symbolism, and worth an exercise in commentary.

The Reuben of *Jerusalem* has been examined with considerable care by Karl Kiralis, who takes him as representative of male frustration in the poem.[6] The Reuben of Genesis is a rather feckless being (brilliantly developed by Thomas Mann in his Joseph-saga), associated with the story of the mandrakes, fit symbols of the vegetative man, as Frye remarks. Hand is Reuben's Spectre; the saving imagination or immortal part in Reuben Blake calls Merlin, possibly remembering the fate of that British prophet, sealed into stone after yielding to the blandishments of the Female Will. The sending of Reuben over Jordan by Los is an attempt to give the Merlin in the natural man a chance by setting a limit beyond which even utterly natural man cannot fall. Los tries to shape the fallen senses in Reuben; they are fallen already but have no clear form. As in *Milton*, where the poet resists the temptation to cross the river, the passage over Jordan from the east symbolizes the fall of man. Los transforms this fall from death into sleep by the mercy of establishing the one creative aspect of the *completed* fall: the setting of a limit to contraction.

On plates 30 and 32 (or 34 and 36 in the unrevised sequence) Blake sets this myth forth with characteristic irony. Poor Reuben flees back across the Jordan each time Los sends him over because he has become too grim a reality for the beings he encounters on the other side. Each time Los sends him back it is with another sense clearly organized in contraction, a truth that those living in delusion cannot bear (though in vain, for once they see him they "became what they beheld" and so learn the reality of their condition). This happens four times because every sense except touch has been marred in the fall. Touch, here as elsewhere in Blake, remains the sexual gate back to resurrection.

The labor of Los for Reuben is parallel to the finding by "the Divine hand" of the two limits of Satan (opacity) and Adam (contraction) in the bosom of the desperately divided Albion. The "Divine voice" speaks out from Los's furnaces, cursing the State of Satan that Albion has entered, but declaring that Albion as an Individual will not suffer the destruction of a State.

In support of this voice Los again on plate 33 (37), calls on Albion to arouse himself, but in vain. Albion flees, followed by the Divine Vision, and Blake himself now enters the poem, describing the London and the England that he sees as he writes of Albion's flight from salvation. In Blake's vision the cities of England are seen as "Men, fathers of multitudes," and are invoked as saving guardians of Albion.

It is in London that Blake locates the Gate of Los, invisible to "Satan's Watch-fiends," and seen only by emanations or worlds created through art. Albion flees through this Gate, and so stands on the verge of eternal disintegration, abandoning the last fitful tracings of the human vision. Los pleads with him again, but Albion is alienated from brotherhood: "the human footstep is a terror to me."

The remainder of the second chapter consists of three movements, two abortive attempts to save Albion followed by a vision of Beulah that is dominated by a speech of Erin, the bulwark against chaos formed by the faculty for individual creation, the art that a single human can cultivate. The two attempts at rescuing Albion are very different, the first being a massed effort by the cities of England "with kindest violence to bear him back against his will thro' Los's Gate to Eden," while the second is a single effort on Los's part "to search the interiors of Albion's bosom" so as to redeem the deathly sleeper's minute particulars, the precious individualities that no Satanic force can ruin forever.

The first attempt to save Albion begins on plate 36 (40) with Los calling an assembly of "the friends of Albion." The immediate danger is that Albion, having passed into Ulro through the Gate of Los, may become a Satan many times more Satanic than Milton's ambiguous rebel:

> For had the Body of Albion fall'n down and
>   from its dreadful ruins
> Let loose the enormous Spectre on the darkness
>   of the deep
> At enmity with the Merciful & fill'd with
>   devouring fire,
> A nether-world must have reciev'd the foul
>   enormous spirit
> Under pretence of Moral Virtue, fill'd with
>   Revenge and Law.
> There to eternity chain'd down and issuing
>   in red flames
> And curses, with his mighty arms brandish'd
>   against the heavens,
> Breathing cruelty, blood & vengeance, gnashing
>   his teeth with pain,
> Torn with black storms & ceaseless torrents of
>   his own consuming fire.

Much of the power of this is in its contrast with Milton's Satan at the opening of *Paradise Lost*. The greater destruction implicit in Albion's Spectre issues from the pretence to Moral Virtue, the demonism of the Law.

The episode of the twenty-eight saving cities has been read as political allegory by David Erdman.[7] As a part of Blake's myth in

Jerusalem, the episode is coherent and effective even without its references to contemporary events. The dexterity with which Blake handles what in the abstract would be an aesthetically intolerable allegory is evident in the passages concerning the city of Bath. Erdman identifies Bath with Richard Warner, a Whig man of letters resident in that city who published an antiwar sermon that Blake may have read.[8] As an identification this is very probable, and clarifies some aspects of the Bath passages. Primarily Blake's Bath is neither man nor city, but an ambiguous power that can both heal and poison, which suggests an association with the duality of the physical body, an interpretation first ventured by Foster Damon.[9] This ambiguity in Bath extends to the other cities as well, for they "trembled in Death's dark caves" lacking the courage of their own honest convictions. In the aggregate they represent the potential powers of the phenomenal world to become the world of Los, but they have in them all the timidity of only partially redeemed nature. They are afraid to enter into their own Spectres as Los has entered into his; they fear the struggle with their own anxious wills. Their indecisiveness provokes Los into the clearing anger of Rintrah, the wrath of the voice in the wilderness:

> Then Los grew furious raging: "Why stand
>   we here trembling around
> Calling on God for help, and not ourselves,
>   in whom God dwells,
> Stretching a hand to save the falling Man?
>   are we not Four
> Beholding Albion upon the Precipice ready
>   to fall into Non-Entity?

The marvelous appeal of the speech beginning with these lines rouses the cities:

> With one accord in love sublime, & as on
>   Cherubs' wings,
> They Albion surround with kindest violence
>   to bear him back

Against his will thro' Los's Gate to Eden.
    Four-fold, loud,
Their Wings waving over the bottomless
    Immense, to bear
Their awful charge back to his native home;
    but Albion dark,
Repugnant, roll'd his Wheels backward into
    Non-Entity,
Loud roll the Starry Wheels of Albion into
    the World of Death.

The cities, under Los's promptings, seek to become the Cherubim who formed the divine chariot in Ezekiel's vision of the Enthroned Man. By attempting to move Albion back from Ulro to Eden through the gate of Los they hope to achieve a vision of Man as God, but they do not prevail against the Satanic Wheels that Albion employs to roll himself back to chaos. Their failure is due to, and illustrates, the inadequacy of the fallen Will, which "must not be bended but in the day of Divine Power." The exhausted cities suffer the fate of those who saw Reuben cross the Jordan: "they become what they beheld." They assimilate with Albion, and so enter death-in-life with him. Bath utters their elegiac farewell with a lament for the closing to eternity of the western gate of the body.

The brooding Albion now turns on Los, commanding Hand and Hyle, Spectres of reason and nature, to seize the prophet even "as you have siez'd the Twenty-four rebellious ingratitudes," or self-vanquished cities. But though Los stands before his furnaces, waiting to do battle with these dead souls, he is too formidable to be taken by any such direct assault, and the spectral world knows it. Whatever else Blake feared, he had no misgivings about the defensive powers of the alerted imagination.

This evil though ineffectual resolve of Albion against Los precipitates a clash of opposing visions of divinity on plate 43 (29). The Divine Vision appears above Albion's dark rocks, and a voice goes forth upon those rocks proclaiming the eventual salvation of deluded mankind. The ironic counterpoint to this promise is given on the same plate where Albion, in the presence of Vala, falls prostrate before Satan-Urizen, "a Shadow from his wearied intellect." In this abasing worship, man becomes the victim of his own guilty anguish. From his subsequent persecutions only the Spectre of Urthona and Enitharmon escape to the protection of Los, as representatives of the human remnant, a time-ridden male and a space-obsessed female, but all that remain for Los to harbor.

Los now, on plate 45 (31), makes another effort to rescue Albion, a heroic and lonely searching out of the inner abyss of the mortal self:

> Fearing that Albion should turn his back
> against the Divine Vision
> Los took his globe of fire to search the
> interiors of Albion's
> Bosom, in all the terrors of friendship,
> entering the caves
> Of despair & death to search the tempters
> out, walking among
> Albion's rocks & precipices, caves of solitude
> & dark despair.
> And saw every Minute Particular of Albion
> degraded & murder'd,
> But saw not by whom; they were hidden within
> in the minute particulars
> Of which they had possess'd themselves; and
> there they take up
> The articulations of a man's soul and laughing
> throw it down
> Into the frame, then knock it out upon the
> plank, & souls are bak'd
> In bricks to build the pyramids of Heber &
> Terah. But Los
> Search'd in vain; clos'd from the minutia,
> he walk'd difficult.

H. M. Margoliouth has preceded me in calling attention to these lines.[10] If a single passage in *Jerusalem* has in it the kernel of Blake's special excellence as a poet, it is this, though there are greater individual moments in the poem. By the light of creative desire, Los goes within Albion, searching for some evidence of incorruptibility. The powerful paradox, "the terrors of friendship," sums up the relation between imagination and the whole condition of man, set against each other as contraries. Los goes in the faith that there are tempters to be searched out, alien invaders within man. But the faith is unrealistic; the Minute Particulars of man, the irreducible individualities that make up a human, are murdered within man by the hidden Accusers. In a sudden terror of inspiration Blake gives inevitable expression to his grief, in one of the most memorable metaphors I know:

> and there they take up
> The articulations of a man's soul and laughing
> throw it down
> Into the frame, then knock it out upon the
> plank, & souls are bak'd
> In bricks to build the pyramids of Heber &
> Terah.

Terah was the father of Abraham; the Heber here is probably one of his ancestors, or less likely the husband of Jael who slew Sisera in her tent. The Satanic Accusers are brickmakers who reduce individual lineaments into the deadly sameness of units in a structure of bondage. Those emblems of tyranny are involved with the natural religion of primitive man, in Blake's view. Albion is Israel, and so Heber and Terah are his ancestors also. If the Heber here is the Kenite husband of Jael, the allusion is all the stronger, for Albion like Sisera is slain in the tent of his body by the Female Will, and the body of the dead Albion is aptly likened to the tomb of a pyramid.

As Los continues to search in vain, he comes down towards London, for the corpse of Albion is one with the isolated island of Britain. Blake's prophetic bitterness breaks through vividly as he looks at his city through Los's eyes:

> And saw every minute particular, the jewels of
>   Albion, running down
> The kennels of the streets & lanes as if they
>   were abhorr'd:
> Every Universal Form was become barren mountains
>   of Moral
> Virtue; and every Minute Particular harden'd
>   into grains of sand;
> And all the tendernesses of the soul cast forth
>   as filth & mire.

This is Blake's most passionate protest against the eighteenth century's esteem for generalization. For Blake there is only one Universal Form: the Human Form Divine, man as he was and as he might be. The intellectual tyranny that hardens the human world into materiality is one with the impulse that piles up the rock of Urizenic law or mountain of Moral Virtue. Surely Blake is justifiably personal in identifying his Lambeth with the Bible's Bethlehem, remembering his own sojourn amid "dens of despair in the house of bread." In the darkness and horrid solitude of the unheeded prophet, Blake feels the helplessness of just anger when it knows that vengeance is forbidden to it:

> What shall I do? what could I do, if I could
>   find these Criminals?
> I could not dare to take vengeance; for all
>   things are so constructed
> And builded by the Divine hand that the
>   sinner shall always escape,
> And he who takes vengeance alone is the
>   criminal of Providence.
> If I should dare to lay my finger on a
>   grain of sand
> In way of vengeance, I punish the already
>   punish'd. O whom
> Should I pity if I pity not the sinner who
>   is gone astray?

O Albion, if thou takest vengeance, if thou
    revengest thy wrongs,
Thou art for ever lost! What can I do to
    hinder the Sons
Of Albion from taking vengeance? or how shall
    I them perswade?

Los-Blake is stating the great moral admonition of the poem, a
Christian commonplace but invested here with all the passion in
the poet's capability. The prophetic fear of Los is that an Albion who
learns the truth of his fall may imprison himself permanently by the
Urizenic impulse towards revenge.

With Los's cry of helplessness, the revised second chapter begins
its final movement. Los hears the lamenting voice of Jerusalem, and
the mocking accusations turned against Jerusalem by Vala. The Spectre sons of Albion rear "their Druid Patriarchal rocky Temples"
around their father's limbs, but he is received into the arms of temporal mercy and given "a Couch of repose," formed by the books of
the Bible, the imaginative revelation that rests man in the dark cycles
of his history.

What remains, as at the conclusion of the first chapter, is a lamentation in Beulah, but raised here to the heights of Blake's rhetorical
power as he conveys the reverberations felt by the daughters of
Beulah as they experience "the manner of the terrible Separation"
between Albion and Jerusalem. Erin, the emblem of personal vision,
the poetic possibility latent in all men, ends the chapter with a long
and complex speech on the condition of unredeemed man. The
function of her speech is to explain what it is in man that resists his
own imaginative promptings. She finds the cause where Blake had
always found it, in the limitations of the fallen senses, and in the
wilful refusal of man to expand those senses even to the limits of
their fallen power.

Against this self-betrayal, Erin holds out the hope she incarnates:
"the Body of Divine Analogy." The terrible surfaces can be removed
from Albion only if the Prolific overcomes the Devouring, if the
natural can be humanized through an excess of the exuberant delight that is poetic beauty. The Lord Jehovah, clearly not his Urizenic debasement, builds the body of Moses in the valley where

the stony Moses of the Law was buried. In that valley Blake's Milton sculpted Adamic flesh upon the cold bones of Urizen. Erin implicitly summarizes the insistent argument of all Blake's poetry, which is that the work of creation by any artist of universal power and sympathy can clear away some encrustation from the natural creation and so demonstrate that the natural man is only an analogy of man, a resemblance in a dream of an actuality waiting to be perceived.

The Shadowy Female's Triumph, Chapter III

Blake begins *Jerusalem's* third chapter with an address to the Deists, or what he takes to be the religious orthodoxy of his own time. The address is in fact made to State Christianity or the established religion of any nation at any time, and is perfectly applicable to European and American society right now. The Deists are those engaged in "calling the Prince of this World, God: and destroying all who do not worship Satan under the Name of God." Since all professedly Christian societies, then and now, follow the law of "Vengeance for Sin," they are not Christian in Blake's view, just as *no* organized church is Christian to Blake, for all men in the aggregate manifest "Self-Righteousness, the Selfish Virtues of the Natural Heart."

This prophetic judgment is implicit throughout Blake, and explicit everywhere in *Jerusalem*. The attack on "Voltaire, Rousseau, Gibbon, Hume" made by Blake is not to be understood as a defence of customary modes of religion, for Blake's protest against the Enlightenment is a very individual one. He defends impartially both monks and Methodists against the rationalists and naturalists, but he had nothing in common with the Church or with the revivalists. In the "enthusiasm" of superstition he found another analogy of his imaginative faith, and was moved to deny that every virtue had passed away from individuals among "the Spiritually Religious," passionately as he dissented from every orthodox theology, and from every ritualized act of worship.

Simply and finally, Blake claims that "those who Martyr others or who cause War are Deists." With this use of persuasive definition one cannot quarrel; it is a proper weapon for the poet. When Blake inverts his own definition in the ballad following, and blames particular Deists for causing war, one must conclude he is being somewhat outrageous. The wars caused by Gibbon and Voltaire are known only to Eternity; historically we have nothing for which to blame them. Yet, here as elsewhere, it would be foolish to expect or desire Blake to be fair to his intellectual contraries. Blake was a poet and a polemicist, a magnificently inventive thinker who was burdened by the unique responsibility for saving vision, or so he firmly believed. His critics can be fair for him; his business was not to reason and compare, but to create.

His creation begins again as he opens Chapter III with Los weeping vehemently over Albion by the waters of the Thames. For the city of Los is "continually building & continually decaying desolate"; there are no static achievements in the New Jerusalem of inspired art. Blake would not have agreed with Yeats in his disciple's ironically qualified conviction of the permanence of forms in Byzantium. The work of Los is constant because art wins no lasting victories, however powerfully it impinges upon the recalcitrance of nature.

As Blake's Chapter III of *Jerusalem* deals with the culmination of history in his own time, its theme is the triumph of error. The antagonists' role is changed in this section of the poem from the sons to the even more formidable daughters of Albion. Another crucial change is in Albion himself, for he has now turned his hatred and desire for vengeance from Los to his own sons as he watches them "assimilate with Luvah" or move through the emotional cycles of Orc, the fallen Luvah or natural man.

Unable to recover his emanative world and oppressed by hatreds, Albion cannot get free of his Spectre, now given the alternative name of Arthur, first of the English kings. Even as *America* identified Urizen and King George, so now *Jerusalem* locates the Satanic principle in political as well as spiritual tyranny. Blake sees the tyranny in his own time as now operative both in England and in Napoleonic France, for Shiloh (from which a saviour comes) is the emanation of France even as Jerusalem is of England, and both Shiloh and Jerusalem, the liberties of their peoples, are desolations. In the political allegory, "Luvah is France," even as his temporal form Orc was violent political revolution, whether American or French, in Blake's minor poems.

On plate 55 the remnant of Eternity provides for Albion by electing the Seven Eyes of God, a symbolism I have discussed before. The election is preceded by a declaration of faith in the integrity of the continued human capability for imaginative existence:

> Let the Human Organs be kept in their perfect
>   Integrity,
> At will Contracting into Worms, or Expanding
>   into Gods,
> And then, behold! what are these Ulro Visions
>   of Chastity?
> Then as the moss upon the tree: or dust upon
>   the plow:
> Or as the sweat upon the labouring shoulder:
>   or as the chaff
> Of the wheat-floor, or as the dregs of the
>   sweet wine-press:
> Such are these Ulro Visions, for tho' we sit
>   down within
> The plowed furrow, list'ning to the weeping
>   clods, till we
> Contract or Expand Space at will: or if we
>   raise ourselves
> Upon the chariots of the morning, Contracting
>   or Expanding Time:
> Every one knows, we are One Family: One Man
>   blessed for ever.

The quiet beauty of these lines is in their mature acceptance of the reality of mundane experience without for a moment acknowledging the primacy of experience over vision. Man is a worm of seventy inches and seventy winters or a god in his perceptions "at will" though his will alone cannot free him from the dialectic of his divided perceptions. Blake does not despise "these Ulro Visions" any more than he contemns dust on the plow or sweat on his own laboring shoulder, but he does not write poetry about them either (Erdman is the great champion of the opposing view here, as his adroit reading of the passage under discussion indicates).[11] The

imaginative Eyes which belong at once to God and to Man sometimes sit down within the plowed furrow in *Jerusalem*, but mostly
they expand time, and raise themselves upon the chariots of the
morning.

As they plow up mundane reality, the Seven state the unity of
Blake's ethic and his aesthetic:

> He who would do good to another, must do it
>   in Minute Particulars:
> General Good is the plea of the scoundrel,
>   hypocrite & flatterer,
> For Art & Science cannot exist but in
>   minutely organized Particulars
> And not in generalizing Demonstrations of
>   the Rational Power.
> The Infinite alone resides in Definite &
>   Determinate Identity;

For Blake, in *Jerusalem*, the Minute Particulars are Mutual For-
givenesses, and to this challenge the female will makes its reply
through the daughters of Albion:

> What may Man be? who can tell! But what
>   may Woman be?
> To have power over Man from Cradle to
>   corruptible Grave.

This is the lesson set forth in deathly perfection by *The Mental
Traveller*. Los replies to the daughters in an ironic imitation of their
feminine speech rhythm (56:30–37), but the triumph is theirs as
they recall that every Divine Vision has been hidden by them "with
Curtain & Veil & fleshly Tabernacle." Looking back to the Church
Blake called Paul, Los sees the vision of "Three Women around the
Cross," a triple female will claiming the vegetative body of Luvah-
Jesus, and a confirmation of the daughters' exultant claim. The rit-
uals of marriage and church alike are condemned in the voices of
the fallen cities rising out of the stormy Atlantic of their now-chaotic
state:

What is a Wife & what is a Harlot? What
    is a Church & What
Is a Theatre? are they Two & not One? can
    they Exist Separate?
Are not Religion & Politics the Same Thing?
    Brotherhood is Religion,
O Demonstrations of Reason, Dividing Families
    in Cruelty & Pride!

Blake's genius for aphorism is so evident in this that one's pleasure
in the rhetorical turn here can obscure the immense bitterness of
these quite open questions. Unless religion is the relationship between man and man, the brotherhood of dialogue that precludes
self-appropriation, then are not religion and politics one, modes of
self-aggrandizement? The earlier questions are so assured in their
rhetorical balance that one wonders if Blake knew of an answer. In
any case they ought to be taken to heart by any reader who thinks,
like John Crowe Ransom, that Blake "foundered on sweet cake."[12]
    Though the Divine Vision has gestured towards Albion, he flees
from his own salvation, plowing even as Satan harrowed in *Milton*,
and with the same consequences:

But Albion fled from the Divine Vision with
    the Plow of Nations enflaming,
The Living Creatures madden'd and Albion
    fell into the Furrow, and
The Plow went over him & the Living was
    Plowed in among the Dead.
But his Spectre rose over the starry Plow.
    Albion fled beneath the Plow
Till he came to the Rock of Ages, & he
    took his Seat upon the Rock.

Blake's mastery of metaphor is still little acknowledged, though
Frye has commented upon it.[13] Here, in five lines, Blake so employs
one of his giant metaphors as to present his complex poem in an
epitome. To plow up mundane reality is the work of Rintrah or Los,
or of Christ in the ultimate reference. When Albion usurps this

station the Living Creatures (literally, the Zoas or Albion's unfallen functions) madden with a redundant energy and Albion loses control. From being the master of the process to being its victim is a sudden transformation, and when he has been plowed in, what is living and what is dead in him momentarily lie planted together. Yet the terror of this experience is instructive; his Spectre rises from him, and his remnant flees beneath to rest upon the only rock that Blake will allow to be providential. There, in the midst of his tribulations, imaginative mercy can begin to be operative upon him. His position is made a Center of vision, and is "rolled out into an Expanse," Blake's very indirect way of saying that Albion is now at the vortex. That is, he can be saved if he is visualized properly, and so freed from the world that his distorted outlook has englobed around him. But he will not be seen by the eye of salvation until plate 95, when at last he will move into wakefulness upon his rock.

The plate immediately following Albion's flight to the Rock of Ages opens with the fierce fantasia of a dance of death, as a blood-drunk daughter of Albion reels "up the Street of London," signaling a war between Los and Urizen to determine whether the mundane world is to belong to Generation or to death. The struggle is continuous, and always indecisive, but throughout this dark war for the future the daughters of Los remain at their wheels of life, generating the substance of the human.

The crisis of Albion's emanation comes on in the midst of these struggles and this inconclusive creation. On plate 60 the Song of the Lamb of God is heard, seeking to lead Jerusalem back to her heritage of liberty. Jerusalem is "clos'd in the Dungeons of Babylon," caught in the insane bondage of self-accusation, unable to be convinced of the reality of forgiveness. To comfort her, and to free her from the delusions of the turning mills of Satan, the Divine Voice tells her Blake's version of the story of Joseph and Mary. This account (on plate 61) is not particularly shocking to readers today, but even now it has not lost all of its direct force. Blake was not the man to accept a divinity born of a virgin; only Satan would enter through such a subterfuge, in Blake's view. His Mary is "a Harlot & an Adulteress" to the eyes of Moral Virtue, but a singing river of the waters of life as she flows into the arms of the forgiving Joseph.

Blake's Jerusalem, like his mother of Christ, is a Magdalen; as such

she presents herself to the Divine Vision on plate 62, and as such she
is accepted. But the massèd forces of the female will are not repentant, and their ghastly triumph is detailed in its frightening particulars
throughout the remainder of the third chapter, from plates 63 through
75. In this procession of iniquity Blake records the depths of
vision, images of a world without apparent hope, an age wracked
by exploitation, war, and selfishness masked in the righteousness
and mutual self-congratulations of governments and churches.
Blake's age, the present age, all ages; the reader can amuse himself,
very grimly, by fitting contemporary equivalents to the protagonists
of Blake's apocalyptic chant. In our time he would have ventured
the identity "Luvah is Russia," or whatever other earthly enemy the
state-church hated with self-destructive passion.

The triumph of the shadowy female will begins on plate 62, even
as Jesus warns Jerusalem she faces "a long season, & a hard journey
& a howling wilderness" before she will see him again. Fires begin
to blaze on the Druid sacrificial altars, and the wheels of Albion's
sons move on in their rage. The dance of death is associated with the
northern religion of Thor and Friga, and is enacted "across the
Rhine, along the Danube" where the wars against Napoleon are
being waged. Vala appears as the coalition of all the daughters of
Albion, to proclaim that man is "Woman-born and Woman-nour-
ish'd & Woman-educated & Woman-scorn'd." She finds her home in
the Spectre's bosom, and takes into her keeping the spindle of Necessity wielded by Tirzah, the mother of man's mortal part. Under
her fateful turnings Luvah is transformed into a Druid victim, "to
die a death of Six thousand years bound round with vegetation."
Encouraged by her dominance, the sons of Urizen leave the tools
of peace for the weapons of corporeal war, and Blake laments the
fate of the impressed warriors of England.

> We were carried away in thousands from
>   London & in tens
> Of thousands from Westminster & Marybone
>   in ships clos'd up,
> Chain'd hand & foot, compell'd to fight
>   under the iron whips
> Of our captains, fearing our officers more
>   than the enemy.

The Spectre sons of Albion cry to Vala, now become a goddess of battles, invoking her as patroness of "blood and wounds and dismal cries, and shadows of the oak," emblem of Druidic error to Blake. These Spectres perform a "Giant dance" (which Blake thought the literal meaning of the name Stonehenge) as they howl round their victims:

> For a Spectre has no Emanation but what he
> imbibes from decieving
> A Victim: Then he becomes her Priest & she
> his Tabernacle.

The reason cannot create, according to Blake, but devours the life of other energies. Yet the devouring is not done with impunity, for their victim is Luvah, whose emanation in the eternal world was the unfallen form of the Vala they worship. By absorbing the world of Luvah, they have become the temple of Vala: "The tremblings of Vala vibrate thro' the limbs of Albion's Sons." They too become what they behold, and so assimilate to the spasms of their victim. Essentially this complex incident is an allegory of the agony of reason when it attempts to deceive passion and so forgets its proper function. The dance of Albion's sons becomes a dance of madness, of minds like Swift's, martyred to reason, as Blake would have understood Swift's fate.

The crazed sons of Albion remain "immense in strength & power," and build an enormous altar to Natural Religion, a Babel-Stonehenge, "rocks piled on rocks reaching the stars." With this "building of eternal death, whose proportions are eternal despair" Blake associates Vala's "Two Covering Cherubs, afterwards named Voltaire & Rousseau." These are "frozen Sons of the feminine Tabernacle of Bacon, Newton and Locke," and they preside over the maiming of Luvah, who is "France, the Victim of the Spectres of Albion." By now we know precisely what this means as Blake's reading of intellectual and political history. As Covering Cherubs Voltaire and Rousseau were once, like the prince of Tyre in Ezekiel, guardians of the truth. But they have fallen into truth's jailors, thus realizing their heritage from the restrictive theoreticians of the Enlightenment. Following their inadequate account of reason and nature, the Revolution collapsed into murderousness, and their nation now suffers the vengeance of the Spectres of Albion.

Plate after plate, passage after passage, the litany of destructions mounts up, in one of the most controlled rhetorical progressions in Blake's poetry. As the ritual dance goes on, it acquires unmistakable overtones of sado-masochism on the part of the daughters of Albion:

> The Daughters of Albion clothed in garments
>   of needle work
> Strip them off from their shoulders and
>   bosoms, they lay aside
> Their garments, they sit naked upon the
>   Stone of trial.
> The Knife of flint passes over the howling
>   Victim: his blood
> Gushes & stains the fair side of the fair
>   Daughters of Albion.
> They put aside his curls, they divide his
>   seven locks upon
> His forehead, they bind his forehead with
>   thorns of iron,
> They put into his hand a reed, they mock,
>   Saying: "Behold
> The King of Canaan whose are seven hundred
>   chariots of iron!"
> They take off his vesture whole with their
>   Knives of flint,
> But they cut asunder his inner garments,
>   searching with
> Their cruel fingers for his heart, & there
>   they enter in pomp,
> In many tears: & there they erect a temple
>   & an altar.
> They pour cold water on his brain in front,
>   to cause
> Lids to grow over his eyes in veils of tears,
>   and caverns

To freeze over his nostrils, while they feed
    his tongue from cups
And dishes of painted clay. Glowing with
    beauty & cruelty
They obscure the sun & the moon: no eye can
    look upon them.

The power of this is more than the flinching effect inherent in its subject matter. The knife of flint suggests a reference to the Aztec sacrifices, the king of Canaan is probably Sisera who was slain by Jael, and the references to the mocking of Jesus by the soldiers are unmistakable. The larger context of the passage is Druidic (meaning as always what Blake took to be Druidic). But what follows is Blake's own reminder of dark moments in *The Mental Traveller* and in *Milton*, when the old woman numbered every nerve of the babe and when Urizen sought to force on Milton an icy intellectual baptism. Frye remarks of this "fantasia on the Crucifixion" that its point "is to show that Jesus also was killed as a Luvah in the role of the dying Albion."[14] The Spectral Accuser slays the saving Imagination so as to keep Man in the posture of a perpetually dying god; "six months of mortality, a summer: & six months of mortality, a winter," is Blake's ironic comment on the consequences. In this frenzy of sacrifice, the world begins to reel in a chaotic helplessness of natural disorder. "The Sun forgets his course, like a drunken man he hesitates," but to no effect: "he is hurried afar into an unknown night." The hesitation marks a shudder in the natural world, poised on the edge of a full appearance of the Shadowy Female, Rahab and Tirzah in their absolute form.

On plate 68 the Adam of this world of murderous necessity, the accusing Skofield, is revealed as the Spectre of Israel's son Joseph, sold into Egypt after being bound upon the stems of the vegetative world. Seeing Joseph, the capable man among Jacob's sons, bound down by the five senses, the Warriors cry out a song of masochistic frenzy as searing as any in poetry, and expressing fully Blake's insight that war is a sexual perversion. In their joy of perverted love the males conjoin into one "Polypus of Roots of Reasoning," Blake's symbol for the vegetated life at its blindest and most helpless.

As the debasement of life proceeds, it corrupts even Beulah, abrogating the generosities of that state, marring every image of finality implicit in a human marriage. Turning from Female Love, Blake remembers Milton's account of angelic love in *Paradise Lost*, VIII, 620–29, as finding no obstacle "of membrane, joint, or limb, exclusive bars," and so desperately visualizes an Eternity where:

> Embraces are Cominglings from the Head even
> to the Feet,
> And not a pompous High Priest entering by a
> Secret Place.

Whatever the genetic motivation of these lines, the mythic insight is startling. The Holy of Holies in the Jerusalem Temple is suddenly apprehended as another Mystery of the Female Will, existing to glorify the sexual power of women. To rise through an increase of sensual fulfillment into the state of Eden where comminglings are total is to enter a world where sacred centers will have no place, for the sanctuary of Eden "in the Outline, in the Circumference, & every Minute Particular is Holy."

But the poem is still very much in our world, where the darkness clusters more and more into opaque forms, still indefinite but doomed, like the Satan of *Milton*, to "resist form in vain." The Sons of Albion take the form of the aggregate Hand, appearing as a Triple Accuser, again like the accusers of Job, of Socrates, and of Bunyan's Faithful:

> His bosom wide & shoulders huge, overspreading
> wondrous,
> Bear Three strong sinewy Necks & Three awful &
> terrible Heads,
> Three Brains in contradictory council brooding
> incessantly,
> Neither daring to put in act its councils,
> fearing each other,
> Therefore rejecting Ideas as nothing & holding
> all Wisdom

To consist in the agreements & disagreements
    of Ideas,
Plotting to devour Albion's Body of Humanity
    & Love.

The Accuser, who is God of this World, is interested in uniformity, in securing agreements and punishing dissenters, for conformity belongs to the indefinite, to the deformity of indecisiveness that
makes for evil. Blake's own Spectral Accuser "in the Oak Groves of
Albion" is the triple form "named Bacon & Newton & Locke," for
it is from their visions of reality that he so radically dissents.

Within the triple Accuser is its Emanation who will not yet come
forth to her manifestation, Rahab as threefold temptress, portrayed
in a marvelous expansion of *The Crystal Cabinet*:

Imputing Sin & Righteousness to Individuals,
    Rahab
Sat deep within him hid: his Feminine Power
    unreveal'd,
Brooding Abstract Philosophy, to destroy
    Imagination, the Divine-
Humanity: A Three-fold Wonder, feminine,
    most beautiful, Three-fold
Each within other. On her white marble &
    even Neck, her Heart,
Inorb'd and bonified, with locks of shadowing
    modesty, shining
Over her beautiful Female features, soft
    flourishing in beauty,
Beams mild, all love and all perfection,
    that when the lips
Recieve a kiss from Gods or Men, a threefold
    kiss returns
From the press'd loveliness; so her whole
    immortal form, three-fold,
Three-fold embrace returns: consuming lives
    of Gods & Men,

In fires of beauty melting them as gold &
    silver in the furnace.
Her Brain enlabyrinths the whole heaven of her
    bosom & loins
To put in act what her Heart wills. O who
    can withstand her power?
Her name is Vala in Eternity: in Time her
    name is Rahab.

Sin and righteousness belong to the states of being through which
all men must pass, but Rahab the harlot, type of the church's claim
to exclusiveness in salvation, is the inward conviction that destroys,
whether she persuades to an unalterable sense of damnation or of
election. As in *The Crystal Cabinet* she consumes all who embrace
her, with endearments that are a demonic semblance of the paradisal pleasures of Beulah.

Now, just before the revelation of Rahab as Antichrist, Blake
ventures on a final survey of the world of Albion's sons, and parcels
out Britain among them in the catalogues of plates 71 and 72.
Even on these plates, where the lists are hardly a poetic virtue in
their own right, the intensity of Blake's negative passion continually
breaks forth into memorable speech. The assignment of Selsey
(Chichester, where Blake was tried) to Hand the reasonable Accuser
is accompanied by the forceful reminder that "you bear your Heaven
and Earth, & all you behold" in your own bosom. Everything that is
outer in nature is inner in the world of imagination, and so the
catalogue of cities enforces the point that their indwelling spirits
are the murderous sons of Albion.

In the midst of these divisions we are shown Los weeping and
calling for divine help, but no longer addressing himself to Albion,
for fear that any admonition would cause the dying Man to turn
his back finally against the vision that will redeem him. Perhaps
there is, in this, a hint on Blake's part of his own isolation, as these
are among the years of which he said: "I am hid." The outspoken
prophecies of *America* and *The Song of Los* have been replaced by a
sublime allegory not too explicit to the Idiot Questioner rejected by
Blake's *Milton*.

Against the mundane divisions of Albion's sons Blake sets, on plate 72, the divisions of the heavenly Jerusalem, with its gates guarded by her sons, the Sons of Eden. Worth notice is the gentle irony by which Blake gives the safe "Gate towards Beulah" into the keeping of the mystics and quietists, "Fenelon, Guion, Teresa," for these are "the gentle Souls" not fit for the strenuous warfare of contraries in Eternity.

A rapid description of Los's City on plate 73 is followed by the reminder of the saving limits of opaqueness and contraction, and by Los's creation of a line of patriarchs, prophets, and poets to counter a line of tyrants "created by Rahab & Tirzah in Ulro." As the age darkens into blindness, the signs of the time of troubles that precedes apocalypse begin at last to appear. Blake beholds "Babylon in the opening Streets of London," and tells "how Reuben slept on London Stone," the Stone of Night of the Lambeth poems. The daughters of Albion admire Reuben's beauty and "cut the fibres of Reuben," an ambiguous act presumably meant to free him for their purposes, but which results in his rolling apart like the poor mandrake he is and taking root again in Bashan, a region which includes a petrified lake of basaltic lava, a grim emblem for his condition. The other sons of Jacob also roll apart, "to dissipate into Non Entity," including the ironic fate of Rachel's sons, the favored Joseph and Benjamin, who "are fix'd into the land of Cabul," a place name so employed in I Kings 9:13 as to mean "good for nothing."

In the midst of these rootings Blake sees a youthful form of Erin, the poetic vision, arise from the Four Zoas as Dinah, Jacob's daughter, for whom her brothers slew the Shechemites. The appearance of Dinah, "beautiful but terrible," is a presage of the arming of individual poetic power for the conflicts with Rahab that are to come.

On plate 75 Rahab is revealed as "Mystery, Babylon the Great: the Abomination of Desolation: Religion hid in War," the Whore who must be exposed for *the* Revelation to begin. All the symbols of Antichrist are gathered together on plate 75: the Cup of Rahab in the hand of Bath, the natural healer now become a poisoner in a parody of the communion cup; the twenty-seven delusory Heavens and their Churches; the cycles of history threatening to turn round again from the twenty-seventh to the first cycle, "and where Luther ends Adam begins again in Eternal Circle." But if error stands totally revealed, then truth will return to confront it:

> But Jesus breaking thro' the Central Zones
>   of Death & Hell
> Opens Eternity in Time & Space: triumphant
>   in Mercy.

Blake has reached again the point previously described at the end of Night VIII of *The Four Zoas*, the nadir of vision that precedes a resolution. Poetically the third chapter of *Jerusalem* must be judged an immense advance on the eighth Night of *The Four Zoas*; the increase in representational subtlety is extraordinary. The horrors of the earlier vision were external compared to the encroachments of Rahab and her brethren on the inwardness of the reader here in *Jerusalem*. Blake has prepared his reader for the final thrust upon his moral consciousness that will constitute the imaginative resolutions of the last chapter of *Jerusalem*.

Los-Blake-Jesus, Chapter IV

The opening address of Chapter IV is "to the Christians," for the chapter is definitive of Blake's Christianity, and he at least knew how far that was from orthodox formulations, or rather how far they were from the truth of his Everlasting Gospel. "Devils are False Religions," and so the ironic vocabulary of the *Marriage* is now overturned. But Blake's ironies continue: the next motto is "Saul, Saul, Why persecutest thou me?", directed now not to Saul of Tarsus but to the Church of Paul, one of the delusive cycles of false religion.

In the address itself Blake is very direct: "I know of no other Christianity and of no other Gospel than the liberty both of body & mind to exercise the Divine Arts of Imagination," this "liberty" being the Jerusalem of the poem. The passionate humanism of Blake is rarely more emphatic than this: "What is the Divine Spirit? is the Holy Ghost any other than an Intellectual Fountain?" One remembers Blake's assertion that "the Fool shall not enter into Heaven let him be ever so Holy." A blank-verse poem follows the address, based on Lear's agonized:

> You do me wrong to take me out o' the grave:
> Thou art a soul in bliss; but I am bound
> Upon a wheel of fire, that mine own tears
> Do scald like molten lead.

Blake assimilates Lear's wheel to the starry wheels of the Satanic sons of Albion:

> I stood among my valleys of the south,
> And saw a flame of fire, even as a Wheel
> Of fire surrounding all the heavens: it went
> From west to east against the current of
> Creation, and devour'd all things in its loud
> Fury & thundering course round heaven & earth.
> By it the Sun was roll'd into an orb
> By it the Moon faded into a globe
> Travelling thro' the night; for from its dire
> And restless fury Man himself shunk up
> Into a little root a fathom long.

The current of creation follows the path of the sun, but the wheel of fire devours the prolific energies of nature. By the wheel's movement the infinite bodies of sun and moon dwindle into globes, and Man becomes a vegetative being measured in terms of a watery materialism:

> And I asked a Watcher & a Holy-One
> Its Name; he answered: "It is the Wheel of
>   Religion."
> I wept & said: "Is this the law of Jesus,
> This terrible devouring sword turning every
>   way?"
> He answer'd: "Jesus died because he strove

> Against the current of this Wheel; its Name
> Is Caiaphas, the dark Preacher of Death,
> Of sin, of sorrow & of punishment:
> Opposing Nature! It is Natural Religion."

The Watcher is like the watchmen to whom the Hebrew prophets cried, asking them "what of the night?" The High Priest of state religion gives his name to the Wheel, which by a fine irony opposes nature's current and yet is "Natural Religion," justified by an appeal to what supposedly is. The poem ends with the assertion that "Hell is open'd to Heaven," which means that the Wheel can be stopped and reversed into the current of creation. In that hope Blake is moved to the quatrains that conclude this preface, in which "England's green & pleasant bowers" are urged to receive again the Lamb of God for "now the time returns again."

That the time is now would not seem evident from the actual opening of Chapter IV, in which the Spectres of Albion's sons revolve over the Sleeping Humanity of their father, seeking to devour him. But the new spirit present in the poem is also evident, for Los is now greatly effective against them, dashing in pieces their self-righteousnesses, "as the Potter breaks the potsherds," an image out of Isaiah (30:14) where man's iniquity is thus broken by God.

Though Los's power is augmented, the Spectres fight on, besieging Erin, and supporting the rule of their "Mother Vala" as Rahab, making of Deism a universal religion. In such a world Jerusalem is "disorganiz'd" and finally becomes an evanescent shade, an image of lamentation wandering amid scenes of bondage. This lamentation is heard throughout plate 79 and at the beginning of plate 80, picturing an isolated England, "a narrow rock in the midst of the sea," instead of the universal land of Eternity, when "London cover'd the whole Earth, England encompass'd the Nations." The policy of imperialistic expansion, as Blake thought he saw it raging in England's wars, is of course an "analogy" or parody of this vision, a demonic displacement of uniting love by the female will to selfish possession. As Jerusalem wanders on, she recalls the lost unity of Israel and England, when "Medway mingled with Kishon: Thames reciev'd the heavenly Jordan." As she reviews her past relation to the nations, she is unable to see in America the golden mountains of Atlantis, for these too are sunk into the abyss of a watery world. She sums up her condition as being "shrunk to a narrow doleful form in the dark land of Cabul," good for nothing but a sense of loss. After this nadir of being, she is reduced to a helpless and un-comprehending appeal to Vala. Taken as the tribulations of a being external to us, this ululation would be wearisome, but is in fact appallingly poignant, for this sufferer is our own lost spiritual free-dom, our hope for autonomous imaginative development, the mother of the Minute Particulars of vision in every man.

The response of Vala is not the mocking cruelty that we expect, but a lamentation as desperate as Jerusalem's. For the times draw near, the torment of nature grows unendurable, and the thick cloud of history seems ready to discharge itself. Vala admits her guilt in the murder of Albion, but attributes her murderousness to Luvah, to whom she was both mistress and daughter. Answering the prompt-ings of desire she slew the humanity of man, a shuddering inter-pretation of the dealings between phenomenal beauty and its ad-mirer. Though she is affrighted by the death she has wrought, "never to be reviv'd" as distinguished from the slain she receives in the wars of love, she remains determined in her own guilt. The body of Albion is kept "embalm'd in moral laws," the dressings of death that Jesus put aside when he came forth from the tomb. Vala is a vegetation-goddess waiting for her dying-god Luvah to return to her, and she fears that a revived Albion would slay her beloved again. In one of the frightening ironies that are the staple of *Jerusalem*, Vala prays to Jesus to pity her "and seek not to revive the Dead." She prays against life while she waits for life, unable to under-stand that the death of the One Man is the death of all.

The wars of death go on, with Rahab retreating into the dis-guises of the indefinite. But that she has been once revealed creates divisions and devourings within the camp of death itself; the daugh-ters of Albion have become newly self-conscious, aware of their own iniquity and the precariousness of their selfish loves. What follows this demonic awareness is one of Blake's most impressive mythopoeic interludes, the fall of Hand and Hyle, reason and nature seduced to their own destruction by the delusive forms they have fashioned in the self-enjoyings of self-denial.

This myth begins on plate 80 with Hand sleeping and his emanation Cambel dividing from him and then reducing him more and more into the fibrous being of the vegetative state. Gwendolen, the emanation of Hyle, first compels him to howling privation, and then reduces him to a second infancy in preparation for a rebirth into the natural prison of her love. Gwendolen states the motive of this transformation: she has rejected Merlin, the immortal imagination of Albion's sons; she has destroyed Reuben who had enough of the spirit of organic Orc to seek to bind her Will; and she has stripped off the many-colored covering of the Joseph sold-into-bondage; and is all this labor to have been for nothing? Hyle is a cruel warrior, but the experienced female will desires total dependence upon itself, and a weeping infant is its proper prey and beloved. The cries of Vala, added to those of Jerusalem, have been a warning even to the cruel sisters:

> I have heard Jerusalem's groans; from Vala's
>   cries & lamentations
> I gather our eternal fate. Outcasts from
>   life and love,
> Unless we find a way to bind these awful
>   Forms to our
> Embrace, we shall perish annihilate; discover'd
>   our Delusions.
> Look! I have wrought without delusion. Look!
>   I have wept,
> And given soft milk mingled together with the
>   spirits of flocks
> Of lambs and doves, mingled together in cups and dishes
> Of painted clay; the mighty Hyle is become a
>   weeping infant:
> Soon shall the Spectres of the Dead follow my
>   weaving threads.

She has "wrought without delusion" only in the ironic sense of the greater delusion of a virgin birth. Her sisters learn from her, absorbing the ultimate lesson of a falsehood, her account of a supposed plot of Enitharmon and Los to annihilate the sisters. But she has forgotten "that Falsehood is prophetic" in a double sense, and her attempt to create by a lie issues in a destruction. The natural babe she expects to see in the reborn Hyle does not appear as a "lovely wayward form" like the human babe at the close of *The Mental Traveller*. Instead, when she draws aside the covering veil, she exposes a winding worm. Screaming, she flees upon the wind, while the deserts tremble at the wrath of the worm that has come upon them as an omen of natural destruction.

Yet Cambel is moved very differently by this new incarnation, and trembles only with envy, for the winding worm, unable to rise from nature, is her ideal for her beloved Hand. The emanation of natural philosophy is not so vicious as this outer form of spectral reason, who proceeds "to form the mighty form of Hand according to her will."

The ultimate sense in which the Falsehood of Gwendolen proves prophetic is demonstrated in her repentance, as she labors "in the eddying wind of Los's Bellows," an inspiring wind not of natural origin, "to form the Worm into a form of love by tears & pain." This is the first sign in *Jerusalem* of a prophetic change of heart that is unequivocal (the conviction of guilt on Vala's part was clearly more ambiguous). As the other sisters begin to give themselves to his furnaces, Los is comforted, and for the first time in his fallen existence identifies himself with Urthona, "keeper of the Gates of Heaven" because those are the auricular nerves with which fully humanized man hears the harmonies of poetry and music.

This realization of his personal identity provokes a crisis in Los, more intense for being closer to the sources of his poetic power than his earlier struggles with his own Spectre. His love for Albion draws him down into the generative world, even as Milton's love for his emanation scattered in the deep led to a descent into our world that seems Eternal Death to those who have achieved a perspective beyond the vortex of space and time. Yet the first evidence of actual "Corruptability" now appears on Albion's limbs, so that Los must resolve never more to leave the sleeper's side, "but labour here incessant till thy awaking." The prophet's fear is that he will forget Eternity under these conditions, and become the worm of mortality or infant horror like Hyle and Hand. With great courage, he overcomes these fears, and resolves to continue as a Watchman, while the work of planting "the seeds of Cities & Villages in the Human bosom" goes forward.

In these labors, Los is not alone, for his Spectre "remains attentive," and "alternate they watch in night; alternate labour in day," a moving portrait of integration, of Blake working both as man and as poet to bring time to its fulfillment, and watching, in both guises, for a sign of the morning. The signs are there, though as readers of the poem we cannot recognize them until we look back from the last plate. Frye, noting this aspect of the poem, remarks on the contrast between Blake's refusal to work up to the climax here, and the tremendous climax of *The Four Zoas*.[15] In this deliberate suppression of crisis, Frye sees a key to the structure of *Jerusalem* as being that of a reversal of perspective, the "analogy" of nature turned inside out to produce the world of imagination.[16] As an insight into *Jerusalem* I do not think that this can be bettered, but there is nevertheless a clear and powerful thematic progression in the fourth chapter of *Jerusalem*, just as there is in the earlier parts of the poem. I am attempting to suggest that the continuity of *Jerusalem* is not so radically different from that of much other poetry as its most distinguished critics have thought it to be, even though it does away both with most narrative progressions and with any kind of a conventional climax.

As Los stands at his watch, he hears the lamentation of the repenting but now badly confused daughters of Albion. They weep in Babylon, "on Euphrates," once Albion's land, for the Euphrates was one of the rivers of Eden. They see a double vision, contrasting the lovely land where the daughters of Beulah walked with their present world, from which Hand and Hyle even have vanished in any recognizable form. Their song recalls the plangency of Psalm 137, when the children of Israel wept by Babylon's waters. As it continues they see London begging in the streets of Babylon, a London who is blind and age-bent and led by a child as he weeps. With a start we remember this as the illustration to the *London* of *Songs of Experience*, which conveys the entire meaning of that angry prophetic lyric in a single image and demonstrates again the deliberate and radical unity of the canon of Blake's poetry.

The daughters hear also "the voice of Wandering Reuben" as it echoes from street to street in all the cities of Europe, including

Paris, Madrid, and Amsterdam, which may mean that Reuben has now become Blake's version of the Wandering Jew. The daughters' extraordinary song ends with a reappearance of Hand the Accuser, now grown from a winding worm into "the Double Molech & Chemosh," two heathen gods to whom infants were sacrificed. In their desperation the daughters react in contradictory ways; they both woo the advancing Hand "all the night in songs" and they call on Los to come forth to "divide us from these terrors & give us power them to subdue." In hysterical fear they retrogress and unite into one again with Rahab. But their terror is now providential, and the prophecy that masked itself as Gwendolen's Falsehood is utterly fulfilled as an analogy of vision:

> Terrified at the Sons of Albion they took the
>   Falsehood which
> Gwendolen hid in her left hand: it grew &
>   grew till it
> Became a Space & an Allegory around the Winding
>   Worm.
> They nam'd it Canaan & built for it a tender
>   Moon.
> Los smil'd with joy, thinking on Enitharmon, &
>   he brought
> Reuben from his twelvefold wand'rings & led him
>   into it,
> Planting the Seeds of the Twelve Tribes &
>   Moses & David:
> And gave a Time & Revolution to the Space, Six
>   Thousand Years.
> He call'd it Divine Analogy, for in Beulah the
>   Feminine
> Emanations Create Space, the Masculine Create
>   Time & plant
> The Seeds of beauty in the Space; list'ning to
>   their lamentation
> Los walks upon his ancient Mountains in the
>   deadly darkness,

Among his Furnaces directing his laborious
    Myriads, watchful
Looking to the East, & his voice is heard
    over the whole Earth
As he watches the Furnaces by night & directs
    the labourers.

Canaan is the mundane Israel, the land that the Divine Vision
takes to itself in marriage and so creates as the emanative world
of Beulah. The daughters take the Falsehood as a lie against being,
as protection against Hand, but because they take it up it grows as
a Space of mercy and an Allegory of salvation around the Worm.
The land they make is generative, and will worship the tender Moon
of a female deity, but such worship is an analogy or inversion of the
Beulah vision of restful love. Los smiles with joy because he recognizes this, and thinks on Enitharmon with sexual longing and joyous expectation. By bringing Reuben from his twelvefold wander-
ings he is taking all the tribes, that is to say all men, out of their
ordeal in the wilderness and planting them in the "Divine Analogy"
of the whole cycle of history. The analogy exists already, as soon
as Los recognizes it; his work is to make it divine by establishing the
dialectic for it of Innocence and Experience, Beulah and Generation,
which makes it directly analogical of the Eternal alternation of contraries between Beulah and Eden.

A finely serene passage, the very first of its kind in this anguished poem, now follows, in which Jerusalem and Vala cease to
mourn, and the ancient mountains bow their crowned heads. The
effect of this sudden quiet, in which "the Stars stand still to hear,"
is very moving, and an aesthetic experience I find unique in literature. Out of that awed silence a Song of Los rises, a vision of the
New Jerusalem and of the River of Life and Tree of Life. The passage at the beginning of plate 86 describing Jerusalem is especially
beautiful, and remarkably Shelleyan, being very close to the descriptions of Asia, the emanation of Prometheus, in *Prometheus Unbound*:

Thy forehead bright, Holiness to the Lord, with
    Gates of pearl
Reflects Eternity beneath thy azure wings of
    feathery down
Ribb'd delicate & cloth'd with feather'd gold
    & azure & purple,
From thy white shoulders shadowing purity in
    holiness!
Thence feather'd with soft crimson of the
    ruby bright as fire,
Spreading into the azure Wings which like a
    canopy
Bends over thy immortal Head, in which Eternity
    dwells.

The Song ends with a haunting echo of the Song of Solomon, and Los works on in his fierce intimations of triumph, his creation "concentering in the majestic form of Erin." But he does not enjoy these fruits of his hard labor for long. His own crisis with his own emanation has been long in abeyance, and now it comes upon him. Enitharmon appears to him, enticing him into a fantasia of desire, flight, and pursuit previously enacted in Night I of *The Four Zoas*. The figure of Enion, the lost mother of Innocence, returns as a sad presiding spirit for this episode. The pattern of strife here is familiar to us, but Los's reaction to Enitharmon's perversities is refreshingly new, for this is a mature prophet of Experience, not a wayward lover of Innocence. He suffers, but he does not yield, and he insists calmly on the necessity for his dominion.

The Spectre of Urthona, who all this while has labored with Los against his own will, smiles sullenly at this strife, priding himself on being the cause of their divisions in the sense that their mundane prides are keeping them apart. This spectral rejoicing prepares the way for a revelation of the dominant Spectre, the Antichrist itself. For the Covering Cherub now to appear is an omen of a greater revelation, and the last line of the following passage is (in its full context) one of Blake's greatest, for it contains the full dialectic by which the uncovering of Antichrist suggests the revelation of Christ,

who on the third day abandons his rejected corpse to the devouring
dragon of death and re-enters the visionary prolific of more abundant
life:

> Thus was the Covering Cherub reveal'd,
>   majestic image
> Of Selfhood, Body put off, the Antichrist
>   accursed,
> Cover'd with precious stones, a Human Dragon
>   terrible
> And bright, stretch'd over Europe & Asia
>   gorgeous.
> In three nights he devour'd the rejected
>   corse of death.

The Cherub's brain "incloses a reflexion of Eden all perverted,"
another instance of the analogy or inverted vision. In this demonic
reflection there appear the parodies we have encountered all through
the poem: Egypt on the Gihon, the river of paradise fallen into
the Nile; the Sea of Rephaim, which means ghosts or shades, and
is equated with the Red Sea; the Minute Particulars in slavery, solid-
ified into the disorganization of uniformity in the bondage of the
Egyptian brick-kilns; and "the Dragon of the River," Leviathan, emblem of the tyranny of nature over man.

Within the Cherub there appears the great Whore Rahab, and into
this combined form of natural tyranny, "Religion hid in War," the
sons of Albion mingle; "they become One Great Satan." Against this
fully revealed abomination Los is able to become truly the prophet
armed. On plate 91 he speaks in a complete consciousness of his
powers, knowing what needs to be known, resolving what needs to
be resolved. This is, to me, the greatest passage in all of Blake, the
gathering together of wisdom gained only through a lifetime of internal conflict never evaded, and poetic insight absolutely disciplined:

> It is easier to forgive an Enemy than to
>   forgive a Friend.
> The man who permits you to injure him deserves
>   your vengeance:

He also will receive it; go Spectre! obey
    my most secret desire
Which thou knowest without my speaking. Go
    to these Fiends of Righteousness,
Tell them to obey their Humanities & not
    pretend Holiness
When they are murderers: as far as my
    Hammer & Anvil permit.
Go, tell them that the Worship of God is
    honouring his gifts
In other men: & loving the greatest men
    best, each according
To his Genius, which is the Holy Ghost in
    Man; there is no other
God than that God who is the intellectual
    fountain of Humanity.
He who envies or calumniates, which is
    murder & cruelty,
Murders the Holy-one. Go tell them this,
    & overthrow their cup,
Their bread, their altar-table, their
    incense & their oath,
Their marriage & their baptism, their
    burial & consecreation.
I have tried to make friends by corporeal
    gifts but have only
Made enemies. I never made friends but by
    spiritual gifts,
By severe contentions of friendship & the
    burning fire of thought.
He who would see the Divinity must see him
    in his Children,
One first, in friendship & love: then a
    Divine Family, & in the midst
Jesus will appear; so he who wishes to see
    a Vision, a perfect Whole,
Must see it in its Minute Particulars.

To comment adequately upon this would be to bring to bear upon it the whole of Blake's life and works, but a few lesser observations can be made more briefly. The opening lines of this speech recall *A Poison Tree*, and the whole of the Satan-Palamabron episode in *Milton*. The definition of the worship of God as "honouring his gifts in other men" is quoted directly from the speech of a Devil in the last Memorable Fancy of *The Marriage of Heaven and Hell*. With the identity of Genius and the Holy Ghost in Man we return to the opening address of Chapter IV, but the vehement overthrowing of the ritual paraphernalia of Christian worship is newly expressed in Blake, though it echoes the lament of Urizen-Jehovah to the Archbishop of Paris in *The French Revolution*, and follows on also from Blake's Milton in his taking off the robe of the promise. Yet none of this is to be understood as mere iconoclasm, for Blake is not an image breaker but a visionary who desires to invert the analogy of religion into the liberating truth of the autonomous imagination. It is "their" cup, "their" bread, and so on that must be overthrown, when "they" are the "Fiends of Righteousness," the Angels satirically castigated in the *Marriage*. There are no Righteous, and the Elect must be transformed by the Reprobate into the Redeemed, the agents of transformation being the strife of contraries, the "severe contentions of friendship & the burning fire of thought." Inexhaustible to meditation, this speech of Los is Blake's testament, the summation of his apocalyptic humanism and a glorious epitome of the "beautiful laughing speech" that Yeats praised in him.

In the thematic continuity of *Jerusalem* the most crucial aspect of Los's great speech is that it is directed to the Spectre of Urthona, to everything in Blake as a man that impeded Blake as a poet by nervous fear. The Spectre has been obedient but sullen; now he is subdued completely, but only after a final struggle:

> The Spectre builded stupendous Works,
>   taking the Starry Heavens
> Like to a curtain & folding them according
>   to his will,
> Repeating the Smaragdine Table of Hermes
>   to draw Los down

Into the Indefinite, refusing to believe
    without demonstration.
Los reads the Stars of Albion, the Spectre
    reads the Voids
Between the Stars: among the arches of
    Albion's Tomb sublime,
Rolling the Sea in rocky paths: forming
    Leviathan
And Behemoth; the War by Sea enormous &
    the War
By Land astounding: erecting pillars in
    the deepest Hell
To reach the heavenly arches. Los beheld
    undaunted, furious
His heav'd Hammer; he swung it round &
    at one blow
In unpitying ruin driving down the pyramids
    of pride,
Smiting the Spectre on his Anvil & the
    integuments of his Eye
And Ear unbinding in dire pain, with many blows
Of strict severity self-subduing, & with many
    tears labouring.

The Smaragdine Table of Hermes is a central document of occult
tradition, and what needs to be emphasized about this passage is
that Blake the poet *rejects* it while his Spectre is shown as attempting
to use it as one more trap of the corporeal understanding to draw
imagination down into an indefinite abyss. Blake is rejecting all
Hermeticism here even as he rejected Swedenborg, Behmen, and
Paracelsus in *The Marriage of Heaven and Hell*. No amount of insistence on this point is likely to stop the continuous flow of writings
on Blake's relation to arcane traditions, yet it is hard to see how
Blake himself could have been clearer, more emphatic, or more
scornful on this subject. A lunatic fringe of enthusiastic occult Blak-
eans is likely to abide as the left wing of Blake studies until the
veritable apocalypse, and all one can do is to counsel students and
readers to ignore them.

The Spectre, reading the Newtonian voids between the stars, learns from them the lesson of Mystery and forms in accordance with that lesson the two Jobean kings over all the children of pride, the earthly tyrants of Mystery, the great beasts Leviathan and Behemoth. These are one with the Covering Cherub, the natural barrier between visionary desire and apocalyptic completion. When Los at one blow destroys these pyramids of pride he unbinds also the eye and ear of his Spectre, stripping away the natural covering that restricts the senses. The Spectre is altered, but at great pain to Los, as the pains of struggle must have been surpassingly great to Blake:

> Terrified Los sat to behold, trembling &
>   weeping & howling:
> I care not whether a Man is Good or Evil;
>   all that I care
> Is whether he is a Wise Man or a Fool. Go,
>   put off Holiness
> And put on Intellect, or my thund'rous
>   Hammer shall drive thee
> To wrath which thou condemnest, till thou
>   obey my voice.

After this, there is no more struggle with the Spectre. But the separation from Enitharmon, the poet's emanation, remains to be healed. She is terrified: "The Poet's Song draws to its period & Enitharmon is no more." This is the cry of a female will, fearing an end to separate female existence, and Los offers her no comfort as he reads in the revelation of Mystery the Signal of the Morning. On plate 94 the poem moves into that morning as "England who is Britannia awoke from Death on Albion's bosom," fainting seven times even as the Shunammite's son sneezed himself seven times into revived life. Britannia is the England of Blake's hoped-for New Age, Jerusalem as she might once more be. The voice of her startled awakening pierces Albion's clay-cold ear, and he moves upon his rock:

> The Breath Divine went forth upon the morning
>   hills. Albion mov'd

Upon the Rock, he open'd his eyelids in pain;
      in pain he mov'd
His stony members, he saw England. Ah!
      shall the Dead live again?

As a risen body he moves to restore the four Zoas, his components, to their proper functions, but Urthona is already at work in the newly integrated "Great Spectre Los." The praise for "Urthona's Spectre" is not just for Blake the man, but for all men who as artists have kept their vision in time of trouble:

Compelling Urizen to his Furrow & Tharmas
      to his Sheepfold,
And Luvah to his Loom: Urthona he beheld,
      mighty labouring at
His Anvil, in the Great Spectre Los unwearied
      labouring & weeping.
Therefore the Sons of Eden praise Urthona's
      Spectre in songs,
Because he kept the Divine Vision in time of
      trouble.

With plate 96 the essential humanism of this apocalypse is revealed. Jesus appears, and "Albion saw his Form a Man, & they conversed as Man with Man." The appearance of Jesus "was the likeness & similitude of Los," the fourth man of Daniel's vision, walking safe in the fiery furnace of the creative imagination. Albion casts out his "Selfhood cruel," and Jesus defines his death and resurrection for Albion: "This is Friendship & Brotherhood: without it Man Is Not." The few words contain the essence of Blake's theme as a poet.

The Covering Cherub comes upon them, and his darkness overshadows and divides them. Fearing for his friend Los-Jesus, Albion sacrifices himself in the furnaces, and by this act "the Furnaces became Fountains of Living Waters." Albion is fully restored as Man, and calls to Jerusalem to awake and come away with him, echoing in this call the beautiful salute to the spring in the Song of Solomon.

The bow of burning gold that Blake called for in his prefatory stanzas to *Milton* now is taken out of Infinitude by Albion's hand.

As this great bow, emblem of an art of finality, sends its arrows of intellect and desire through the wide heavens the innumerable chariots of the Divine manifest themselves, bearing "Bacon & Newton & Locke, & Milton & Shakspear & Chaucer," a vision of contraries prepared for the mental wars of the restored state. These men of intellect and desire are shaped like the four-faced Cherubim of Ezekiel's vision, with as many eyes as are called forth by "the Human Nerves of Sensation, the Four Rivers of the Water of Life." Their converse is rendered in a nervous and alert diction, marvelous in its vivification of what elsewhere would seem abstractions:

> And they conversed together in Visionary
>   forms dramatic which bright
> Redounded from their Tongues in thunderous
>   majesty, in Visions
> In new Expanses, creating exemplars of
>   Memory and of Intellect,
> Creating Space, Creating Time according to
>   the wonders Divine
> Of Human Imagination throughout all the
>   Three Regions immense
> Of Childhood, Manhood & Old Age; & the all
>   tremendous unfathomable Non Ens
> Of Death was seen in regenerations terrific
>   or complacent, varying
> According to the subject of discourse, &
>   every Word & Every Character
> Was Human according to the Expansion or
>   Contraction, the Translucence or
> Opakeness of Nervous fibres: such was the
>   variation of Time & Space
> Which vary according as the Organs of
>   Perception vary: & they walked
> To & fro in Eternity as One Man, reflecting
>   each in each & clearly seen
> And seeing, according to fitness & order.

Word and vision are one here, with the image evident immediately it is uttered. The mind so directly creating space and time, regenerates even the nonexistence of death, inventing it or destroying it at will. In the presence of a Word altogether humanized, the forms of individuals accomplish the last paradox of being, according to desire, One Man, the perfect freedom of humanistic communion, of dialogue and mutual vision. There remains only the pure serenity of the end of the song of *Jerusalem:*

> All Human Forms identified, even Tree, Metal,
>   Earth & Stone, all
> Human Forms identified, living, going forth,
>   & returning wearied
> Into the Planetary lives of Years, Months,
>   Days & Hours, reposing
> And then Awaking into his Bosom in the Life
>   of Immortality.
>
> And I heard the Name of their Emanations:
>   they are named Jerusalem.

This is not our cycle of Innocence and Experience that is being described, but the eternal alternation of contrary states, the living and going forth of Eden, and the returning wearied and reposing of Beulah. The identification of all forms as human is one with hearing the beloved creation of those forms as the name of Jerusalem, for the liberty of all things is to be human.

Conclusion: The Old Blake

After *Jerusalem*, Blake wrote very little poetry, and devoted himself to his work as painter and engraver. The most considerable poem
left in manuscript from his later years is *The Everlasting Gospel*,
a series of notebook fragments on the theme of the necessity for
the forgiveness of sins. There are powerful passages among these
fragments, but they do not add anything to *Jerusalem* as imaginative
thought, and Blake did not bother to arrange them in any definite
form. The rhetorical directness of some of the fragments has made
them popular, but their very freedom from the inventiveness of
Blake's mythmaking has the effect of rendering them poetically un-
interesting.

This is not true of Blake's last engraved poem *The Ghost of Abel*,
a dramatic scene composed in 1822 as a reply to Byron's drama,
Cain. Byron's Cain fights free of natural religion and its fears only
to succumb to a murderous dialectic by which every spiritual emancipation of a gifted individual is paid for through alienation from
his brethren, the consequence being that a dissenter from the orthodoxy of negations in moral values is compelled to become an unwary
Satanist. Blake's brief drama begins where Byron's ends, with Abel
slain and Cain gone forth as a wanderer. The Ghost of Abel demands a life for a life, and then sinks down into the grave, from
which it rises again to be revealed as Satan crying for the blood of
men. A thoroughly imaginative Jehovah sends this Satan to self-annihilation, and the little play ends with an angelic chorus celebrating
the covenant of the forgiveness of sins. Blake's very subtle point is
that the covenant of Christ, as he interprets it, takes man beyond

the "cloven fiction" of moral good and moral evil, the "hateful siege of contraries" experienced by Milton's Satan on Mount Niphates, and into the clarification of seeing that only a part of what is called moral good is actually good to the imagination or real life of man. Vengeance and every similar mode of hindering another can have no part in an imaginative morality, and for Blake there is no other morality worthy of the name. *The Ghost of Abel*, which makes surprisingly effective use of Blake's long line, the fourteener, as a medium for dramatic dialogue, is the true coda to Blake's poetry, rather than *The Everlasting Gospel*, for it makes explicit the moral basis of the laconic *Marriage of Heaven and Hell*.

At about the time he wrote *The Everlasting Gospel*, Blake re-engraved a little emblem-book, *The Gates of Paradise*, which he had first engraved as early as 1793, adding a number of rhymed couplets and an epilogue in two quatrains to the engravings and their inscriptions. The Gates of Paradise are "Mutual Forgiveness of each Vice," and the story told in pictures and text alike is a version of the Orc cycle. But the epilogue is something rarer, an address "To the Accuser who is The God of This World," and one of Blake's most perfect short poems:

> Truly, My Satan, thou art but a Dunce,
> And dost not know the Garment from the Man.
> Every Harlot was a Virgin once,
> Nor can'st thou ever change Kate into Nan.
>
> Tho' thou are Worship'd by the Names Divine
> Of Jesus & Jehovah, thou art still
> The Son of Morn in weary Night's decline,
> The lost Traveller's Dream under the Hill.

The tone of this is unique in Blake, and I have not found the equivalent in any other poet. There is enormous irony here, but mitigated by a gentle and mocking pity for the great antagonist, the Satan adored as Jesus and Jehovah by the religious of this world. Blake is past argument here; he has gone beyond prophetic anger and apocalyptic impatience. The Accuser is everywhere and at all times apparently triumphant, yet he is a delusion and so but a dunce.

He cannot distinguish the phenomenal garment from the Real Man, the Imagination, and his spouse Rahab is only a delusion also. States change, individuals endure. The god of the churches is still that light-bearer, son of the morning, who fell, and he is now in his weary night's decline as history moves to a judging climax. The vision of a restored man, Blake's vision, is the clear sight of a Mental Traveller in the open world of poetry. The Accuser is the dream of a lost traveller in the phenomenal world, but Blake has found his way home, and need not dream.

Notes

CHAPTER ONE

1. See the discussion of Blake's poems to the seasons in W. K. Wimsatt, Jr.'s *The Verbal Icon* (University of Kentucky, 1954), pp. 112–13.

2. Spenser's influence on *Poetical Sketches* is studied in detail in Margaret Ruth Lowery's *Windows of the Morning* (New Haven, 1940), pp. 88–107.

3. The name "Beulah" is taken from Isaiah 62:4. There are full discussions of Blake's Beulah in Milton Percival's *William Blake's Circle of Destiny* (New York, 1938), pp. 52–59 and in my *The Visionary Company* (New York, 1961), pp. 15–27.

4. The best study of Blake's *King Edward the Third* is in David Erdman's *Blake: Prophet Against Empire* (Princeton, 1954), pp. 60–79.

CHAPTER TWO

1. Northrop Frye, *Fearful Symmetry* (Princeton, 1947), p. 192; Erdman, p. 107.

2. Leslie Stephen, *History of English Thought in the Eighteenth Century* (New York, 1876, reprinted 1927), Vol. I, p. 32.

3. Ibid., p. 32.

4. *The Complete Writings of William Blake*, edited by Geoffrey Keynes (London, 1957), p. 393.

5. Stephen, p. 372.

6. J. Middleton Murry, *William Blake* (London, 1933), p. 15.

7. Ibid., p. 28.

CHAPTER THREE

1. S. Foster Damon, *William Blake: His Philosophy and Symbols* (New York, 1924), p. 306.
2. Frye, p. 242.
3. The name "Ijim" is from Isaiah 13:21, where it refers to the satyrs who will dance in the ruins of Babylon. See Frye, p. 243.
4. Wallace Stevens, *Opus Posthumous* (New York, 1957), p. 165.

CHAPTER FOUR

1. A good account of the nature of pastoral poetry can be found in Frank Kermode's introduction to his anthology, *English Pastoral Poetry* (London, 1952). W. W. Greg's *Pastoral Poetry and Pastoral Drama* (London, 1906), is the standard study of English pastoral poetry.
2. The Virgilian tradition of European pastoral is studied in E. R. Curtius, *European Literature and the Latin Middle Ages* (New York, 1953), pp. 190–202.
3. *The Pilgrim's Progress*, towards the close of the First Part.
4. *The Faerie Queene*, Book III, Canto VI, Stanza XLII.
5. Arthur Barker, *Milton and the Puritan Dilemma, 1641–1660* (Toronto, 1942), p. 318.
6. Peter F. Fisher, *The Valley of Vision* (Toronto, 1961), p. 205.
7. Damon, p. 312.

CHAPTER FIVE

1. Erdman, p. 127.
2. *Complete Writings*, ed. Keynes, p. 90.
3. Northrop Frye, *Anatomy of Criticism* (Princeton, 1957), pp. 311–12 and p. 365.
4. *Complete Writings*, ed. Keynes, p. 91.
5. John Burnet, *Early Greek Philosophy* (New York, fourth edition, 1930), p. 136.
6. A. C. Swinburne, *William Blake* (Bonchurch Edition, London, 1926), p. 251.
7. Frye, *Fearful Symmetry*, p. 198.

8. C. S. Lewis, *A Preface to Paradise Lost* (London, 1942), p. 92.
9. Chatterton, *The Dethe of Syr Charles Bawdin*, ll. 133–36.
10. *Complete Writings*, ed. Keynes, p. 88.
11. Philip Rieff, *Freud: The Mind of the Moralist* (New York, 1961), p. 64.
12. Damon, p. 94.
13. Swinburne, p. 263.

CHAPTER SIX

1. *Paradise Lost*, Book III, l. 44.
2. John Wisdom, broadcast talk on "Paradox and Discovery," BBC Third Programme, Nov. 1, 1958.
3. Erdman, pp. 211–27.
4. H. M. Margoliouth, *William Blake* (London, 1951), p. 93.
5. Frye, p. 241.

CHAPTER SEVEN

1. *Beowulf*, ll. 111–14, where *orcneas* means "monsters."
2. Erdman, p. 239, n. 32.
3. Frye, p. 224.
4. Damon, pp. 336–37; Frye, p. 440, n. 27. See Also G. M. Harper, *The Neoplatonism of William Blake* (Chapel Hill, 1961), pp. 219–27.
5. Erdman, p. 232.
6. Jeremiah 22:29; Milton, *The Ready and Easy Way*.
7. Northrop Frye, "Blake's Introduction to Experience," *The Huntington Library Quarterly*, vol. xxi: Number 1: November, 1957, p. 65.
8. See Frye's comment on this illustration in his "Poetry and Design in William Blake," *The Journal of Aesthetics and Art Criticism*, X (September, 1951), reprinted in *Discussions of William Blake*, ed. by John Grant (Boston, 1961), p. 47.
9. Two useful readings of *The Tyger*, each very different from my own, may serve to instance the rich ambiguity of the poem: Hazard Adams, "Reading Blake's Lyrics: *The Tyger*" and John Grant, "The Art and Argument of *The Tyger*," both available in *Discussions of William Blake*, ed. Grant. R. F. Gleckner's *The Piper and the Bard* (Detroit, 1959) also has a useful discussion of the poem.
10. From the song of Enitharmon on plate 5 of *Europe*.

11. Frye, *Fearful Symmetry*, p. 228.

12. The best treatment of Blake's Druid symbolism is in Fisher's *The Valley of Vision*, and in the same scholar's "Blake and the Druids," reprinted in Grant's *Discussions*.

13. Erdman, pp. 193–207.

14. Murry, pp. 95–96.

15. Erdman, p. 206.

16. Murry, p. 96.

17. See Fisher, *The Valley of Vision*, p. 51, for the association in Blake between rational analysis and Druidic ritual murder.

18. Frye, p. 254.

19. Frye, p. 255.

CHAPTER EIGHT

1. I have ventured a comparison of aspects of *The Book of Urizen*, Coleridge's *Hymn before Sunrise*, and Shelley's *Mont Blanc* in my *Shelley's Mythmaking* (New Haven, 1959), pp. 15–18.

2. Proverbs 8:27; *Paradise Lost*, VII, 226–31.

3. Fisher, p. 195, sees Fuzon as the "fusion" of the energetic and rational aspects of man, "the spirit of Orc acting through reason." Fuzon is perhaps best regarded as a Blakean version of the "fatal child" fearfully expected by Zeus, a child who will rise and attempt to dethrone his divine father.

4. Frye, p. 214, associates Fuzon and Absalom.

CHAPTER NINE

1. *William Blake's Vala*, edited by H. M. Margoliouth (Oxford, 1956).

2. Letter to Dr. Trusler, 23 August 1799, in *Complete Writings*, ed. Keynes, p. 793.

3. *Complete Writings*, ed. Keynes, p. 611.

4. From the Notebook; printed in *Complete Writings*, p. 596.

5. Blake lists the Seven Eyes in *The Four Zoas*, VIII, 398–406, in *Milton* 13:14–27, and in *Jerusalem* 55:31–33. Damon gives a full account of them (p. 389), to which little need be added. Their names are Lucifer, Moloch, Elohim, Shaddai, Pachad (Isaac's "fear" as sworn to by Jacob in Genesis 31:53), Jehovah, and Jesus. Lucifer and Moloch are Druidic de-

ities; the Elohim create Adam as the Limit of Contraction; Shaddai fixes Satan as the Limit of Opacity; Pachad, as its name may indicate, still abides in the fear of human sacrifice though that age is past. Jehovah and Jesus are the Mosaic and Christian dispensations. The Eighth Eye sometimes mentioned by Blake is a direct emblem of apocalypse.

6. Revelation 4:5. See also Revelation 5:6, where Jesus is a unified image of the Seven Eyes.

7. W. B. Yeats, "William Blake and the Imagination" (1897), reprinted in *Essays and Introductions* (New York, 1961), p. 114.

8. *The Magi*, from *Responsibilities* (1914).

9. Zechariah 8:17; Job 28:12–13.

10. Frye (p. 279) speaks of Enion's song as containing "a thought which can lead only either to madness or apocalypse," a valid statement of Blake's intentions in the poem. But the dilemma is partly the result of Blake's absolute identification of prophecy and apocalypse, a heroic misunderstanding of the nature of Hebraic prophecy. Enion's song is Jobean, but would find no place in Isaiah or Amos, who refused to yield up history to the Accuser to the extent that Blake did.

11. *The Visionary Company*, p. 87.

12. Murry, pp. 153–71; Frye, p. 298.

13. Mark Schorer, *William Blake: The Politics of Vision* (New York, 1946, 1959), pp. 277–78.

14. Frye, p. 298.

15. D. J. Sloss and J. P. R. Wallis, in their edition of *The Prophetic Writings of William Blake* (Oxford, 1926), Vol. I, p. 258 n., trace the name "Luban" to the antiquarian Jacob Bryant's association of Mount Baris or Luban with Ararat.

16. "Cathedron" may be a combination of cathedral and Catherine, the name of Blake's wife. Whatever the genesis of the word, one does well to consider its meaning from its context in Blake's poetry, and not from its supposed formation. The same principle holds for all the new names in Blake's mythology.

17. Frye, p. 125.

18. Erich Auerbach, "Typological Symbolism in Medieval Literature," *Yale French Studies*, 9, p. 4.

19. *Complete Writings*, ed. Keynes, p. 604.

20. *Northern Antiquities* (London, 1770), Vol. II, pp. 160–62. Translated by Bishop Percy from the French of Paul Henri Mallet, this is almost certainly Blake's source for Norse mythology.

21. Frye, pp. 308–9.

CHAPTER TEN

1. W. B. Yeats, A *Vision* (New York, 1938, 1956), gives an interpretation of the babe's birth in *The Mental Traveller* on p. 106. Compare this with the use of a passage from *The Second Coming* on p. 263 of *A Vision*.

2. The most suggestive reading of *The Mental Traveller* is by Frye in *Anatomy of Criticism*, pp. 322–23, where it is treated as an example of an ironic encyclopaedic form, akin to *A Vision*, Robert Graves's *The White Goddess*, and *Finnegans Wake*.

3. The symbolism of *The Crystal Cabinet* is best understood in conjunction with the poem included by Blake in his letter to Thomas Butts, 22 November 1802 (*Complete Writings*, pp. 816–18), where the threefold vision "in soft Beulah's night" is contrasted with the fourfold vision "in my supreme delight" of creativity, and with the "twofold always" of ordinary experience and the "Single vision & Newton's sleep" of Ulro.

CHAPTER ELEVEN

1. Frye, "Notes for a Commentary on *Milton*," in *The Divine Vision*, ed. V. de Sola Pinto (London, 1957), p. 130 n.

2. Frye, *Fearful Symmetry*, p. 332.

3. The fullest account of the Blake-Hayley relationship is in Morchard Bishop's biography, *Blake's Hayley* (London, 1951), especially in chapters XVII–XIX. Good as this is, it is perhaps overly partial to Hayley.

4. *William Cowper, Esqre*, in *Complete Writings*, p. 551.

5. Notes on Spurzheim's *Observations on Insanity*, in *Complete Writings*, p. 772. The legends of Blake's "madness" never seem to cease, despite all scholarly rebuttal. Blake would have been ironically amused at this, as at so many of his posthumous versions, from a happy mystic to a vehement sadist. Blake's poems exist to indicate that most men lead insane lives, prisoners of insanely unimaginative concepts and conventions. The people who still think Blake to have been mad are merely defending themselves from the keenest diagnostician of their own maladies.

6. *Complete Writings*, p. 803.

7. Ibid., p. 819.

8. There is an excellent study of this phenomenon by M. H. Abrams,

"The Correspondent Breeze: A Romantic Metaphor," in *English Romantic Poets*, ed. Abrams (New York, 1960), pp. 37–54.

9. *Fearful Symmetry*, pp. 299–303.

10. Frye, "Notes for a Commentary on *Milton*," p. 133 n.

11. *Fearful Symmetry*, p. 350; Hazard Adams, *Blake and Yeats: The Contrary Vision* (Ithaca, 1955), pp. 106–08.

12. Percival, *Blake's Circle of Destiny*, p. 232.

13. Frye, "Notes . . . on *Milton*," p. 136.

14. Murry, pp. 226–27.

15. Frye, "Notes . . . on *Milton*," p. 127.

16. Damon, p. 416.

CHAPTER TWELVE

1. The second line of the passage quoted is a recovery by David Erdman of one of Blake's deletions. The line, "Saying, we are not One: we are Many, thou most simulative . . . ," is crucial for the passage's meaning.

2. Erdman, p. 376.

3. *Fearful Symmetry*, p. 377.

4. Damon, p. 441.

5. Frye's most persuasive account of Blake's Biblism is in "Blake After Two Centuries," *University of Toronto Quarterly*, XXVII (Oct. 1957), pp. 10–21, reprinted in *English Romantic Poets*, ed. Abrams, pp. 55–67.

6. Karl Kiralis, "A Guide to the Intellectual Symbolism of William Blake's Later Prophetic Writings," *Criticism*, vol. I, no. 3, Summer, 1959, p. 200.

7. Erdman, pp. 439–44.

8. Ibid., p. 440.

9. Damon, p. 451.

10. Margoliouth, p. 157.

11. Erdman, "Blake: The Historical Approach," *English Institute Essays: 1950*, ed. A. S. Downer (New York, 1951). Reprinted in *Discussions of William Blake*, ed. Grant, p. 25.

12. See Ransom's poem, *Survey of Literature*.

13. *Fearful Symmetry*, p. 338.

14. Ibid., p. 398.

15. Ibid., pp. 357–58.

16. Ibid., pp. 380–84.

Index